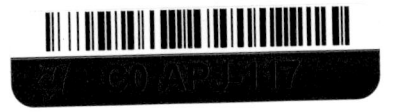

History of the Life and Times of James Madison, Volume 1

William Cabell Rives

LIFE AND TIMES

OF

JAMES MADISON.

assured of my great & affectionate esteem

James Madison

HISTORY

OF THE

LIFE AND TIMES

OF

JAMES MADISON.

By WILLIAM C. *abell* RIVES.

VOLUME I.

BOSTON:
LITTLE, BROWN AND COMPANY.
M DCCC LIX.

RIVERSIDE, CAMBRIDGE:

STEREOTYPED AND PRINTED BY

H. O. HOUGHTON AND COMPANY.

PREFACE.

THE following work has been undertaken from no ambition of authorship, to which the active and diversified pursuits of the writer's life present every possible discouragement. It was felt, however, that some account of the character, opinions, and actions of the man who contributed more largely and effectively, though unobtrusively, to the formation of the institutions under which we live than any of his contemporaries, and who was the elective head of the Government at a period of external difficulties and trials which gave the United States definitively a rank among nations, was a *desideratum* in the history of the country.

Many valuable and authentic materials for such a work having recently come into the hands of the writer by a public charge confided to him, and others being placed at his disposal by private courtesy, he was led to consider it a duty, so far as his other occupations would per-

mit, to attempt the execution of a task, which
surmises without foundation represented him to
have entered upon, at a much earlier period.
It is only within the last two years that his
thoughts have been turned to the subject; and
his application to it during that period has met
with almost daily interruptions, and sometimes
long suspensions, from the necessary calls of
other duties.

The first volume of the work is now submitted
to the public. It belongs more, perhaps, to the
department of History than of Biography, though
partaking of the character of both. From the
nature of Mr. Madison's career, it was impossible
to isolate him from the public events of the
times in which he lived and acted; and a copious development of contemporary transactions
has been often found indispensable to display, in
its proper light, the part he bore in those transactions. We have thus been led, it will be seen,
into a fuller history, than is probably elsewhere
to be found, of the Congress of the Confederation during the four years Mr. Madison was an
active member of that body (from 1780 to
the definitive Treaty of Peace,) — embracing the
most important period of the War of the Revolution, and deeply interesting passages in our

political and diplomatic annals, which have hitherto received comparatively but little illustration.

In this and every other portion of the work,
we have relied only on original, and, in some
instances, unpublished documents; and in re-
mounting to the *sources* of our History, apocry-
phal versions of it, which have become current
by repetitions upon trust from one writer to
another, have not unfrequently been rectified by
the lights of contemporary evidence.

In reviewing these great scenes of our early
national struggles, we have not felt ourselves at
liberty to suppress anything which the truth of
history required to be uttered or disclosed. And
on the other hand, we have not been unmindful,
we trust, of the obligations of justice and candor
due to all the illustrious actors of the time. We
have endeavoured, in forming our judgments, to
guard against every influence but that of truth,
and to give way to no impressions but such as
the facts transmitted to us would, of themselves,
naturally produce upon every unbiassed mind;
keeping always before our eyes the great moral
law of History—*Ne quid falsi dicere audeat, ne
quid veri non audeat.*

SEPTEMBER, 1859.

CONTENTS.

CHAPTER I.

CHAPTER II.

CHAPTER III.

CHAPTER IV.

CHAPTER V.

CHAPTER VI.

CHAPTER XII.

CHAPTER XIII.

CHAPTER XVI.

CHAPTER XVII.

CHAPTER XVIII.

CHAPTER XIX.

CHAPTER XX.

LIFE AND TIMES

OF

JAMES MADISON.

CHAPTER I.

Connection of History and Biography — Birth and Family of Madison — Pioneers of Virginia — Education — Princeton College — Excitements produced by early Disputes between the Colonies and Mother Country — Dr. Witherspoon — Distinguished College Associates.

ALTHOUGH the Life of a Statesman derives a large portion of its interest from the public events with which it is associated, yet it would be a narrow and mistaken view of the welfare of society, and of the philosophy of human affairs, which should limit our curiosity and inquiries to the mere exterior, and, as it were, professional, history of public men. The laws by which the Divine Ruler of the universe has decreed an indissoluble connection between public happiness and private virtue, whatever apparent exceptions may sometimes delude our short-sighted judgments, never fail in the end to vindicate their supremacy and immutability. The great interests of States, of Republics especially, are conducted by the instrumentality of numerous individual agents; and as these are virtuous, competent, and wise, or vicious, faithless, or incapable, the commonwealth prospers, or sooner or later falls into ruin and decay.

The personal character and history, then, of public men, their moral principles, their intellectual qualities and attainments, the circumstances which have contributed to form and discipline them in either respect, become a most important branch of historical inquiry, and, by a natural and just relation, go hand in hand with the great public questions in which they have borne a distinguished part.

Of the statesmen of America, few have had a more important agency in the great scenes of our national story, both foreign and domestic, than James Madison. the fourth President of the United States, and none, it is believed, so leading a part in the formation and establishment of the great constitutional compact of government and union which crowned the labors of our revolutionary fathers, and forms the vital bond of our present national existence. An attempt to trace his career, with reference both to its public results and the principles and influences which guided and controlled it, will, it is hoped, meet with an indulgence from the patriotic sympathies of the country, none the less on account of the extraordinary modesty of the illustrious actor, which ever prevented him from speaking of himself, or avowing his own just and indisputable claims.

James Madison was born on the 16th day of March, 1751, at the house of his maternal grandmother, Mrs. Conway, on the northern bank of the Rappahannock river, in the county of King George, Virginia. The residence of his parents was in the county of Orange, fifty or sixty miles distant; but his birth took place during a visit of his mother to her ancestral home in the " Northern Neck " of Virginia — a designation which was originally,[1] and is still popularly, confined to the narrow peninsular region lying on tide-water between the Potomac and Rappahannock rivers, and hallowed as the birthplace of a long line of illustrious worthies,—the Washingtons, the Lees, the Masons, the Monroes, the Jones', and others,—whom it has given, from its fruitful bosom, to the service of the country. He was thus, from the moment and by the accident of his nativity, brought into close proximity and fellowship with many of those with whom he was destined to be afterwards associated in some of the most eventful passages of his future life and of the public history.

His father, bearing the same name with himself, was a large landed proprietor, occupied

[1] See Hening's Statutes at Large, vol. i. p. 352, and vol. iii. pp. 26 and 27.

mainly with the care and management of his extensive rural concerns. A large landed estate in Virginia, consisting of distinct and sometimes distant plantations, with the general supervision of the agents and laborers employed on each, and the negotiations incident to the periodical sale of their produce and purchase of their supplies in remote markets, was a mimic commonwealth, with its foreign and domestic relations, and its regular administrative hierarchy. It called for the constant exercise of vigilance, activity, humanity, sound judgment, and wise economy; and was thus a school, both of virtue and intelligence, in which many of the patriots of that day were trained for public usefulness. It does not appear, however, that the father of Mr. Madison was ever engaged in political pursuits. He was a leading man in the affairs of his county, and held, during the period of the revolutionary war, the ancient traditional office of *County Lieutenant*, derived from the institutions of the mother country, the duties of which he performed with patriotic zeal and diligence.

The name and family of Madison are coeval with the foundation of the Colony. The pious researches of kindred have ascertained that a patent was taken out for land "between the North and York rivers," on the shores of the Chesapeake Bay, as early as 1653, by John Madison, who was the father of John, and he the father of Ambrose, the paternal grandfather of the President. More recent historical inquiries conducted, with a view to general information, by a distinguished member of the Historical Society of Virginia,[1] led to the discovery of a document, in the State Paper Office at London, containing a list of the Colonists in 1623, on which the name of Captain Isaac Madison appears, only seventeen years after the landing at Jamestown. This Captain Isaac Madison was, doubtless, identical with the "Captain Madyson," whose achievements in war with the "salvages," in the year 1622, are specially mentioned in the first authentic history of the Colony, by its gallant and heroic preserver, Captain John Smith.[2] The family, arriving among the earliest of the emigrants in the new world, and planting itself on the shores of the Chesapeake, extended its scions, in little more than a century, to the waters of the Mississippi, braving, with heroic constancy, the hardships of a then unbroken wilderness, and the terrors of Indian ferocity and revenge against the intruding and progressive white man.

Among the papers of President Madison is a letter addressed to his father in 1753 by John Madison, the pioneer of the western branch of the family, who had then recently established himself in the transmontane region of Virginia.

[1] See Report of the Executive Committee of the Virginia Historical Society in 1856, by Conway Robinson, Esq.

[2] Smith's History of Virginia, book IV.

It presents so lively a picture of the dangers, distresses, and hardships of our ancestors who first occupied that portion of the State, and of the mingled bravery and tenderness, resignation and magnanimity, which they displayed in their trials, that some passages of it are here inserted, as belonging, of right, to the domain of history. From familiarity with danger, the intrepidity of the writer seems sometimes to turn almost to recklessness.

"Four families, on their flight from a branch of New River, this minute passed by my house, who say that five men were murdered at the house of Ephraim Voss on Roanoke since the death of Col. Patton. 'Tis shocking to think of the calamity of the poor wretches who lived on the Holston and New rivers, who for upwards of a hundred miles have left their habitations, lost their crops and vast numbers of their stock. Could you see, dear friend, the women who escaped crying after their murdered husbands, with their helpless children hanging on them, it could but wound your very soul."

"As the Governor has been pleased to appoint Captain Andrew Lewis the Lieutenant of this county, I expect I shall see his instructions at court. Perhaps he may fall upon some measures to put a stop to the inroads of those barbarians, without giving the people below the trouble of marching over; of which I will write to you by Mr. Semple."

"I am extremely obliged to all my good friends for the guns sent. Pray tell them they shall be carefully returned, as soon as I can be otherwise provided. I am also much obliged to you for your kind invitation, and much to my good aunt for the concern she expressed to Mr. Johnston for our welfare. But when I consider what a train I have, I cannot think of being so troublesome. Besides, should I lose my all with my life, I think my children had as well go hence, whilst in a state of innocency.

"I am, with the greatest esteem,

"Your affectionate kinsman,

"JNO. MADISON."

"August 19, 1753."

In a postscript, after reciting some further outrages of the Indians, he concludes with the following characteristic passage :—

"I verily believe they are determined on our destruction. However, as they come in small parties, if they will be so kind as to stay till I have finished my fort, may Heaven send me a few of them. Perhaps I may defray all expenses. Farewell."

From the writer of this letter, who was the first cousin of President Madison's father, sprang the Right Reverend James Madison, the first Bishop of the Protestant Episcopal Church of Virginia, and long the distinguished head of William and Mary College; Col. George Madison of Kentucky, who served with brilliant distinction in the war of 1812, and was subsequently governor of that State; and several other brothers who enjoyed a large share of the esteem and consideration of their countrymen. The annals of the State, of the Army, and of the Church have thus, all in their turn, been illustrated by the name of Madison.

The father of President Madison resided, during his whole life, upon the Montpelier estate, which became afterwards the residence of his son, as it had been of his own father, Mr. Ambrose Madison. It was always the seat of hospitality, rendered doubly attractive by the picturesque grandeur of its mountain scenery, and the heartiness and cordiality of its possessors. The mother of Mr. Madison, Eleanor Conway, must in her day have added largely to the attractions of the social, as she undoubtedly did, in the highest degree, to the happiness, comfort, and usefulness of the domestic scene. Nothing is more touching and beautiful in the life of her illustrious son than the devoted tenderness for his mother with which her virtues and character inspired him—ever recurring with anxious thoughtfulness, in the midst of his most important occupations, to her delicate health, and after the close of his public labors, personally watching over and nursing her old age with such pious care that her life was protracted to within a few years of the term of his own. His father was, no less, the object of his dutiful and affectionate attachment and respect.

The correspondence between them, from the period of young Madison's being sent to Princeton
College in 1769 to the installation of the matured and honored statesman in the office of
Secretary of State in 1801, when the father
died, has been carefully preserved, and shows
how much they were bound to each other by
sentiments of mutual confidence and respect,
even more than by ties of natural affection.

James Madison was the eldest of a family of
seven children who attained years of maturity—
four sons and three daughters. His brothers,
Francis, Ambrose, and William, enjoying, in the
main, the same opportunities of liberal education
with himself, were led by circumstances or taste
after the close of the revolutionary war, in the
military duties of which two of them bore a
part, to prefer the paths of private life, in which
they were warmly esteemed and beloved. His
sisters, superadding accomplishments and solid instruction to natural charms, married gentlemen
of the highest respectability and intelligence,
and adorned with their virtues and graces the
spheres of life in which they moved.

James, being the eldest of the sons, was the
first to pass through the ordeal of the scholastic
training which his father, appreciating its advantages so much the more from having been deprived of them, in a great degree, by the rude
and imperfect state of education in his own
youth, was honorably anxious to secure to his

children. His novitiate was passed at a school of much reputation in the county of King and Queen, conducted by an erudite Scotchman of the name of Donald Robertson. In this school, he was instructed mainly in the Greek, Latin, French, and Spanish languages. He seems to have retained in after life a very lively impression of the erudition of his preceptor, as we find the following memorandum indorsed by him on a letter received in 1804, when he was Secretary of State, from a certain Isaac Robertson, preferring his claims to a share of the public patronage: "The writer is son of Donald Robertson, the learned Teacher in King and Queen County, Virginia." It was probably from this Mr. Robertson that Mr. Madison originally derived, with much sound learning, a somewhat rugged and inharmonious pronunciation of the French language, for which he always apologized as his *Scotch-French*—a dialect not likely to be improved by the subsequent instructions and example of the learned and patriotic Dr. Witherspoon.

After leaving the school of Mr. Robertson, young Madison prosecuted his studies at home, under the tuition of the Rev. Thomas Martin, the established minister of the parish, who lived, at the time, in the family at Montpelier. This gentleman was from New Jersey, though he had near connections in North Carolina, where one of his brothers then resided, and afterwards became governor of that State. He appears to have been a man of both learning and piety; and while preparing his youthful pupil for college, acquired a strong hold on his friendship and esteem. What were the precise circumstances which determined the collegiate destination of young Madison to Princeton, instead of Williamsburg, where most of the young men of Virginia were then educated, is, perhaps, at this day, not very accurately known. It has been suggested that the unhealthiness of the latter place, particularly for those reared in the mountain climate of Virginia, was the chief motive of the decision made in favor of the former. But it is highly probable that the unhappy divisions which existed, about that time, between the Board of Visitors of William and Mary College and its Faculty, together with the unpopularity of the President, the Rev. Mr. Horrocks, who, in the excitement which then prevailed on the disturbing question of an American Episcopate, was suspected of too eager aspirations to the mitre,[1] contrasted with the harmonious councils and rising reputation of Nassau-Hall, under the rule of Dr. Witherspoon, whose name had just brought to that institution the prestige of a European renown, were not without their due share of influence on the choice finally made.

The following letter of Mr. Madison, then a

---

[1] See History of Old Churches and Ministers in Virginia, by Bishop Meade, vol. I. pp. 168–173, and 175, in note.

youth of eighteen years of age, addressed to
his late preceptor, just after his introduction to
the academic shades of Princeton, presents so
pleasing a picture of his amiable nature, of his
literary ardor, and of the nascent graces of a
pen destined, in its maturity, to be among the
most polished of the age, that we cannot withhold it from the reader, especially as it happens
to be the one of the earliest date now extant.

"NASSAU-HALL, August 10th, 1769.

"REVEREND SIR: I am not a little affected at
hearing of your misfortune, but cannot but hope
the cure may be so far accomplished as to render your journey not inconvenient. Your kind
advice and friendly cautions are a favor that
shall be always gratefully remembered: and I
must beg leave to assure you that my happiness, which you and your brother so ardently
wish for, will be greatly augmented by both
your enjoyments of the like blessing."

"I have been as particular to my father as I
thought necessary for this time, as I send him
an account of the institution, &c., wrote by Mr.
Blair, the gentleman formerly elected President
of this college. You will likewise find two pamphlets, entitled, 'Britannia's Intercession for John
Wilkes, &c. &c.,' which, if you have not seen,
may perhaps divert you."

"The near approach of Examination occasions
a surprising application to study on all sides;

and I think it very fortunate that I entered college immediately after my arrival. Though I believe there will not be the least danger of my getting an Irish hint, as they call it, yet it will make my future studies somewhat easier; and I have, by that means, read over more than half Horace, and made myself pretty well acquainted with prosody, both which will be almost neglected the two succeeding years."

"The very large packet of letters for Carolina, I am afraid, will be incommodious to your brother on so long a journey, to whom I desire my compliments may be presented, and conclude with my earnest request for a continuance of both your friendships, and sincere wishes for your recovery and an agreeable journey to your whole company.

"I am, sir, your obliged friend

"And humble servant,

"JAMES MADISON."

"To the REV. THOS. MARTIN.

"P. S. Sawney tells me that your mother and brothers are determined to accompany you to Virginia. My friendship and regard for you entitle them to my esteem; and assure them that, with the greatest sincerity I wish, after a pleasant journey, they may find Virginia capable of giving them great happiness. J. M."

The young Virginian, invested with the *toga virilis* of anticipated manhood, we now see launched

on that disciplinary career which is to form him
for the future struggles of life. The moment is
one not only of deep interest in his own personal fortunes, but of a most marked and stirring character in the history of the world. The
year 1769 witnessed the fatal renewal of the
controversies between the British Colonies in
America and the mother country, which were
thenceforward to go on with increasing complication and violence till they terminated in the
disruption of the empire.

The scheme of George Grenville for taxing
unrepresented America, abandoned by the short-
lived Whig administration of Lord Rockingham,
had been already revived by the arrogant temer-
ity of Charles Townshend, accompanied with the
odious machinery of a Board of Trade, new-fan-
gled courts of admiralty, and arrangements for
quartering British troops on the Colonies. The
two Houses of Parliament, in a joint address to
the King, had just had the folly to repeat their
determined adhesion to all these pernicious measures, to which they added the fresh provocation
of calling upon the Ministers to put in action an
obsolete and unconstitutional statute for bringing home, for trial and punishment in England,
those who should be accused of offending against
the unlimited supremacy claimed by them in
America. The House of Burgesses of the Colony to which young Madison belonged had, at
its session in the month of .May preceding the

date of his letter given above, adopted Resolutions of patriotic and indignant remonstrance against these proceedings, and was instantly dissolved. The example of Virginia was promptly followed, with noble spirit, by Massachusetts and several of the other colonies; and their legislative assemblies were, in like manner, arbitrarily and rudely dissolved.

These agitating events, which marked the year 1769 in America, were, by a singular coincidence, matched with scenes of corrresponding excitement, occurring at the same time in the domestic politics of England. The memorable Resolution of the House of Commons, nullifying the election of John Wilkes for the County of Middlesex, which, in its antecedents and consequences, convulsed the British nation with one of the most violent and protracted constitutional struggles it has ever known, dates from this eventful year. Besides the parliamentary debates of surpassing power to which, in conjunction with the American question, it gave rise, and in which the great names of Chatham, Camden, Burke, and Fox were in constant battle-array against those of Mansfield, North, Wedderburne, and their ministerial compeers, it caused the Press to teem with a brood of controversial pamphlets, which found their way to America, and of which two, we have just seen, were sent home by young Madison for the perusal of his father, and of the learned and excellent gentleman who was lately his tutor. But, among the political writers of the day, one rose to a splendor and height of renown which will forever signalize the year 1769, as that in which the letters of *Junius* to the Public Advertiser first made their appearance, and drew upon the mysterious combatant, whose impenetrable mask has never yet been lifted, the mingled wonder, admiration, and imitative zeal of the age.

Amid such thronging excitements, both in the Colonies and the metropolitan seat of empire, to arouse and stir the youthful minds of America, it was a happy circumstance for them and the country that so superior a spirit as that of Dr. Witherspoon then directed the instruction and discipline of one of its chief establishments of learning. It was only the year before Mr. Madison's entrance into the college of Princeton, that this truly great man, and ardent lover and champion of American freedom, as he afterwards approved himself, was called to preside over it. At the ripened age of forty-six years, he brought with him the learning and science of his native country in its meridian glory, while it was yet illustrated and adorned by the living lights of Smith, Hume, Reid, Kaimes, Robertson, and Blair; a spirit of profound philosophy, imbibed from the companionship of these master minds; a sympathy and attachment for popular rights, nurtured in the contests he had waged against the claims of privilege and patronage in his mother church; a practical wisdom and talent for affairs acquired by the experience of life; and a purity, manliness, and conscientious courage and energy, all his own.

These rich gifts he laid on the altar of his adopted country, and devoted in an especial manner, while the continuance of the public tranquillity permitted, to the service of the Institution over which he presided. Among the important reforms he introduced into the system of studies there, were an enlargement of the mathematical course, a special attention to metaphysical science, which had recently made such marked advances under the lead of the great minds of his own country, an extension of the course of moral philosophy, so as to embrace the general principles of public law and politics, a course of history, and regular instruction, practical and theoretic, in the canons of criticism and taste, and the art of literary composition. In these peaceful but fruitful fields, he labored earnestly and faithfully for the intellectual and moral training of the youth of America, till he was called by the course of events and the confidence of the country to play a more conspicuous and responsible part on the stage of public affairs. Thenceforward, as one of the *working men* and most active patriots of the Revolution, his name stands in imperishable connection, not only with the Declaration of American Independence, and the Articles of Confederation and

2 *

perpetual Union, of both of which he was a signer, but with all the great acts of the old Congress, from the beginning to the close of the glorious struggle.

The following letter from young Madison to his father gives us a familiar home view of his *Alma Mater*, where he was now beginning to lay the deep foundations of his future usefulness and distinction, (with an incidental mention of names which afterwards became historical,) that will be none the less interesting for the youthful *naïveté* of the writer.

"NASSAU-HALL, September 30th, '69.

"HONORED SIR: I received your letter by Mr. Rosekrans, and wrote an answer; but as it is probable this will arrive sooner which I now write by Dr. Witherspoon, I shall repeat some circumstances, to avoid obscurity."

"On Wednesday last, we had the annual Commencement. Eighteen young men took their Bachelor's degrees, and a considerable number their Master's degrees. The degree of Doctor of Laws was bestowed on Mr. Dickinson, the Farmer,[1] and Mr. Galloway, the Speaker of the Pennsylvania Assembly[2]—a distinguished mark of honor, as there never was any of that kind conferred before in America. The Commencement began at 10 o'clock, when the President

---

[1] Author of the Farmer's Letters, so justly celebrated.

[2] This gentleman afterwards tarnished all his honors by defection from the American cause.

walked first into the church, the Board of Trustees following, and behind them those that were to take their Master's degrees, and last of all, those that were to take their first degrees.

"After a short prayer by the President, the head oration, which is always given to the greatest scholar, was pronounced by Mr. Samuel Smith, son of a Presbyterian minister in Pennsylvania. Then followed the other orations, disputes, and dialogues, distributed to each according to his merit; and, last of all, was pronounced the valedictory oration, by Mr. John Henry, son of a gentleman in Maryland. This is given to the greatest orator.

"We had a very great assembly of people, a considerable number of whom came from New York. Those at Philadelphia were most of them detained by races, which were to follow the next day. . . . .

"The Trustees have appointed Mr. Caldwell, a minister at Elizabethtown, to take a journey through the Southern Provinces, as far as Georgia, to make collections, by which the college fund may be enabled to increase the Library, provide an apparatus of mathematical and philosophical instruments, and likewise to support professors, which would be a great addition to the advantages of this college. Dr. Witherspoon's business in Virginia is nearly the same, as I conjecture, and perhaps to form some acquaintance, to induce gentlemen to send their sons to this college. . . . .

"I feel great satisfaction at the assistance my uncle B—— has derived from the Springs, and I flatter myself, from the continuance of my mother's health, that Dr. Shore's skill will effectually banish the cause of her late indisposition.

"I recollect nothing more at present worth relating; but as often as opportunity and anything worthy your attention may occur, be assured you shall hear from

"Your affectionate son,

"JAMES MADISON.

"COL. JAMES MADISON, Orange Co., Va."

Mr. Madison continued his residence as an undergraduate at Princeton for three years, during which time, by a diligence and ardor in the prosecution of his studies which cost him a serious detriment to his health, he completed the entire course of instruction there. In 1771, at the age of twenty years, he closed his collegiate career with the degree of Bachelor of Arts. There can be no doubt that the intellectual training through which he passed in this institution, the habits and associations he formed there, the example, both literary and personal, as well as the instructions, of its distinguished head, exerted a very large influence in moulding the character of his mind and shaping his future destiny.

We have seen how liberal and expansive a field of inquiry was opened to the student by the additions which Dr. Witherspoon made to the previous *curriculum* of the college. The increased attention paid to the study of the nature and constitution of the human mind, and the improvements which had been lately introduced into this fundamental department of knowledge by the philosophical inquiries of his own countrymen, constituted a marked and most important feature of Dr. Witherspoon's reforms. Mr. Madison formed a taste for these inquiries, which entered deeply, as we shall hereafter have occasion to remark, into the character and habits of his mind, and gave to his political writings in after life a profound and philosophical cast which distinguished them, eminently and favorably, from the productions of the ablest of his contemporaries.

Whatever tendency there might be supposed to be in these studies to encourage too speculative a turn of mind was effectually counteracted by the lessons of experience derived from the study of history, a course of which, we have seen, was at the same time instituted by Dr. Witherspoon. To those who may be inclined to question the importance of metaphysical, as well as historical, knowledge to public men, we may be permitted to cite the testimony of one who ranked among the most able and successful, as well as brilliant, statesmen of his age and country, and who, in lamenting that the race of statesmen-lawyers was extinct—that there were no longer Clarendons and Bacons—declared there would be none such any more till men found leisure and encouragement to climb up to the vantage-ground of science, and when that happens, "one of the vantage-grounds to which men must climb," he adds, " is metaphysical, and the other historical, knowledge." [1]

Nor was it the able and judicious instruction of the college only that contributed to form the character of the future statesman, legislator, debater, and writer. There was in the kindred zeal, and high scholarship and attainments of his college associates, much that impelled him forward in his unremitting efforts of self-discipline and improvement. The young Smith mentioned by him in the letter we have just read, as the distinguished scholar to whom the "head oration" was assigned at the college commencement, was the Rev. Dr. Samuel Stanhope Smith, who afterwards became so celebrated for his literary and philosophical works, succeeding Dr. Witherspoon, whose daughter he married, in the presidency of Princeton College, after having presided with great reputation over that of Hampden Sidney

---

[1] See Lord Bolingbroke's Works, (Letters on the Study and Use of History, Lett. v.) He developes his idea, and shows the reason and justness of it, in the following sentence :—

" They must pry into the secret recesses of the human heart, and become well acquainted with the whole moral world, that they may discover the abstract reason of all laws ; and they must trace the laws of particular States, especially of their own, from the first rough sketches to the more perfect draughts,—from the first causes or occasions that produced them, through all the effects, good and bad, that they produced."

in Virginia. He was the intimate friend and correspondent of Mr. Madison during the whole period of their lives.

The young Henry of Maryland mentioned by him, as the gifted orator who pronounced the "valedictory" on the same occasion, became in after life successively member of the Congress of the Confederation, senator of the United States, and governor of his State; and he and Mr. Madison were thus destined to renew, upon the theatre of their common public duties, the acquaintance of their early days. Among his college contemporaries were also Brockholst Livingston, future judge of the supreme court of the United States; William Bradford of Pennsylvania, future attorney-general of the United States under the administration of Washington; Hugh Henry Brackenridge of the same State, distinguished alike as a jurist and a writer; Aaron Burr, future Vice-President of the United States; and Morgan Lewis of New York, Aaron Ogden of New Jersey, and Henry Lee of Virginia, all three, after distinguished military and civil careers, becoming the chief magistrates of their respective States.

The young men who filled the halls of Princeton College at this period, as at a later day, were animated with a high spirit of public liberty and a jealous love of constitutional freedom. Breathed into them, as these sentiments were, by their great preceptor, there was everything in the mighty issues of the time, and the lofty

and sublime eloquence with which those issues
were discussed on both sides of the Atlantic, to
fan and invigorate the sacred fire.   One of the
fruits of this patriotic excitement was the formation among the students of a new society which
nobly survives to this day,—the "American Whig
Society,"—of which Mr. Madison is reputed to
have been one of the principal founders.   In a
letter to his father, dated "Nassau-Hall, July 23
1770," he relates, in the following language of
youthful fervor, two significant incidents which
give honorable proof of the high spirit of resistance to the unconstitutional encroachments of
the mother country, which then actuated the
body of students of Princeton College.

"We have no public news but the base conduct of the merchants in New York, in breaking
through their spirited resolutions not to import,
a distinct account of which, I suppose, will
be in the Virginia Gazette before this arrives.
Their letter to the merchants in Philadelphia,
requesting their concurrence, was lately burnt by
the students of this place in the college yard, all
of them appearing in their black gowns, and the
bell tolling.—The number of students has increased very much of late.   There are about a
hundred and fifteen in college and the grammar
school, (twenty-two commence this fall,) all of
them in American cloth."

It is a matter of natural and interesting inquiry to learn what were the personal relations

formed between the eminent man who was the head of this seat of learning and patriotism, and the pupil upon whom, more than any other, he seems to have impressed the distinctive characteristics of his own mind; for no intelligent reader, acquainted with their works, can fail to remark how much the same clearness of analytical reasoning, the same lucid order, the same precision and comprehensiveness combined, the same persuasive majesty of truth and conviction clothed in a terse and felicitous diction,[1]

---

[1] The style of Mr. Madison, like that of Dr. Franklin and others of the best writers of that age of American literature, seems to have been formed by early familiarity with the writings of Addison. The following letter addressed by him, at a later period of his life, to a nephew in whose studies he took a lively interest, contains such valuable hints on this subject that, for the benefit of the young men of the country, as well as for its intrinsic excellence and the beautiful tribute it pays to the merits of the Spectator, and of Addison in particular, we insert it here.

"MONTPELIER, Jan. 4, 1829.

"When I was at an age which will soon be yours, a book fell into my hands which I read, as I believe, with particular advantage. I have always thought it the best that had been written for cherishing in young minds a desire of improvement, a taste for learning, and a

lively sense of the duties, the virtues, and the proprieties of life. The work I speak of is the Spectator, well known by that title. It had several authors, at the head of them Mr. Addison, whose papers are marked at the bottom of each by one of the letters in the name of the muse, *Clio.* They will reward you for a second reading, after reading them along with the others.

"Addison was of the first rank among the fine writers of the age, and has given a definition of what he showed himself to be an example. 'Fine writing,' he says, 'consists of sentiments that are natural, without being obvious;' to which adding the remark of Swift, another celebrated author of the same period, making a good style to consist 'of proper words in their proper places,' a definition is formed, which will merit your recollection when you become qualified, as I hope you will one day be, to shine forth in the productions, whether written or spoken, of both. Such intellectual affinities, joined to moral worth, could not but form a strong bond of friendship, and of mutual confidence, attachment, and respect between them. These sentiments are warmly manifested by the pupil in a letter written from Princeton to his father the 9th October, 1771, in which he says:

"I should be glad if your health and other circumstances should enable you to visit Dr. Witherspoon during his stay in Virginia. I am persuaded you would be much pleased with him, and that he would be very glad to see you."

Dr. Witherspoon continued to feel a lively interest in the studies and pursuits of his pupil, after the formal connection of the latter with the college was terminated. Young Madison, appreciating at its just value the aid of so enlightened a guide and counsellor, and desiring also to avail himself of the riches of the college library, determined, after his graduation, to pass one year more at Princeton as a private student. The preceptor and the pupil were destined to meet again, after a lapse of nine years, in the supreme councils of the country, as coworkers in the great cause of national independence and national union.

employ your pen for the benefit of others, and for your own gratification.

"I send you a copy of the 'Spectator,' that it may be at hand when the time arrives for making use of it, and as a token also of all the good wishes of your affectionate uncle.   J. M."

CHAPTER II.

Madison leaves Princeton and returns to his Father's Residence in
Virginia — His Studies and Pursuits at Home — Correspondence
with his College Friend, Bradford of Philadelphia — Religious Sentiments — Traits of Personal Character — Progress of Controversy
with the Mother Country — Persecution of Baptists in Virginia
excites Indignation of Madison — Early Champion of Religious
Freedom — Established Church in Virginia — Conduct and Influence of its Members in the Contest for Independence.

In 1772, Mr. Madison, then twenty-one years
of age, returned to take up his residence under
the paternal roof in Virginia. Here his love of
study followed him; and he divided his time
between an extensive course of reading for his
own improvement, and the amiable office of instructing his younger brothers and sisters in the
rudiments of literature. The temporary lull in
our controversies with the mother country happily enabled him, for a year or two, to give
himself up to these peaceful and edifying pursuits with but little distraction.

The port duties imposed upon the Colonies,
after the repeal of the Stamp Act, had in their
turn been repealed also, with the single exception of the duty of three pence on tea, which,

contemptible as it was in amount, was obstinately retained by the infatuation of Lord North, as a symbol of the legislative supremacy of England; he madly declaring that a *total repeal*, which was urged by some of the ablest of his colleagues in the Cabinet, as well as by the leaders of the opposition in Parliament, "was not to be thought of, till America is prostrate at our feet." America wisely contented herself, for a season, with a calm but effectual resistance by associations generally entered into, and for the most part religiously kept, not to consume any tea of British importation, so long as it was the subject of unconstitutional taxation.

A brief period of comparative tranquillity ensued. During this interval we find Mr. Madison, from the bosom of the peaceful retirement in which he was prosecuting his studies with no other discouragement than that of the feeble health he had brought with him from Princeton, cultivating the pleasures of ingenuous friendship in a free epistolary intercourse with some of his late college companions. Among these was young Bradford of Philadelphia, whose name has been already mentioned. He was two or three years the junior of Mr. Madison; but congenial tastes and sentiments formed a strong, mutual attachment between them. The subsequent career of Bradford, first as a gallant officer of the army during a portion of the revolutionary contest, afterwards successively attorney-general, and judge of the supreme court, of Pennsylvania, and finally attorney-general of the United States under the administration of Washington, in which high position his days were prematurely ended, shows how worthy he was of the friendship he inspired.

A cordial and unreserved correspondence was kept up between these two young friends for several years after they left their *Alma Mater*, from which we propose to offer some extracts as illustrative alike of the early character of Mr. Madison and of the contemporary history of the country. We give entire the first letter, as revealing the inmost sentiments of Mr. Madison's mind on topics of the deepest interest to human life, in a mingled tone of philosophy and friendship, and with an unstudied Addisonian grace, which prefigured the future sage in the youthful friend.

"ORANGE, Virginia, Nov. 9, 1772.

"MY DEAR B——: You moralize so prettily that, if I were to judge from some parts of your letter of October 13, I should take you for an old philosopher, that had experienced the emptiness of earthly happiness; and I am very glad that you have so early seen through the romantic paintings with which the world is sometimes set off by the sprightly imaginations of the ingenious. You have happily supplied by reading and observation the want of experiment; and therefore I hope you are sufficiently guarded

3 *

against the allurements and vanities that beset us
on our first entrance on the theatre of life. Yet
however nice and cautious we may be in detecting the follies of mankind, and framing our economy according to the precepts of wisdom and
religion, I fancy there will commonly remain
with us some latent expectation of obtaining
more than ordinary happiness and prosperity,
till we feel the convincing argument of actual
disappointment: though I will not determine
whether we shall be much the worse for it, if
we do not allow it to intercept our views towards a future state, because strong desires and
great hopes instigate us to arduous enterprises,
fortitude, and perseverance.

"Nevertheless, a watchful eye must be kept
on ourselves, lest, while we are building ideal
monuments of renown and bliss here, we neglect
to have our names enrolled in the annals of
heaven. These thoughts come into my mind,
because I am writing to you and thinking of
you. As to myself, I am too dull and infirm
now to look out for any extraordinary things in
this world, for I think my sensations for many
months have intimated to me not to expect a
long or healthy life; though it may be better
with me after some time, but I hardly dare expect it, and therefore have little spirit or elas-
ticity to set about anything that is difficult in
acquiring, and useless in possessing after one has
exchanged time for eternity. But you have

health, youth, fire, and genius to bear you along through the high track of public life, and so may be more interested and delighted in improving on hints that respect the temporal, though momentous, concerns of man.

"I think you made a judicious choice of history and the science of morals for your winter's study. They seem to be of the most universal benefit to men of sense and taste in every post, and must certainly be of great use to youth in settling the principles and refining the judgment, as well as in enlarging knowledge and correcting the imagination. I doubt not but you design to season them with a little divinity now and then, which, like the philosopher's stone in the hands of a good man, will turn them and every lawful acquirement into the nature of itself, and make them more precious than fine gold.

"As you seem to require that I should be open and unreserved, (which is, indeed, the only proof of true friendship,) I will venture to give you a word of advice, though it be more to convince you of my affection for you than from any apprehension of your needing it. Pray do not suffer those impertinent fops that abound in every city to divert you from your business and philosophical amusements. You may please them more by admitting them to the enjoyment of your company; but you will make them respect and admire you more by showing your indignation at their follies, and by keeping them at a becoming distance. I am luckily out of the way of such troubles; but I know you are surrounded with them, for they breed in towns and populous places as naturally as flies do in the shambles, because there they get food enough for their vanity and impertinence.

"I have undertaken to instruct my brothers and sisters in some of the first rudiments of literature; but it does not take up·so much of my time but I shall have leisure to receive and answer your letters, which are very grateful to me, I assure you, and for reading any performances you may be kind enough to send me, whether of Mr. Freneau or anybody else. I think myself happy in your correspondence, and desire you will continue to write as often as you can, as you see I intend to do by the early and long answer I send you. You are the only valuable friend I have settled in so public a place, and I must rely on you for an account of all literary transactions in your part of the world.

"I am not sorry to hear of Livingston's getting a degree. I heartily wish him well, though many would think I had but little reason to do so; and if he would be sensible of his opportunities and encouragement, I think he might still recover. L—— and his compeers, after their feeble but wicked assault upon Mr. Erwin, in my opinion, will disgrace the catalogue of names; but they are below contempt, and I spend no more words about them.

"And now, my friend, I must take my leave of you, but with such hopes, that it will not be long before I receive another epistle from you, as make me more cheerfully conclude and subscribe myself your sincere and affectionate friend,

"JAMES MADISON, JR.

"To Mr. WILLIAM BRADFORD, JR., }
  at the Coffee-House, Philadelphia." }

"P. S. Your direction was right. However, the addition of 'Jr.' to my name would not be improper."

The reader will not have failed to remark the elevated strain of religious sentiment which pervades the preceding letter. The advice which young Madison gave his friend to season his other studies with a due attention to the oracles of Divine Truth was faithfully observed by himself. Among his early manuscripts, which have come down to us, are minute and elaborate notes made by him on the Gospels and the Acts of the Apostles, which evince a close and discriminating study of the sacred writings, as well as a wide acquaintance with the whole field of theological literature. In one of these notes, referring to a chapter of the Acts of the Apostles, where the Bereans are mentioned as "more noble than those in Thessalonica, in that they received the word with all readiness of mind, and searched the Scriptures daily whether these things were so," he commends their conduct "as a noble

example for all succeeding Christians to imitate
and follow." After the manner of the Bereans,
he seems to have searched the Scriptures daily
and diligently; and we give below, from the
mass of his annotations, a few brief excerpts, as
specimens of the manner in which he conducted
and recorded his researches.[1]

Nor were his studies in this vital and momentous branch of the relations of humanity,
confined to the text of the Holy Scriptures. He
explored the whole history and evidences of
Christianity on every side, through clouds of
witnesses and champions for and against, from
the Fathers and schoolmen down to the infidel
philosophers of the eighteenth century. No one

[1] In a paraphrase on the Gospel of St. John, referring to the
passage in which Mary Magdalene
is represented as looking into the
Holy Sepulchre and seeing two
angels in white, one sitting at the
head and the other at the feet,
where the body of the Saviour
had lain, he makes the following
reflection:—

"Angels to be desired at our
feet as well as at our head—not
an angelical understanding and a
diabolical conversation — not all
our religion in our brains and
tongue, and nothing in our heart
and life."

In the same spirit, commenting
on the chapter of Acts, where Je-
sus says to St. Paul, who had fallen
to the earth under the light which
shined round about him from heav-
en, "*Arise*, and *go* into the city,
and it shall be told thee what thou
shalt *do*," he subjoins this as the
proper deduction from the passage: "It is not the *talking*, but
the *walking* and *working* person
that is the true Christian."

On doctrinal points, the following brief memoranda and refer-
ences taken from many others of
a like character, may serve to show
both his orthodoxy and his pene-
tration :—

" Omnisciency — God's fore-
knowledge doth not compel, but
permits to be done." Acts, ch. II.
v. 23.

" Christ's divinity appears by St.
John, ch. xx. v. 28."

" Resurrection testified and witnessed by the Apostles. Acts,
ch. IV. v. 33."

not a professed theologian, and but few even of those who are, have ever gone through more laborious and extensive inquiries to arrive at the truth. So vast and so unwonted was the research which, during this period of his life, he had bestowed on religious investigations, that, when the University of Virginia was established, he was called on by its eminent founder for a list of theological writers, ancient and modern, to fill that department of the university library. The catalogue he furnished will ever remain a memorial alike of his learning and of his just appreciation of the paramount importance of this great province of human reason and faith.[1]

What was the result in his mind of these profound and laborious inquiries, prosecuted with all the freshness and energy of his intellectual powers, appears very significantly, although incidentally, in a letter written by him two years later to his young Pennsylvanian friend. Speaking of the celebrated Tracts of Dean Tucker on the dispute between England and her American colonies, which he had just then read with much satisfaction at the practical solution of the controversy recommended by that author, in a voluntary separation of the two countries, Mr. Madison adds:—

"At the same time, his ingenious and plausible defence of parliamentary authority carries in it such defects and misrepresentations as confirm

[1] See Appendix, A.

me in political orthodoxy, after the same manner as the specious arguments of infidels have established the faith of inquiring Christians."

To return, however, to the order of time in following this familiar and confidential correspondence, so full of characteristic traits. We find two letters of Mr. Madison addressed to his friend Bradford during the year 1773, which, being a year of unusual political tranquillity for the times, the correspondence of that date claims our attention chiefly by its personal details, and the unstudied revelations it gives, by the way, of the character of the writer. In a letter of the 28th of April, 1773, his love of truth and plain dealing strikingly appears in the following passage:—

"I am glad you disclaim all punctiliousness in our correspondence. For my own part, I confess I have not the face to perform ceremony in person; and I equally detest it on paper, though, as Tully says, it cannot blush. Friendship, like all truth, delights in plainness and simplicity; and it is the counterfeit alone that needs ornament and ostentation. I am so thoroughly persuaded of this, that, when I observe any one over-complaisant to me in his professions and promises, I am tempted to interpret his language thus: 'As I have no real esteem for you, and for certain reasons think it expedient to appear well in your eye, I endeavour to varnish falsehood with politeness, which I think I can do in so ingenious a manner that so vain a blockhead as you cannot see through it.' "

Another passage in the same letter, in which he expresses a manly disdain at malice and detraction, is a fit pendant to the preceding.

" I have not seen," he says, " a single piece against the Doctor's address.   I saw a piece advertised for publication in the Philadelphia Gazette, entitled ' Candid Remarks, &c.,' and that is all I know about it.   These things seldom reach Virginia, and when they do, I am out of the way of them.   I have a curiosity to read those authors who write ' with all the rage of impotence,' not because there is any excellence or wit in their writings, but because they implicitly proclaim the merit of those they are railing against, and give them an occasion of showing by their silence and contempt that they are invulnerable."

In the conclusion of his letter, he tells his friend : " My health is a little better, owing, I believe, to more activity and less study, recommended by physicians.   I shall try, if possible, to devise some business that will afford me a sight of you once more in Philadelphia, within a year or two.   I wish you would resolve the same with respect to me in Virginia, though within a shorter time."

On the 6th of September, of the same year, he writes another but very brief letter to his friend, in which he mentions, with great gratification, a

visit that had just been paid him by a gentleman who was one of his tutors at Princeton.
How congenial the sentiments of friendship and
affection were to his ingenuous nature, is shown
by the following simple effusion of the heart:—

"This will be handed you by Mr. Erwin, who
has been kind enough to extend his journey thus
far, and whose praise is in every man's mouth
here for an excellent discourse he this day
preached for us. He will let you know everything that occurs to me worth mentioning, at
commencement, or Philadelphia if you should
not attend commencement. Gratitude to him
and friendship to you and others, with some
business, perhaps, will induce me to visit Philadelphia or Princeton in the spring, if I should
be alive and should have health sufficient."

The year 1774 opened with questions of the
deepest import to American liberty. The British
ministry, foiled in their attempt to raise a revenue in America from the duty on tea by the
private associations so extensively entered into
against its use, had recently fallen upon a new
expedient for the accomplishment of their object. They entered into an arrangement with
the East India Company, exempting them from
the heavy export duty which had been hitherto
imposed on the shipment of tea from England;
in consideration of which the Company was to
send out to the Colonies large cargoes of that
commodity, which, being thus enabled to sell at

much cheaper rates than before, including the
duty charged upon it in America, it was thought
they could not fail to introduce again into the
consumption of the country, and so succeed at
last in levying the unconstitutional tribute. Under this arrangement, numerous ships of the
Company laden with tea arrived, about the close
of the preceding year, at New York, Philadelphia, Charleston, and Boston.

The people of America, filled with indignation
at this politico-commercial confederacy, resolved
to defeat it by preventing the landing of the obnoxious cargoes. The peace-loving Quaker city
of Philadelphia, in which Mr. Madison's friend
resided, took the lead on this occasion.[1] A public meeting of its inhabitants was held, in which
bold and vigorous resolutions were adopted, declaring the new plan of importation to be
an "attack upon the liberties of America," calling
on every good citizen to oppose the attempt,
and denouncing any one who should directly or
indirectly countenance it as " an enemy of his
country." At the same time, a committee was
appointed to call upon the consignees of the
company, and insist. upon the resignation of
their agency. The demand was immediately
complied with; and the odious tea ships, with
their offensive contraband, sailed back from the
Delaware to the Thames without having once

---

[1] See Annual Register for 1774, p. 49, and Belsham's Great Britain,
vol. VI. p. 40.

broken bulk. Similar proceedings were adopted at New York, and with the like result. At Charleston, after much opposition, the tea was allowed to be unloaded, but without entry at the custom-house, and deposited in damp cellars, where it was finally rendered worthless by the effect of the humidity to which it was exposed.

At Boston, events of a yet graver character grew out of the resistance to the new ministerial device. Every effort to prevail on the consignees of the East India Company to decline their agency had failed. The Governor and the officers of the customs, anxious to recommend themselves to the ministry by their zeal, interposed every obstacle to the voluntary return of the tea ships. The spirit of popular indignation, chafed by official opposition, had recourse to more summary methods of redress; and a number of persons, in the disguise of Indians, entered on board the East India ships, and emptied the tea chests into the ocean.

This memorable occurrence took place on the 16th of December, 1773, and was undoubtedly, in the immediate sequence of events which it produced, the proximate cause of the American Revolution. It kindled at once an unmeasured and intemperate resentment in the government of the mother country that hurried it headlong into violent and arbitrary measures, which, in their turn, aroused and united all America in determined resistance to these accumulated acts of tyranny and oppression. The bill for closing the port of Boston; fundamental alterations in the colonial government of Massachusetts in violation of her charter; a virtual indemnity granted to any crimes which might be committed in that province under color of official authority; and new orders for quartering troops on America, were the acts of ministerial vengeance which followed in quick succession upon the events in Boston.

But, in the midst of these great questions, was another of not less interest to the rights and destinies of man, which affected the mind of Mr. Madison the more painfully, perhaps, because it came home to his native land. It was the vital question of religious freedom. The original colonial polity of Virginia had been founded in that mistaken connection of Church and State, which was then the universal practice of all nations and of all religious parties. Even the Puritans of New England, who came to America to escape religious persecution in the mother country, were no sooner established in their new abode than they fell into the same abuse, and set the example of fierce intolerance against all other sects than their own.

The colonists of Virginia left their native land in cordial amity with the civil and religious government of their fathers. They were content to bring with them the single guarantee of the "liberties, franchises, and immunities" of free born

4 *

Englishmen; and in the institutions of every kind established by them in the new world, they sought to conform, as near as might be, to the model furnished by the father-land. The government of the colony was, indeed, expressly instructed to administer its various functions " as near to the common laws of England and the equity thereof as may be," and, in religion, to provide that " the service of God and the Christian faith be preached, planted, and used according to the doctrine and rites of the Church of England."[1]

The Church of England, though necessarily modified in its transplantation, thus became the established Church of Virginia; and from time to time, laws of more or less stringency were passed to enforce conformity to it. At the period to which Mr. Madison's correspondence now brings us, the Baptist dissenters fell particularly under the persecution of the dominant authority; and in the county of his own residence, (Orange,) as well as two of the adjacent counties, (Spotsylvania and Culpeper,) several of their ministers had been confined in jail for the alleged offence of disturbing the public peace by their preaching and mode of worship.[2]

These brief historical reminiscences seemed an indispensable preface to the following extracts of a letter addressed by Mr. Madison to his

[1] See Charter and Instructions in Hen. Stat. vol. I. pp. 57–76.

[2] See Semple's History of the Virginia Baptists, pp. 15, 381, 382, 415, 416, 427, 428.

young Pennsylvanian friend on the 24th of January, 1774, and which, we doubt not, will interest the reader as well by the fervid love of liberty with which they glow, as by the justness and depth of the reflections they contain.

"I congratulate you on your heroic proceedings in Philadelphia with regard to the Tea. I wish Boston may conduct matters with as much discretion, as they seem to do with boldness. They appear to have great trials and difficulties by the reason of the obduracy and ministerialism of their governor. However, political contests are necessary sometimes, as well as military, to afford exercise and practice, and to instruct in the art of defending liberty and property.

"I verily believe the frequent assaults that have been made on America, (Boston especially,) will in the end prove of real advantage. If the Church of England had been the established and general religion in all the Northern colonies, as it has been among us here, and uninterrupted harmony had prevailed throughout the continent, it is clear to me that slavery and subjection might and would have been gradually insinuated among us. Union of religious sentiment begets a surprising confidence, and ecclesiastical establishments tend to great ignorance and corruption, all of which facilitate the execution of mischievous projects.

"But away with politics! Let me address you as a student and philosopher, and not as a

patriot now. I am pleased that you are going
to converse with the Edwards and Henrys and
Charles' who have swayed the British sceptre,
though I believe you will find some of them
dirty and unprofitable companions, unless you
will glean instruction from their follies, and fall
more in love with liberty by beholding such detestable pictures of tyranny and cruelty. . . . . .

"I want again to breathe your free air. I
expect it will mend my constitution and confirm
my principles. I have, indeed, as good an at-
mosphere at home as the climate will allow, but
have nothing to brag of as to the state and liberty of my country. Poverty and luxury prevail
among all sorts; pride, ignorance, and knavery
among the priesthood; and, vice and wickedness
among the laity. This is bad enough; but it is
not the worst I have to tell you. That diabolical, hell-conceived principle of persecution rages
among some; and, to their eternal infamy, the
clergy can furnish their quota of imps for such
purposes. There are, at this time, in the adjacent country, not less than five or six well-mean-
ing men in close jail for publishing their religious
sentiments, which, in the main, are very ortho-
dox. I have neither patience to hear, talk, or
think of anything relative to this matter; for I
have squabbled and scolded, abused and ridiculed
so long about it to little purpose that I am without common patience. So I must beg you to pity
me, and pray for liberty of conscience to all."

There is no form of tyranny so revolting to
the feelings of human nature as that which is
exercised over the mind of man; and no species
of mental tyranny so odious as that which seeks
to enslave the conscience in matters of religion.
The sentiments of generous indignation expressed
by Mr. Madison at the instances of religious persecution which had occurred in his own State, and
almost under his eyes in his own neighbourhood,
do honor alike to his heart and understanding.

But there may be reason to question whether,
under the excitement so natural to a well
principled mind in such circumstances, the picture drawn by him is not somewhat over-
charged. That there were some honorable exceptions to the character given by him of the
clergy of the Established Church, there can be
no ground to doubt from the contemporary accounts which have reached us; and that the laity
were not universally, or, we would fain believe,
generally infected with the malignant spirit of
persecution described by him, seems to be sufficiently shown by the noble and catholic public
letter of President Blair, son of the commissary,
written only five or six years before this period,
while he was the acting governor of the colony,[1]
and also by the fact that many of the laity, two
years only after the date of Mr. Madison's letter,
as members of the legislature concurred in the

[1] See this admirable letter in Semple, pp. 15, 16, and also in Campbell's Virginia, p. 139.

repeal of the laws by which the establishment was sustained.[1]

Nor were the Baptist dissenters exposed, in every part of the State, to the same measure of persecution. In some extensive regions, they were exempt from all legal molestation.[2] The country in which Mr. Madison resided seems to have been, in a particular manner, the focus in which the scorching rays of persecution were converged, and directed, with their intensest heat, against this devoted sect. No wonder, then, that he should have been deeply outraged by such a spectacle, and that contrasting it, as he naturally did, with the general peace and happiness of the colony in which his friend lived, and where the principle of universal and unlimited freedom of religion had been established from the first, he should have taken a somewhat gloomy and desponding view of the state of society in his native land.

The opinion expressed by Mr. Madison in the preceding letter, that " if the Church of England had been the established and general religion in all the northern colonies, as it has been with us here, and uninterrupted harmony had prevailed throughout the continent," the ultimate loss of liberty might and probably would have ensued, deserves to be attentively considered, as it embraces a great general principle, profoundly medi-

---

[1] Semple, pp. 26, 27, and also Jefferson's Writings, vol. i. p. 32.

[2] Semple, p. 294.

tated, to which he ever attached the highest importance, and which may be said to be, in an especial manner, the corner-stone of his political creed.

It was not that there was anything in the principles or constitution of the Church of England, as it existed in this country, which he deemed intrinsically deleterious to the public liberty, but it was, as the context shows, "the union of religious sentiment" enforced by law, which the general establishment of that or any other Church in all the colonies would have produced, that he deprecated as dangerous to liberty. The unfettered and spontaneous diversity of opinions, of sects, of parties, of interests, in both politics and religion, he held to be the only practical security for the equal liberty of all, by the mutual vigilance and inspection they would exercise over each other, and the mutual forbearance they would finally learn to practise from an experience of that security. We shall hereafter have occasion to trace the consistent influence of this leading and fruitful principle, in his views and conduct on all the various and difficult problems of constitutional and legislative organization which he had to deal with in his long and eventful career.

That there was nothing in the Church of England, as it existed in this country, essentially hostile to public liberty, the history of the colony, where it was first established and most

widely spread its roots, satisfactorily proves.
Virginia was, in an especial manner, the nursery
of freedom in the new world. By the exercise
of a bold initiative, she early established a representative assembly of her own, and through
that assembly, proclaimed the great constitutional principle of immunity from taxation except by her own consent. During the period
of the intestine troubles in the mother country,
she virtually assumed and exercised all the powers of independent self-government. She set the
example of an appeal to arms in vindication of
her rights a century before the final struggle for
national independence; and in every stage of
that great struggle, she was certainly behind
none of her sister colonies in the energy and
boldness with which she sustained the common
cause. It cannot be said, therefore, that the
Church of England, as it existed in Virginia,
had extinguished or even depressed the spirit
of liberty.

Whatever tendencies of that kind might have
belonged to it in its native and original constitution, were excluded by the modifications it
underwent here. The political elements of the
Church were not, and could not be, transplanted
into American soil. Here were no bishops appointed by the king and holding seats in the
upper branch of the legislature, and pledged to
an interested and unhallowed alliance between
the altar and the throne. Neither were there

any rights of *patronage* which could fill our churches, without regard to the wishes or consent of the people. Vestries, originally chosen by the people of each parish, exercised the right of admitting, rejecting, or displacing ministers, according to their own views of duty and propriety, and steadily resisted the formality of inductions, which were supposed to give the incumbent a legal freehold paramount to the will of the congregation.[1] Discussions and controversies, on this point, often arose between the vestries and the Governor or commissary, and trained the leading men of the colony, in the school of parochial freedom, to habits and principles of political independence.

The vestries, though primarily ecclesiastical bodies, and expressly required to "subscribe to be conformable to the doctrine and discipline of the Church of England," were also invested with various functions of a civil and municipal character. They were empowered to lay and collect taxes within the limits of their jurisdiction for local purposes, to provide for the poor, to cause the lands to be "processioned,"[2] to "present," through their churchwardens, offences against the laws and public order, and to make appoint-

---

[1] See Beverly's History of Virginia, p. 229. Also Lord Culpeper's statement in Chalmers's Annals of the Colonies, p. 356.

[2] Formerly, the laws of Virginia required the periodical appointment of persons, in every term of four or five years, to go around and re-mark the limits of every separate tract of land. This was called "processioning" the lands.

ments of all necessary subordinate officers in the execution of these duties.[1] They were thus clothed, to a considerable extent, with the power of the purse, the guardianship of property, and the censorship of morals, and united in their hands legislative, executive, and judicial trusts. It was natural that the men of education, property, and character in their respective districts should be chosen into these bodies; and it is impossible to form a just idea of the social, religious or political condition of Virginia, at the period of which we are speaking, without adverting to their composition, and the influence they exerted.

The vestry-men of that day, we shall find, were the Washingtons, the Lees, the Randolphs, the Masons, the Blands, the Pendletons, the Nelsons, the Nicholas', the Harrisons, the Pages, the Madisons, and other names, far too numerous to recapitulate in detail, which stand among the first on the roll of our revolutionary worthies. In these men, and such as these, were the effective and controlling powers of the Church; for the laity, and not the clergy, were the rulers here. If they showed an attachment to the Church of their fathers, it was not because of the laxity and abuses which had crept into it, but, in despite of those abuses, for the sake of those sol-

[1] For the qualifications and duties of Vestry-men, see Laws of Virginia, edition 1752, pp. 2, 4, 119, 220, 304, 305, 336, 337, and edition 1769, p. 350.

emn and impressive forms of worship, that noble and exalted liturgy, which, in the religious services at the opening of the first Congress, we are told by one of themselves, made so profound and thrilling an impression upon the members, who, by habit and education, had been most prepossessed against it.[1]

[1] See Correspondence and Diary of John Adams, in his Works, vol. II. pp. 368, 369, and Irving's Life of Washington, vol. I. pp. 400–401.

The whole scene of the assembling of the first Continental Congress in Philadelphia, in May 1774, was a most imposing and extraordinary one. When the members met together, gifted as they were with the highest moral and intellectual qualities, there was yet, as Mr. Adams writes, "such a diversity of religions, educations, manners, and interests among them as it seemed impossible to unite in one plan of conduct." Upon the organization of the body, it was proposed that its daily proceedings should be opened with prayer; but it was immediately suggested that, as the delegates were of different religious sects, they might not consent to join in the same form of worship. Upon this, Mr. Samuel Adams, who was a strong Congregationalist, arose and said that "he would willingly join in prayer with any gentleman of piety and virtue, whatever might be his cloth, if he was a friend to his country," and moved that the Rev. Mr. Duché;

a distinguished Episcopalian clergyman of Philadelphia, should be invited to officiate as chaplain. The following morning, which was the 7th of May, Mr. Duché attended, and commenced his ministration by reading, as he did with great solemnity, the morning service of the Episcopal Church. The Psalm for the day was the 35th:—

"Plead thou my cause, O Lord, with them that strive with me; fight thou against them that fight against me.

"Lay hand upon the shield and buckler, and stand up to help me," &c., &c.

Mr. Adams thus describes the effect in a letter to his wife: "You must remember this was the morning after we heard the horrible rumor of the cannonade of Boston. I never saw a greater effect upon an audience. It seemed as if Heaven had ordained that psalm to be read on that morning."

It may well be conceived that the devout humility of Washington, who, according to Irving, while others stood, knelt, (a spectacle itself of touching sublimity,) added not a little to the effect.

If the policy of the mother country had planted a principle of intolerance and persecution in our laws, it was not such men as those we have mentioned who could be swayed by a narrow and illiberal spirit of bigotry,—far less by a slavish submission to tyranny of any sort. Without denying to other religious denominations their full and glorious share in the early struggles for political liberty in Virginia, it would be to blot out the records of history not to recognize the patent fact that the leaders and chief actors here, (with one or two exceptions, and those not belonging to any religious profession,) were members of the Established Church, nobly sustained by the patriotism, moral and intellectual power, and military courage of their Christian brethren of other persuasions.[1]

In a letter of the 1st of April, 1774, to his friend Bradford, Mr. Madison recurs again to the subject of the religious persecution in Virginia, which weighed so heavily on his heart. As nothing can give a juster idea of the elevated and catholic spirit of his mind than the sentiments expressed by him on this the most vital question affecting the rights of humanity, we subjoin a few extracts from it, in addition to those cited from the previous letter:—

"Our Assembly is to meet the first of May,

[1] Mr. Jefferson, cited in Wirt's Life of Patrick Henry, p. 125, says that "Henry, the Lees, Pages, Masons, &c., were the boldest" and most forward spirits in the movements which led to the Revolution. They were all of the Established Church.

when it is expected something will be done in behalf of the Dissenters. Petitions, I hear, are already forming among the persecuted Baptists; and I fancy it is in the thought of the Presbyterians also to intercede for greater liberty in matters of religion. For my own part, I cannot help being very doubtful of their succeeding in the attempt. The affair was on the carpet during the last session; but such incredible and extravagant stories were told in the House of the monstrous effects of the enthusiasm prevalent among the sectaries, and so greedily swallowed by their enemies, that I believe they lost footing by it. And the bad name they still have with those who pretend too much contempt to examine into their principles and conduct, and are too much devoted to the ecclesiastical establishment to hear of the toleration of the dissentients, I am apprehensive, will be again made a pretext for rejecting their requests.

"The sentiments of our people of fortune and fashion on this subject are vastly different from what you have been used to. That liberal, catholic, and equitable way of thinking, as to the rights of conscience, which is one of the characteristics of a free people, and so strongly marks the people of your province, is but little known among the zealous adherents to our hierarchy. We have, it is true, some persons in the legislature of generous principles both in religion and politics; but number, not merit, you know, is

5 *

necessary to carry points there. Besides, the clergy are a numerous and powerful body, have great influence at home by reason of their connection with and dependence on the bishops and crown, and will naturally employ all their arts and interest to depress their rising adversaries; for such they must consider dissentients, who rob them of the good-will of the people, and may in time endanger their livings and security.

"You are happy in dwelling in a land where those inestimable privileges are fully enjoyed; and the public has long felt the good effects of this religious, as well as civil, liberty. Foreigners have been encouraged to settle among you. Industry and virtue have been promoted by mutual emulation and mutual inspection; commerce and the arts have flourished; and I cannot help attributing those continual exertions of genius, which appear among you, to the inspiration of liberty, and that love of fame and knowledge which always accompanies it. Religious bondage shackles and debilitates the mind, and unfits it for every noble enterprise, every expanded prospect. How far this is the case with Virginia, will more clearly appear when the ensuing trial is made."

In the just reflections and noble sentiments of the preceding paragraph, we see the foreshadowing of the powerful and convincing arguments which, at a future day, were to proceed from the pen and tongue of Mr. Madison in the triumphant vindication of religious freedom; for it was upon his motion, as we shall hereafter have occasion to point out, that the principle was asserted in its true breadth, and upon its legitimate grounds, in the Virginia Bill of Rights,—from him came the Memorial and Remonstrance of 1785, the decisive battle fought in the great contest,—and by his able advocacy and exertions it was that, in the legislative session of the same year, the celebrated Declaratory Act, drawn by Mr. Jefferson, at last became a law.

NOTE. A question has been much mooted as to the relative number of churchmen and dissenters in Virginia, at the period of the Revolution. A loose conjecture of Mr. Jefferson, in the "Notes on Virginia," that the latter formed, at that time, two thirds of the population of the Colony, has been followed by several historical writers, native and European. [See Howison's History of Virginia, vol. II. p. 186, and Grahame's History of the United States, vol. I. p. 113.] Mr. Jefferson afterwards changed his estimate to a simple majority. [Jefferson's Writings, vol. I. p. 31.] But either estimate is obviously erroneous, and is so treated by his intelligent biographer, Professor Tucker. [See Life of Jefferson, vol. I. pp. 19 and 97.] It is shown by contemporary authorities of great respectability that, about the middle of the century, there were but few dissenters in Virginia.

Even as late as 1760, Burnaby, an inquisitive and well informed English traveller, says: " There are very few dissenters of any denomination in this province." [See " Travels in the Middle Settlements of North America in 1759 and 1760."] It is difficult to conceive how, from such a limited number at that time, they could have risen in so short an interval, and in the face of the strong discouragements presented by the laws of the Colony for the support of the Established Church, to a majority at the breaking out of the Revolution. The opinion of Mr. Madison, reported by Professor Tucker, is doubtless more to be relied on : " That the proportion of dissenters in Virginia, at the breaking out of the Revolution, was considerably less than one half of those who professed themselves members of any church."

CHAPTER III.

AT the session of the legislature in May, 1774,
which followed the date of the foregoing letter,
the headlong course of political events, which
were then rapidly verging to a perilous crisis,
precluded the consideration of all other subjects.
The news of the Boston Port Bill was received at
Williamsburg very soon after the Assembly met.
It made a profound and ominous impression;
and the following day, the House of Burgesses
passed a resolution setting apart the 1st of June,
when this vindictive measure was to take effect,
to be observed as a day of fasting, humiliation,

and prayer to implore the Divine' interposition for averting the calamity of civil war, and to give the people of America one heart and one mind firmly to oppose every invasion of their rights. This resolution was too significant in its language and spirit to be agreeable to the representative of royalty, and the House of Burgesses was immediately dissolved by the governor, Lord Dunmore.

The members, by common consent, reassembled in the long room of the Raleigh Tavern called the "Apollo," then the headquarters of patriotism, and formed themselves into an association to oppose the unconstitutional taxation of the British Parliament by discouraging the use of tea and of all commodities brought in by the East India Company,—denouncing the act lately passed for shutting up the harbour and commerce of Boston "in our sister Colony of Massachusetts Bay" as a "dangerous attempt to destroy the liberty and rights of all North America,"—declaring an attack made on one of the Colonies, to compel a submission to arbitrary taxes, an attack on all,—and finally recommending the appointment of deputies from the several Colonies, to meet annually in general Congress at such place as shall be thought most convenient, "there to deliberate on those general measures which the united interests of America may, from time to time, require." At a subsequent meeting of the members, a resolution was adopted inviting a convention of delegates at Williamsburg on the 1st day of August next, to consider what further measures may be necessary for the protection of American liberty, and to appoint deputies to the proposed Continental Congress.

While these measures were taken by the patriots of Virginia against the oppressions of the mother country, a cruel and bloody war was waging upon her western frontiers by the red men of the forest. It was in the midst of these complicated troubles that Mr. Madison, having just returned from a visit to his friends in Pennsylvania and New Jersey, renewed his correspondence with his Philadelphia friend. On the first of July, 1774, he writes to him as follows:—

"I am once more got into my native land, and into the possession of my customary employments, solitude and contemplation; though I must confess, not a little disturbed by the sound of war, bloodshed, and plunder on the one hand, and the threats of slavery and oppression on the other. From the best accounts I can obtain from our frontiers, the savages are determined on the extirpation of the inhabitants, and no longer leave them the alternative of death or captivity. The consternation and timidity of the white people, who abandon their possessions without making the least resistance, are as difficult to be accounted for, as they are encouraging to the enemy. Whether it be owing to the unusual cruelty of the Indians, the want of the necessary implements and ammunition for war, or to the ignorance and inexperience of many who, since the establishment of peace, have ventured into those new settlements, I can neither learn, nor with any certainty conjecture. However, it is confidently asserted that there is not an inhabitant for some hundreds of miles back, (which have been settled for many years,) except those who are forted in or embodied by their military commanders. The state of things has induced Lord Dunmore, contrary to his intentions at the dissolution of the Assembly, to issue writs for a new election of members, whom he is to call together on the 11th of August.

"As to the sentiments of the people of this Colony with respect to the Bostonians, I can assure you I find them generally very warm in their favor. The natives are very numerous and resolute, are making resolves in almost every county, and I believe are willing to fall in with the other Colonies in any expedient measure, even if that should be universal prohibition of trade. It must not be denied, however, that the Europeans, especially the Scotch, and some interested merchants among the natives, discountenance such proceedings, as far as they dare, alleging the injustice and perfidy of refusing to pay our debts to our generous creditors at home. This consideration induces some honest, moderate folks to prefer a partial prohibition, extending only to the *importation* of goods."

The next and last letter we have, (though others doubtless were written, and may perhaps still be in existence,) in the interesting correspondence we have been following, is of the 20th of January, 1775. In the six months' interval, which had elapsed since the date of the previous letter, events of the deepest moment had passed. A feeling of profound indignation had been aroused among the people by the news of the Boston Port Bill and the dissolution of the Assembly; and meetings were held in a large majority of the counties of Virginia, denouncing those proceedings in the stern, unmitigated language of freemen, and calling for efficient measures of retaliation and self-protection.

The Convention of Virginia met in Williamsburg on the 1st of August, 1774, and entered into a solemn association and agreement by which they pledged themselves "under the sacred ties of honor and love of country," and recommended the same engagement to be entered into by their constituents, not to import any goods, wares, and merchandise from Great Britain after the 1st of November next; to cease from exporting thither all American productions after the 10th day of August, 1775, if the grievances of the Colonies should not, by that day, be fully redressed; to have no dealings with any merchant who should not subscribe to their association, and to consider all such persons as enemies of the country.

On the 5th of September the Continental Congress met in Philadelphia. They adopted a solemn Declaration of American rights, concluding with an explicit demand of the repeal of all the acts of Parliament, (which were enumerated at length,) that had been passed in violation of those rights; entered, "for themselves and their constituents," into a non-importation, non-consumption, and non-exportation agreement, upon the model of that of Virginia; and finally put forth those masterly State Papers which have been immortalized by the eloquent applause of Chatham and by their own transcendent merits.[1]

While the Continental Congress was yet in session, Virginia met her savage foes in the memorable and decisive battle of Point Pleasant, and closed one war, just in time to prepare for another and graver.

[1] It was on the occasion of making his motion, (20th of January 1775,) for the withdrawal of the troops from Boston, that Lord Chatham spoke thus of the proceedings of the Congress of 1774:

"When your lordships look at the papers transmitted us from America; when you consider their decency, firmness, and wisdom, you cannot but respect their cause and wish to make it your own. For myself, I must declare and avow that, in all my reading and observation, and history has been my favorite study,—I have read Thucydides, and have studied and admired the master States of the world,—that for solidity of reasoning, force of sagacity, and wisdom of conclusion, under such a complication of difficult circumstances, no nation or body of men can stand in preference to the General Congress at Philadelphia. I trust it is obvious to your lordships that all attempts to impose servitude upon such men, to establish despotism over such a mighty continental nation, must be futile, must be vain."

See another version of the same noble panegyric, which, with precisely the same sentiments, varies somewhat in language, in Belsham's History of Great Britain, vol. VI. p. 99.

It was under these circumstances that Mr.
Madison wrote to his friend Bradford on the
20th of January, 1775 :—

"We are very busy at present, in raising men
and procuring the necessaries for defending ourselves and our friends in case of a sudden invasion. The extensiveness of the demands of the
Congress, and the pride of the British nation,
together with the wickedness of the present ministry, seem in the judgment of our politicians to
require a preparation for extreme events. There
will by the Spring, I expect, be some thousands
of well-trained, high-spirited men ready to meet
danger, whenever it appears, who are influenced
by no mercenary principles, but bearing their.
expenses, and having the prospect of no recompense but the honor and safety of their country.

"I suppose the inhabitants of your province
are more reserved in their behaviour, if not
more easy in their apprehensions, from the prevalence of Quaker principles and politics. The
Quakers are the only people with us, who refuse
to accede to the continental association. I cannot forbear suspecting them to be under the
control and direction of the leaders of the party
in your quarter; for I take those of them that
we have to be too honest and simple to have
any sinister or secret views, and I do not observe anything in the association inconsistent
with their religious principles. When I say
they refuse to accede to the association, my

meaning is, that they refuse to sign it,—that being the method used among us to distinguish friends from foes, and to oblige the common people to a more strict observance of it. I have never heard whether the like method has been adopted in the other governments.

"I have not seen the following in print, and it seems so just a specimen of Indian eloquence and mistaken valor that I think you will be pleased with it. You must make allowance for the unskilfulness of the interpreter." [He then gives the "Speech of Logan, a Shawanese chief, to Lord Dunmore," in the same words (with a few very slight variations) in which it afterwards appeared in Mr. Jefferson's Notes on Virginia.] [1]

The foregoing letter of Mr. Madison leads to the correction of a prevalent historical error with regard to the time when military preparations were begun in Virginia for the vindication by force, if it should prove necessary, of the rights asserted by the Colonies. The hitherto accredited account is, that the resolutions for arming and embodying a portion of the militia, moved by Mr. Henry in the convention which assembled in Richmond, on the 20th of March, 1775, and adopted by that body, sounded the first note of preparation for an impending con-

[1] The last paragraph of this letter of Mr. Madison was published without his name, a few weeks after its date, together with the speech of Logan, in a newspaper of New York of the 16th of February, 1775, as "an extract of a letter from Virginia." See American Archives, 4th series, vol. i. p. 1020.

flict of arms; and that, down to that time, the older and more cautious leaders had been supinely relying, and were even then disposed to rely, upon the vain and delusive remedies of "petition, commercial non-intercourse, and passive fortitude." Such is the view presented by an eloquent biographer of Mr. Henry,[1] who, with a commendable bias in favor of the patriotism, spirit, and sagacity of his illustrious subject, has not been sufficiently on his guard against the tendency of that bias to depreciate, in comparison, both the general spirit of the times, and the merits of other illustrious actors in the same eventful scenes. But the truth of history, however it may slumber for a season in unknown or forgotten documents, awakes at last, and deals impartial justice to all.

The letter of Mr. Madison proves, that, two months at least in advance of Mr. Henry's proposition, there was a general concurrence of public men in the necessity of "preparation for extreme events," and that a military organization was already in progress in Virginia, which, by the Spring, would offer to the country "some thousands of well-trained, high-spirited men, ready to meet danger, whenever it appears."

In a most valuable and authentic repository of original documents, we find a letter from a gentleman in Maryland to his correspondent in Glasgow, dated as early as the 1st of November,

[1] See Wirt's Life of Patrick Henry, pp. 114–124.

1774, in which the following statements are made : " The province of Virginia is raising one company in every county, which will make a body of six thousand men. They are all independent; and so great is the ambition to get among them, that men who served as commanding officers last war and have large fortunes, have offered themselves as private men."[1] And in the same collection is an official letter from Lord Dunmore, governor of Virginia, to the Earl of Dartmouth, secretary for the Colonies, dated Williamsburg, 24th of December, 1774, in which the Governor says : " Every county is now arming a company of men, whom they call an independent company, for the avowed purpose of protecting their committees, and to be employed against government, if occasion require. The committee of one county has proceeded so far as to swear the men of their independent company to execute all orders which shall be given them from the committee of their county."[2]

Nor was this an irregular popular movement, without the well-considered and deliberate sanc-

[1] See American Archives, 4th series, pp. 953 and 1062.

[2] Although a committee of the House of Burgesses in June, 1775, in an elaborate report on the causes of the public disturbances which had then arisen, complained of this letter of Lord Dunmore, and impeached some of its statements, yet an intelligent historian, who investigated with great care and industry the transactions of these times, and had also the advantage of consulting living contemporary testimony on the subject, expresses his decided " conviction, *upon proofs altogether satisfactory to his mind,*" that the leading fact stated by Lord Dunmore was true, and that " at

tion of the leading men of the country. In the address of the Continental Congress to the inhabitants of the Colonies, in the month of October preceding, which was the work of a distinguished Virginia patriot, Richard Henry Lee, after detailing the measures of a pacific character which had been adopted by that body, the following significant and impressive counsel was given. " But we think ourselves bound in duty to observe to you that the schemes agitated against these Colonies have been so conducted as to render it prudent that you should extend your views to mournful events and be, in all respects, prepared for every contingency." That the contingency of an appeal to arms, with the necessity of 'preparation for it, was in the mind of Washington at this time, is proved by his enthusiastic declaration. in open convention that " he was ready to raise, and subsist at his own expense, a body of one thousand men," for the defence of the liberties of the country.[1]

The noble resolves of the Virginia officers, at a meeting held by them in the bosom of the western forest on the 5th day of November, 1774, just after they had terminated their glorious campaign against the Indians, pledging themselves, their swords still unsheathed, " to

the time of writing his letter, a company of men was arming in almost every county, if not in every county, in the Colony." See Continuation of Burk's History of Virginia by Skelton Jones, 4th Burk, p. 41, in note.

[1] See Works of John Adams, vol. II. p. 360.

exert every power within them for the defence of American liberty," [1] sufficiently testified the spirit with which they were animated, and their readiness for any contingency. The same spirit pervaded the ranks of civil life.

Its general diffusion, even at an earlier date, was evinced in a striking manner by the simultaneous publication of two patriotic appeals from different writers, which appeared on the same day (28th of July, 1774,) in Williamsburg: one by the celebrated civilian and jurist, Thomson Mason, telling his countrymen that, if their peaceful and constitutional efforts for redress should fail, "you must draw your swords in a just cause, and rely upon that God, who assists the righteous, to support your endeavours to preserve the liberty he gave, and the love of which he hath implanted in your hearts as essential to your nature." The other by an anonymous but most able and eloquent writer, concluding with this bold and lofty invocation: "Let us, then, protest against the authority of Parliament in every case whatever; let us forbid our magistrates to be governed by their acts, on pain of incurring the just indignation of an injured people; and above all, let us remember, in times of necessity, that with the sword our forefathers obtained their constitutional rights, and by the sword it is our duty to defend them." [2]

[1] American Archives, (4th series,) vol. I. p. 962.   [2] Idem, pp. 647 and 653.

With these evidences before us of the spirit of the times, and the well-attested fact that an imposing military organization had already taken place in Virginia, under the auspices of the several county committees, of which a large majority of the convention were doubtless active members, the assertion that the convention shrank back in terror and alarm from the comparatively tame proposition of Mr. Henry for embodying, arming, and disciplining a portion of the militia, and that it required "his steadier eye and deeper insight," his "firm and manly heart," to push them from the precipice, to which they still clung with "suppliant tenderness,"[1] must appear rash indeed.

If there were enlightened and leading members of the convention who opposed the adoption of Mr. Henry's resolutions, it must have been because, with the knowledge they possessed of the extensive military organization which had already taken place and was still going on in Virginia, they considered them unnecessary for any practical purpose,—that, by a needless proclamation of our preparations to the adverse party, who would thus be stimulated to arm in turn, their adoption would prove injurious to the relative strength of the Colonies,—and that, if any new measure were called for, it ought to be of a more vigorous and efficient character. Accordingly, that faithful and well-tried patriot, Robert

---

[1] Wirt's Life of Patrick Henry, *ubi supra*.

Carter Nicholas, classed among the halting and laggard opponents of Mr. Henry's resolutions, the moment they were carried by a vote of the convention, rose and moved the substitution of a more efficient system of defence by raising ten thousand regulars, instead of embodying a portion of the militia.[1]

In rectifying, by the testimony of Mr. Madison and others, an historical error which does injustice to many of the truest patriots of Virginia, as well as the spirit of her people in a crisis of great public trial, no design has been entertained of derogating, in any degree, from the proud merits of Mr. Henry. His, indeed, was a distinguished and splendid *rôle*. By his ever memorable resolutions in opposition to the Stamp Act, and the lofty eloquence with which he sustained them, he struck a timely blow which resounded through America and the world, and roused a spirit that never slumbered till its great work was accomplished. The moment was opportune and critical; and he seized it with a

---

[1] At the succeeding convention in July, 1775, the more efficient system proposed by Mr. Nicholas was actually adopted. As this gentleman, with Mr. Pendleton, Mr. Bland and others, has been reproached with backwardness in the earlier movements of the Revolution, it is gratifying to find so thorough a champion of the cause as George Mason bearing the strongest testimony to his zeal and decision. Writing to General Washington on the 14th of October, 1775, of the proceedings of this convention, he says: " Our friend the Treasurer (R. C. Nicholas) was the warmest man in the convention for immediately raising a standing army of not less than four thousand men, upon constant pay." See Sparks's Washington, vol. III. p. 152, in note.

bold and felicitous energy that belonged to his ardent and impassioned nature.

His was the temperament and the genius of the great popular orator, that fitted him to lead at such a moment, and, like Aaron, to proclaim the divine message of freedom to his countrymen, and of wrath and denunciation to their oppressors. There were others, like Moses,[1] not possessing this superlative gift of eloquence, but prepared, when the proper time should come, to act their several parts, even the highest, in the great drama of national deliverance, with a foresight, fortitude, and wisdom that could be surpassed by none.[2]

[1] The following scriptural parallel is strikingly illustrative and true to nature, and is often reproduced in the men of action and men of speech in great national emergencies:—

"Moses said unto the Lord, O my Lord, I am not eloquent, but slow of speech, and of a slow tongue." Exodus, chap. iv. v. 10.

"The Lord said, Is not Aaron the Levite thy brother? I know that he can speak well." v. 14.

"Thou shalt speak unto him, and put words in his mouth." v. 15.

"And he shall be thy spokesman unto the people, and he shall be, even he shall be to thee instead of a mouth, and thou shalt be to him instead of God." v. 16.

[2] Among the papers of Mr. Madison is a letter addressed to his father by Mr. Pendleton, which

justice to that venerable public servant and to those who, like him, opposed Mr. Henry's resolutions on the Stamp Act as inexpedient, requires should not remain unknown. The Stamp Act, which was passed in March, 1765, did not go into operation till the month of November following. When it went into operation, the courts of Virginia universally ceased from the transaction of civil business, in order to avoid the necessity of giving effect to the obnoxious act. After the lapse of a few months, however, such were the inconveniences of a total occlusion of the courts, that the question was presented whether they ought not to be reopened, and, in that case, whether, in their judicial proceedings, they should give effect to the provisions of the Stamp Act. Mr. Pendleton, a lawyer by profession,

Another error, akin to that just noticed, is that the great movements of the Revolution in Virginia had a purely democratic origin, to which the men of large estates, stigmatized as the "Landed Aristocracy,"[1] were for the most part strangers, if not enemies. This version of our history is of comparatively recent date, but has received countenance from names of so much respectability in our literature and politics,[2] that,

was at the same time a magistrate of his county, and as such a member of the county court. In the discharge of his judicial functions, he at once took the bold ground of treating the Stamp Act as a nullity, in consequence of the want of constitutional authority in Parliament to pass it. This was going a step beyond Mr. Henry's resolutions. He thus announces to his friend his determination, and the reasons of it :—

"We must resolve to admit the stamps, or proceed without them, for to stop all business must be a greater evil than either..... For my own part, I never have or will enter into noisy and riotous companies on the subject. My sentiments I shall be always ready to communicate to serious men. As a magistrate, I have thought it my duty to sit, and we have constantly opened court; and I shall not hesitate to determine what people desire me and run the risk of, themselves; and having taken an oath to decide according to law, shall never consider that Act (Stamp Act) as such, for want of power, I

mean constitutional authority in Parliament to pass it. On this principle, upon a matter being proposed at last court within the act, I informed the court it was so, and then put a general previous question whether they would proceed in any business desired, notwithstanding that act. They generally expressed their intention to proceed this Spring, but thought it was best to wait awhile longer as they had hitherto stopped.— Were I applied to for an attachment, or any other thing within my office out of court, I would grant it at the party's risk as to the validity of it; for I am not afraid of the penalty, at least so much as of breaking my oath." Manuscript Letter of Edmund Pendleton to James Madison, Sr., dated Feb. 15, 1766.

[1] See Wirt's Life of Patrick Henry, pp. 44 and 54.

[2] Mr. Grigsby, in his Discourse on the Virginia Convention of 1776, and Ex-President Tyler, in his Oration at Jamestown delivered May, 1857.

in the retrospect of our annals into which the early life of Mr. Madison leads us, it appears inexcusable not to pause for a moment to inquire how far it is justified by contemporary testimony.

A simple roll-call of the names which, along with Mr. Henry's, will ever stand most conspicuous in the records of this august era of Virginia patriotism, would, of itself, seem a sufficient answer to so novel a theory. What were Washington, the Lees, the Masons, the Pages, the Nelsons, not to mention others their numerous and gallant compeers in every part of the Colony, but large landed proprietors, holding, as such, a deep stake in the liberties and happiness of the country. If such men were, in a certain sense, an aristocracy, it was an aristocracy pledged by its very nature to the general good, and constituted, by the advantages of superior fortune and education, the vigilant sentinels and faithful guardians of the common safety. They were the natural leaders of the people in a crisis of public danger; and the people willingly and of their own choice, without jealousy or distrust, followed their lead.

That such was the constitution of society in Virginia, both politically and morally, at the period of the revolutionary struggle, and indeed long after, a careful study of our history will indisputably prove. If we look at the composition of the county committees which, at the

time of which we are now speaking, were intrusted with large and almost dictatorial powers
to provide for the public safety, we shall see
that it was the men of estates, of property and
education, who were invariably placed upon them
by the public voice. In the county of Mr. Madison's birth and residence, we find that on the
22d of December, 1774, a month preceding the
date of his letter given above, his father, probably the largest proprietor of the county, was
made chairman of the committee, and that the
names of Taylor, Barbour, Taliaferro, and other
well known proprietors, appear upon the list of
its members; and his own, "James Madison, Jr.,"
though then a young man of twenty-three years
only, also among them,—an honorable distinction
accorded to his early patriotism and ability, and
a presage of his future services to the country.

The names of Archibald Cary, Robert Carter
Nicholas, Peyton Randolph, George Wythe, Benjamin Harrison, and others, with whom the possession of property was not supposed to infer
an indifference to liberty, appear upon these
county committees as early as the year 1774.
George Washington, whose large fortune certainly did not impair the force of his patriotism,
was chairman of the county committee of Fairfax; and at a meeting of that committee, held
on the 17th of January, 1775, Col. Washington
presiding, resolutions were passed for arming
and organizing the militia of the county, in

which the same considerations were set forth, and in the same language, which were afterwards employed by Mr. Henry in the resolutions moved by him in the convention, and for which, as we have seen, he has been specially applauded as the originator of a bold and necessary measure, in advance of all his contemporaries.[1]

With what noble and generous zeal these patriotic men of fortune in Virginia devoted themselves to the vindication of American rights in the day of peril, is shown by the contemporary testimony already cited. Many of them, accord-

[1] That the reader may the better judge of this coincidence, which could hardly have been accidental, we annex one of the Fairfax resolutions, (which, it will be perceived, was avowedly but an echo to an opinion expressed by the Maryland Convention,) and the corresponding resolution offered by Mr. Henry in the Virginia Convention :—

Fairfax Resolution, adopted 17th of January, 1775.

" *Resolved,* That this committee do concur in opinion with the Provincial Committee of Maryland that a well-regulated militia, composed of gentlemen, freeholders, and other freemen, is the natural strength and only stable security of a free government, and that such militia will relieve our mother country from any expense in our protection and defence, will obviate the pretext for taxing us on that account, and render it unnecessary to keep standing armies among us,—ever dangerous to liberty."

See Am. Arch. (4th series,) vol. I. p. 1145.

Mr. Henry's Resolution, offered 23d of March, 1775.

" *Resolved,* That a well-regulated militia, composed of gentlemen and yeomen, is the natural strength and only security of a free government; that such a militia in this Colony would forever render it unnecessary for the mother country to keep among us, for the purpose of our defence, any standing army of mercenary soldiers, always subversive of the quiet and dangerous to the liberties of the people, and would obviate the pretext of taxing us for their support."

See Journal of Virginia Convention of 1775, p. 5.

ing to one of the statements quoted above, though " men of large fortunes " and having served " as commanding officers in the last war," entered the ranks of these volunteer companies as privates. The volunteers, in general, according to Mr. Madison, were " high-spirited men, bearing their own expenses, and having no prospect of recompense but the honor and safety of their country." Such an aristocracy as this was worthy to lead, as the only precedence it claimed was a precedence of danger, of responsibility, of sacrifice.[1]

[1] Among the many examples of the self-sacrificing devotion of this noble class of patriots in Virginia, none was more remarkable than that of General Thomas Nelson, whose statue it has been recently determined to place in the illustrious group, which is to form the *entourage* of the Washington monument at Richmond. After having signed the Declaration of Independence, as one of the delegates of Virginia in Congress, he returned to his native State to uphold it by his services and exertions in the council and in the field. He was placed in command of the militia of the State, and also elected governor, at the most critical period of the war, immediately preceding the surrender of the main body of the enemy's forces at Yorktown.

The extraordinary exertion required of Virginia at that time, and the low state of her finances and public credit, imposed upon her governor a weight of responsibility, which it required a Roman spirit to meet. General Nelson gave himself and all he had, freely and unhesitatingly, to the cause. While nothing could be obtained for the supply of the army upon the exhausted credit of the State, his personal engagements were readily accepted and never withheld. In this manner, the whole of his princely fortune was absorbed in the payment of his liabilities for the public. When the country, in the enjoyment of independence, became prosperous and powerful, his descendants thought it not unbecoming to ask of the public councils some retribution of the immense and generous sacrifices of their ancestor.

It was upon this occasion that Mr. Madison, appealed to for his recollection of the services and losses of General Nelson in the cause of the country, returned the following answer, which is so glowing and just a tribute to his merits, and to those of another of our

The exhibition of so fervid and manly a love of liberty by the Virginians of this epoch has been thought, by one of the writers already alluded to,[1] to be entirely inconsistent with the received accounts of the predominance of the Cavalier element in the early emigrations to the Colony. But if there be any historical fact beyond the reach of modern disputation, this,

revolutionary worthies, whom he gracefully associates with him, that we cannot deny our readers the gratification of its perusal.

"MONTPELIER, Nov. 7, 1833.

"I regret that my absence from the State during his meritorious services as a military commander and governor, deprived me of the opportunity of having any personal knowledge of them. But my general acquaintance with his character, and the impressions left by whatever was of public notoriety, make me readily confide in the statements of the petition, and inspire a sincere wish that it may be favorably received.

"My personal acquaintance with General Nelson was limited to a few opportunities at an early stage of the Revolution. It was sufficient, however, to disclose to me his distinguished worth. He was excelled by no man in the generosity of his nature, in the nobleness of his sentiments, in the purity of his revolutionary principles, and in an exalted patriotism that ensured every service and sacrifice that his country might need.

"With this view of the subject, it could not but accord with my best sympathies that nothing which may be due to the ancestor may be withheld from the heirs to it. I must be allowed to add that the gratification will be increased by the knowledge that the benefit will be shared by the descendants of Governor Page, whose memory will always be classed with that of the most distinguished patriots of the Revolution. Nor was he less endeared to his friends, among whom I had an intimate place, by the interesting accomplishments of his mind and the warmth of his social affections, than he was to his country by the evidence he gave of devotion to the republicanism of its institutions.

"With great and cordial respect,   JAMES MADISON."

[1] In differing from so learned and patriotic a writer, our tribute of thanks is none the less for his pious and admirable labors in commemoration of departed patriots and worthies, whose services and examples form an inseparable part of the national inheritance.

undoubtedly, is one. At the time of the settlement of Virginia, as well as before and after, the Puritan controversy had divided the English nation into two great parties,—the one demanding change and reform, especially in the Church; the other adhering to the established order of things, both in Church and State. The latter did not, in point of fact, receive the name of Cavalier till a somewhat later period, when it was given as the antitheton of Roundhead, applied to its adversary.[1] But in historical disquisitions of the present day, the two parties are known from their origin under the denominations of Puritan and Cavalier.

No fact is better established than that the early English emigrants to Virginia, for the first half century of her history, with here and there an exception serving only to prove the general rule, were "loyal subjects to both King and Church."[2] It could not but be so; for the stringent laws of the Colony from the beginning, with regard to Church conformity, rendered it altogether an uninviting abode to persons of other sentiments, while the subversion of Throne and Church in England, during the civil wars which soon followed, furnished a new and superadded motive for the Cavaliers to seek an asylum in a land where their principles and

---

[1] According to Clarendon, these party designations were first applied in the year 1641. See History of the Rebellion, book IV.

[2] Jefferson. See his Writings, vol. I. p. 31.

predilections were unproscribed. Down to the period of the Restoration, then, the great mass of the emigration from England to Virginia must have been, as unquestionable historical proofs show that it was, of the Cavalier strain; and this is farther demonstrated by the general and joyous enthusiasm with which that event was hailed in Virginia.

At that time the population of Virginia had acquired a stable character. It approached to forty thousand;[1] and the natural increase upon such a stock by children born upon the soil, whose multiplication had been, fourteen years before, the subject of special and touching thanksgiving in an act of the Colonial Assembly,[2] insured the future and steady growth of the Colony, with no other than the ordinary accessions from abroad. Virginia was now the cherished home and abiding place of her inhabitants; and all classes, native and adopted, united in zealous and filial efforts to build up her prosperity, and to watch over and guard her interests and rights.

After the Restoration, there came in a few,

---

[1] It actually surpassed that amount a few years after, (in 1671,) according to the official statement of the governor, Sir William Berkeley. See his Answers to Enquiries of the Lords of the Committee of the Colonies in Chalmers, p. 325, and II. Hen. Stat., pp. 511–517.

[2] " God Almighty, among many his other blessings, hath vouchsafed increase of children to this Colony, who are now multiplied to a considerable number," was the language of the Assembly in the act of 1646, here alluded to. Hen. Stat., vol. I. p. 336.

and but a few, of the Oliverian soldiers; soon after, some of the followers of the Duke of Monmouth, who were banished to Virginia; then came the interesting band of Huguenots, who were concentrated in a single settlement on the James River, above its Falls; and then a number of Scotch-Irish and German families, who settled for the most part in the transmontane valley of Virginia. They were all valuable accessions to the progressive development of the Colony; but the main stream of emigration continued to be from England and Scotland, and of those who brought with them loyal attachments to the constitution of England, in both Church and State.

If we descend from this general historical view of the early population of Virginia to the genealogy of individual families, we are met by the indisputable fact that many of the leading and most distinguished patriots of the Revolution were the descendants of men who had sealed, with their blood in the field of battle, their loyalty to Charles I. in his contest with the Long Parliament. Washington's grandfather was the first cousin of the Colonel Henry Washington who, in 1643, so gallantly led a forlorn hope for the King at the taking of Bristol, and three years afterward, with desperate courage, defended a feeble and reduced garrison, to the last extremity, against the overwhelming forces of Fairfax. The paternal ancestor of George Mason raised a corps for the service of the King, which he led in person against the troopers of Cromwell, and continued to adhere to the royal standard with unshaken fidelity, till the "crowning mercy" of the field of Worcester crushed the last hopes of the Cavaliers, and drove him, with other gallant spirits, to seek a new home in the distant and unsubdued Colony of Virginia.

The Cavalier blood of the noble Falkland, who offered up his life on the plains of Newbury, a costly sacrifice to a romantic sentiment of loyalty and honor, flowed in the veins of a Virginia patriot, Archibald Cary,[1] than whom Liberty never had a firmer friend, or Tyranny a more determined foe. The Lees, the Blands, the Carters, the Randolphs, the Digges', the Byrds, and others among the foremost patriots of the day, whose genealogies either curiosity or filial piety may have explored, were of well known Cavalier descent.

This new interpretation of the early annals of Virginia, so contrary to hitherto received accounts and well attested history, seems to have arisen from a strange and exaggerated misconception of the character of the Cavalier. The Cavalier, it is said, was a slave,—doubly a slave to King and Church. How does this picture

[1] It was Archibald Cary, then Speaker of the Senate, whose stern purpose and republican firmness are supposed to have had great influence in defeating the project of creating a *Dictator* in Virginia, during the first year of the revolutionary war. See Girardin, Burk's Hist. of Va., vol. IV. p. 190, and Wirt's Life of Henry, p. 205.

accord with the sober testimony of history? What is the judgment of English historians, even of the school of politics most decidedly opposed to the pretensions of the King in his memorable contest with the Parliament? The great oracle of that school, and the most admired historical writer of the present day, says: "Many men, whose virtues and abilities would have done honor to any cause, ranged themselves on the side of the King."[1] The biographer of the great parliamentary leader, Hampden, while celebrating with noble zeal the just praises of that incomparable patriot and statesman, does not hesitate to say that there stood opposed to him, and on the side of the King, many "who were high-minded and steady friends of liberty."[2]

Among them were Falkland, of whom we have just spoken; the virtuous Southampton, whose father had been the watchful guardian and unflinching champion of Virginia freedom in the ardent conflicts of the London Company; the chivalric Sir Bevill Grenvil,[3] whose name, for generosity and elevation of spirit, must ever be linked in glorious companionship with that of Falkland; Sir Ralph Hopton, Lord Capel, the Marquis of Hertford, and others, some of whom, it is well known, had firmly coöperated with the

[1] Macaulay, Hist. Eng. vol. I. p. 88.

[2] Lord Nugent, Life of Hampden, vol. II. p. 190.

[3] See some incidents of his career, and a noble letter written by him to his friend, Sir Joseph Trelawney, in Nugent, vol. II. pp. 192-198.

opponents of arbitrary power in all those great measures by which, during the first nine months of the Long Parliament, the cause of British constitutional freedom was vindicated, and, as they hoped, entrenched against the danger of future assault. When, a few months afterwards, the "Grand Remonstrance" sounded the signal of what seemed to many an approaching revolution, men, who were before united on the ground of the constitution, separated, more perhaps according to their hopes and fears than their principles, and some rallied to the side of the monarchy, while others embraced that of the Parliament.[1]

[1] The class of country gentlemen, who had gradually risen to great influence and power, played a most important part on the one side and the other in the mighty questions which were then at issue. Lord Macaulay, whose bold and striking generalizations occasionally substitute brilliant fancy sketches for sober historical portraits, has, it seems to us, in the sweeping comprehensiveness of the language used by him, given rather a delusive picture of the country gentleman of the seventeenth century; whom he describes, even those of large fortunes and collegiate educations, as coarse, vulgar, sensual, ignorant of the refinements of society, and destitute of every liberal and cultivated taste.

This picture may be true to a certain extent, with reference to the reign of Charles II., when a sudden and rapid degeneracy of manners had taken place under the licentiousness brought in by the restored monarch, as well as from the demoralizing effect of the previous civil convulsions. But if we may credit the actual testimony of contemporary witnesses, and not the "lighter literature," which is cited by him as equal, if not higher, authority, the picture this great historical writer has drawn of the country gentleman of the seventeenth century, bears but little resemblance to the improved and cultivated country life of the time of Charles I., when it showed, perhaps, as much genuine refinement as it has ever since attained.

Let any one read the charming accounts he will find in the autobiography of Clarendon, of the elegant hospitality exercised by Falkland in his paternal seats of

Without entering into the national dissensions in England farther than to render the homage due to the truth of history, we cannot but say, while sympathizing as republicans with the popular leaders in that great civil contest,—always excepting him whose guilty ambition, notwithstanding many great qualities, made him in the end the chief of apostates, as he was the profoundest of dissemblers,—that there were among the Cavaliers also brave and noble and free spirits. Certain it is that their descendants in America, who were almost exclusively, as we have seen, the settlers of Virginia during the first half-century of her existence, were here the vigilant and faithful guardians of the rights, liberties, and interests of the people of the Colony. Hand in hand with the constantly recurring manifestations of their loyalty to the King, they firmly and unremittingly asserted those "liberties, franchises, and immunities of natural-born Englishmen" which they brought with them to America under the plighted faith of their charters, and

Tew and Burford; of the polished reunions of science, letters, virtue, and taste in the circle of friends who habitually resorted to him there; with the like accounts which have come down to us of the social life and rural enjoyments of Hampden, and the occasional glimpses we meet with in some of the works of Lord Bacon, of the dawn of a new era of taste and manners; and we shall be much more inclined to follow the authority of Swift, who gave it as his opinion, founded on what he had heard from some who lived in those times, as well as what he had read of them, that "the highest period of politeness in England was the peaceable part of King Charles the First's reign." See Hints towards an Essay on Conversation, by Dean Swift.

which they never ceased to claim and vindicate as their indefeasible birthright.

At the very moment of adopting a solemn Declaration filled with expressions of the most zealous loyalty and gratitude to the King for his protection, and "his many royal favors and gracious blessings," and protesting their unwillingness (to use their own language) "to degenerate from the condition of their birth, being born under a monarchical, and not a popular and tumultuary government," they repeat and "confirm," in terms of peculiar energy, the great constitutional principle, already boldly proclaimed by them, of immunity from taxation except by their own consent.[1]

Again, upon the pages of the Colonial Statute Book we find an enactment, by which any aspersion upon the memory of the late King (Charles I.) is made a highly criminal offence, and the questioning of the title of his son and heir to the supreme government of the Colony declared to be high treason, preceding, by an interval of only two years, that great Charter of the liberties of the Colony obtained by these same Cavaliers, with arms in their hands, from the commissioners of the Parliament;—a charter by which were solemnly guaranteed to the colonists "all such freedoms and privileges as belong to the free-born people of England"; their "Grand Assembly" recognized as the legitimate

[1] Hen. Stat. vol. I. pp. 232 and 242.

representative and guardian of their rights; freedom from taxes, except such as they should impose, acknowledged; and "neither forts nor castles to be erected, nor garrisons to be maintained without their consent"; the same freedom of trade "with all nations" secured to Virginia as the people of England enjoy; and finally, a full and total indemnity granted from "all acts, words, or writings done, spoken, or written against the Parliament or Commonwealth of England from the beginning of the world to this day."[1] Thus did the Virginians of that day unite with the faith and loyalty of Cavaliers, the free spirit and sturdy independence of the ancient barons of England.

This brief review of the early history of Virginia seemed indispensable, not only for the reestablishment of historical truth, but as furnishing the necessary key to the conduct of her patriots and statesmen at the period of which we are treating. Virginia still fondly cherished her connection with the mother country; she was loyal to the King as the constitutional head of the empire; but she was proud and jealous of the birthright of English freedom, which she claimed as her undoubted heritage. These blended feelings, expressed in all the acts of her public authorities, received nowhere a nobler utterance

---

[1] See convention entered into with the Parliamentary Commissioners in 1651, Hen. Stat. vol. L pp. 363-368, and Jefferson's Notes on Virginia, p. 214.

than in the frank and unstudied language of the
Virginia militia officers at their meeting, already
referred to, after the victorious close of their
campaign against the Indians. There are, perhaps, no better exponents of the true popular
feelings of a country than its citizen-soldiers,
called momentarily from the pursuits of civil life
by a crisis of public danger.

The following resolution was unanimously adopted on the occasion alluded to :—

"*Resolved*, That we will bear the most faithful
allegiance to His Majesty King George the Third,
whilst His Majesty delights to reign over a brave
and free people; that we will, at the expense of
life and everything dear and valuable, exert ourselves in support of the honor of his crown, and
the dignity of the British empire. But as the
love of liberty and attachment to the real interests and just rights of America outweigh every
other consideration, we resolve that we will
exert every power within us for the defence of
American liberty, and for the support of her just
rights and privileges, not in any precipitate, riotous, or tumultuous manner, but when regularly
called for by the unanimous voice of our countrymen."

Here was the heart and mind of Virginia truly
and manfully spoken. It gives the index to her
character at this great epoch of her history.
There was a reverence for authority; an hereditary attachment to the institutions derived from

the mother country; a loyalty to the King, so
long as he was content to "reign over a brave
and free people;" an undeviating adherence to
law and order even in her resistance to oppression, which did not extinguish, but raised and
ennobled, her proud spirit of independence, and
her indomitable love of liberty.

If some of these were Cavalier traits, we have
no need to be ashamed of them, as being undoubted historical facts; and if the truth of history requires us to add some others, of the same
origin perhaps, to the social portraiture of our
ancestors;—a genial fondness for sports and
diversions,[1] an elastic joyousness of temper, a

[1] Nothing, perhaps, is better fitted to give an idea of the social temperament and habits of the Virginians of the middle of the last century, and to establish, if farther evidence were wanted, the genuineness of their Cavalier de-scent, than the following festive programme, taken from the Virginia Gazette of October, 1737:—

"We have advice," says the editor, "from Hanover county, that on Saint Andrew's Day, there are to be Horse-Races and several other Diversions for the Enter-tainment of the Gentlemen and Ladies at the Old Field near Captain John Bickerton's in that county, (if permitted by the Hon. Wm. Byrd, esquire, Proprietor of the said Land,) the substance of which is as follows, viz:

"It is proposed that 20 Horses or Mares do run round a three miles Course for a Prize of Five Pounds. That every Horse shall be entered with Mr. Joseph Fox, and that no person be allowed to put up a Horse unless he hath subscribed for the Entertainment and paid half a Pistole.

"That a Hat of the value of 20s. be cudgelled for, and that after the first challenge made, the Drums are to beat every Quarter of an Hour for three Challenges round the Ring, and none to play with their left hand.

"That a Violin be played for by 20 Fiddlers; no person to have the liberty of playing unless he bring a fiddle with him. After the prize is won, *they are all to play together and each a different tune*, and to be treated by the company.

sympathetic nature, a free and uncalculating hospitality, and too great proneness to inaction and self-indulgence, except when the public cause summoned to exertion;—we shall have arrived at the outlines of a character, which, although not in all respects free from the animadversions of the moral censor, yet, in the mixed and imperfect condition of humanity, forming a whole that might well be the basis of high deeds and noble aspirations.

"That 12 Boys, of 12 years of age, do run 112 yards, for a Hat of the cost of 12 shillings.

"That a Flag. be flying on said Day 30 feet high.

"That a handsome Entertainment be provided for the subscribers and their wives; and such of them as are not so happy as to have wives, may treat any other lady.

"That Drums, Trumpets, Hautboys, &c., be provided, to play at said Entertainment.

"That after Dinner, the Royal Health, His Honor the Governor's, &c., are to be drunk.

"That a Quire of Ballads be sung for by a number of Songsters, all of them to have Liquor sufficient to clear their Wind-Pipes.

"That a pair of Silver Buckles be wrestled for by a number of brisk young men.

"That a pair of handsome Shoes be danced for.

"That a pair of handsome Silk Stockings of one Pistole value be given to the handsomest young Country Maid that appears in the field. With many other Whimsical and Comical Diversions, too numerous to mention.

"And as this mirth is designed to be purely innocent, and void of offence, all persons resorting there are desired to behave themselves with decency and sobriety; the subscribers being resolved to discountenance all immorality with the utmost rigor."

From the number of competitors on the violin, each bringing his own violin, the genius for that instrument must have been widely diffused, as well as highly appreciated, at that day in Virginia; and when it is recollected that Jefferson and Henry were both ready performers, it would seem, contrary to the notion of Themistocles, that a man might play on the fiddle, and be, at the same time, capable of raising a small to be a great State.

CHAPTER IV.

IN the preceding chapter we have seen the
commencement of preparations in Virginia for
the contingency, which seemed daily becoming
more and more probable, of an appeal to arms
in vindication of the rights of America. These
preparations were soon justified by grave and
signal events. In Massachusetts, an expedition

8 *

set on foot by Governor Gage, to destroy some
military stores collected at Concord, brought on
a conflict of arms, in which many lives were lost
on both sides, and which made the 19th of April,
1775, ever memorable as the date of the first
overt act of war in the controversy between the
mother country and the Colonies. Governor
Dunmore in Virginia, pursuing the same policy of cutting off the means of defence from
America, but with far less of military boldness in
its execution, caused a party of marines from
the Magdalen sloop of war, lying in James River,
to land on the 20th of the. month, and under
cover of the night, to take from the magazine
in Williamsburg fifteen or twenty barrels of gunpowder, and transfer them on board that vessel.

This proceeding of the governor kindled a
flame of indignation and excitement in every
part of the Colony, as the intelligence of it was
communicated from place to place. In Fredericksburg, on the 24th of April, as soon as information of what had occurred was received there,
a meeting of the Independent Company of the
town was called, at which a resolution was adopted
to hold themselves in readiness to march, as
light-horse, to Williamsburg on the following
Saturday, (the 29th,) "for the purpose of recovering the gunpowder and securing the arms in
the magazine."[1]   At the same time, a letter was

---

[1] See letter to Capt. William Grayson of Prince William County,
in American Archives, (4th series,) vol. II. p. 395.

drawn up by the officers of the company, Hugh Mercer, George Weedon, Alexander Spotswood, and John Willis, (of whom the three first-named afterward bore distinguished parts in the war of the Revolution,) and sent by express to the independent companies of the neighbouring counties, inviting their coöperation. A letter was also addressed by these gentlemen to Col. George Washington, informing him that "the gentlemen of the Independent Company of Fredericksburg think this first public insult is not to be tamely submitted to, and determine, with your approbation, to join any other bodies of armed men, who are willing to appear in support of the honor of Virginia, as well as to secure the military stores yet remaining in the magazine. It is proposed to march from hence on Saturday next for Williamsburg, properly accoutred as light-horsemen." [1]

This invitation to the independent companies of the neighbouring counties was nobly responded to; and before the day fixed for the departure to Williamsburg, "fourteen companies of light-horse, consisting of upwards of six hundred well armed and disciplined men, friends of constitutional liberty and America," assembled in Fredericksburg, prepared to vindicate the honor of Virginia and the cause of constitutional freedom at every hazard.[2] In the mean time, a letter was received from the Hon. Peyton Randolph, late

[1] American Archives, (4th series,) vol. II. p. 387. [2] Ibid. p. 443.

speaker of the House of Burgesses, and President of the Continental Congress, acquainting the gentlemen congregated at Fredericksburg that the governor had given "full assurance" of satisfaction in the affair of the gunpowder, and advising that "they should proceed no farther at this time." In consequence of this information and advice, a council of the officers and other deputies of the several independent companies was held to deliberate on the course which it was proper for them, under these circumstances, to pursue. It was determined, in deference to the advice given from so venerable and patriotic a source, to proceed no farther at this time; but "considering," they said, "the just rights and liberty of America to be greatly endangered by the violent and hostile proceedings of an arbitrary ministry, and being firmly resolved to resist such attempts at the utmost hazard of our lives and fortunes, we do now pledge ourselves to each other to be in readiness, at a moment's warning, to reassemble, and by force of arms to defend the law, the liberty, and rights of this, or any sister Colony, from unjust and wicked invasion." This noble and spirited declaration was countersigned with the significant motto, "God save the Liberties of America," as opposed to the traditional and stereotyped formula of "God save the King," with which the proclamations of the governor invariably concluded.

A few days after these proceedings in Fredericksburg, Patrick Henry put himself at the head of the independent company of Hanover, and marched towards Williamsburg with the view of demanding compensation for the gunpowder removed by the orders of the governor, or, as it was expressed at the time, "making reprisals upon the King's property sufficient to replace the gunpowder taken out of the magazine." The King's receiver-general, having charge of all the fiscal resources of the crown in the Colony, being thus a principal object of the movement, a detachment was sent to his residence in King William County; but not finding him there, they rejoined the main body of the company at Doncastle's ordinary, sixteen miles from Williamsburg. Here the whole party remained till the following morning, when the receiver-general, Mr. Corbin, sent up from Williamsburg his bill of exchange for £330, the estimated value of the gunpowder, for which Mr. Henry gave his receipt in due form, and he and his companions returned in peaceful triumph to their county.

This striking and lucky *coup de main*,[1] — the

---

[1] It seems impossible to characterize in any other terms this fortunate adventure of Mr. Henry. While its success excited much enthusiasm among the people, there were those who, comparing the result with the inadequacy of the means employed to produce it, and adverting also to the pause of Mr. Henry at Doncastle's ordinary, did not spare, in their criticisms, either the terrified royal governor, or the triumphant popular leader. The late Governor Page was, at the time, a member of Lord Dunmore's council, — the only one who stood out against his arbitrary measures, — and was a witness of

success of which must have been owing, in no
small degree, to the really imposing military demonstration that had taken place at Fredericksburg, and which showed there was a large and
effective force ready "at a moment's warning to
reassemble" and supply Mr. Henry's deficiency of
numbers,—drew upon the Hanover volunteers
and their distinguished leader the warm and enthusiastic plaudits of the people. Nowhere were
these sentiments more boldly and energetically
expressed than by the county committee of Orange, of which the father of Mr. Madison was
chairman, and he himself, as we have seen, a
member, and, without doubt, the member selected,
on this occasion, to give expression to their sentiments, as we find their resolutions among his
papers, and in his own handwriting.

After resolving that "the resentment shown
by the Hanover volunteers, and the reprisals
they have made on the King's property, highly

the progress and termination of
the whole affair. In a brief autobiographical memoir, drawn up in
answer to the inquiries of a friend,
he says :—

"I advised the governor (Lord
Dunmore) to give up the powder
and arms he had removed from the
magazine. But he flew into an
outrageous passion, smiting his fist
on the table and saying, 'Mr. Page,
I am astonished at you.' I calmly
replied I had discharged my duty,
and had no other advice to give.
As the other councillors neither
seconded nor opposed me, he was
greatly embarrassed. As I was
never summoned to attend another board, I might well suspect
I was suspended from my office;
but as I cared nothing about that,
I never inquired whether I was or
not. Patrick Henry, afterwards
so famous for his military parade
against Dunmore, did actually
bully him, but they appeared to
me to be mutually afraid of each
other." See the Memoir in the
Virginia Historical Register, vol.
III. p. 142.

merit the approbation of the public, and the thanks of this committee," they determine that "an address be presented to Captain Patrick Henry and the gentlemen Independents of Hanover." This address, as the production of Mr. Madison's pen, and as evincing the high spirit of resistance to tyranny which warmed and animated his bosom amid the thickening dangers of the crisis, we give in full.

                                    "MAY 9, 1775.

"GENTLEMEN : We, the committee for the county of Orange, having been fully informed of your seasonable and spirited proceedings in procuring a compensation for the powder fraudulently taken from the country magazine by command of Lord Dunmore, and which it evidently appears his lordship, notwithstanding his assurances, had no intention to restore, entreat you to accept their cordial thanks for this testimony of your zeal for the honor and interest of your country. We take this opportunity also to give it as our opinion that the blow struck in the Massachusetts government is a hostile attack on this and every other Colony, and a sufficient warrant to use violence and reprisal in all cases in which it may be expedient for our security and welfare.

"JAMES MADISON, Chairman.

JAMES TAYLOR,	THOMAS BARBOUR,
ZACHARIAH BURNLEY,	ROWLAND THOMAS,
JAMES MADISON, JR.,	WILLIAM MOORE,
JAMES WALKER,	LAWRENCE TALIAFERRO,
HENRY SCOTT,	THOMAS BELL."

The committee of Orange was particularly distinguished at this period of public danger, among the county committees of the Colony, for the boldness, energy, and public spirit which marked all its proceedings. To the instance just given may be added another of peculiar and remarkable character. It had been represented to the committee that a Rev. Mr. Wingate was in possession of various pamphlets reflecting very injuriously on the conduct and motives of the Continental Congress, and in other respects adverse to the public cause. They immediately held a meeting to demand of Mr. Wingate the surrender of these anti-American publications; but finding him unwilling to give them up, except on conditions inconsistent with the objects they had in view, they at length "peremptorily insisted, with a determination not to be defeated in their intentions."

When at last the pamphlets were yielded, the committee took time to examine them, and adjourned to meet again at the court-house of the county on Monday, the 27th of March, 1775. The following resolution, the production, doubtless, of their accomplished penman, and instinct with the spirit he had early imbibed in defence of American rights, was then adopted:—

"*Resolved*, That as a collection of the most audacious insults on that august body (the grand Continental Congress,) and their proceedings, and also on the several Colonies from which they were deputed, particularly New England and Virginia,—of the most slavish doctrines of provincial government, and of the most impudent falsehoods and malicious artifices to excite divisions among the friends of America,—these pamphlets deserve to be publicly burnt, as a testimony of the committee's detestation and abhorrence of the writers and their principles."

The record then continues: "Which sentence was speedily executed in the presence of the Independent Company of Orange, and other respectable inhabitants of the said county, all of whom joined in expressing a noble indignation against such execrable publications, and their ardent wishes for an opportunity of inflicting on the authors, publishers, and abettors the punishment due to their insufferable arrogance and atrocious crimes."

Things were now rapidly hastening to a decisive issue in Virginia. After the affair of the gunpowder, the governor lost all hold on the confidence and respect of the Colony. His language as well as conduct, when he had somewhat recovered from the impression made on his nerves by the bold military front exhibited by the independent companies throughout the Colony, became more arrogant and offensive than ever. He issued a proclamation denouncing "the outrageous and rebellious practices" which had taken place, and threatening with "the vengeance of offended majesty" those who should hereafter be found engaged in them. On the occasion of some trivial commotion in Williamsburg, he sent a message to the magistrates of the city, threatening "to lay the town in ashes," and at the same time holding over the heads of the people the menace of "proclaiming freedom to the slaves and devastating the Colony."[1] Notwithstanding these offensive proceedings on the part of the governor, he again called the Assembly together,—which had not been convoked since the sudden dissolution in May, 1774,—to consider the "conciliatory proposition" of Lord North.

The meeting took place in the capitol at Williamsburg on the 1st of June, 1775; and the session was opened with a speech of studied, but hollow and deceptive, courtesy from the governor. The House of Burgesses was organized with a scrupulous observance of all the stereotyped regal formalities. By *command* of the governor, they attended his excellency in the council-chamber; received his permission, or rather order, to choose a speaker; afterwards waited upon him to present their speaker, who was graciously approved; and then they laid claim to "their ancient rights and privileges of freedom of debate, exemption from arrest, and protection for their estates," all of which were "granted and allowed to them upon their petition" by the King's sub-

[1] See Report of Committee of House of Burgesses on the causes of the late Disturbances, in American Archives, (4th series,) vol. II. pp. 1209-1215.

stitute and representative. As this was the last
rehearsal of mimic royalty on the theatre of
Virginia, these few particulars of the scene may
be worth a passing commemoration. A resolution was then adopted, by which, with great dignity, the House assured his lordship that they
would take into their most serious consideration
the important matters contained in the speech,
and "proceed with that coolness and deliberation
which ought to influence the counsels of a free
and loyal people."

Hardly was this exchange of ceremonious respects concluded, when an incident occurred
which produced a sudden and entire change in
the face of affairs. Two or three young men
of the town, who had entered the magazine to
furnish themselves with arms, were grievously
wounded by the explosion of a spring-gun, which
had been secretly contrived, by the orders of
Lord Dunmore, to take vengeance of such a
trespass, if it should be attempted. So vindictive and treacherous a proceeding, in the midst
of smiling overtures of peace and conciliation,
naturally excited a lively feeling of indignation;
but there was no act, or even demonstration, of
violence by any portion of the people. The
guilty conscience of the governor, however, con-
jured up ideal dangers to himself and to his
family; and on the night of the 8th instant, he
secretly withdrew from the palace in Williamsburg, and placed himself on board his Majesty's

ship of war, the Fowey, riding at anchor in York River. From this floating and frowning citadel he proposed thenceforward to conduct his intercourse with the Assembly. This was submitted to for awhile, under repeated protests and remonstrances from the Assembly; but when at length the rejection of the ministerial plan of conciliation, in a series of well reasoned and eloquent resolutions from the pen of Mr. Jefferson, put an end to all show of respect on the part of the governor, the breach between him and the representatives of the people daily became wider and more embittered.

To an address from the House of Burgesses,— justifying one of their measures from certain captious objections taken to it by the governor, and entreating him to meet them on the following day at the capitol in Williamsburg, for the purpose of giving his assent to such of the bills and resolves passed by them as he should approve,— he curtly replied by reiterating his objections to the obnoxious measure, refusing to meet them at the capitol, and informing them that he would receive them the following day, "at twelve of the clock at his present residence," on board his Majesty's ship of war, the Fowey. The House immediately resolved itself into a committee of the whole House to take into consideration the state of the Colony and the governor's answer; and, by an unanimous vote, declared "his lordship's message, requiring them to attend him on board one of his Majesty's ships of war, to be a high breach of the rights and privileges of the House." Protesting their unshaken loyalty to the King, and the determination "to the utmost of their power and at·the risk of their lives and property to maintain and defend his government in this Colony, as founded on the established laws and principles of the constitution," they affirm that the proceedings of the governor "give them great reason to fear that a dangerous attack may be meditated against the unhappy people of this Colony," whom they therefore advise "to prepare for the preservation of their property and their inestimable rights and liberties with the greatest care and attention."

In stern and ominous silence they then adjourned to the 12th day of October next. But when that day arrived, the Colony was placed in flagrant war with its oppressors; and the proceedings of the 24th of June, 1775, proved to be the last scene of the last act of the "House of Burgesses" in Virginia,—an honorable and dignified close of its existence, in keeping with many glorious antecedents.

A convention of delegates, chosen by the people under the recommendation of the preceding convention, soon took the place of the regular and yet legal representative body. They assembled in Richmond on the 17th day of July, 1775, and immediately adopted measures for the defence and protection of the Colony. Two regi-

ments of regular troops were ordered to be
raised for immediate service, and sixteen battal-
ions of minute-men to be organized, and trained
and exercised periodically within their respective
districts, to be ready, at a minute's warning, to
unite with the regular force in case of need. In
addition to these provisions for the general defence of the Colony, half-a-dozen detached companies were to be raised and stationed at Pitts-
burg, Wheeling, and other designated points for
the protection of the western frontiers. Mr.
Henry, then one of the delegates to the Continental Congress, but who returned to Virginia
about this time, was appointed colonel of the
first regiment, and, as such, commander-in-chief
of all the colonial forces. This honor, however,
was not conferred on him without a close contest with a gentleman of high civil and military
merit, Hugh Mercer, who upon the first ballot
obtained one vote more than Mr. Henry.[1]

[1] This military appointment conferred on Mr. Henry appears to
have been the occasion of a good
deal of dissatisfaction and criticism
at the time. Girardin, who, in
writing his continuation of Burk,
had the advantage of daily and
unreserved personal communications with Mr. Jefferson, as well
as free access to all his papers,
(see Jefferson's Writings, vol. I.
p. 41, and vol. IV. p. 251,) says:—

"The elevation of Patrick Henry to the chief command of the
regular colonial forces was, in the
opinion of many, one of those hasty
measures into which the efferves-
cence of gratitude not unfrequently
betrays even public bodies. From
the national councils, where his
usefulness was preëminently conspicuous, that gentleman was called
to an important military station,
with the duties of which he must,
in the nature of things, have been
mostly unacquainted; whilst, by
an unhappy reaction, the country
lost the services of some able officers, whom the pride of former
rank would not suffer to act under

In concurrence with these measures, a committee of safety was appointed, consisting of eleven of the most experienced and honored members of the convention,[1] to whom large discretionary powers were given in the direction of the military force, and, in general, for all those executive functions of government which were now considered in abeyance, at least, by the hostile attitude of the royal governor. The convention closed a session of earnest and efficient practical labors for the care of the public liberty and safety, by the promulgation of a document, simple and unadorned as it was truthful, "setting forth the cause of their meeting, and the necessity of immediately putting the country into a posture of defence for the better protection of their lives, liberties, and properties." After glancing, in general terms, at the long course of ministerial despotism which had been exercised over the Colonies, and a review, more in detail,

him,—a loss peculiarly to be lamented in the infancy of an arduous struggle, and at a time when Virginia counted only a few military characters possessed of the qualifications necessary for discharging their duty with honor to themselves and security to the common cause." Burk's History of Virginia, vol. IV. p. 103.

[1] The members who received this high proof of the confidence of the convention were Edmund Pendleton, George Mason, John Page, Richard Bland, Thomas Ludwell Lee, Paul Carrington, Dudley Digges, William Cabell, Carter Braxton, James Mercer, and John Tabb. In the election of the committee of safety, at the succeeding convention in December, 1775, in the place of George Mason, who retired on account of infirm health, and of Carter Braxton, just elected delegate to the Continental Congress, were chosen Joseph Jones and Thomas Walker; and the other members were all reappointed.

of the odious malversation of the governor, and stating the necessity which was thus imposed upon them of adopting measures of self-protection and defence, they conclude with the following earnest protestation :—

"But lest our views and designs should be misrepresented or misunderstood, we again, and for all, publicly and solemnly declare before God and the world that we do bear faith and true allegiance to His Majesty, King George the Third, our only lawful and rightful sovereign; that we will, so long as it may be in our power, defend him and his government, as founded on the laws and well known principles of the constitution; that we will, to the utmost of our power, preserve peace and good order throughout the country, and endeavour, by every honorable means, to promote a restoration of that friendship and amity, which so long and happily subsisted between our fellow-subjects in Great Britain and the inhabitants of America; that as, on the one hand, we are determined to defend our lives and properties, and maintain our just rights and privileges at every, even the extremest, hazard, so, on the other, it is our fixed and unalterable resolution to disband such forces as may be raised in this Colony, whenever our dangers are removed, and America is restored to that former state of tranquillity and happiness, the interruption of which is so much deplored by us and every friend to either country."

While these events were passing in Virginia, the second Continental Congress had assembled in Philadelphia. Coming together after the fatal effusion of blood at Concord and Lexington, they entered at once upon the consideration of the measures which the commencement of hostilities by the commander-in-chief of the royal, or, as they were yet called, ministerial troops, rendered indispensably necessary. On the 26th of May, 1775, they unanimously adopted a resolution, that "for the express purpose of securing and defending the Colonies, and preserving them in safety against all attempts to carry the oppressive and unconstitutional acts of Parliament into execution by force of arms, these Colonies be immediately put into a state of defence." At the same time, declaring that "they most ardently wish for a restoration of the harmony formerly subsisting between our mother country and these Colonies, the interruption of which must, at all events, be exceedingly injurious to both countries," they resolved, that, "with a view to the promotion of so desirable a reconciliation by all the means not incompatible with a just regard for the undoubted rights and true interests of the Colonies, a humble and dutiful petition be presented to His Majesty," and that a "negotiation for accommodating the unhappy disputes which had arisen be made a part of the said petition."

It is known that the suggestion of a second

petition to the King was exceedingly distasteful to many of the patriots of the day, but from a spirit of deference and conciliation towards those who desired it, it was not opposed; and a most respectable contemporary authority [1] has expressed the opinion that its effect in the end, when it came to be known that it had been treated with silent disregard by the Throne and ungraciously rejected by Parliament, was to rally all shades of patriotic sentiment in America to a firmer and more united support of the national cause.

On the 15th of June, Congress resolved that "a general be appointed to command all the continental forces raised and to be raised for the defence of American liberty," and proceeded at once to the eventful choice. Who that General was the world knows, and to the latest ages will remember. They, then, by successive resolutions determined upon the number and description of the troops to be raised, appointed four major-generals, eight brigadiers, and an adjutant general, to act under the orders of the commander-in-chief, and voted, for the support of the army, three millions of dollars in bills of credit, for the redemption of which the faith of the confederated Colonies was solemnly pledged.

Among the most important of the papers which this august body, after the example of its predecessor, thought fit to put forth, was "a declaration by the representatives of the United

---

[1] See Ramsay's History of the American Revolution, vol. i. p. 273.

Colonies of North America, now met in Congress
at Philadelphia, setting forth the causes and necessity of their taking up arms." This noble
paper was the joint production of Mr. Dickinson
and Mr. Jefferson; but being debated paragraph
by paragraph, and carefully considered by Congress before its adoption, it must be regarded
as speaking the genuine and most deliberate
sense of that body.

After declaring that "the arms we have been
compelled by our enemies to assume we will,
in defiance of every hazard, with unabating
firmness and perseverance, employ for the preservation of our liberties, being with one mind
resolved to die freemen rather than live slaves,"
they proceed to say, "we mean not to dissolve that union which has so long and so
happily subsisted between us, and which we sincerely wish to see restored; .... we have not
raised armies with ambitious designs of sep-
arating from Great Britain and establishing independent States. .... In our own native land, in
defence of the freedom that is our birthright,
and which we ever enjoyed till the late violation of it, for the protection of our property,
acquired solely by the honest industry of our
forefathers and ourselves, against violence actually offered, we have taken up arms. .... We
shall lay them down, when hostilities shall cease
on the part of our aggressors and all danger of
their being renewed shall be removed, and not

before." They conclude with an appeal to the
Supreme Ruler of the Universe " to protect us
happily through this great conflict, to dispose
our adversaries to reconciliation on reasonable
terms, and thereby to relieve the empire from
the calamities of civil war."

These expressions of a sincere desire of reconciliation with the mother country, while arming
in defence of their rights,—which marked the
proceedings of all the other Colonies, as well as
of Virginia and of their common representative,
the Continental Congress,—were treated in England as hypocritical and treacherous. The King
himself, in the speech at the opening of Parliament on the 26th of October, 1775, went so far
as to say that " the Americans meant only to
amuse by vague expressions of attachment to
the parent state, and the strongest protestations
of loyalty to me, whilst they were preparing for
a general revolt;" and that " the rebellious war
now levied is manifestly carried on for the purpose of establishing an independent empire."
Not a few of the ablest political writers in England [1] charged the Colonies with harbouring the
design of independence, even before the present
dispute; and it has been quite common for
European historians of the American Revolution,
who are not unfriendly to the cause of the
Colonies, viewing the subject through the medium of diplomatic usages and traditions familiar

[1] Such as Chalmers, Dr. Johnson, and Soame Jenyns.

to the old world, to consider the earnest professions of a desire for a reconciliation with the
mother country on terms consistent with their
constitutional rights, which were so emphatically
made at this time, both by the general Congress
and the several colonial assemblies, as nothing
more than the trite, conventional language of
diplomacy.[1]

Such a representation does injustice alike to
the original spirit and object of this great movement, to the sincerity of both leaders and people,
and to contemporary evidence of the highest
character. General Washington, writing to his
friend M'Kenzie, from the midst of the counsels
and deliberations of the first Congress which met
at Philadelphia in September, 1774, and of which
he was silently the ruling spirit, says: "I am
well satisfied that no such thing as independence
is desired by any thinking man in North America; on the contrary, it is the ardent wish of
the warmest advocates for Liberty that peace
and tranquillity, on constitutional grounds, may
be restored, and the horrors of civil war prevented."

Mr. Jefferson, who was a member both of the
Virginia convention of 1775, and of the second
Continental Congress, the proceedings of each of
which bodies we have given above, in writing
to his friend John Randolph, immediately after
their adjournment, uses a language which de-

[1] Both Botta and Grahame adopt this interpretation.

serves so much the more consideration with reference to this question, as being that of a leader who, by the course of events, finally became one of the earliest and most zealous champions of independence. "I hope," he says, "the returning wisdom of Great Britain will ere long put an end to this unnatural contest. There may be people to whose tempers and dispositions contention is pleasing, and who, therefore, wish a continuance of confusion; but to me it is, of all other states but one, the most horrid. My first wish is a restoration of our just rights; my second, a return of the happy period when, consistently with duty, I may withdraw myself totally from the public stage, and pass the rest of my days in domestic ease and tranquillity, banishing every desire of ever hearing what passes in the world. Perhaps, (for the latter adds considerably to the warmth of the former wish,) looking with fondness towards a reconciliation with Great Britain, I cannot help hoping you may be able to contribute towards expediting this good work."

This was the language, in a confidential correspondence excluding every possible motive for dissimulation, of a jealous and ardent friend of liberty, the author of the "Summary View of the Rights of British America," soon to become the immortal penman of the Declaration of Independence itself, who had just left the deliberations of the two assemblies which, in arming for the defence of their rights, still invoked the return of peace and union upon those constitutional grounds which could alone insure a lasting or useful harmony.

It would be easy to multiply proofs of the same character, even to redundancy. Instead of that, we prefer to give the deliberate and well considered opinion of one who was a most intelligent and deeply interested observer of the events of the times, though then too young to take an active lead in them, and who, appealed to, in the retirement which closed his long career, for his judgment on this disputed point of our history, gave the following answer, reflecting, with the lights of truth, the characteristic modesty and dignity of the writer.

"My first entrance on public life," says Mr. Madison, in replying to his distinguished querist,[1] "was in May, 1776, when I became a member of the convention in Virginia which instructed her delegates in Congress to propose the Declaration of Independence. Previous to that date, I was not in sufficient communication with any under the denomination of leaders to learn their sentiments or views on that cardinal subject.

"I can only say, therefore, that so far as ever came to my knowledge, no one of them ever avowed, or was understood to entertain, a pursuit of independence, at the assembling of the first Congress or for a considerable period there-

[1] Letter to Mr. Jared Sparks, 5th of January, 1826.

after. It has always been my impression that a reëstablishment of the colonial relations to the parent country, as they were previous to the controversy, was the real object of every class of the people, till despair of obtaining it, and the exasperating effects of the war and the manner of conducting it, prepared the minds of all for the event declared on the 4th of July, 1776, as preferable, with all its difficulties and perils, to the alternative of submission to a claim of power at once external, unlimited, irresponsible, and under every temptation to abuse from interest, ambition, and revenge. If there were individuals who aimed at independence, their views must have been confined to their own bosoms, or to a very confidential circle."

The difficulty which English and other foreign writers have had in giving faith to the language of the American Colonies and their representative assemblies at this time, seems to have arisen from some notion of an inherent incompatibility of the attitude of armed resistance with the preservation of existing political ties. But is such a state of things any novelty in the annals of English freedom? Did not the barons at Runnymede, with arms in their hands, and their military retainers encamped around them, obtain the great charter of English liberty without a dissolution of the government, or a temporary renunciation, even, of their allegiance to the sovereign from whom it was demanded and received? Was it not an express stipulation in that same charter that, if any of its articles should be thereafter violated by the King, the barons should have the right to levy war against him, until full satisfaction be made?

So frequent and familiar indeed are such examples in the early struggles of our British ancestors, that their great constitutional lawyer, John Selden, when asked by what law he justified the right of resistance, replied, "By the *custom* of England, which is part of the common law." What was the Revolution of 1688, from which Englishmen proudly date the final and triumphant establishment of the national freedom, but an armed movement of the nation in vindication of their constitutional rights, without any subversion of existing institutions, and followed by a solemn compact with the sovereign pledging him to the maintenance and security of those institutions, as recognized and established?

There was no want, then, either of logical consistency, or of honest sincerity, in the ends and aims professed by the American Colonies in the first stage of the contest on which they had entered. The full enjoyment of constitutional freedom and the redress of wrongs were the objects for which they took up arms. But when, in the progress of the struggle, it became apparent that these objects were not to be obtained, and that unconditional submission to the authority claimed

by the mother country was the sole and degrad-
ing condition of peace, a higher and more uncompromising object emerged to view; and by
degrees, all minds were prepared for the bold
and grand alternative of independence.

The measures adopted by the British Parliament, at its first session after the proceedings of
the Continental Congress already noticed, contributed decisively to the change of public feeling
in America. The petition to the King, to which
no answer had been given by ministers, was laid
before Parliament, where it was rejected by an
overwhelming majority; and in the debate to
which it gave rise in the House of Lords, Lord
Dartmouth, late Secretary of State for the Colonies, in excusing himself for returning no answer
to the petition, said that "although the terms
of it were unexceptionable, there was every reason to believe that the softness of its language
was intended to conceal the most traitorous designs."

The Prime Minister soon introduced and carried a bill, under the title of a "Bill to prohibit
all Trade and Intercourse with the Colonies during the present Rebellion," which authorized the
indiscriminate capture, either in port or on the
high seas, of all American vessels; forfeited both
vessel and cargo to the captors; and directed that
the crews and all persons found on board the
captured vessels should be at once entered upon
his Majesty's ships of war, and be there com-

pelled to serve, as if they had been regularly enlisted seamen, against their brethren in America. A virtual declaration of war, with aggravations unknown to the law of nations in case of foreign war,— this measure was accompanied with the actual preparation of large armaments, both naval and military, and the engagement of *foreign* mercenary troops, for the avowed reason of excluding the operation of those sympathies and scruples which might arise between fellow-subjects in such a contest.

It is impossible for an American, or even an Englishman, who reads at this day the proceedings of that memorable session of Parliament which so madly forced on the issue of independence, not to render the homage of his admiration to the Roman firmness of that small band in either House, which stood up against the headlong torrent of ministerial and national delusion, and sustained the cause of constitutional liberty and the Colonies, under the almost certain penalty of being denounced as sympathizers with treason and rebellion, if not traitors and rebels themselves.[1] Such was the glorious and

[1] When the bill for "prohibiting trade and intercourse with the Colonies during their present rebellion" came up to the House of Lords, it was met there, as it had been in the other House, in a spirit of bold and undaunted opposition. The Duke of Richmond pronounced it to be a measure which, both in its principle and its provisions, was fraught with all manner of injustice and cruelty; and added, "I do not think the people of America in rebellion, but resisting acts of the most unexampled cruelty and oppression." Here he was loudly called to order; and one of the ministerial

never to be forgotten part acted by the Duke of Richmond, the Marquis of Rockingham, the Bishop of Peterborough, the Dukes of Manchester, Cumberland, and Grafton in the House of Lords, and by General Conway, Lord John Cavendish, Colonel Barré, Mr. Hartley, Mr. Fox, and Mr. Burke in the House of Commons.

While these vindictive measures of the British ministry and Parliament were producing their natural effect on the sensibilities and reflections of the people of all the Colonies, there were peculiar causes in operation in Virginia · which were rapidly preparing a thorough revulsion in the sentiments of loyal attachment to the mother country, for which she had been once so distinguished. The royal governor, Dunmore, giving way to the resentments which his recent contro-

lords, Denbigh, undertook .to reprimand him by declaring that those "who defend rebellion are themselves little better than rebels, and that there is but little difference between the traitor, and him who openly or privately abets treason." The Duke disdainfully replied by telling his lordship that "he was not to be deterred by loud words from the performance of his duty, and that he neither modified nor retracted anything he had said."

On another occasion during this same eventful session of Parliament, several of the opposition members of the House of Commons, Col. Barré and Mr. Burke particularly, having eulogized in warm terms the heroism and magnanimity of Montgomery, Lord North censured them for bestowing such unqualified praises on one who was a rebel; when Mr. Fox rose, and with a noble manliness and elevation of spirit, said, "The term rebel applied by the noble lord to that excellent person was no certain mark of disgrace, and therefore he was the less earnest to clear him of the imputation; for that all the great asserters of liberty, the saviours of their country, the benefactors of mankind in all ages, had been called rebels; that they even owed the constitution which enabled them to sit in that house to a rebellion."

versy with the legislative authority of the Colony
had kindled in his bosom, now organized, with
the vessels of war that were under his control,
a most disgraceful system of piratical warfare
against those whom it was his duty to conciliate
and protect. Collecting, on board his buccaneering fleet, a few deluded followers, and as many
African slaves as he could seduce from their .
masters by promises of freedom, he ravaged the
shores of the rivers which were open to him,
plundered the property and burnt the dwellings
of the inhabitants, and at length attempted the
destruction of their towns. Repulsed at Hampton by a greatly inferior but gallant force assembled in haste for its defence, he ventured to land
his motley array, reinforced with some companies of regulars, to meet the provincial troops
at King's Bridge, where he was again defeated;
and then took an ignominious revenge by laying the chief seaport of the Colony, Norfolk, in
ashes.

In the prosecution of these barbarous and disgraceful hostilities, he had issued, on the 7th of
November, 1775, a proclamation calling upon all
persons capable of bearing arms "to repair to
his standard, or be looked upon as traitors to
His Majesty's crown and government," and declaring free all negroes, who shall join him "for
the more speedily reducing this Colony to a
.proper sense of their duty to His Majesty's
crown and dignity." An outrage of so deep a

dye as this, could admit of no aggravation from the superaddition of any other official iniquity: but it so happened that discoveries, just then made, proved that this infamous viceroy, while inviting the fellowship and coöperation of slaves as allies in a war of extermination against their masters, was at the same time, through his congenial instrument, Connolly, preparing to bring down the merciless savages of the forest, not only upon the western frontiers, but into the very heart, of the Colony.[1] Such were the multiplied enormities of this chosen representative of royalty in America, that Washington, in a letter of the 26th of December, 1775, to Richard Henry Lee,[2] speaking of the "diabolical schemes" of Dunmore, says that "nothing less than depriving him of life or liberty will secure peace

---

[1] A letter of the Earl of Dartmouth to Lord Dunmore, dated the 2d of August, 1774, contains the following significant passage, which shows that this unscrupulous and vindictive agent of ministerial tyranny relied upon the employment of Indians and negroes as a regular means of sustaining the authority of his government, even before the occurrence of any open rupture with the inhabitants of the Colony.

"The hope," says the approving minister to the guilty governor, "you held out to us in your letter of the 1st of May, that, with a supply of arms and ammunition, you should be able to collect from among the Indians, negroes, and other persons, a force sufficient, if not to subdue rebellion, at least to defend government, was very encouraging; but I find by your letters delivered to me by Lieutenant Collins, that you have been obliged, from the violence of the times, menaced by one branch of the legislature and abandoned by the other, to yield up all the powers of government and retire yourself on board the Fowey." See American Archives, (4th series,) vol. III. p. 6.

[2] American Archives, (4th series,) vol. IV. p. 465.

to Virginia; as motives of resentment actuate his conduct, to a degree equal to the total destruction of the Colony."

Under the influence of these various and powerful causes of alienation from the mother country, the public mind of America began to advance rapidly, though with unequal steps in both individuals and communities, to the stern and magnanimous resolve of final separation. The question of independence was now freely canvassed, not only in the consultations of patriots and in the conversations of friends and neighbours, but openly through the public press. In this state of things, in the month of April, 1776, delegates were elected by the several counties of Virginia to a new convention, which assembled in Williamsburg, on the 6th day of the following month. Of this body, destined to take so important a lead on the great question which then occupied the minds and hearts of all America, Mr. Madison, at the age of twenty-five years, was chosen a member for his native county of Orange.

CHAPTER V.

WHEN it became manifest that the last and only security for the rights of America was in the valor of her sons, and the Colonies were all arming for the contest, Mr. Madison kindled with the military ardor of his countrymen, and earnestly desired to join the army. A very large proportion of those who had been his intimate friends and associates at Princeton, where we have seen the spirit of patriotic resistance to the encroachments of the mother country run so high, had obtained commissions in the army;[1] and one of his brothers, Ambrose, four years younger than himself, had likewise done so. These circumstances, together with the lofty and indignant sense of the wrongs of his country which fired his own bosom, strongly disposed him to the military career. The continued feebleness of his health and constitution, in depriving him of the physical strength necessary for the services of the field, alone prevented the indulgence of the decided bent of his feelings. As a member of the committee of his county, however, he had shown too much zeal for the cause of American liberty, with high power, moral and intellectual, to defend and promote its interests, not to have attracted the notice of his fellow-citizens; and by their spontaneous voice,

[1] In an oration of the Hon. W. C. Alexander, (24th of August, 1857,) "On the Influence of Princeton College on the Liberty, Independence, and Greatness of the United States," it is stated that four fifths of her alumni passed from her walls into the revolutionary army. As a further illustration of the wide influence of that ancient institution, through her alumni, on the early destinies of America, the same authority states that nearly one fifth of the signers of the Declaration of Independence, and an equal proportion of the members of the convention which formed the constitution of the United States, and of the first Congress under it, were also graduates of Princeton College.

he was summoned from his studious retirement
to represent them in the convention of 1776.

He was probably, with one or two exceptions,
the youngest member of that body.   It was an
assembly of the conscript fathers of the Colony,
called together by a crisis of the most momentous character to take counsel for the public
liberty and safety.   Richard Bland, the Lees,
(Thomas Ludwell, and Richard Henry,) George
Mason, Patrick Henry, Edmund Pendleton, Robert Carter Nicholas, George Wythe, Archibald
Cary, and others, whose names had been long
familiar, and were now consecrated in the general confidence and affection, as leaders and
oracles of public opinion, were there to lend the
aid of their ripened wisdom and experience.
Mr. Pendleton was chosen to preside over their
deliberations; and, in taking the chair, he reminded the convention, in terms of impressive
gravity and dignity, that they were met "at a
time truly critical; ... when almost all the powers of government have been suspended for near
two years; ... and it will become us to reflect
whether we can longer sustain the great struggle we are making, in this situation."

These pregnant words plainly pointed to the
necessity of organizing a new and independent
government, and of finally severing the ties
which had hitherto (for the last two years, in
form only,) bound the Colony to the mother
country.   On the following day, (8th of May,)

it was ordered that the convention would, on the 10th instant, resolve itself into a committee of the whole house to take into their consideration the state of the Colony. This order was put off from day to day until the 14th instant, when it was executed; and Mr. Archibald Cary, chairman of the committee of the whole house, reported that, "having had the state of the Colony under their consideration, but not having time to go through the same, the committee directed him to move for leave to sit again." On the succeeding day, the 15th of May, 1776, the convention again resolved itself into a committee of the whole on the state of the Colony; and after some time spent therein, the president resumed the chair, and Mr. Cary reported that the committee of the whole had come to certain resolutions, "which he read in his place, and then delivered in at the clerk's table, where the same were again twice read, and unanimously agreed to, one hundred and twelve members being present." [1]

These resolutions recapitulate, in a brief and vigorous summary, the wrongs experienced from the King and Parliament of Great Britain, especially the last crowning outrage, by which the Colonies are declared to be out of the protection of the parent state, their ' properties subjected to confiscation, their people, when "captivated," compelled to join in the murder and

[1] Journal of the Convention, p. 15.

plunder of their relations and countrymen, fleets and armies raised, and the aid of foreign troops engaged to assist these destructive purposes; and then passing to the proceedings of the King's representative in the Colony, which they characterize as "a piratical and savage warfare," they declare that no alternative is left but "abject submission to the will of these overbearing tyrants, or a total separation from the crown and government of Great Britain, uniting and exerting the strength of all America for defence, and forming alliances with foreign powers for commerce and aid in war." They conclude with solemnly instructing the delegates of Virginia in the general Congress, "to propose to that body to declare the united Colonies free and independent States, absolved from all allegiance to or dependence on the crown or Parliament of Great Britain, and that they give the assent of this Colony to such Declaration, and to whatever measures may be thought proper and necessary by the Congress for forming foreign alliances, and a confederation of the Colonies."

This was the first decided movement of a competent authority, in any of the Colonies, in favor of independence. The Provincial Congress of North Carolina had, it is true, on the 12th day of the preceding month, passed resolutions which "empowered their delegates in Congress to concur with the delegates of the other Colonies in declaring independence and forming foreign alliances." But, however meritorious and patriotic those resolutions were, they simply gave to the North Carolina delegates the power, if they thought proper to exercise it, to concur in a measure which might or might not be brought forward by others; while the resolutions of Virginia imposed upon her representatives the obligation to propose that measure unconditionally, and to take, in her name, all the responsibility of a courageous and unhesitating lead.

Accordingly her delegates, in pursuance of their instructions, brought forward in Congress, on the 7th day of June, a resolution declaring that "these united Colonies are, and of right ought to be, free and independent States; that they are absolved from all allegiance to the British crown, and that all political connection between them and the state of Great Britain is and ought to be totally dissolved." This resolution was earnestly debated on the 8th and 10th of June; on the last of which days, without coming to a final decision upon it, a select committee was appointed to "prepare a declaration to the effect of the said resolution." As it had encountered a good deal of opposition in quarters where it was hoped the delay of a few weeks would produce a more favorable sentiment towards it, its farther consideration was postponed to the 1st of July.

On that and the following day, the debate upon it was renewed. The resolution, as pro-

posed by the delegates of Virginia in pursuance
of their instructions, was then finally adopted by
the House; and two days later the declaration,.
prepared in conformity to the resolution, proclaiming in fit and noble language the birth of
a great republican empire in America, springing
from the tyranny and oppression of its European
parent, received in the bosom of Congress its last
sanction by the individual and responsible signatures of the delegates of the several Colonies.[1]

The great act of national independence as proclaimed by the Congress of the United Colonies,
—an event of which the immeasurable influence
upon the destinies of the human family is everywhere acknowledged,—being thus connected in
an unbroken line with the instructions of the
Virginia convention of 1776 to their delegates
in Congress, every circumstance relating to the
origin and history of those instructions becomes
matter of rational and patriotic interest. Though
they were entered upon the journal of the convention as unanimously adopted, one hundred
and twelve members being present, there is reason to believe that they did not pass with the
entire concurrence of all the members. This,
besides being the natural inference from the circumstance of their being under the consideration
of the committee of the whole for two days, is

---

[1] For a full account of the proceedings in Congress relative to
independence, see Journal of Old
Congress, vol. i. pp. 368, 369, and
392–396, and Jefferson's Writings,
vol. i. pp. 10–16, and 96–100.

positively affirmed in the contemporary correspondence of a distinguished member.[1] That there were shades of difference in the convention among those friendly to independence, as to the mode of giving effect to it, appears from a letter of Major-General Lee, who, being at Williamsburg in the exercise of his military command, during the sitting of the convention, wrote to General Washington on the 10th of May, "A noble spirit possesses the convention. They are almost unanimous for independence, but differ in their sentiments about the mode; two days will decide it."[2]

[1] Manuscript Letter of George Mason to R. H. Lee of the 18th of May, 1776, wherein he says, "the opponents being so few that they did not think fit to divide, or contradict the general voice." This letter is in the archives of the Virginia Historical Society.

[2] See American Archives, (4th series,) vol. VI. p. 406. A letter addressed by General Lee to Patrick Henry, bearing date only three days before the one to General Washington cited above, has raised a doubt whether Mr. Henry was not among those who hesitated about the Declaration of Independence at this time. In that letter, which is a very remarkable one, as well for its ability as for the incidental disclosures made by it, (see it at length in American Archives, 5th series, vol. I. pp. 95-97,) the writer combats, with great clearness and force, certain objections which appear to have been urged by Mr. Henry, in a conversation of the day previous, against an immediate Declaration of Independence.

It will be seen, from a statement of Mr. Edmund Randolph hereafter referred to in the text, that the instructions of the Virginia convention of the 15th of May, in favor of a declaration of independence by Congress, were actually sustained in debate by Mr. Henry; from which the natural inference would be that his mind had been entirely relieved from the doubts he entertained at the time of his conversation with General Lee. And yet, in a letter written by him to Mr. John Adams on the 20th of May, five days after the adoption of those instructions, he repeats and dwells upon the apprehension that France might be seduced to take sides against the Colonies by

By what pen the instructions of the Virginia convention were drawn, is a question suggested as well by the intrinsic dignity and importance of the paper, as by the fact of its being the basis of the proceedings of Congress, which terminated in independence. Like the great Declaration itself, it has not escaped criticism, though in a somewhat different sense.[1] As a grave public act, however, without aspiring to the ambitious graces of studied composition, it is characterized by an appropriate clearness and condensation; a sobriety, yet energy, of statement marking firm resolve; and an unaffected and even Doric simplicity of language, which well consorts with the inherent grandeur of the cause.

That there was no spirit of self-seeking or

---

an offer from England to divide the territories of America between them;—an apprehension that formed the principal subject-matter of the objections, which appear to have been urged by him, in his conversation with General Lee, against an immediate declaration of independence.

In the letter to Mr. Adams, Mr. Henry also says, "the confederacy" (meaning, as the context proves, the conclusion of articles of confederation among the States,) "must precede an open declaration of independence, and foreign alliances;"—a condition which, as things turned out, if inflexibly adhered to, would have postponed the declaration of independence near five years. It would almost seem that Mr. Henry had an idea of an *open* declaration of independence as something different from what the instructions of the Virginia convention, which had been sustained by him, absolutely required her delegates in Congress to propose. See the letter to Mr. Adams in "Works of John Adams," vol. IV. pp. 201, 202.

[1] See Letter of George Mason to R. H. Lee, referred to above, and also the letter of Patrick Henry to John Adams, of the 20th of May, 1776.

vanity connected with the production of this
important paper, is evinced by the circumstance
of its authorship being unknown to many of the
members of the convention itself.   It appears
from a letter addressed by Mr. Madison in after-
life to Mr. Jefferson, with the laudable purpose
of rescuing from oblivion the part borne by each
actor in this great scene of our history, that,
though a member himself of the body from
which these instructions proceeded, he was left
wholly to conjecture with regard to their particular origin.   The following is an extract of
the letter referred to, dated the 6th of September, 1823 :—

" The friends of R. H. Lee have shown not
only injustice in underrating the draught, (of the
Declaration of Independence,) but much weakness in overrating the motion in Congress preceding it; all the merit of which belongs to the
convention of Virginia, which gave a positive
instruction to her deputies to make the motion.
It was made by him as next in the list to Peyton Randolph, then deceased.   Had Mr. Lee been
absent, the task would have devolved on you.
As this measure of Virginia makes a link in the
history of our national birth, it is but right that
every circumstance attending it should be ascertained and preserved.   You probably can best
tell where the instruction had its origin, and by
whose pen it was prepared.   The impression at
the time was that it was communicated in a

letter from yourself to Mr. Wythe, a member of the convention."

To this letter we have not the answer of Mr. Jefferson; but the entire omission of the conjecture it contained in later letters of Mr. Madison, referring to the same subject, authorizes the conclusion that it did not receive confirmation from the authentic source to which he appealed.

It seems now to be established by the unquestionable testimony of a contemporary actor that Edmund Pendleton, the president of the convention, was the draughtsman of this memorable act. In a funeral eulogy on the occasion of his death in 1803, recently brought to light by the researches of a most devoted and able inquirer into our State history, the orator, Edmund Randolph, who was a member of the convention of 1776, distinctly affirms that "the resolution which passed the convention for declaring independence was drawn by Mr. Pendleton, proposed by General Nelson, and enforced by Mr. Henry." [1] The revelation adds new lustre to the fame of Pendleton.

This gentleman, whose patriotism was always above suspicion, had, nevertheless, united with the steady firmness of his resistance to the arbitrary measures of the mother country, so much of the native coolness, deliberation, and prudence of his character, that the more ardent spirits of

---

[1] See the Virginia Gazette of the 2d of November, 1803. To Mr. Grigsby belongs the merit of evoking this posthumous testimony.

the day were sometimes dissatisfied with, if they did not venture openly to reproach, him. The offence, too, which, as chairman of the committee of safety, in a question of great delicacy, he had been so unfortunate as to give to the personal friends of Mr. Henry, had arrayed against him, at one time, the prejudices and animosity of a strong and powerful party. To every ingenuous mind, therefore, cherishing with equal loyalty and regard the fame of all our illustrious patriots, it cannot but be matter of sincere gratification to find the name of Pendleton connected, in the closest possible relation, with the first great and decisive movement in favor of independence; thus furnishing, for the instruction of rulers and people, a new proof that prudence, which a great English statesman has pronounced "not only the first in rank of virtues, political and moral, but the director, the regulator, the standard of them all," does not exclude boldness, but is often, as the same profound genius has said, another name for "courageous wisdom."[1]

On the same day and by the same act by which the convention pronounced their eventful decision in favor of independence, they resolved with like unanimity that "a committee be appointed to prepare a Declaration of Rights and such a Plan of Government as will be most likely to maintain peace and order in this Col-

[1] Burke. Appeal from New to Old Whigs, and Letters on a Regicide Peace.

ony, and secure substantial and equal liberty to the people." It is a circumstance which renders the 15th of May, 1776, yet more memorable, that the Continental Congress, on that day, adopted a preamble and resolution setting forth, in language almost identical with that of the Virginia convention, that "as the whole force of Great Britain, aided by foreign mercenaries, is to be exerted for the destruction of the good people of these Colonies," it has become necessary to suppress the exercise of every kind of authority under the British crown, and that all the powers of government be henceforward exerted under the authority of the people of the Colonies, for the preservation of peace, liberty, and safety; and recommending to the respective assemblies or conventions of the Colonies to proceed at once to the organization of such governments.[1] The convention of Virginia, guided by the intuitive suggestions of its own patriotism and forecast, had already entered upon the task, at the very moment Congress was advising it, and days before the recommendation of the latter could have been known in Virginia.

The committee appointed for the performance of this master work consisted originally of twenty-eight members, embracing the most eminent and well known names of the convention, Archibald Cary, Robert Carter Nicholas, Patrick Henry,

[1] See Journals of old Congress, vol. I. pp. 339 and 345.

Richard Bland, Thomas Ludwell Lee, John Blair, Meriwether Smith, James Mercer, and others, who, if less known to fame, had nevertheless given solid proofs of practical wisdom and capacity for government. On the day following the appointment of the committee, Mr. Madison, who, through the veil of his inexperience and modesty, had just begun to attract the notice of the convention, was, on special motion, added to it; and it was not till one day later that George Mason, destined to be the great leader in the labors of the committee, was, in like manner, made a member of it. One already so well known to the country, for his great abilities and experience, could not have been pretermitted in the original formation of the committee but for his absence at the time of its appointment; having been detained from his seat by an attack of his constitutional malady, the gout.

The difficulty of the task intrusted to the committee corresponded with its dignity and importance. The first written constitution for a free, sovereign, and independent state which the history of the world had yet called forth, was now to be framed, and adjusted to new and untried circumstances. New Hampshire and South Carolina had, a few months before, adopted temporary and provisional governments, "during the continuance of the dispute with the mother country," and in view of an ultimate "reconciliation," which both of them, at the time, earnestly invoked. But these essays were so crude and imperfect, and bore such evident marks of the precarious and equivocal circumstances in which they were formed, that they could furnish no guide, or even useful hint, for the foundation of a permanent and self-existent government.

Mr. Adams, at the request of one of the delegates of Virginia in Congress, had written a small tract, containing "Thoughts on Government," which was sent to Virginia; and another of the Virginia delegates had himself prepared a sketch of a constitution, founded on principles less democratic, which he addressed to the convention through the public journals, under the anonymous signature of "A Native."[1] It does not appear that either of these contributions, however well meant, and though the former received the hearty approbation of Mr. Henry, afforded any essential aid to the deliberations of the committee. The plan prepared by Mr. Jefferson, and forwarded through Mr. Wythe, arrived after the committee had made their report, and too late to be seriously considered.

The first part of their task, as we have seen, was the preparation of a Declaration of Rights. The proper office of such a declaration, as it was conceived by the committee, was not merely to

[1] The tract of Mr. Adams is to be found in his Works, vol. IV. p. 193, and the communication of "A Native," in American Archives, (4th series,) vol. VI. pp. 748–754.

proclaim an abstract theory of the rights of man, natural or civil, but to lay down the great fundamental principles of just and free government, and to assert those inviolable safeguards which experience, as well as reason, had shown to be indispensable for the protection of public and private liberty. In this extent, the task demanded the maturest judgment, the largest wisdom, the discipline and training of the most thorough statesmanship.

In George Mason, all these requisites were happily united. He had now attained the full meridian of life. He had taken a lively interest in every stage of the controversy with the mother country; and his pen, while he was yet a private citizen, and clung with fond preference to the endearments of domestic life, had been often and ably employed in vindicating the rights of the Colonies. For the first time, he was drawn from his retirement to supply the place of Washington as one of the members for Fairfax County in the convention of 1775, when the latter was appointed commander-in-chief of the army. In that convention, he so distinguished himself by his great abilities, untiring energy and fervid patriotism, that he was placed second to Pendleton on the committee of safety; and he was also most honorably elected a delegate to the Continental Congress in the place of Mr. Bland, which situation, however, he was forced by domestic considerations to decline.

He now came forth again from his cherished
retirement to participate in the common counsels for the public safety. He was the type of
that enlightened and patriotic class of country
gentlemen, who sedulously eschew the political
scene, except when imperiously summoned to it
by the voice of duty and public danger. This
circumstance, doubtless, strongly commended him
to the confidence of his associates, while his
well known wisdom and ability,—the fruit of
long study and observation,—qualified him in an
especial manner for the lead that was assigned
him.

Though not a lawyer by profession, no man
was more profoundly versed in the constitutional
lore, and the legislative and political history, of
the parent state. This was the school in which
he imbibed his free principles, with the strong
conservative sentiments to which, in his case,
they were so closely allied. In a letter written
to a friend and relative in England in 1778, while
avowing his determination to " risk the last penny
of his fortune and the last drop of his blood
on the issue of independence," he says that " no
man had been more warmly attached to the
Hanover family, and the Whig interest of England, than I was, and few men had stronger
prejudices in favor of that form of government
under which I was born and bred." [1]

[1] See Letter to Col. George Mercer in Virginia Historical Register,
vol. II. p. 30.

When we look at the Declaration of Rights
prepared by him, and which, with a few alterations, was unanimously adopted by the convention, we shall find it a condensed, logical, and
luminous summary of the great principles of
freedom inherited by us from our British ancestors; the extracted essence of Magna Charta,
the Petition of Right, the acts of the Long Parliament, and the doctrines of the Revolution of
1688 as expounded by Locke,—distilled and concentrated through the alembic of his own powerful and discriminating mind. There is nothing
more remarkable in the political annals of America than this paper. It has stood the rude test
of every vicissitude; and while Virginia has already had three different constitutions, the Declaration of Rights of 1776 has stood, and yet
stands, without the change of a letter, at the head
of each one of them, however difficult it may
be to reconcile with its principles some of the
provisions of the later constitutions. At the
same time, its leading articles have been adopted
into the constitutional acts of many of the other
States, and also into those amendments of the
constitution of the United States, which were
deemed by the first Congress, that met under it,
indispensable to complete the fabric of American
liberty and Union. What a commentary is this,
alike upon the largeness of British freedom in
its original spirit and purity, and upon the conservative genius and character of American lib-

erty, as conceived by the founders of our institutions.[1]

Every circumstance, relating to such a muniment of traditional freedom, is of public and lasting interest. The committee chosen to prepare it and a plan of government was, as we have seen, originally appointed on the 15th of May, and on the 18th, Mr. Mason was added to it. On the 27th of May, Mr. Archibald Cary, the chairman, reported the Declaration as agreed to by the select committee; and it was ordered to be printed for the perusal of the members of the convention. The original draught presented to the committee by Mr. Mason has, happily, been preserved among his papers, and is now, in his own handwriting, carefully enshrined, as it deserves to be, in the public library of the State. By a comparison of that draught with the paper reported by Mr. Cary, of which we find a printed copy among the papers of Mr. Madison, (the only one, perhaps, now extant,) we are enabled at once to see the few verbal alterations made in it by the committee.

In addition, however, to the fourteen articles which composed Mr. Mason's draught, the committee reported three others; of which one condemned retrospective or *ex post facto* laws; an-

[1] In support of these views, we beg leave to commend to the reader an admirable Discourse of Professor Washington on the Virginia Constitution of 1776, delivered before the Historical Society of Virginia, in January, 1852.

other general warrants, and the third declared the right of the people of Virginia to uniform government, and inhibited the erection of any separate or independent government within her limits. On the 10th of June, the convention resolved itself into a committee of the whole to take into consideration the Declaration of Rights as reported by the select committee; and certain amendments to it were made in committee of the whole, which were agreed to by the convention on the following day, and the day after, (the 12th of June,) the declaration as thus amended was unanimously adopted by the convention.

In regard to the verbal alterations in Mr. Mason's draught which had been made by the select committee, it is a proof of the admirable precision with which his work was done that the convention, in almost every instance, restored the original version, and rejected the modifications of the committee. Of the three additional articles proposed by the committee, that which related to retrospective or *ex post facto* laws was rejected;[1] but the other two respecting general warrants and uniform government were adopted

---

[1] It is a curious coincidence connected with the decision of the convention on this article, showing the probable influence of Colonel Mason in producing it, that twelve years afterwards, in setting forth his objections to the Federal Constitution, he included in those objections that clause of the instrument which absolutely and unconditionally prohibits all *ex post facto* laws, whether by Congress or the legislatures of the States. See his Objections, &c., in Sparks's Washington, vol. ix. pp. 544–547.

with slight variations, and form a part of the Declaration, as it now stands.

There was one amendment made by the convention, however, which merits special notice, both on account of the importance of the principle involved, and the connection of Mr. Madison with it. The last article of Colonel Mason's draught related to the vital subject of religious freedom. Setting forth, that religion, or the duty which we owe to our Creator, and the manner of discharging it, can be directed only by reason and conviction, not by force or violence, it proceeded to declare that "all men should, therefore, enjoy the fullest toleration in the exercise of religion, according to the dictates of conscience, unpunished and unrestrained by the magistrate, unless, under color of religion, any man disturb the peace, the happiness, or the safety of society." This article was reported by the select committee without the suggestion of any amendment, and came before the convention precisely as it stood in Colonel Mason's draught.

To Mr. Madison, however, there seemed to be both a dangerous and illogical implication in the use of the word *toleration*, as well as in the clause which admitted the restraining and punitive interposition of the civil magistrate in cases where the peace of society might be supposed to be endangered. Toleration belonged to a system in which there was an established Church, and where a certain liberty of worship is granted, not of right but of grace, to dissenting denominations; and the exception to this granted liberty, in cases where the peace of society might be alleged to be in danger of being disturbed, was one which, in the hands of the dominant power, might be easily so construed as to impair, if not annul, the grant.

These considerations impressed themselves so deeply upon the mind of Mr. Madison, that, though his remarkable modesty and the deference he habitually paid to superior age and experience made him most reluctant to offer any suggestion of his own to the convention, yet an overruling sense of duty, with a profound and settled attachment to the principle of religious freedom in its utmost latitude, impelled him to propose, in committee of the whole, an amendment to the Declaration, as it came from the hands of Colonel Mason and of the select committee. Instead of affirming that "all men should enjoy the fullest toleration in the exercise of religion, &c.," his amendment asserted the inherent and indefeasible right, by nature, to freedom of religion, declaring that "all men are equally entitled to the full and free exercise of it, according to the dictates of conscience;" and to close the door more effectually against the dangers of an abusive exercise of the authority of the civil magistrate under the clause of exception in Colonel Mason's draught, it added that "no man or class of men ought, on account of religion, to be invested with peculiar emoluments or privileges, nor subjected to any penalties or disabilities, unless, under color of religion, the preservation of equal liberty and the existence of the state are manifestly endangered."

The result of Mr. Madison's motion was that the term *toleration* was excluded from the Declaration of Rights, and the assertion of an absolute and equal right in all to the free exercise of religion, as proposed by him, substituted in its place ; and the qualifying clause of the original draught, admitting the interposition of the civil magistrate in cases where the peace, happiness, or safety of society might be supposed to be in danger of being disturbed, was wholly omitted.[1]

[1] That the reader may have the whole of this interesting matter under his eye at the same moment, we present here in parallel columns the draught of Colonel Mason, and the amendment of Mr. Madison, and subjoin underneath the article of the Declaration, as finally adopted :—

Draught of Colonel Mason.

" That religion, or the duty we owe to our Creator, and the manner of discharging it, can be directed only by reason and conviction, not by force or violence : and therefore, that all men should enjoy the fullest toleration in the exercise of religion, according to the dictates of conscience, unpunished and unrestrained by the magistrate unless, under color of religion, any man disturb the peace, happiness, or safety of society."

Amendment of Mr. Madison.

" That religion, or the duty we owe to our Creator, and the manner of discharging it, being under the direction of reason and conviction only, not of violence or compulsion, all men are equally entitled to the full and free exercise of it, according to the dictates of conscience, and, therefore, that no man or class of men ought, on account of religion, to be invested with peculiar emoluments or privileges, nor subjected to any penalties or disabilities unless, under color of religion, the preservation of equal liberty and the existence of the state be manifestly endangered."

Thus early were the wisdom and vigilant love of liberty of Mr. Madison, — then a young man, for the first time a member of a deliberative body, and of an extreme modesty, resembling in that, as in all his moral attributes, the great character of Washington, — incorporated with one of the noblest and most enduring monuments of American freedom and constitutional law. The term toleration had been admitted into the draught of Colonel Mason, doubtless, from his long familiarity with the leading precedents of English legislation, and with the great works of Locke, Hoadly, and others, by whom it had been used in a sense of unusual liberality for the country and times in which they wrote. Subjected, however, to a logical analysis, it embraced a dangerous fallacy; and Mr. Madison, in advance of his contemporaries, perceived the lurking mischief, and extirpated it from the American code.

A celebrated writer, an early champion of American independence, has since given utterance to the same views of the subject in language of peculiar pungency and force. "Toleration," he says, "is not the opposite of intolerance, but is the counterfeit of it. Both

The article, as finally adopted, is as follows :—

" That religion, or the duty we owe to our Creator, and the manner of discharging it, can be directed only by reason and conviction, not by force or violence, and, therefore, all men are equally entitled to the free exercise of religion, according to the dictates of conscience."

are despotisms. The one assumes to itself the right of withholding liberty of conscience, the other of *granting* it." [1]   An English author, yet more profound, and not less an admirer of American institutions, has recorded similar opinions in the following grave and weighty language.

"In liberty of conscience, I include much more than toleration.   Christ has established a perfect equality among his followers.   His command is that they shall assume no jurisdiction over one another, and acknowledge no master besides himself.   It is, therefore, presumption in any of them to claim a right to any superiority or preëminence over their brethren.   Such a claim is implied, whenever any of them pretend to *tolerate* the rest.   Toleration can take place only where there is a civil establishment of a particular mode of religion; that is, where a predominant sect enjoys exclusive advantages, and makes the encouragement of its own mode of faith and worship a part of the constitution of the state, but at the same time thinks fit to suffer the exercise of other modes of faith and worship. Thanks to God, the new American States are, at present, strangers to such establishments." [2]

The changes here noticed in Colonel Mason's draught of the Declaration of Rights having taken place in committee of the whole, the Journal of

---

[1] See Paine's Rights of Man, p. 58.
[2] Observations on the American Revolution, by Dr. Price, p. 28.

the convention, according to the usual mode of keeping that record, furnishes no clue to the history of them. But among Mr. Madison's papers, as we have already stated, is a printed copy of the Declaration in the form in which it was reported by the select committee, corresponding, in the article relating to religion, precisely with the original draught of Colonel Mason; and upon that copy is inscribed in the handwriting of Mr. Madison, evidently of contemporaneous date with the printed paper, the amendment proposed by him, as we have given it above. On a manuscript copy of the Declaration made by Mr. Madison at a later period of his life, and exhibiting in parallel columns the instrument in the form in which it was reported by the select committee, and also in that in which it was finally adopted by the convention, is the following note subjoined by him to the last article:—

"On the printed paper, here literally copied, is a manuscript variation of this last article making it read"—(Here the amendment proposed by him is incorporated.) "This variation," he adds, "is in the handwriting of J. M., and is recollected to have been brought forward by him with a view, more particularly, to substitute for the idea expressed by the term 'toleration,' an 'absolute and equal right' in all to the exercise of religion according to the dictates of conscience. The proposal was moulded into the last article in the Declaration as finally established, from which the term 'toleration' is excluded." [1]

We have been thus minute in tracing the history of the amendment proposed by Mr. Madison to the Declaration of Rights, not only to render the tribute due to the early wisdom and sagacity of the youthful statesman, but because the amendment itself forms an era in the history of American liberty. In discarding a term hitherto consecrated, in some degree, as a symbol of liberty, but intrinsically fallacious, and fraught with dangerous implications, it erected a new and loftier platform for the fabric of religious freedom. It planted, at the same time, the germ of all those measures which were afterwards pursued, and finally consummated mainly, as we shall see, through his agency, for removing every civil distinction,—privileges on the one hand, or disabilities on the other,—founded on religious opinion, and covering the rights of conscience under the broadest possible shield of legislative protection.

The fundamental principles of free government being thus agreed upon, the next thing was to embody them in a practical and organized plan of government. To the same committee which had been charged with the preparation of the Declaration of Rights, was confided also, as we

[1] In the Appendix B will be found the Bill of Rights in its three several stages—the original draft of Mr. Mason, the version reported by the select committee, and the form in which it was adopted by the convention.

have seen, the framing of the constitution, or plan of government. Of what passed in the interior deliberations of the committee we have but little knowledge. Patrick Henry, who was a member of it, writing to Mr. John Adams on the 20th of May, five days after the appointment of the committee, says: " Our convention is now employed in the great work of forming a constitution. My most esteemed republican plan has many and powerful enemies."

He then comments with no small severity upon the *projet* of a constitution, (the same to which we have already referred,) which had just been published under the auspices of Mr. Braxton, one of the delegates of Virginia in Congress, and of which that gentleman was supposed to be the author. It proposed a triennial house of representatives, a council for life, and a governor during good behaviour, (to be chosen by the house of representatives,) and having the power of appointment to the most important public offices. It was framed with the nearest possible approximation to the aristocratical and monarchical features of the British model, on which the writer pronounced the highest eulogium.

That such a proposal should have revolted the republican sentiments of Mr. Henry, is not at all surprising. We cannot, however, avoid being surprised when, recurring to the difficulty and importance of the work devolving on the convention, he adds: "I cannot count upon one coadjutor of talents equal to the task. Would to God that you and your Sam Adams were here!" At the time of inditing these lines, Mr. Henry probably had at his side, in his committee-room, colleagues who, if inferior in learning to his correspondent, were in depth of wisdom and true statesmanship far his superiors; and one of them, George Mason, was well known to Mr. Henry.

Mr. Adams had communicated to Mr. Henry a small tract, prepared at the instance of Mr. Wythe and Richard Henry Lee, containing his "Thoughts on Government," and the outline of such a constitution as he would recommend. The outline proposed a representative assembly to be annually chosen by those who owned a certain quantity of land; and that this assembly should annually choose out of its own body, or the community at large, twenty or thirty persons to form a council, which should constitute a distinct and coequal branch of the legislature with itself; and that these two should, by joint ballot, annually elect a governor, who was to have a negative upon the laws, and also the power, with the advice of a privy council, of appointing to all the offices of state. Without subjecting this scheme, of which Mr. Henry expressed his hearty approbation, to any formal criticism, it is obvious to remark that, attaching as Mr. Adams did the highest possible importance to the separation of the legislative department into two distinct and independent branches, which he pronounced to be the vital and indispensable condition of a free government, it is a somewhat crude, if not contradictory provision in his plan which gives the annual and absolute election of one branch to the other.

The only surviving trace we have of the deliberations of the select committee, upon the plan of government they were charged with preparing, is a printed copy among Mr. Madison's papers, of a plan which appears from a note in his handwriting, to have been "laid before that committee, and by them ordered to be printed for the perusal of the members of the House." This plan provides that the legislative department be formed of two distinct branches, one to be called the lower house of assembly, to consist of two members for each county, chosen annually by the qualified voters; the other the upper house, to consist of twenty-four members, to be chosen for four years by an intermediate body of deputies elected by the people in the respective districts, and the members to be so arranged into classes that one fourth of the number shall go out at the end of every year, and be then ineligible for four years. The right of suffrage is limited, in the first instance, to freeholders possessing a certain estate of inheritance, but accompanied with a provision that it be extended, in future, to leaseholders for a

13*

term of seven years at least, and to housekeepers, being fathers of three children in the country.

The governor or chief magistrate, it provides, shall be chosen annually by joint ballot of the two houses, not to continue in office longer than three years successively, and then to be ineligible for the next four years. He is to exercise the executive powers of government in general, with the advice of a council of state, and with the like advice, to appoint justices of the peace and officers of the militia, and to commission clerks, sheriffs, and coroners upon the nomination of the respective courts. The council of state shall consist of eight members to be chosen by joint ballot of the two houses, and two of the members to be removed by vote of their own board at the end of every three years, and to be then ineligible for the next three years. The judges of common law, chancery, and admiralty, and the attorney-general, shall be chosen by joint ballot of the two houses, and continue in office during good behaviour, and the treasurer be chosen annually in the same mode.

Such is the outline of the plan submitted to the select committee and ordered by them to be printed, as we find it among the papers of Mr. Madison. How far and in what respects it was modified by the select committee in their report to the convention, we are without the means of ascertaining, as no copy of that report can now be found.[1] It was on the 24th of June that the select committee reported the plan as agreed to by them to the convention. On the 26th, 27th, and 28th of June, it was under the consideration of the convention in committee of the whole. On the last of these days, it was reported from the committee of the whole to the convention, with amendments, and the plan, together with the amendments, ordered

[1] A copy of the printed paper originally laid before the select committee, and obtained probably from Mr. Madison, was published near thirty years ago in the "Literary Museum" of the University of Virginia. (See No. of 23d of September, 1829.) It is there published under the title of "A plan of government laid *before the committee of the house*, which they have ordered to be printed for the perusal of the members;" which might, naturally enough, lead to the inference that it was the plan reported by the select committee to the convention, referred to the committee of the whole house and by them ordered to be printed; and as such, it is commented upon by the editors of the Museum. Mr. Madison, however, has with the pen corrected this title in the copy remaining among his papers, so as to make it read, according to the citation in the text, "A plan of government laid before *the committee appoint-* ed for that purpose, which they have ordered to be printed for the perusal of the members of the house." This reading evidently excludes, as it was intended to do, the supposition that the printed paper was the report made by the select committee to the convention, and referred to the committee of the whole. The journal of the convention shows there was no order for the printing of the report of the select committee of a plan of government, as there was in the case of the Declaration of Rights. The editors of the Museum are also mistaken in saying that this paper which they call a Report, (considering it as the report of the select committee to the convention,) is dated June 24, 1776. That, according to the journal of the convention, was the day when the select committee made their report to the convention. But the paper referred to is without any date whatever.

to be transcribed and read a third time. On the 29th of the month, the plan of government so transcribed was read the third time and unanimously adopted.

On comparing the constitution, as adopted, with the plan submitted to the committee, we recognize a pervading likeness in their general features, and yet material variations in particular provisions.[1] The most striking of these variations is in the manner of electing the senate, substituting a direct for an intermediate election—in the periodical removal of two members of the privy council by a vote of the houses of assembly, instead of their own board—a more jealous limitation of the powers of the governor—and a precise and permanent definition of the right of suffrage by reference to the existing law, which made it consist in the possession of a freehold estate in twenty-five acres of improved, or a hundred of unimproved, land. There were a few additional articles, not found in the original plan, among which the most noticeable, perhaps, is the disqualification of all persons holding lucrative offices, and all ministers of the gospel of every denomination, to be members of either house of the assembly or of the privy council.[2]

[1] To facilitate a more minute and satisfactory comparison of the two instruments, they will both be found in the Appendix, C.

[2] The article of the adopted constitution, which excludes ministers of the gospel from political station, has been the subject of criticism

In looking back to the Virginia constitution of 1776, with all the lights which the intermediate experience of eighty years has shed on the science of popular government, we cannot but be struck with the reach of practical wisdom and sagacious statesmanship exhibited in its construction. It was a system which, while resting on the general principle of the sovereignty of the people and equal rights, was so organized as to combine justice and moderation with power, and to erect barriers against every species of arbitrary authority, whether of one, the few, or the many. It set limits even to the sovereignty of the people itself by declaring that there are certain inherent, individual rights which no human power can lawfully invade; and in the ordinary and regular action of the constituted authorities, it provided the most efficient security against abuse, not merely by dividing the whole government into separate and distinct departments according to the nature of

---

by speculative writers, particularly Turgot in his celebrated letter to Dr. Price on the American constitutions. Mr. Madison even, in a letter addressed by him in 1788 to Mr. John Brown, one of the first senators of Kentucky in the Congress of the United States, takes exception to it as an apparent departure from the principle which condemns all civil disabilities and incapacitations on account of religion. On the other hand, it seems indispensable to carry out, in practice, the great and vital problem of the separation of Church and State. Experience has fully vindicated the wisdom of the provision in preserving the purity and respect of the sacred office; in most striking contrast with its desecration by worldly passions and contentions, wherever the political arena has been thrown open to clerical champions.

their respective functions, but by dividing each department into branches, whose concurrence should be necessary to utter the deliberate sense of that particular organ of the public will. The department, whose great province it is, in the administration of justice, not only to protect private right and punish public wrong, but to maintain the balance of the constitution itself by passing upon the validity of the acts of the other departments, was endowed with the firmness and independence necessary for the proper discharge of its high functions by the tenure of good behaviour alone.

While every department of the government was derived, directly or indirectly, from a popular origin, the right of suffrage was exercised by those who, by a fixed ownership, however small, in the soil of the country, were attached by "a permanent common interest" to the society, whose destinies they controlled. Nor was this great and naturally virtuous body of electors,—the middle classes of society, removed alike from the temptations of riches or poverty,— called upon to fill, by their own immediate choice, all the various grades of public magistracy. After the election of their representatives in the legislative department, upon which mainly devolved the guardianship of the public interests, it was thought that the choice of most of the other public functionaries, whether local or general, might safely and wisely, and greatly to the relief of the people themselves, be left to intermediate agencies created by their will and possessing their confidence.

He is no true friend of popular government or popular liberty who is for calling the sovereign power of the people into action for every occasion, whether great or small, and thus disturbing that calm, deliberate, and impartial revision, at stated times, of the conduct of public servants, which is the highest and most essential attribute of popular sovereignty, as it is the best preservative of freedom. The necessary consequence of so frequent and teasing a recurrence to the popular suffrage is to weary and disgust the people with its exercise, and to enslave them to the habitual guidance of party leaders and managers, who cover, and hardly cover, their own interested and selfish ends under a pretence of public zeal.[1]

[1] The following reflections of a most able and profound political writer who, being the native of a Republic, (Geneva,) had the amplest opportunities of becoming practically acquainted with the subject of which he treats, deserve to be constantly present to the minds of all true friends of popular government.

"Here, also, we must remark the error of those who, as they make the liberty of the people consist in their power, so make their power consist in their action. When the people are often called to act in their own persons, it is impossible for them to acquire any exact knowledge of the state of things. The event of one day effaces the notions which they had begun to adopt on the preceding day; and amidst the continual change of things, no settled principle, and above all, no plans of union, have time to be established among them. You wish to have the people love and defend their laws and liberty;—leave them, therefore, the necessary time to know what laws and liberty are, and to agree in their opinion con-

The men who framed the constitution of 1776 were men versed in the history of popular governments, as well as profoundly conversant with the principles of human nature, and the character, circumstances, and genius of the people for whom they acted. They had studied the ancient democracies, and knew well the vices and infirmities by which they were led to the worst of tyrannies. They had no design of adding another to the list of these disastrous and discredited experiments. Their purpose was to found, not a democracy upon the ancient model, but a republic,[1] in which the people exercised their

cerning them. You wish an union, a coalition, which cannot be obtained but by a slow and peaceable process ;—forbear, therefore, continually to shake the vessel.

" When the people are too frequently called to move, each individual is obliged, for the success of the measures in which he is then made to take a concern, to join himself to some party ; nor can this party be without a head. The citizens thus grow divided among themselves, and contract the pernicious habit of submitting to leaders. They are, at length, no more than the clients of a certain number of patrons." De Lolme on the Constitution of England, book II. chap. 14.

[1] Aristotle, who, of all writers ancient or modern, has given most attention to the various modifications of which government is susceptible, having studied and described, in a work now lost, the constitutions of one hundred and fifty different States of Greece and her colonies, considered democracy not a regular and legitimate form, but a corruption, of popular government. The genuine form of a government, founded on free, popular principles, in his view, was a balanced republic, acknowledging the supremacy of law and aiming at the common good of all classes, including minorities, as well as majorities. It was this which he distinguished particularly by the name of Πολιτεια, or a free State ; and the corruption of it he called a democracy, between which and a tyranny he traced a close resemblance. See his Politics, book III. chap. 7, and book IV. chap. 2 and 4.

It was not without a knowledge of this important distinction that the able and wise men, who form-

rightful power through delegated and responsible agencies; to each of which was marked out its proper province of action by the constitution, the supreme law, binding both upon the people and their agents, until changed by a like solemn and authentic act of the public will.

In this republican form of polity, contradistinguished from democracy, the authors of the constitution of 1776 saw the highest guarantee, not only for the public order and happiness, but for popular liberty itself. The distinction has been fearfully but most instructively illustrated by the democratic experiments which, since their day, have been added to the lessons of history, in that fruitful but sanguinary hot-bed of political theories and revolutions,—France. The present imperial ruler of that country has said, "France is democratic, not republican. By democracy, I mean the government of an individual by the will of all,—by a republic, I mean the government of a number, in obedience to a certain system." [1]

ed the constitution of the United States, provided in that instrument for the guarantee of a "republican" form of government to each State of the Union.

The subject of the Grecian democracies, and of democracy in general, has been most ably treated in a paper of the late Hugh S. Legare, attorney-general of the United States, in whom the states-man and the scholar were so admirably blended. See his Works, vol. i. pp. 364-442.

[1] These aphorisms, the result of much thought and deliberation, were delivered by Louis Napoleon in a conversation with Colonel Vaudrey, recorded in the preface to the English edition of his *Idées Napoleoniennes*. They are substantially repeated in the body of

There cannot be a more striking proof of the real merits and essential wisdom of the constitution of 1776 than that, in an age of change and revolution, it firmly maintained its ground, for a period of fifty-four years, against the persevering assaults of a host of critics and theorists, sustained by the authority of some of the highest names in the State; and, when at last it was superseded by a new experiment, which in its turn has given place to another, that there is hardly now a thinking man of any party in Virginia who would not gladly exchange the modern structure and all its imagined improvements for the ancient constitution just as it was, with only a necessary readjustment of the representation to the changes which have taken place in the local distribution of the population. "Government," our wise ancestors thought with Burke, "was a practical thing, made for the happiness of mankind, and not to furnish out a spectacle of uniformity to gratify the schemes of visionary politicians." [1]

To what leading character in the convention we were mainly indebted for a work of so much practical wisdom, is an inquiry naturally prompted

that work, and especially in the passage where he says,—"La nature de la démocratie est de se personnifier dans un homme;" the nature of democracy is to personify itself in one man. See Œuvres de Louis Napoleon Bonaparte, vol. I. pp. 202, 208, and note, and pp. 222, 223.

[1] Burke's Letter to the Sheriffs of Bristol in 1777, on the Affairs of America,—abounding in lessons of political wisdom.

by a sentiment of filial respect for our ancestors, as well as by the search of historic truth in whatever relates to an event so important. The belief has been hitherto almost universal that the first draught of the constitution of 1776 was from the same able and luminous pen which produced the Declaration of Rights. The papers of Mr. Madison, without authoritatively settling the question, furnish some materials of speculation and conjecture, which it would not be proper to overlook. In the evening of his life, and amid the leisure of his philosophical retirement, he seems to have turned, with lively interest, to the reminiscences of this the opening scene of his public career and associations. In a paper, in which he retraces the proceedings of the Virginia convention in relation to independence and the formation of a State constitution, he embodies a copy of the first draught of the constitution, the outlines of which we have given above, and subjoins to it the following note :—

"It is not known with certainty from whom this first draught of a plan of government proceeded. There is a faint tradition that Meriwether Smith spoke of it as originating with him. What is remembered by J. M. is that George Mason was the most prominent member in discussing and developing the constitution in its passage through the convention. The preamble is known to have been furnished by Thomas Jefferson."

At a period probably subsequent to this note,
which is without date, one of the grandsons of
Colonel Mason, desiring to prepare a biographical
memoir of his illustrious ancestor, applied to Mr.
Madison for the aid of his personal recollections.
From Mr. Madison's answer, dated the 29th of
December, 1827, we give the following extract,
which, while recounting (with his habitual modesty as to himself) the distinguished part borne
by Colonel Mason in all the labors of the convention of 1776, has a particular bearing on the
question we are now considering :—

"The biographical tribute you meditate is
justly due to the merits of your ancestor,
Colonel George Mason. It is to be regretted
that, highly distinguished as he was, the memorials of them on record, or perhaps otherwise
attainable, are more scanty, than of many of his
contemporaries far inferior to him in intellectual
powers and public services. It would afford me
a pleasure to be a tributary to your undertaking.
But although I had the advantage of being on
the list of his personal friends, and, in several
instances, of being associated with him in public
life, I can add little for the pages of your
work.

"My first acquaintance with him was in the
convention of Virginia in 1776, which instructed
her delegates to propose in Congress a 'Declaration of Independence,' and which formed the
'Declaration of Rights,' and the 'Constitution'

for the State. Being young and inexperienced,
I had, of course, but little agency in those proceedings. I retain, however, a perfect impression
that he was a leading champion for the Instruction; that he was the author of the 'Declaration,' as originally drawn, and, with very slight
variations, adopted; and that he was the master-
builder of the constitution, and its main expositor and supporter throughout the discussions
which ended in its establishment. How far he
may have approved it, in all its features as
established, I am not able to say; and it is the
more difficult to make the discovery now, unless
the private papers left by him should give the
information, as, at that day, no debates were
taken down, and as the explanatory votes, if
there were such, may have occurred in committee of the whole only, and of course, not appear
in the journals. I have found, among my papers,
a printed copy of the constitution in one of
its stages, which, compared with the instrument
finally agreed to, shows some of the changes it
underwent; but in no instance, at whose suggestion or by whose votes.

"I have also a printed copy of a sketched
constitution which appears to have been the
primitive draught on the subject. It is so different, in several respects, from the constitution
finally passed, that it may be more than doubted
whether it was from the pen of your grandfather. There is a tradition that it was from

14 *

that of Meriwether Smith; whose surviving papers, if to be found among his descendants, might throw light on the question. I ought to be less at a loss than I am in speaking of these circumstances, having been myself an added member to the committee. But such has been the lapse of time that, without any notes of what passed, and with the many intervening scenes absorbing my attention, my memory cannot do justice to my wishes. Your grandfather, as the journal shows, was, at a later day, added to the committee, being, doubtless, not present when it was appointed, as he never would have been overlooked." [1]

[1] Though not relating to the particular subject discussed in the text, we cannot forbear adding here two other paragraphs of this letter of Mr. Madison, in order to complete his view of the distinguished character of Col. Mason; and also to show that, notwithstanding the wide difference of opinion which afterwards arose between them in regard to the constitution of the United States, and which may have somewhat chilled their personal relations at the time, it did not affect, in the slightest degree, the generous award of a noble and elevated sense of justice.

"The public situation," Mr. Madison proceeds to say in the letter cited above, "in which I had the best opportunity of being acquainted with the genius, the opinions, and the public labors of Col. Mason, was that of our co-service in the convention of 1787, which formed the constitution of the United States. The objections which led him to withhold his name from it have been explained by himself. But none who differed from him on some points will deny that he sustained, throughout the proceedings of the body, the high character of a powerful reasoner, a profound statesman, and a devoted republican.

"My private intercourse with him was chiefly on occasional visits to Gunston, when journeying to and from the North, in which his conversations were always a feast to me. But though in a high degree such, my recollection, after so long an interval, cannot particularize them in a

The variations between the first draught of the constitution as submitted to the select committee, and the constitution as finally adopted, will probably present themselves to different minds with different impressions of their importance. Most readers will perhaps be less struck with these variations, than with the resemblance of the two instruments in their general structure, and the coincidence in the order and arrangement of their several parts. And when the long prevalence of the opinion that Colonel Mason was the author of the first draught of the constitution, as well as its leading champion and supporter in the form in which it was adopted, is considered, the public mind will be naturally slow to admit now a different hypothesis.[1] If the author of the

form adapted to biographical use. I hope others of his friends still living, who enjoyed more of his society, will be able to do more justice to the fund of instructive observations and interesting anecdotes for which he was celebrated."

[1] Mr. Madison's own impression, at an earlier period, seems to have been that the first draught of the constitution was by Col. Mason. See his letter to Gen. Washington of the 18th of October, 1787, where he incidentally speaks of the constitution of Virginia as having been drawn by Col. Mason, (Sparks's Wash. vol. IX. pp. 547–549,) and also his letter to Judge Woodward of the 11th of September, 1824.

It is proper, however, to add that to a copy of this last letter among Mr. Madison's papers is subjoined a note, under date of July, 1826, referring to the paper quoted in the text as containing a "more recollected view of the matter."

For those who may be curious to pursue this inquiry, there is one circumstance which, though small in itself, is not unworthy of consideration. In the long disputed question of the authorship of the *Icon Basiliké*, or the still disputed one of the Letters of Junius, it might have been deemed of weight sufficient to turn the scale. In the first draught of the constitution of Virginia, the word "judicative" is used instead of judicial, in speaking of

primitive draught, and the "master-builder of the constitution, and its main expositor and supporter," as Mr. Madison says Colonel Mason was, should have been different persons, while to the first we must accord a just share of praise for conception and combination, he who perfected and finished the plan, and, by the concurring testi-

the three great departments of government. In the first draught of the Bill of Rights, the known production of George Mason, the word judicial, and not judicative, is used in precisely the same connection. The select committee, to which Col. Mason's draught of the Bill of Rights was submitted, reported a version of it differing in several particulars from his, and among other alterations, they struck out the word judicial, and substituted judicative. This report, there is reason to believe, was drawn by Meriwether Smith.

He was the second upon the committee; and the chairman, Col. Archibald Cary, is not likely to have drawn it. Moreover, there is a letter extant of George William Smith, at one time lieutenant-governor of Virginia, and son of Meriwether Smith, in which he says he had a draught of the Declaration of Rights in the handwriting of his father. This was, in all probability, the draught reported by the select committee, in which the word "judicative" was used for judicial.

The same characteristic and not happily chosen word was, as we have seen, used in the first draught of the constitution of Virginia, and would seem to indicate a common origin for that draught and the altered draught of the Bill of Rights as reported by the select committee. If Meriwether Smith was the author of the one, he may be presumed to be the author of the other. There is no known instance in which Col. Mason used the word judicative for judicial; and the convention, in acting both on the constitution and the Bill of Rights, adopted judiciary as the appropriate word. It may also be remarked, in addition to this curious piece of presumptive evidence, that Col. Mason, in his most admirable letter of the 2d of October, 1778, to Col. George Mercer, while expressly mentioning that the Bill of Rights was drawn by him, speaks of the constitution in general terms, as an instrument by which "*we* have endeavoured to provide the most effectual securities for the essential rights of human nature, in civil and religious liberty," without any intimation that the original draught of it proceeded from his pen. [See this letter in Virginia Historical Register.]

mony of all, "bore the heat and burden of the day" in its exposition and defence, and carried it triumphantly through the convention, will, in the estimation of mankind, have achieved by far the most solid and lasting claim on the gratitude of his country. If they should have been one and the same person, the double glory is a rich and overflowing fund, which the rightful possessor may well afford to divide with able and meritorious co-laborers in the same cause.

That there were many such in the convention, we need only to look over the list of members, and to recollect the length of time (from the 15th of May to the 29th of June) during which the subject of a plan of government was under consideration, either in committee or before the whole body, to be entirely satisfied. Such veteran statesmen as Richard Bland, Edmund Pendleton, Patrick Henry, Robert Carter Nicholas, Thomas Ludwell Lee, Archibald Cary, not to mention others whose wisdom and capacity were acknowledged by being called to fill some of the most important offices under the new government, could not have been idle and unassisting spectators, when so great a work was in hand as laying the foundations of the first free and balanced republican government, without privilege or caste, which the world had yet seen. Richard Henry Lee and George Wythe also returned from their duties in Congress in time to take part in the closing deliberations of the convention on the constitution.

In this review must be included likewise Meriwether Smith, to whom a vague tradition, as we have seen, has ascribed the first draught of the constitution. Though his name is little familiar to the present generation, he was undoubtedly a man of mark in his day, as is sufficiently attested by the circumstance of his being named second on the committee appointed to prepare the Declaration of Rights and a plan of government, as well as by the many public offices,—councillor of state, delegate to the Congress of the Confederation, the convention of Annapolis, and the ratifying convention of Virginia of 1788, and member of the legislature,—which he afterwards filled.

Nor can we suppose, notwithstanding the modest self-disqualification of Mr. Madison, that, "young and inexperienced" though he was, his well-trained mind, and those of his two youthful and rising colleagues, Edmund Randolph and Henry Tazewell, were not earnestly directed to this great work; while the reserved corps of grave, practical men, whose business was not so much to speak as to think and act, calmly watched and controlled every step of its progress. The character, thought, wisdom, and patriotism of an entire generation of superior men were thus stamped and moulded into the constitution of 1776; and it is the immortal praise of

George Mason to have been the acknowledged leader of such an assembly, and the accredited exponent and champion of its principles.

Immediately after the adoption of the constitution, and on the same day, the convention proceeded to the election of the governor and council, upon whom the executive administration of the new government was to devolve. Mr. Henry was chosen governor; and from his letter of acceptance we are authorized to conclude that the constitution just adopted fulfilled entirely his conception of that "most esteemed republican plan," which, in his letter to Mr. Adams, he said he had so much at heart. To the convention, he says: "I shall enter upon the duties of my office, whenever you, gentlemen, shall be pleased to direct, relying upon the known wisdom and virtue of your honorable House to supply my defects, and to give permanency and success to that system of government which you have formed, and which is so wisely calculated to secure equal liberty and to advance human happiness." After making further provisions for military defence, and providing for the election of the senatorial branch of the new legislature, the convention, on the 5th day of July, adjourned to meet in Williamsburg on the first Monday in October following, then to serve as a House of Delegates, in virtue of the annual election of April last, and, with the Senate, form the General Assembly of the Commonwealth of Virginia.

CHAPTER VI.

ON the 7th day of October, 1776, commenced in Williamsburg, under the auspices of the new constitution, the first session of the independent Legislative Assembly of Virginia. A remarkable and providential series of military successes had attended the first year of the contest with the armed tyranny of the mother country. The able generalship of Washington had forced the British army to abandon its stronghold at Boston; an imposing expedition against Charleston, the principal seaport of the South, under the command of Sir Henry Clinton, had been signally repulsed; in North Carolina and Virginia, discomfiture had everywhere attended the arms of the enemy; and from the latter State, the infamous and revengeful Dunmore, with his piratical bands, had been at last driven out with total and pitiable overthrow. But the tide of fortune now began to ebb; and the disastrous battle of Long Island, and the expulsion of the American army from the city of New York by the overwhelming superiority of the enemy's forces concentred there, commenced that mournful succession of reverses which tried, to the uttermost, the great soul of the commander-in-chief, and called for the united fortitude, courage, and wisdom of all America.

In the midst of these circumstances of general anxiety, the new republican legislature of Virginia entered upon their labors. Their attention was first turned to certain alterations in the internal and domestic policy of the State, which seemed indispensable to place it in harmony with the principles of the new government. Of these, the most urgent was some measure for the equal extension of the benefits of religious freedom to every class of citizens; and to this vital reform the consideration of the legislature was earnestly called by numerous petitions. Another measure which the republican genius of the new government was thought urgently to demand was the abolition of the system of entails, which, by locking up large and overgrown estates in a prescribed and unalterable succession, beyond the power of alienation, tended to build up a permanent and artificial aristocracy in the country.

In these measures, Mr. Jefferson, who had resigned his seat in the Continental Congress and was now a member of the House of Delegates for the county of Albemarle, was naturally and properly the leader. His generous sentiments of liberty, his large philosophic views, the distinction he had acquired, both in the colonial and continental councils, as a bold and vigorous champion of American rights, and the laurels with which he was crowned as the author of the Declaration of Independence, rightfully assigned him that lead. He and Mr. Madison now, for the first time, met. The close intimacy of half a century which afterwards subsisted between them,—never dimmed by a shade of jealousy or coolness, though admitting the utmost freedom, and sometimes diversity of opinion, in their fraternal communications with each other, as we shall have occasion to see,'—forms a rare example of generous and elevated friendship, amid the contentions and vicissitudes of public life, that does honor to human nature.

How entirely Mr. Madison concurred with Mr. Jefferson, on the present occasion, in the two great measures espoused by the senior statesman, the part he had borne in engrafting the principle of religious freedom, in its broadest latitude, on the Virginia Declaration of Rights, as well as the catholic sentiments so nobly expressed in his correspondence with Bradford, and the high republican tone of his principles manifested alike in private and in public, furnish the fullest assurance. But his youth and diffidence prevented him from embarking in a debate, in which the "steadfast, able, and zealous" coöperation of the veteran Mason,—"himself a host," as Mr. Jefferson gracefully acknowledges,—rendered other allies on the floor of the House superfluous. We cannot forbear to record here what Mr. Jefferson, in the brief memoir of his own life, has said of the first appearance in the public councils of the youthful statesman, whose modesty, in keeping back, only the more fully matured the consummate powers he afterwards displayed.

"Mr. Madison," he says, "came into the House in 1776, a new member and young; which circumstances, concurring with his extreme modesty, prevented his venturing himself in debate before his removal to the council of state in November, 1777. From thence he went to Congress, then consisting of few members. Trained in these successive schools, he acquired a habit of self-possession, which placed at ready command the rich resources of his luminous and discriminating mind and of his extensive information, and rendered him the first of every assembly afterwards of which he became a member. Never wandering from his subject into vain declamation, but pursuing it closely in language pure, classical, and copious, soothing always the feelings of his adversaries by civilities and softness of expression, he rose to the eminent station which he held in the great national convention of 1787; and in that of Virginia, which followed, he sustained the new constitution in all its parts, bearing off the palm against the logic of George Mason and the fervid declamation of Mr. Henry. With these consummate powers, was united a pure and spotless virtue, which no calumny has ever attempted to sully."

The measure brought forward by Mr. Jefferson
for the abolition of entails was finally carried in
the form in which he proposed it; though not
without earnest opposition from able and honest
men, whose natural temper and habitual caution
made them averse to all sudden change.

On the question of the general and equal extension of the benefits of religious freedom, the
struggle was long and arduous. Finally, it was
agreed in committee of the whole to repeal all
laws which restrained, by penal enactments, the
freedom of religious opinion or worship; to exempt dissenters from taxes or contributions for
the support of the Established Church; and to
dispense with any future provision of legal salaries for ministers, — reserving to the present
incumbents of parishes the arrears of salaries
actually due to them, and to them and their
congregations the use and enjoyment of existing
glebes, churches, and chapels, with their appen-
dages.[1]

A select committee of seventeen, of whom Mr.
Madison was one, together with Mr. Jefferson,
Mr. Mason, Mr. Nicholas, and others of the older
members of the House, was appointed to bring
in a bill in pursuance of the resolutions adopted.
The bill reported, which soon received the sanction of both branches of the legislature and became a law, embodied all these provisions; but

[1] See Journal of House of Delegates, October session, 1776,
pp. 62, 63.

expressly reserved for future determination the
question of a general assessment for the support
of religious teachers of the various denominations;
and instead of repealing, suspended only the acts
of Assembly providing salaries for ministers.[1]
This suspension was renewed from session to
session until 1779, when there was a definitive
repeal of all laws which provided salaries for
ministers, and when there was a negative decision also on the question of a general assessment.
But the latter question was, four or five years
afterwards, revived in a very imposing form,
under the auspices of venerable and distinguished
names: and it was reserved for Mr. Madison, as
we shall see, upon his return into the legislature
after a service of several years in the national
councils, to become the powerful and successful
champion in opposition to it, and to consummate,
in the maturity of manhood, that great struggle
for religious freedom in his native State, which
he commenced a youth.

With a view to other necessary and yet more
extensive reforms in the existing legislation of
the State, and to adapt it to the new republican
institutions, Mr. Jefferson, at this session of the
Assembly, proposed the appointment of a committee of five persons, to be chosen by joint
ballot of the two Houses, whose duty it should
be to revise all the laws of the State, to modify
and mould them in such manner as they should

[1] Hen. Stat. vol. ix. pp. 164–166.

deem expedient, and to submit them, in the appropriate form of bills, to the consideration of a future legislature. The proposition was adopted; and Thomas Jefferson, Edmund Pendleton, George Wythe, George Mason, and Thomas Ludwell Lee were chosen to constitute the committee. The work was one of equal difficulty and importance, and called for a rare union of industry, skill, learning, and practical wisdom. The Herculean labor devolved upon the three first-named gentlemen; and they submitted the results of it in a digest of one hundred and twenty-six bills to the General Assembly at the session of May, 1779.

The engrossing public cares and events of the war prevented any action of the legislature on these bills, with the exception of a few of a more urgent character, (which were taken up from time to time and passed,) until the return of peace. Here again it devolved upon Mr. Madison, at a later period of his career, and in the full-grown energy of his powers, to put the finishing hand to labors of patriotism and wisdom, at whose inception he had assisted with the modest intelligence of the youthful but well-trained statesman. Mr. Jefferson, in the autobiographical memoir already referred to, says: "The main body of the work" (the report of the revisers) "was not entered on by the legislature until after the general peace, in 1785, when, by the unwearied exertions of Mr. Madi-

son, in opposition to the endless quibbles, chi-
caneries, perversions, and delays of lawyers and
demi-lawyers, most of the bills were passed by
the legislature with little alteration."

Various other measures, connected with the
internal policy of the State and demanded for
its good government, were matured and adopted
by this Assembly; but the increasing urgency of
the national danger at length summoned its earnest attention to measures, of which all America
was the object. The American army, after the
forced abandonment of New York, was rapidly
reduced in numbers by successive though not
decisive actions, by the loss of Fort Washington
and its numerous garrison, and, more than all,
by the discouragement and expiring terms of
service of large bodies of troops. In this state
of things, the commander-in-chief found it necessary to pass to the other side of the Hudson,
and finally to retreat to the banks of the Delaware, where, when he arrived, his whole force
had dwindled to less than three thousand men,
in the face of a numerous and well-appointed
foe.

The General Assembly of Virginia had already
provided for a large increase of its military establishment, both for State and continental service: but when this intelligence reached it,
measures were instantly taken to send on reinforcements to the continental army, and to stimulate, by every possible means, the recruiting of

new levies. On the 20th of December, a few days only after the retreat of the army to the banks of the Delaware, and under the impression of that disastrous news, — rendered yet more painful by the inexplicable capture of General Lee, — the House of Delegates resolved itself into a committee of the whole to take into consideration "the state of America" (the usual formula was the "state of the country"). On the following day, the committee reported a series of resolutions which were immediately adopted by the House, evincing the deep sense that was felt of the gravity of the crisis, and the prompt determination of Virginia to bear her full share of its burdens and perils.

Nothing, perhaps, marks more strongly the readiness to make every sacrifice to the common cause, than that the representatives of the people, — with all the jealousy then felt in Virginia of executive power, and which was engraven upon the front of the political institutions she had just adopted,[1] — invested the governor and council with unlimited power to call forth any amount of military force they should judge necessary and proper, in addition to that already

[1] Besides the jealous limitation of executive power in the constitution itself, the governor was required, in the oath of office prescribed to be taken by him, to " solemnly promise and swear that I will peaceably and quietly resign the government to which I have been elected, at the several periods to which my continuance in the said office is or shall be limited by law and the constitution." See this form of oath in Ordinances of Convention of 1776, p. 7.

provided by law; to determine its destination, whether "to join the continental army or to march to the assistance of any of our sister States"; and to provide for its pay, equipment, and support by a *carte blanche* to draw upon the treasury. The governor was requested to transmit, by express, copies of these resolves to the neighbouring States of Maryland and North Carolina, "in order to satisfy them," as the Assembly declared, "that we are exerting ourselves in defending the liberties of America"; and at the same time, a resolution was adopted, instructing the delegates of Virginia in Congress to recommend to that body the expediency of "investing the commander-in-chief of the American forces with more ample and extensive powers for conducting the operations of the war," and to use their influence also "in exhorting the legislatures of the several States to adopt the most speedy and effectual methods for calling their military force into action."[1]

Congress, — which had then removed from Philadelphia to Baltimore, — on the 27th of December, six days after the recommendation of the legislature of Virginia, passed a resolution conferring the proposed enlargement of powers on the commander-in-chief. Only the day before the adoption of this resolution, but too recently to be known to Congress at the time of its passage,

[1] For these various proceedings, see Journal of House of Delegates, October session, 1776, pp. 106–108.

Washington, by one of the boldest and most brilliant *coups de main* on record, and which showed that he was Marcellus or Fabius by turns, as the interests of the great cause committed to his hands required, recrossed the Delaware, and, by an impetuous onset, captured a large detachment of the enemy's army at Trenton;—a success which he followed up a .few days afterwards, with equal brilliancy and spirit, by another at Princeton, enabling him to resume a position, if not of equality, yet of confidence and self-reliance, face to face with the hosts that stood opposed to him.

On the day of their proceedings mentioned above, the General Assembly of Virginia adjourned, after a laborious and most important session of three months. At that time its meetings were semi-annual,—in May and in October. A new election of delegates took place annually in April. At the ensuing election of 1777, Mr. Madison was outvoted by candidates who brought to their aid a species of influence unfortunately not uncommon in that day, but against which he was firmly principled. The practice of *treating* at elections was one which, in England, had long and rankly flourished in spite of prohibitory enactments; and it had been transplanted, with the representative institutions which it tended to vitiate and corrupt, to the virgin soil of the new world. Mr. Madison, believing, to use his own language, that "the reputation and success of representative government depended on the purity of popular elections," resolved to give no countenance to a practice which he deemed so destructive of it; and he declined, therefore, to follow the example of his competitors in courting the suffrages of the electors by offering them treats. He fell a victim, as others have done before and since, to the inflexibility of his principles; but his self-respect raised him above the mortification of defeat. In a paper containing some reflections on the importance of maintaining the purity of popular elections, he has incidentally given an account of this early experience of his political life, which we cannot do better than to present in his own words to the reader.

"In Virginia, where the elections to the colonial legislature were septennial, and the original settlers of the prevailing sentiments and manners of the parent nation, the modes of canvassing for popular votes in that country were generally practised. The people not only tolerated, but expected and even required to be courted and treated. No candidate, who neglected those attentions, could be elected. His forbearance would have been ascribed to a mean parsimony, or to a proud disrespect for the voters.

"The spirit of the Revolution and the adoption of annual elections seeming to favor a more chaste mode of conducting elections in Virginia, my way of thinking on the subject determined me to attempt, by an example, to introduce it. It was found that the old habits were too deeply rooted to be suddenly reformed. Particular circumstances obtained for me success in the first election, at which I was a candidate. At the next, I was outvoted by two candidates, neither of them having superior pretensions, and one particularly deficient in them; but both of them availing themselves of all the means of influence familiar to the people. My reserve was imputed to want of respect for them, if to no other unpopular motive."

It is gratifying to know that the fellow-citizens of Mr. Madison, who appreciated at their just value the gradually unfolding talents and virtues of their young countyman, did not tamely acquiesce in the loss of his services to the public cause by means so unworthy. A petition of "sundry freeholders of the county of Orange" was presented to the House of Delegates at its succeeding session, complaining of the corrupt influence through which one of the new delegates, by whom Mr. Madison had been superseded, was elected, and praying that "the said election be set aside." The petition was referred to the committee of privileges and elections; but for the want of adequate proof to sustain the allegations of the petition, which in such cases it is extremely difficult to obtain with the requisite precision, the proceeding was unavailing, except as a perpetual protest upon the legislative records of the country against a dangerous abuse, of which one of her sons, so well qualified to serve her, and destined to be one of her chief ornaments, was the early though temporary victim.[1]

Unambitious and retiring as the youthful statesman was, his merits were too well known to those with whom he had been associated in the public service to allow his ostracism to be of long duration. At the autumnal session of the legislature in this same year, (on the 13th of November, 1777,) he was chosen by the joint ballot of the two Houses to be a member of the Council of State. This body, under the new constitution, as has been already stated, consisted of eight members, who participated with the governor in the exercise of all the executive powers of the government, and without whose "advice" he could perform no official act. In the earlier times of the new government, none but such as were distinguished for patriotism, talents, and influence were chosen into the Council of State.[2]

---

[1] Journal of House of Delegates, May session, 1777, pp. 14 and 67.

[2] A striking illustration of the opinion formerly entertained of the mature qualifications suitable for a member of the executive council, is found in a letter of Judge Pendleton to Mr. Madison, dated the 25th of November, 1782, mentioning the election of young Mr. Marshall, (afterwards Chief Justice,)—at that time a year older than Mr. Madison was, when he was chosen into the same body. The passage is curious also as a reminiscence of a distinguished public character: "Young Mr. Marshall is elected a Councillor in the room of Mr. Bannister, who resigned. He is clever, but I think too young for that department, which he should rather have earned as a retirement and reward, by ten or twelve years hard service in the Assembly." Manuscript Letter.

Among those who, at this time, held seats in that body were John Page, Dudley Digges, and Dr. Thomas Walker, all of whom had been members of the general committee of safety; and with them were John Blair, Nathaniel Harrison, and others well known by their public characters. It is a farther and flattering proof of the consideration entertained for Mr. Madison at this time in the General Assembly, that he was nominated for his new post without his knowledge or wish; and was elected by a handsome majority, though brought into competition with such men as Meriwether Smith, John Bannister, and Lewis Burwell, all his seniors, and of long established reputation.[1]

The governor and council, in addition to the regular executive functions devolved upon them by the constitution, were now invested, by special acts of the legislature, with extraordinary powers of great delicacy and importance, adapted to a state of war and the critical posture of public affairs, — as we have seen in the instance of the resolutions adopted by the Assembly just a year ago. The same powers, substantially, were renewed from session to session, during the continuance of the public danger.

The moment at which Mr. Madison came into the body, was one full of urgency and interest. The general elation produced by the splendid success of Saratoga was naturally mingled with

[1] Journal of House of Delegates, October session, 1777, pp. 24, 25.

a feeling of depression at the occupation of Philadelphia by the enemy, and with painful anxiety for the situation of the patriot army in its winter quarters at Valley Forge. As the seat of war, too, was gradually being transferred more to the South, the state of things demanded more and more of vigilance in that direction, and gave increased importance to the powers, both ordinary and extraordinary, with which the executive of Virginia was clothed.

It was, perhaps, a providential event in Mr. Madison's career that he was removed from a numerous, popular assembly, where his natural diffidence would have long withheld him from any active participation in its proceedings and debates, to a smaller and more quiet body, whose deliberations being of a less formal character,—uniting the ease of colloquial with the earnestness, occasionally, of forensic discussion,—he was drawn out, from time to time, to take part in them. He thus gradually acquired a habit of self-possession in the enunciation of his views, which was alone wanting to make him as lucid and powerful in debate, as he was clear and profound in thought, and copious and overflowing in information. The council chamber, in this manner, became to him, not only a scene of useful and patriotic labor, but a school of training which prepared him for some of the highest and most enduring triumphs of his public life.

We cannot forbear introducing here, as an ingenuous tribute to the blended modesty and worth of the new councillor of State, an extract from a letter addressed to him, soon after his election, by one of his early college friends, the Rev. Samuel Stanhope Smith, who, a native son of Pennsylvania, was now the president of Hampden Sidney College in Virginia.

"This is the first time I have had an opportunity to write to you since your election to your new and honorable office. I rejoice that your country has been able, in spite of all your modesty, to discern your merit, and that she has had virtue enough to place you in a station where your talents will not be useless to her; although I could wish you had the same opinion of yourself that others have, and then I confess I should be glad to see you a degree or two lower, but where your services would be more important. For I am really afraid that the Assembly doth not sufficiently consult her own dignity, while so many of her most deserving members are distributed among the honorable and profitable offices of State, and so few are left who can give a lustre to her councils, or authority to her decisions, or even, perhaps, guide her deliberations with regularity and prudence. You are better acquainted, however, what reason there is to fear any loss of dignity in our own legislature, or in our representation in the Congress of the States."

This passage forms only the introduction to a letter of some twenty pages, in which the learned writer submits to the criticism and revision of his friend his matured and profoundly meditated views on a great question of moral and intellectual philosophy,—the long controverted one of the freedom or fatalism of human actions. They are, in substance, the same which were, many years after, embodied by him in his Lectures on Philosophy, when president of Princeton College.[1] Dr. Smith was the eloquent and able champion of free agency; and in the letter to Mr. Madison, he has discussed the subject with a depth of learning and reflection, and in some respects with an originality of views, which we have never seen surpassed. It is no small proof of Mr. Madison's proficiency in metaphysical studies, to which we have heretofore alluded, that so profound a thinker should have sought his judgment upon the result of his meditations.

The letter proceeds: "Perhaps it may prove a relaxation to you, in the midst of other business, to attend to a few metaphysical speculations. I would not have troubled you on such subjects, if I had not known your taste for them, and your quick discernment of every error or mistake, and even of every hint that may lead to the discovery of truth. I promise myself this benefit at least, that I shall see some

[1] See Lectures on Moral and Political Philosophy by Dr. Samuel Stanhope Smith, vol. I. p. 275.

mistakes or superficial reasonings that I am not aware of at present, and that I may receive some clue that may serve to exercise my thoughts anew, and lead to a more perfect investigation of the truth.

"You have frequently attacked me on that knotty question of liberty and necessity, that has so much embarrassed philosophers, and has raised such furious war among 'divines. I have lately had occasion to write on several philosophical subjects, and among others, on this question. I send you the result of my thoughts upon it; not at length, but with the utmost conciseness I am able, knowing that you are so well acquainted with the subject, that it is sufficient barely to state my opinion, without any long detail of the reasonings that support it, which are apt to grow tedious, where they are not necessary. I write with the prospect of my own improvement and not of your information; and, therefore, beg in return your candid animadversions on my scheme, with your own thoughts on the same subject."

We have not the answer of Mr. Madison, which could not fail to interest philosophical inquirers; but the tenor of it may be inferred from a subsequent letter of Dr. Smith, in which he says:—

"I have read over your theoretical objections against the doctrine of moral liberty, for practically you seem to be one of its disciples. I remember the manner in which you have formerly expressed yourself upon that intricate subject; and, indeed, they express the difficulties that occurred to me in attempting to solve it."

It is a spectacle refreshing to humanity to see two such minds turning away, for the moment, from the exciting controversies of international war to explore, by the calm lights of philosophy, a question concerning the moral destinies of man. But our particular purpose in referring to this correspondence was to exhibit Mr. Madison's early familiarity with those abstract truths that lie at the basis of all systems of human government and legislation, and that gave a breadth and comprehensiveness to his views, which, united with practical sagacity and wisdom, raised him to the exalted rank he was destined to occupy among the statesmen of America and the world.

Mr. Henry was in the second year of his administration as governor of Virginia, when Mr. Madison took his seat in the Council of State as one of his constitutional advisers and assistants. These two gentlemen, who in after-times were to be placed in such marked opposition to each other on public questions of the greatest moment, had already met in the convention of 1776, of which they were both, as we have seen, members. But the difference of years, with the natural modesty and reserve of Mr. Madison, probably rendered their acquaintance at that time a slight one. They were now brought into closer relations; and it is gratifying to know that sentiments of cordial respect and esteem soon sprang up between them. The amiable and ingenuous disposition for which Mr. Madison was always distinguished, and which formed so fitting an ornament of his youthful talents, could not but commend him to the regard of Mr. Henry.

It so happened, too, that he was the only member of the Executive Council, at that time, who was versed in foreign languages; and the number of foreign officers then in the service of the country, Virginia particularly, and in constant communication with the executive, — together with other occasions, occurring from time to time, to maintain a correspondence with foreign states or their agents, — made it indispensable for the governor often to call in the aid of the youthful and accomplished councillor.[1] These occasions

---

[1] Mr. Madison used to relate, as a ludicrous instance of the tenacity with which the French, in the commencement of their intercourse with us, transferred the forms and traditions of their monarchical régime to the unaccustomed republican institutions of America, that letters were not unfrequently addressed to the governor as "Son Altesse Royale, Monsieur Patrick Henri, Gouverneur de l'Etat de Virginie." He related also the following anecdote as illustrative of the total want of acquaintance of our Gallic friends, at that day, with the most obvious and familiar usages of representative government. One of them, attending a session of the House of Delegates, discovered much curiosity to know by what right and for what end the Speaker seemed to be invested with a supreme control over the order of proceedings in the body. After listening very earnestly to the explanation given, to wit, that the Speaker was the presiding officer, chosen by the body itself, to maintain order and decorum in its proceedings by enforcing conformity to certain established rules, he

were so frequent that the legislature, at a sub-sequent session, provided specially for the establishment of an office of foreign correspondence.[1] But Mr. Madison's personal and confidential aid was always freely given at the call of the governor; and his general skill and facility as a writer, concurring with the governor's known aversion to the labors of the pen, caused his aid to be so frequently sought in the preparation of other papers, as well as the foreign correspondence, that he bore with many the title of *Secretary*, as well as *Councillor* of State.[2]

Among the most urgent of the duties incumbent at this time upon the governor and council was the execution of the measures adopted by the legislature, at their late session, for completing the State's quota of troops for the continental service, and for contributing its aid, in every possible mode, to an early and vigorous commencement of the next campaign. For these purposes, new recruits were to be raised, and in default of them, drafts to be made from the militia; volunteers, also, were to be encouraged, embodied, and officered; and arms, accoutrements, clothing, and provisions of every kind, to be obtained and distributed for the supply of the

exclaimed, with an air of sudden illumination and satisfaction, " Enfin, Monsieur, Je vous comprends; c'est un Prince du Sang!"

[1] See Hen. Stat. vol. IX. p. 467.

[2] These facts are stated upon the authority of Mr. Jefferson, who often related them in conversation with his friends.—See also Campbell's Introduction to the History of Virginia, p. 167.

troops. It is an honorable proof of the paramount regard for the common cause, which then actuated the councils of Virginia, that troops, raised for her special protection, were ordered at once into the continental service.

The language of loyalty to the general interest of the confederacy in which the legislature prefaced the provision for raising volunteers, over and above the legal quota of troops which the State was bound to furnish, deserves also to be cited. "Whereas," say they, "it is of the greatest importance to the American cause to open the next campaign as early as possible; and, in order to render its operations more decisive and effectual, that the army under the command of his excellency General Washington should be reinforced by an additional number of troops to be raised for that purpose in this Commonwealth": They then proceed to offer special inducements to volunteers to engage in this service, and confer upon the governor and council the necessary powers for appointing the higher officers, organizing the troops, and bringing them into the field.[1]

Mr. Madison, who had just then assumed his place in the Council of State, took the liveliest personal concern in the successful execution of these various measures. His father was still the county lieutenant of Orange; but having reached an age when the duties of the office were felt to be burdensome to declining years, he wished

[1] See Hen. Stat. vol. IX. pp. 345–348.

to relieve himself of them in favor of a successor, who should be younger and more capable of exertion. Mr. Madison, apprised of his father's wishes, addressed to him, in a letter from Williamsburg dated the 23d of January, 1778, the following respectful remonstrance.

"Although I well know how inconvenient and disagreeable it is to you to continue to act as the lieutenant of the county, I cannot help informing you that a resignation at this juncture is here supposed to have a very unfriendly aspect on the execution of the draft, and, consequently, to betray at least a want of patriotism and perseverance. This is so much the case, that a recommendation of a county lieutenant this day received by the governor, to supply the place of one who had resigned to the court, produced a private verbal message to the old lieutenant to continue to act, at least as long as the present measures were in execution."

This filial appeal to paternal patriotism was not unheeded; and Colonel Madison continued with unremitting zeal to perform the duties of commanding officer of his county.

An act was passed at the late session of the legislature which empowered the governor and council, in case of the invasion, or apprehended invasion (as a subsequent act provided), of "any sister State," to order to their assistance such corps of the militia as the exigencies of the case should seem to the executive to require.

The preamble to this act contains another noble expression of the comprehensive national spirit that, in advance of any positive compact, animated the bosom of Virginia, at this great epoch, to exert herself for the common cause, — an example which in these days of family feud and mutual alienation, it is refreshing to recall. "Whereas," say the legislature of that day, "the present war between America and Great Britain was undertaken for the defence of the common rights of the American States, and it is, therefore, just that each of them, when in danger, should be aided by the joint exertions of all," &c.; and then follows the full discretionary authority to the governor and council to send military assistance to "any sister State" invaded or threatened with invasion.[1]

By another act of the legislature, passed at the same session, powers were conferred on the governor and council that led to one of the most daring and brilliant military enterprises recorded in the annals of individual or national hardihood, of which the results were of the highest importance to Virginia and the whole confederacy. The frontiers of Virginia and Pennsylvania had been for a long time exposed to sanguinary and desolating incursions of the Indians, which were fomented and encouraged mainly by the British military posts in the Northwest. A bold and adventurous spirit, George Rogers Clarke,

[1] See Hen. Stat. vol. IX. pp. 428 and 477.

a native of Albemarle county in Virginia, inured to scenes of pioneer life, conceived the hardy project of extinguishing these savage cruelties in their source, by striking a blow at once at the enemy's posts on the waters of the Mississippi.

An act was accordingly passed which authorized the "Governor, with the advice of the Privy Council," to organize an expedition "to march against and attack any of our Western enemies," to appoint the proper officers, and give the necessary orders for the expedition.[1] A force of only two or three hundred men could be raised, which was placed under the command of the dauntless and sagacious genius that had suggested the enterprise. With this small but heroic band, he plunged into the Western forest, traversed the Alleghanies, descended the Ohio in rude and frail barks, and penetrating thence through a difficult and almost impassable region of swamps and floods, appeared before the British fort of Kaskaskias on the borders of the Mississippi, surprised and captured it, though defended by greatly superior numbers, and then, without allowing a moment's pause for either repose on the one hand, or alarm on the other, successively reduced several others of the enemy's posts. This sudden and miraculous conquest, — superadding a new title to her chartered rights, — secured to Virginia the ready allegiance

[1] See Hen. Stat. vol. IX. p. 375.

of the inhabitants; and at the following session of the legislature, an act was passed for incorporating into her government the whole country between the Ohio and the Mississippi, under the name of the county of Illinois.[1]

At the same time, a resolution of thanks to the brave commander and his companions in arms was adopted, reciting that "whereas Lieutenant-Colonel George Rogers Clarke, with a body of Virginia militia, has reduced the British posts in the western part of this Commonwealth on the River Mississippi and its branches, whereby great advantages may accrue to the common cause of America, as well as to this Commonwealth," he and the valiant officers and men under his command justly merit "the thanks of this Assembly for their extraordinary resolution and perseverance in so hazardous an enterprise, and for the important services they have rendered their country."[2] Stimulated by the meed of his country's applause, this gallant and daring commander, with a yet smaller band of heroic followers, some months afterwards, (the 24th of February, 1779,) eclipsed even his former achievements by the capture, against every possible odds of fortune, as well as the most formidable obstacles of nature, of Fort Vincennes on the Wabash. With its garrison, he took prisoner the governor of Detroit, Hamilton, the odious

[1] See Hen. Stat. vol. IX. p. 552.
[2] Journal of House of Delegates of the 23d of November, 1778.

patron and instigator of Indian barbarities, whose treatment, under the laws of war, subsequently gave rise to extremely delicate and important questions for the consideration of the governor and council of Virginia, and of the commander-in-chief of the army.[1]

In recurring to the contemporaneous progress of the general contest, we find the first year of Mr. Madison's connection with the executive of Virginia attended by a mixture of political and military events of the highest interest on the national theatre. So decisive an advantage as that achieved by the American arms in the capture of Burgoyne's army, in the autumn of 1777, could not but inspire with new confidence the governments of Europe, who were disposed to regard with sympathy and encouragement the transatlantic struggle for independence. In February, 1778, France concluded treaties both of friendship and commerce, and of alliance, with the United States. This event was hailed with universal joy in America. The news of it was received early in May, and was followed by public demonstrations of the national feeling, in which the army bore an imposing part.

One of the earliest consequences of this event was the evacuation of Philadelphia by the enemy's forces. Sir Henry Clinton was justly apprehensive that the arrival of a French fleet in

---

[1] See Writings of Jefferson, vol. I. pp. 168–171, and 451–459. Also Sparks's Washington, vol. VI. pp. 315–317, and 407.

the Delaware, if not forestalled, might finally cut off his retreat, and literally fulfil what Dr. Franklin had said on first hearing the news of the hostile occupation of Philadelphia: "Say not that the British army has taken Philadelphia, but rather that Philadelphia has taken the British army." On the morning of the 18th of June, the British commander withdrew from Philadelphia, and commenced his long and toilsome march through the Jerseys. On the 29th instant he was brought to action in the memorable and glorious field of Monmouth, where the roused lion of Washington's nature again broke forth with irresistible energy, and in spite of the reluctant and faltering coöperation on the part of the general next in command to himself, he remained in possession of the field of battle.[1]

Sir Henry Clinton continued his retreat, and arrived with his shattered forces in New York the very day that the French fleet under Count d'Estaing made its appearance on the American coast. An unfortunate failure of the necessary concert between the naval force of Count d'Estaing and the American land forces, in a combined attack on the enemy's position in

---

[1] Lafayette, speaking of the bearing of Washington in the battle of Monmouth, says: "Dans cette affaire, mal préparée, mais bien finie, le Général Washington sembla d'un coup d'œil arrêter la fortune; et sa noblesse, sa grâce, sa présence d'esprit ne furent jamais mieux déployées." Mémoires de Lafayette, vol. i. p. 53. See his graphic letter to Judge Marshall, to the same effect, in Life of Washington, vol. i. p. 255.

Rhode Island, prematurely terminated the campaign.

In the midst of these events, a paltry but persevering attempt at reconciliation was set on foot by the British ministry. The news of Burgoyne's surrender had produced as much mortification and dejection in the councils of England, as it had given confidence and boldness to the policy of France. The prime minister, Lord North, it has been said, even wept in announcing the intelligence to the House of Commons.[1] After appealing to the patriotism and loyalty of the people of England for voluntary succours, he brought in three bills, commonly known by the name of the "conciliatory bills;" two of which virtually retracted all the claims of parliamentary power, in which the revolutionary controversy had its origin, and the third provided for the appointment of commissioners who should be duly authorized to treat and agree to a pacification on that basis. The whole scheme, however, proceeded on the assumption that the American States were to return to their colonial dependence upon the British crown.

Copies of these bills were sent to America, as soon as they were introduced, — and before they could be passed through the necessary forms of legislation, — in the hope that they might have the effect of preventing the consummation of the alliance with France. Governor Tryon addressed

1 Belsham, History of Great Britain, vol. VI. pp. 334, 335.

them to General Washington, by whom they were immediately laid before Congress. That body promptly and unanimously resolved that they would hold no conference or treaty with any commissioners on the part of Great Britain, unless they should, as a preliminary, either withdraw their fleets and armies, or acknowledge, in positive and express terms, the independence of the States. These proceedings took place on the 22d of April, 1778; and were ordered, together with copies of the proposed bills, to be forthwith promulgated to the public. They were adopted in entire ignorance of the conclusion of the treaties with France, which did not arrive until a fortnight afterwards, when they were instantly and unanimously ratified by Congress.

The royal commissioners, Lord Carlisle, Governor Johnstone, and Mr. Eden (afterwards Lord Auckland), arrived in Philadelphia about the 1st of June, and addressed a communication to Congress, setting forth, in specious and glozing terms, the objects of their mission. To this communication Congress returned the answer they had already given, when the copies of the "conciliatory bills" were first laid before them, but in yet more decisive and emphatic language. The commissioners still continued their efforts; one of them superadding the attempt to influence individual members by sordid and dishonorable approaches. Finally, it was determined to hold no farther correspondence with them.

Repulsed by the inflexible firmness of Congress, they published a manifesto which was designed to operate, more particularly, on the Assemblies of the respective States. After repeating the various considerations which seemed to them so strongly to invite an acceptance of the insidious propositions with which they were charged, they concluded their appeal by declaring that if the American people should persist in rejecting these propositions and adhering to the connection they had formed with the ancient enemy of both countries, it would be the policy of the British government to render that connection as little profitable as possible to her adversary by henceforward waging a war of desolation upon the country.

So shameless and revolting a declaration, which it is gratifying to know met with a scathing rebuke from the honorable and high-minded men who formed the opposition in both Houses of Parliament, aroused one deep and universal feeling of indignant scorn and defiance throughout America. The commissioners made an insolent attempt to convey copies of their manifesto to the State governments under the protection of flags of truce. In Virginia, the legislature, on being informed by the governor that a British officer, bearing this obnoxious message, had arrived at Fort Henry with despatches from the enemy, which the commanding officer of the fort had refused to receive, adopted a resolution ex-

pressing in warm terms their approbation of the
conduct of the commander of the fort, and
instructing him to order the officer, charged
with the despatches, immediately to depart from
the State, and to inform him that, in future, any
person making a like attempt should be treated
as an enemy to America.[1] Thus ended, in discomfiture and disgrace to the British missionaries
and their patrons at home, the political campaign of 1778, which had gone on hand in hand
with the military.

The year 1779 opened with a new system of
operations on the part of the enemy. Foiled in
all their attempts to effect any general occupation of the country in the face of the American
army at the North, their attention was now
turned to the South, where the comparative
sparseness of the population and the absence of
military preparation and organization opened to
them an easier and less obstructed field for their
operations. An expedition set on foot from New
York, under the command of Lieutenant-Colonel
Campbell, attended by a squadron under Com-
modore Hyde Parker, had taken possession of
Savannah, and being soon afterwards joined by
a larger force from East Florida under the command of Major-General Prevost, the State of
Georgia was speedily reduced, and South Carolina seriously threatened.

[1] See Journal of House of Delegates, under date of the 17th of
October, 1778.

In the month of May, Virginia was honored with a visit from the enemy. An expedition of two thousand men under General Matthew, convoyed by the British admiral, Sir George Collier, in person, made its appearance in Hampton Roads on the 9th of that month. There being no force collected to resist them but the small garrison of Fort Nelson, they landed without difficulty, destroyed the stores accumulated at Portsmouth and Gosport, burnt the little town of Suffolk, and rioted in the wanton destruction of private as well as public property for a week or two, when they returned, with such inglorious laurels as plunder and devastation could give them, to the common rendezvous at New York.

At the time of this invasion, there was in the neighbourhood of Williamsburg a force of two thousand men which had been raised in Virginia for the continental service, and which was now momentarily detained from its destination, in consequence of the irruption of the enemy. On the 20th of the month, however, the House of Delegates passed a resolution that the march of these recruits, which had been ordered by Congress to the South, should not be delayed for the purposes of the State; whose immediate defence, it was declared, should rest on its own militia and regular troops. At the same time, the governor and council were requested to urge forward the march of that portion of the militia of the State which had been already drafted for the succour of South Carolina. In the midst of her own dangers, Virginia did not forget· her obligations to her sister States and to the common cause.[1]

With these events, terminated the administration of Mr. Henry as governor of Virginia. He had fulfilled, under successive annual elections, the whole term of service (three years) admitted by the provisions of the constitution; and Mr. Jefferson was now chosen his successor. Mr. Madison continued a member of the Executive Council a few months more, under the new administration; and the close and more intimate association, commencing in this branch of the public service of their native State, laid the foundation of that long and unbroken friendship which united these illustrious men in all the trials of their future lives, and attended them to the close of their career.

The day after Mr. Jefferson's election, a resolution of an unusual and anomalous character was adopted by the legislature of Virginia. It served, however, to evince her earnest attachment to the common cause, and a strong determination to defeat the machinations of its adversaries, whether foreign or domestic. In the insidious efforts made, during the last year, to regain for England her lost American empire, it was frequently insinuated by the royal commissioners that the ratification of the French alliance by Congress was not binding upon the

[1] See Journal of House of Delegates, May session, 1779, p. 15.

national faith, as the articles of confederation, which gave to that body authority to conclude treaties with foreign powers, had not received the confirmation of *all* the States, which was made necessary to their validity. Maryland had not yet given her signature to them; whereby the compact remained without *full binding* force upon any of the parties.

It was in this state of things that Virginia, with the view of cutting off pernicious intrigues, whether from within or without, to detach her from the French alliance, or to seduce any portion of her people by the dangerous and delusive project of a separate arrangement with the enemy, which the terms of the alliance expressly forbade, determined to silence at once all cavils as to the obligation of the treaty, so far as she was concerned, by a formal ratification of it by her own act and in her own name. Accordingly, on the 2d day of June, 1779, a resolution was passed by the legislature, *nemine contradicente*, declaring that "the treaties of alliance and commerce between His Most Christian Majesty of France on the one part, and the Congress of the United States of America on the other part, ought to be ratified and confirmed, so far as is in the power of this Commonwealth, and the same are hereby ratified, confirmed, and declared binding on this Commonwealth." The governor was, at the same time, requested "to notify to the minister of His Most Christian Majesty, resident at Philadelphia, the above ratification under the seal of the Commonwealth.[1] ·This proceeding, — doubtless an irregularity in a diplomatic and political sense, — stands redeemed to every ingenuous mind by the loyal motives of national honor and inflexible patriotism which dictated it.

It was the earnest desire both of France and the United States to secure the coöperation of Spain in the contest now waging against the vast military and naval power of England. Overtures were early made by Congress through Dr. Franklin at Versailles, who addressed a letter on the subject to Count d'Aranda, the Spanish minister at the same court; and more recently, Mr. Arthur Lee had been accredited directly to Madrid. But the time had not yet come for the cautious and dilatory councils· of the Spanish monarchy to entertain a proposition so doubtful and hazardous. When the King of France had made up his mind to give aid to the American Colonies in their struggle for independence, he indited a letter under his own hand to Charles III., earnestly urging him to take part against the common enemy. The advice, however, was far from being acceptable to his Catholic Majesty; who even complained that, in a matter in which there should have been a previous understanding and friendly concert between the two branches of the house of Bourbon, the King of France had already committed himself, without consulting him.

[1] See Journal of House of Delegates, May session, 1779, p. 82.

Instead, therefore, of entering into the war, the King of Spain offered his mediation to the belligerent powers, to bring about a pacification which would, of course, include the American States. The mediation was cordially accepted by France, and not declined by England. Negotiations were carried on by the mediator for eight or nine months, which the haughty spirit of Great Britain at length brought to an abrupt close; and the King of Spain, no longer able to avoid the obligations of the family compact, in June, 1779, recalled his ambassador from London, with a virtual declaration of war against England.

Apprehensive, however, for the security of his own empire in America, he was not willing to become a party to the alliance between France and the United States, unless the latter should first renounce their claim to the navigation of the Mississippi, and also limit their territorial pretensions within the Alleghany mountains, as their extreme western boundary. France, attaching the highest importance to the naval coöperation of Spain in the American war, and anxious also to restore the cordiality of her relations with her ancient ally, used all her influence with the United States to obtain from them the concessions demanded by Spain as the condition of her accession to the alliance. These concessions, however, involved interests of far too vital a nature to the United States to be easily yielded;

and we shall see that they formed the Gordian knot of the foreign negotiations, as well as of the domestic councils, of the Confederacy for years yet to come. No State was more deeply interested in these questions than Virginia; and by a resolution of her Assembly, adopted the 5th of November, 1779, her delegates in Congress were instructed, "in the pending negotiations with Spain, to use their utmost endeavours to obtain an express stipulation in favor of the United American States, for the free navigation of the river Mississippi to the sea," with a free port and other easements on the shores and at the mouth of the river.[1]

Within a short time after the adoption of this resolution, another act of the General Assembly of Virginia, of a very marked character, served to show how delicate and sensitive were the questions relating to that Western territory, on which Spain had fixed an eye of covetous and ambitious desire. Virginia, in virtue of her chartered limits, as well as, recently, by right of conquest, claimed a large domain, stretching away from the mountain barrier of the Alleghanies to the banks of the Mississippi and the shores of the northern lakes. Some private land companies (the Indiana and Vandalia especially) had set up claims to extensive portions of this territory in opposition to her laws, and appealed to Congress to protect their alleged titles against

[1] See Hen. Stat. vol. x. pp. 535, 536.

the jurisdiction of Virginia. The General Assembly of the State, on the 10th day of December, 1779, adopted a remonstrance, addressed to the Congress of the United States, asserting in strong terms "her exclusive rights of sovereignty and jurisdiction within her own territory"; and, while professing every disposition to make sacrifices to the common interest of America, protesting energetically against any jurisdiction or right of adjudication in Congress on the matter of the above-mentioned petitions, or upon any other matter "interfering with the internal policy, civil government, or sovereignty of the several States, in cases not warranted by the articles of confederation." [1]

It was in the midst of these grave and difficult questions of foreign and domestic policy, and at a most critical and embarrassed period of the great contest for American Independence, that Mr. Madison was sent forth to exert his patriotism and talents on the theatre of the national councils. On the 14th of December, 1779, at the age of twenty-eight years, he was chosen by the General Assembly of Virginia one of the delegates to represent the State in the Congress of the Confederation.

---

[1] See Journal of the House of Delegates of the date referred to. The Remonstrance was, doubtless, drawn by George Mason.

CHAPTER VII.

THE Congress of the Confederation, of which
Mr. Madison was now a member, was the supreme and central authority on which depended
the conduct of the war, the struggle for independence, and every great interest common to
the confederated States. Federal association, in

18 *

some form or other, was so obviously dictated by the circumstances of Colonies planted in a new and distant hemisphere, all springing from a common national parentage, speaking the same language, and governed by kindred institutions, civil and social, that it may be said to be the natural and spontaneous growth of the American soil. Thus arose, as early as 1643, the Confederacy of the "United Colonies of New England," which maintained a virtually independent administration of the affairs of those Colonies, under a nominal subjection to the metropolitan authority of England, for the space of near half a century. The Albany Plan of Union of 1754, embracing all the Colonies from New Hampshire to Georgia, though specially evoked, at the moment, by the prospect of an impending war with France, was the result of the same permanent law of reciprocal attraction and mutual dependence, which binds together, in one harmonious whole, the elements of American greatness.

That plan was lost through the dormant jealousies which even then existed between the mother country and its Colonies; but it was reserved for the master mind which conceived it[1] to propose, in the Congress of 1776, when the final and inevitable rupture had taken place, another scheme of "Confederation and perpetual Union," which became the groundwork on which the system actually adopted by independent

[1] Franklin.

America to maintain her struggle with the parent state was built up. Such, however, was the inherent difficulty of balancing the centripetal and centrifugal forces in the new political system that, though the task was referred in June, 1776, to a committee consisting of one member from each State, which made its report on the 12th day of the following month, the "Articles" were not finally agreed upon in Congress until the 15th day of November, 1777; and they yet wanted the assent of the legislature of one State (Maryland) to complete the unanimous ratification required, when Mr. Madison took his seat in the Federal Assembly.

Under these articles,— which, although not yet complete in point of legal validity, formed, by common consent, the rule of procedure for the federal authority, and the States in their relations with each other,— the general Congress exercised the widest possible range of political functions, legislative, executive, and even judicial. It possessed the power of peace and war; conducted foreign negotiations; received ambassadors and ministers; appointed diplomatic agents of its own, as well as all civil and military officers of the higher grades employed in the service of the United States; exercised a general superintendence and control over the operations of the war; determined the amount and description of the land and naval forces to be raised by the States; fixed the sums of money to be contributed by them for the common defence and other purposes, and appropriated the same; and in short was charged, theoretically at least, with the general interests of the Confederacy in whatever concerned its collective action without, or the preservation of harmony within.

At the same time, it was declared to be a fundamental canon of the Confederacy. that " each State retains its sovereignty, freedom, and independence, and every power, jurisdiction, and right which is not, by this confederation, expressly delegated to the United States in Congress assembled." Upon the vital subjects of finance and military preparation, while Congress was invested with the unlimited power of " borrowing money and emitting bills on the credit of the United States," it could raise neither revenue nor troops by any direct action of its own, but only by requisition upon the States for their respective quotas of each, as apportioned by Congress in the ratio established by the articles of confederation.

Enfeebled, and sometimes frustrated in its best directed efforts, as we shall see Congress not unfrequently was, for the want of a direct power to call forth the resources, fiscal and military, of the country, its sphere of action was yet so extensive and paramount as to demand, in its members, abilities and virtues of the highest order. The number of the body was comparatively small. Each State had but one vote in the common council, and was limited to a representation not exceeding seven, nor less than two, delegates. The delegates were annually chosen by the legislatures of the several States; and the same person was not capable of being a delegate for more than three years in any term of six. It rarely happened that any of the States had more than three or four delegates present at the same time, and frequently some of them had not more than their minimum number in attendance; so that the total number of the body assembled ranged generally from thirty to forty.

After the first two or three years of the war, and especially after the treaty of alliance with France, which inspired in many an over-sanguine confidence that the contest would soon be brought to a successful close, not a few of the leading men of the several States grew weary of the federal service, and withdrew from Congress. General Washington, deeply impressed with the fatal consequences threatened by this abandonment of the federal councils by men of large experience and tried abilities, addressed letters of earnest remonstrance to several of his confidential friends on the subject. Among these was Mr. Benjamin Harrison, of Virginia; and in a letter of the 18th of December, 1778, to that gentleman, who was then Speaker of the House of Delegates of his own State, he pleads thus impressively the claims of the national service.

"As there can be no harm in a pious wish

for the good of one's country, I shall offer it as
mine that each State would not only choose, but
absolutely compel, their ablest men to attend
Congress. . . . . Without this, to how
little purpose are the States individually framing
constitutions, providing laws, and filling offices
with the abilities of their ablest men. These,
if the great whole is mismanaged, must sink in
the general wreck, which will carry with it the
remorse of thinking that we are lost by our own
folly or negligence, or by the desire, perhaps,
of living in ease and tranquillity during the expected accomplishment of so great a revolution,
in the effecting of which the greatest abilities
and the most honest men our American world
affords, ought to be employed. It is much to
be feared, my dear sir, that the States, in their
separate capacities, have but very inadequate
ideas of the present danger. Many persons, removed far distant from the scene of action, and
seeing and hearing such publications only as
flatter their wishes, conceive that the contest is
at an end, and that to regulate the government
and police of their own State is all that remains
to be done; but it is devoutly to be wished that
a sad reverse of this may not fall upon them,
like a thunder clap that is little expected."

This glowing, and even pathetic expostulation
of the great chief, on whose Atlantean shoulders
was cast the main burthen of the contest, had
not all the effect he desired. Mason, Wythe,

Jefferson, Nicholas, Pendleton, Nelson,—to whom, in a subsequent letter to Colonel Harrison,[1] he severally appealed by name,—still remained, from the influence of considerations of a public or private nature, in the councils of the State. Mr. Henry, immediately after the close of his executive administration, was again chosen by the legislature a delegate to the general Congress; but he soon resigned the appointment, without ever having taken his seat under it. Richard Henry Lee, after three years continuous service since his last appointment, had just retired under the obligatory rotation established by a law of the State, as well as the articles of confederation.

Virginia had limited her number of delegates to five; and to fill the vacancies which now existed in her representation, Mr. Joseph Jones, a confidential friend of Washington,—who had already served for a short time in Congress during the year 1777, and now gave up an honorable place as one of the judges of the general court of Virginia to return to that service,—Mr. James Henry, a distant kinsman of the great orator, and Mr. John Walker were appointed, with Mr. Madison, delegates for the current term, which would end the first Monday in November, 1780. The representation was completed by Mr. Cyrus Griffin, one of the old members, who retained his seat under an unexpired term. Mr.

[1] See Sparks's Washington, vol. VI. p. 152.

Madison appeared and took his seat the 20th of March, 1780, Mr. James Henry the 21st of April, and Mr. Jones the 24th of that month. The attendance of Mr. Walker is shown only by the secret journal, and for a short time.

Nothing could have been more gloomy and discouraging than the aspect of public affairs at the period when Mr. Madison entered upon his national career. The main body of the American army was still in winter quarters at Morristown, and almost on the verge of dissolution from the combined effect of short supplies of food and clothing, short terms of enlistment, and the spirit of dissatisfaction, approaching to mutiny, which those causes naturally produced. These brave men were by turns, and for weeks together, without meat or without bread; and in the extremity of their distresses, could not always be restrained from irregular modes of supplying their wants, which the law of self-preservation seemed to excuse, if not to justify. On the 3d of April, 1780, the commander-in-chief wrote to the president of Congress: —

"I think it my duty to touch upon the general situation of the army at this juncture. It is absolutely necessary that Congress should be apprised of it, for it is difficult to foresee what may be the result; and as very serious consequences are to be apprehended, I should not be justified in preserving silence. There never has been a stage of the war in which the dissatisfaction has been so general or alarming. It has lately, in particular instances, worn features of a very dangerous complexion."

This unhappy and critical state of things was the consequence of the almost total loss of public credit, which had at length resulted from the financial system that had been adopted for the prosecution of the war. Many considerations forbidding a large recourse to taxes, which depended, moreover, exclusively on the State governments, Congress resorted to the expedient of issuing, from time to time, bills of credit to meet the expenses of the war; until the amount issued had now reached the formidable sum of two hundred millions of dollars, which, by a resolution of the 1st of September, 1779, they had already determined, should, " on no account whatever," be exceeded.[1] No specific funds having been provided, nor any certain period fixed, for the redemption of these bills, they soon began to depreciate; and at this time they passed, in transactions of business, at the rate of forty dollars in paper for one of specie.

In the hope, at least, of arresting a farther depreciation, if not of ultimately restoring the credit of the circulation, Congress, on the 18th day of March, 1780, just two days before Mr. Madison took his seat in the body, adopted a resolution to substitute for the old issues, as they should come in under the requisition upon the

[1] See Journals of Congress, vol. II. p. 347.

States, new bills to be made payable in specie six years after date, bearing, in the mean time, an interest of five per cent.; and specific funds were to be provided by the several States, as well as the faith of the United States to be pledged, for the punctual payment of both principal and interest.[1] At the same time, the actual rate of depreciation of the bills already issued was recognized and established, by declaring that "gold and silver should be received in payment of the quotas of the several States at the rate of one Spanish milled dollar in lieu of forty dollars of the bills now in circulation;" a regulation which, however intended by Congress, was viewed by many of the public creditors, both foreign and domestic, as a virtual act of national bankruptcy.[2]

The sudden and heavy depreciation of the bills of credit, which now constituted almost the sole pecuniary resource of the United States, by rendering the purchase of supplies, to any material extent, practically impossible, was the immediate cause of the alarming destitution and demoralization into which the army had fallen, under the very eyes of the commander-in-chief, and in spite of almost superhuman efforts of vigilance and providence, on his part, to avert the catas-

[1] See Journals of Congress, vol. II. pp. 442-444.

[2] See complaints of Count de Vergennes, and Mr. Adams's reply, in Diplomatic Correspondence of the American Revolution, vol. v. pp. 208-211, and 213-225; and Life of Witherspoon by Dr. Ashbel Green.

trophe. Congress, despairing of obtaining any means of purchasing supplies in time for the ensuing campaign, on the 25th of February, 1780, adopted the novel and somewhat primitive expedient of calling upon the States to make their contributions to the common treasury in articles of produce, — such as flour, beef, hay, and corn, — instead of money. This rude system of finance was too slow and awkward in its mechanism to bring any immediate or sensible relief; and the crisis of danger and anxiety continued, for the present, without a single circumstance of alleviation. We will leave it, however, to Mr. Madison's pencil to sketch the picture of national embarrassment and distress, which greeted him on his arrival in Philadelphia. On the 27th of March, 1780, he wrote to Mr. Jefferson, then governor of Virginia, in the following terms: —

"Among the various conjunctures of alarm and distress which have arisen in the course of the Revolution, it is with pain I affirm to you that no one can be singled out more truly critical than the present. Our army threatened with an immediate alternative of disbanding or living on free quarter; the public treasury empty; public credit exhausted, — nay, the private credit of purchasing agents employed, I am told, as far as it will bear; Congress complaining of the extortion of the people; the people, of the improvidence of Congress; and the army, of both; our affairs requiring the most mature and systematic measures, and the urgency of occasions admitting only of temporizing expedients, and these expedients generating new difficulties; Congress recommending plans to the several States for execution, and the States separately rejudging the expediency of such plans, whereby the same distrust of concurrent exertions that has damped the ardor of patriotic individuals, must produce the same effect among the States themselves; an old system of finance discarded as incompetent to our necessities, an untried and precarious one substituted, and a total stagnation in prospect, between the end of the former and the operation of the latter.

"These are the outlines of the picture of our public situation. I leave it to your own imagination to fill them up. Believe me, sir, as things now stand, if the States do not vigorously proceed in collecting the old money, and establishing funds for the credit of the new, we are undone; and let them be ever so expeditious in doing this, still the intermediate distress to our army, and hindrance to public affairs, are a subject of melancholy reflection. General Washington writes that a failure of bread has already commenced in the army, and that, for anything he sees, it must unavoidably increase. Meat they have only for a short season; and as the whole dependence is on provisions now to be procured, without a shilling for the purpose, and without credit for a shilling, I look forward with the most pungent apprehensions."

To provide, if possible, some remedy for the distresses of the army, and to devise a more efficient system in the administration of its various departments, as well as to make arrangements for the ensuing campaign, Congress appointed a committee of three of its members to repair to headquarters. They were to consult with the commander-in-chief upon the necessary measures of preparation or reform, which they were authorized, with his advice, to carry at once into effect, or otherwise to report for the consideration of Congress.[1] General Schuyler, then one of the delegates of New York, Mr. Matthews of South Carolina, and Mr. Peabody of New Hampshire, were selected for this important duty. They continued at headquarters, in consultation with the commander-in-chief for six months; and although measures of great intrinsic utility resulted from their joint councils, the fatal want of money and of credit — those indispensable resources of war — continued to embarrass and enfeeble all the operations of the service.

There never had been a period of the war which called for such vigorous and universal exertion. Charleston was invested by the enemy with a large land and naval force, directed in person by the commander-in-chief, Sir Henry Clinton. In the event of its fall, which seemed but

[1] See Journals of Congress, under dates of the 6th and 12th of April, 1780, vol. III. pp. 446, 447, and Secret Journals, under date of the 19th of May, 1780, vol. I. p. 150.

too probable, the whole Southern country would be at once exposed to be overrun by him. The main body of the British army, left under the command of General Knyphausen, continued in possession of the city of New York; and from thence daily threatened the adjacent States, and particularly New Jersey, in which the main body of the American army, under the immediate command of Washington, was quartered.

In these circumstances, nothing could have been more trying and painfully embarrassing than the situation of the American commander-in-chief. His guardian care and vigilance were summoned, at the same moment, to opposite and widely distant points of the compass. His means of every kind were greatly inferior to those of the enemy; who superadded to all his other advantages the absolute command of the water, by which he was enabled to transfer his forces and supplies, with the velocity of the wind, from place to place, while the defenders of the country were doomed to long and toilsome marches, and an almost impracticable transportation by land. Washington sent detachment after detachment from the main body of his army for the defence of the South, and was thus left with a remnant of continental troops reduced to three thousand men, and such reinforcements of militia as he could collect on the spur of the occasion, to face an army greatly superior in numbers and equipments, and so flushed with confidence that its leader, Knyphausen, pushed an incursion into the State of New Jersey to the very verge of Washington's encampment. A few days later, Sir Henry Clinton himself, who had returned to New York immediately after the capture of Charleston, appeared and took command of the expedition.

Thus beset on every hand, Washington was, at the same time, earnestly and anxiously intent on preparations for a great and decisive movement in concert with our allies, which, he flattered himself, would put a victorious close, during the present campaign, to the contest, by giving him possession of the city of New York, and with it of the main body of the British army. Lafayette — who seemed, in some sort, the tutelary genius of American independence — had, after freely hazarding his life for the cause in the fields of Brandywine and Monmouth, gone back to his native country to solicit of its powerful monarch the succours necessary to crown the struggle with final and complete success. He had now returned to America, and brought with him the royal promise of a large reinforcement of both land and naval forces, — already collected at Brest, and soon to depart for the coasts of the United States.

The news diffused hope and joy through the country, and inspired Congress with fresh vigor and resolution. They immediately called upon the States to pay into the treasury, within one month, the sum of ten millions of dollars to enable them to bring into the field an efficient army of coöperation; and, through their committee at headquarters, as well as by direct appeals, they employed every method to stimulate the States to furnish, with the utmost promptitude, the supplies of specific articles required of them for the support of the army.[1] On the 10th day of July, the French fleet, under the command of the Count de Ternay, bringing a body of five thousand troops under General Count Rochambeau, made its appearance at Newport. Nor was this the full extent of the promised succours. Another division of the fleet was soon to leave Brest, and bring with it an additional and nearly equal number of men.

Every thing now exhibited the eagerness of expectation, and, as far as possible, of preparation on the part of the American army for the combined, and as it was hoped, decisive blow. Washington collected his forces, and moved forward to the east of the Hudson, to be nearer to his ally and the object of their joint enterprise. The command of the water was the *sine qua non* of every plan of operation that was in contemplation. This was unfortunately lost by the appearance on the coast, a few days after Count de Ternay, of Admiral Graves with six ships of the line, which gave the naval superiority to the enemy. It was confidently hoped to regain it

[1] See Secret Journal of Congress, vol. I. pp. 149–151.

by the arrival, daily expected, of the second division of the French fleet. At length came the blighting news that the French fleet was blockaded in the harbour of Brest by a large and superior force of the enemy. Hopes were then turned to the French squadron in the West Indies; and urgent letters were addressed to its commander, Count de Guichen, both by Washington and De Ternay, to supply the required naval reinforcement. This last hope vanished. De Guichen had already sailed to Europe; and soon afterwards, the British naval predominance was still farther increased by the arrival at New York of Admiral Rodney, with eleven ships of the line and four frigates.

Thus ended in disappointment, for the present season, the combined movements of the French and American forces, from which so much had been expected; and on which the commander-in-chief had, at one time, fondly set his heart to close in triumph, with the pending campaign, the great contest for American freedom. But the time was not yet. America was to pass through other trials, and to learn still further lessons of wisdom and virtue in the hard school of experience, before she entered into full possession of the prize of national independence for which she was contending.

Disappointment and disasters met her in the South, as well as the North. After the fall of Charleston, Cornwallis swept, like a whirlwind, with his ferocious legions over the Carolinas, till the native bravery and self-taught generalship of the independent borderers of Virginia and of North and South Carolina gave him a check at King's Mountain; and thus opened the way for the future successes of Greene, of Morgan, and of William Washington, of Marion and of Sumpter, and of their heroic brethren in arms. A yet deeper shade was to be added to the picture of national trials and adversities, during this memorable year, by the treason of Arnold; but even in that, the guardianship of Providence was manifested in the timely and critical discovery of a secret impending blow, from which, if it had been permitted to fall, the recovery must have been slow and painful indeed.

The many difficulties and embarrassments of the public service, during the year, were fraught with profitable lessons to every thoughtful American statesman. It was the business of Congress to provide, as far as possible, against their recurrence. A mind, like Mr. Madison's, could not have been inattentive to so grave and exigent a duty. He saw that the primary source of the national disasters was in the disordered state of the public finances; and that there was no hope of repairing these, unless some barrier could be opposed to the flood of depreciated paper money with which the country was inundated. Congress, by its resolution of the 18th of March, had sought to diminish, if not wholly to correct, this evil by drawing in its own issues, as far as it was practicable to do so: and in order to take away from the States the inducement to resort to farther emissions of a like kind, it had called upon them for contributions in specific articles instead of money, nominal or real.   It was designed that these specific supplies should be raised by specific assessments on the tax payers; but instead of that, in many of the States it was attempted to procure them with new bills of credit or certificates of debt issued for the purpose,—thus swelling the mass of depreciated paper money, which already paralyzed the operations of the public administration, as well as the business of the country.

In the month of October, 1780, Mr. Madison addressed a letter from Philadelphia to his colleague, Mr. Jones,—who was then attending a session of the State legislature, of which he was a member at the same time as of Congress,—in which he presses upon his consideration the following important observations:—

" We continue to receive periodical alarms from the commissary's and quartermaster's departments.   The period is now arrived when provision ought to be made for a season that will not admit of transportation, and when the monthly supplies must be subject to infinite disappointments, even if the States were to do their duty.   But instead of magazines being laid in, our army is living from hand to mouth, with a prospect of being soon in a condition still worse. How a total dissolution of it can be prevented in the course of the winter, is, for any resources now in prospect, utterly inexplicable, unless the States unanimously make a vigorous and speedy effort to form magazines for the purpose.

"But unless the States take other methods to procure their specific supplies than have prevailed in most of them, the utmost efforts to comply with the requisitions of Congress can only be a temporary relief. This expedient, as I take it, was meant to prevent the emission of paper money. Our own experience, as well as the example of other countries, made it evident that we could not by taxes draw back to the treasury the emissions as fast as they were necessarily drawn out. We could not follow the example of other countries by borrowing; neither our own citizens nor foreigners being willing to lend as far as our wants extended. To continue to emit *ad infinitum* was thought more dangerous than an absolute occlusion of the press. Under these circumstances, the expedient of specific requisitions was adopted for supplying the necessities of the war. But it is clear the success of this expedient depends on the mode of carrying it into execution. If, instead of executing it by specific taxes, State emissions, or commissary's and quartermaster's certificates, (which are a worse species of emissions,) are recurred to, what was intended for our relief will only hasten our destruction."

Mr. Madison was so impressed with the pernicious consequences of this practice of the States in procuring the specific supplies required of them with new emissions of paper money, (which in another letter to his colleague, of a few days later date, he emphatically pronounced to be "the bane of every salutary arrangement of the public finances,") that, when the estimates for the ensuing year were under consideration, he proposed that Congress should address a formal recommendation to the States to discontinue the use of those emissions. His proposition, he says, met with a cool reception,— not because the practice which it sought to dissuade the States from found any apologists, but, on the contrary, because that practice was considered "so manifestly repugnant to the spirit of the acts of Congress heretofore passed," that it was thought useless to address any farther recommendations to the States upon the subject.

We offer yet another extract from Mr. Madison's correspondence of this period, not merely to show his sense of the paramount importance of a sound and reliable system of national finance, — an object which, we shall see, he earnestly and steadily pursued through the whole of his Congressional career,— but also as developing a great and leading principle of his constitutional creed. Attached by his earliest impressions and most profound convictions to republican government, he studied closely the weaknesses and infirmities which had discredited democratical experiments elsewhere; and while placing our institutions frankly and unreservedly on the fundamental principle of popular sovereignty, he labored to secure them from the danger of those aberrations which, under crude and unbalanced systems, had hitherto exposed the principle itself to more or less of distrust. His great aim was to vindicate and recommend republican government by establishing it on the broad, moral and legal foundations of justice, order, and public faith, and of energy sufficient to give effect to the legitimate decrees of the public will. In the following observations, contained in a letter addressed by him on the 7th of November, 1780, to Mr. Pendleton, then the presiding judge of the High Court of Chancery in Virginia, we trace the dawnings of that policy which produced, a few years later, the Constitution of the United States.

"The want of money is the source of all our public difficulties and misfortunes. One or two millions of guineas, properly applied, would diffuse vigor and satisfaction throughout the whole military departments, and would expel the enemy from every part of the United States. It would also have another good effect. It would reconcile the army and everybody else to our republican forms of government; the principal inconveniences imputed to them being really the fruit of defective revenues. What other States effect by money, we are obliged to pursue by dilatory and indigested expedients, which benumb all our operations, and expose our troops to numberless distresses. If these were well paid, well fed, and well clothed, they would be well satisfied, and fight with more success. And this might and would be as well effected by our governments as by any other, if they possessed money enough;— as, in our moneyless situation, the same embarrassments would have been experienced by any government."

The lessons of the late campaign, enforced by the constant and earnest representations of the commander-in-chief, were not lost upon Congress. They proceeded to reorganize the army on a more effective plan for the operations of the ensuing year. Its aggregate force was to be raised to thirty-five thousand seven hundred and forty-eight rank and file; and the new enlistments were to be made for the whole period of the war,— a point of vital importance, which the commander-in-chief had often, but hitherto in vain, pressed upon the consideration of Congress.[1] To offer more adequate inducements to remain or engage in the service, half-pay for life was promised to all officers who should serve to the end of the war, and it was recommended

[1] Journals of Congress, under date of the 3d and 21st of October, 1780, vol. III. pp. 532, 533, and 538; also Secret Journals, vol. I. p. 206.

to the States to make up to their respective lines the loss sustained by them from the depreciation of the medium in which they had been paid. The States were at the same time called upon, "in the most pressing manner," to have their several quotas of the common force completed, and in the field, by the 1st of January next,—a requisition afterwards urgently and emphatically repeated in consequence of a letter from the commander-in-chief, which was transmitted by Congress to the legislatures or executives of the respective States, who were reminded that "the public safety depended on their complying, without reserve or delay, with the measures adopted for an active and decisive campaign." [1]

While these arrangements were pursued for raising a more effective military force, corresponding provisions were made to place the fiscal resources of the country—an instrument of war no less essential—on a more adequate and satisfactory footing. In addition to the arrears of former requisitions, the States were now called upon to raise by taxes the value of six millions of silver (not paper) dollars; of which a large portion was allowed to be paid in specific supplies for the army at fixed valuations, and the residue in gold or silver, or the new bills of credit redeemable in specie. [2] It being felt that

[1] Resolution of the 22d of December, 1780. Journals of Congress, vol. III. p. 557.

[2] Resolution of the 4th of November, 1780. Journals of Congress, vol. III. p. 542.

no taxation which the present condition of the country admitted of was, in itself, adequate to the extraordinary demands of a state of war, the ministers of the United States at the courts of France and Spain had been already instructed to use their best efforts to negotiate loans in those countries. A mission had also been recently sent to Holland, mainly with a view to pecuniary aids; but the minister, Mr. Henry Laurens of South Carolina, former President of Congress, was captured on the voyage to his destination by a British cruiser, and was now a prisoner in the Tower at London.

The hopes of Congress for pecuniary assistance rested mainly on the friendship and liberality of France, enforced by her common interest in the event of the contest. On the 22d of November, 1780, they addressed to His Most Christian Majesty a letter, distinguished alike by its dignity and frankness, in which they recapitulated the untoward events of the last campaign, set forth, with manly candor, the extent and urgency of their financial wants, and concluded by informing him that "a foreign loan of specie, to the amount of twenty-five millions of livres at least," will be indispensably necessary for the vigorous prosecution of the next campaign: and for the reimbursement of it, they solemnly pledged to His Majesty the faith of the United States, whether it shall please him to become

20 *

their security in the loan, or to advance the amount of it from his royal coffers.[1]

The negotiation, at first, was committed solely to the minister plenipotentiary, Dr. Franklin, who had been resident at Paris from the commencement of diplomatic relations with that country: but to give greater significance and urgency to the objects of it, Colonel John Laurens of the army, one of the staff of the commander-in-chief, was afterwards commissioned for the special purpose of soliciting, in conjunction with Dr. Franklin, the aids asked of His Most Christian Majesty, and of forwarding them to the United States with the least possible delay. He was instructed, at the same time, to use every effort to impress upon the minds of the King and his ministers the necessity of maintaining a naval superiority in the American seas, as the indispensable condition of success to the allied arms in the operations of the ensuing campaign.[2]

[1] Secret Journals of Congress, vol. II. pp. 343–348.

[2] Secret Journals, vol. II. pp. 351, and 366–375.

CHAPTER VIII.

We have already had occasion to mention how desirous both France and the United States were that Spain should become a party to their alliance. This was now more to be desired than

ever, as the junction of her naval armaments
with those of France would, at once, give that
maritime predominance on the American coasts,
to which such vital importance was justly attached. The prospect of regaining the Floridas,
which she had lost in the war of 1756, and, in
that event, their guarantee by the United States
had been held out by a resolution of Congress
as an inducement for her to unite in the contest: but this was upon the express condition
that "the United States should enjoy the free
navigation of the River Mississippi into and from
the sea." [1] Such were the explicit instructions
given to Mr. Jay, who had been appointed minister to Spain in the autumn of 1779. Despatches recently received from him informed
Congress of the earnestness with which the Spanish government still continued to insist on the
renunciation by the United States of their claim
to the free navigation of the Mississippi, as the
sine qua non of His Catholic Majesty's accession
to the alliance. The minister, at the same time,
expressed his own opinion that, if Congress remained firm, Spain would be ultimately content
with such equitable regulations, in the use of the
navigation, as should suffice to guard against
contraband.

These despatches, together with the instructions of the legislature of Virginia to her dele-

[1] See Resolution of the 17th of September, 1779, Secret Journals,
vol. II. pp. 248, 249. See also Idem, pp. 261-263.

gates in Congress of the 5th of November, 1779, by which they were enjoined to use their utmost endeavours to maintain the freedom of the Mississippi, were referred to a select committee. In pursuance of their report, Congress, on the 4th of October, 1780, unanimously resolved that Mr. Jay should adhere to his former instructions respecting the right to the free navigation of the Mississippi (which, if not expressly acknowledged by Spain, was, in no event, to be relinquished by any stipulation on the part of the United States); and with regard to boundaries, that he should adhere strictly to the designation already fixed by Congress, making the Mississippi River the western limit of the territory of the United States above the thirty-first parallel of north latitude.

Two days after the adoption of these resolutions by Congress, a committee was appointed "to draft a letter to the ministers of the United States at the courts of Versailles and Madrid to enforce the instructions given by Congress to Mr. Jay by the resolutions of the 4th instant, and to explain the reasons and principles on which the same are founded, that they may be respectively enabled to satisfy those courts of the justice and equity of the instructions of Congress." Mr. Madison, Mr. Sullivan of New Hampshire, and Mr. Duane of New York, constituted the committee.

The paper, required at the hands of this committee, was one of the greatest delicacy and importance. It was to explain and vindicate the position of the United States on a question deeply affecting, not merely their foreign relations and their prospects of obtaining that external support of which they were so much in need, but their interior union and strength in all future time. It was to be addressed to two of the most eminent men of their country, whose experience and wisdom made them objects of universal respect; and, through them, to two of the most powerful and enlightened governments of the world, on a subject touching the interests and pride of the one, and the sympathies and political affinities of the other, and involved in more or less of difficulty and doubt by the contradictory solutions which the history of different nations presented. It is not a little singular that the preparation of such a paper should have devolved upon the youngest member, probably, of the body to which he belonged. It was drawn by Mr. Madison, reported to Congress on the 17th of October, 1780, immediately agreed to, and transmitted to Dr. Franklin and Mr. Jay as the authorized exposition and defence of the claims of the United States.

The law of nations, with regard to the right of those who inhabit the upper parts of a river flowing through the jurisdiction of a foreign power before it reaches the ocean, to use its navigation into the sea,—the common highway of commerce,—was, at this time, unsettled either by usage or authority. The freedom of the Rhine was established by the treaty of Westphalia in 1648, and was ever afterwards recognized by the general consent of Europe. But by the same treaty the mouth of the Scheldt was allowed to be closed by the United Provinces, within whose limits it fell, against the navigation of the Spanish Netherlands which occupied its upper course, and of all others, beyond the limits of the new republic, who should desire to use it as a channel of communication to the sea.

The Emperor Joseph II., to whom the Low Countries had descended under the arrangements of the Peace of Utrecht, became restless under the restrictions put by the treaty of Westphalia on that avenue to the ocean, which nature seemed to have given to his Flemish subjects in common with their Batavian neighbours; and almost at the same time that our discussions commenced with Spain respecting the navigation of the Mississippi, he boldly demanded, and threatened to assert by force his claim to the free navigation of the Scheldt. He afterwards, however, with characteristic indecision renounced his claim by the treaty of Fontainebleau in 1785; and the freedom of the Scheldt remained, more or less, a vexed question of the public law of Europe, until it was definitively established by the Congress of Vienna.[1]

[1] See Histoire des Traités de Paix, par Kock & Schœll. vol. IV. pp. 70–80, and vol. XI. p. 394.

The question of the navigation of the Mississippi, now in controversy between the United States and Spain, had heretofore been the subject of conventional arrangement, as between other parties. In the treaty of Paris, which terminated the war of 1756 between England on the one hand and France and Spain on the other, the river Mississippi, from its source to its junction with the Iberville, was established as the boundary between the British and French possessions in America,—leaving the Island of Orleans, on the eastern side of the Mississippi below the junction with the Iberville, and the whole country on the western side, to France; and it was stipulated that "the river Mississippi shall be equally free as well to the subjects of Great Britain as to those of France, and expressly that part which is between the said Island of Orleans and the right bank of the river, as well as the passage both in and out of the mouth."[1] By a transfer of Louisiana made to Spain, the year after the treaty of Paris, she succeeded to all the possessions of France on the Mississippi; receiving them, of course, subject to the stipulations of the treaty of Paris, so long as that treaty should be in force.

But the treaty of Paris, it was contended, was abrogated by the war which had since broken out with both France and Spain; and it was, moreover, insisted that the stipulation respecting the free

[1] See 7th Article of the Treaty of Paris.

navigation of the Mississippi, being made in favor of "the subjects of Great Britain," could not be claimed by the people of the United States, as they were no longer British subjects. To these arguments Mr. Madison opposed the great principle of both natural and constitutional law, that the rights of a sovereign are held in trust for the people over whom he rules; and that the sovereignty exercised by the King of England over the people of America not being in virtue of his quality as King of England merely, but because he was recognized by the consent of the people of America as their King also, stipulations made by him respecting America, and as the sovereign of America, should be considered as made for the particular benefit of the American people; and when, from the course of events, they had been driven to resume the sovereignty into their own hands, the rights previously acquired by their conventional sovereign necessarily devolved upon them.

But, independently of all treaty stipulations, Mr. Madison argued with convincing clearness and force, that, according to the general principles of the law of nations, the circumstance of Spain being in possession of both banks of the river at and near its mouth ought not to be deemed "a natural or equitable bar" to the free use of its navigation by the inhabitants of the country above. Such an assumption, he alleged, "would authorize a nation, disposed to take advantage of circumstances, to contravene the clear indications of Nature and Providence, and the general good of mankind." He then instanced the universally acknowledged right of an "innocent passage," even with troops, through the territory of a foreign power; and pressing the argument *a fortiori*, demanded, "if a right to a passage by land through other countries may be claimed for troops, which are employed in the destruction of mankind, how much more may a passage by water be claimed for commerce, which is beneficial to all nations."

The claim of right he reinforced by considerations appealing to the interests of Spain. Looking into the future, he showed how the serious inconveniences resulting to the inhabitants of the great Western basin, from a denial of the free use of the Mississippi, must be a constant and increasing source of disquietude to them, of vigilant and restrictive precautions on the part of Spain, and of mutual irritation and probable collision to both. He exhibited in perspective the unbounded agricultural riches of that vast and fertile region, and pointed out how those riches, if allowed to flow unobstructed through the channel of the Mississippi, might become the basis of a most profitable trade to Spain and France in the exchange of their manufactures and artificial products for the raw produce of Western America; whereas, if that produce should be forced, by the occlusion of the Mississippi, to seek a market through the lakes and the St. Lawrence, or other eastern channels, it would only serve to swell still farther the already great maritime and commercial predominance of their rival and enemy, Great Britain.

We have given this brief outline of Mr. Madison's powerful and persuasive plea for the freedom of the Mississippi, as embodied in the report of the committee of Congress, because it laid the groundwork of all the future discussions on a vital question of national policy, — a question which continued, through many vicissitudes and a long series of years, to agitate the public councils, and in which he was destined, on various occasions, to take a leading and most effective part. The report also embraces an able and expanded view of our claims to Western territory, — drawn from treaty stipulations, principles of public law, and considerations of foreign and domestic policy, — in answer to the jealous and covetous pretensions of Spain; and exhibits marks, equally conspicuous, of the comprehensive and analytical mind of the accomplished author.

This able paper seems at once to have assigned to Mr. Madison, in the estimation of Congress, the rank due to his superior worth and talents. We see him immediately afterwards, and in quick succession, placed on many of the most important committees appointed to prepare instructions to our ministers abroad, . or to hold conferences with foreign ministers residing in the country, and in these duties associated with the oldest and most distinguished members of the body, — Samuel Adams, Dr. Witherspoon, Judge Duane, Mr. McKean, Mr. Burke, and Mr. Matthews.[1]

It is not without a painful feeling we are compelled to record the fact that the position thus nobly taken by Congress on the right to the free navigation of the Mississippi, and so ably sustained by the pen of Mr. Madison, was soon afterwards, under the stress of a supposed political necessity, temporarily abandoned. The progress made by the British arms in the Southern States, after the fall of Charleston, had excited serious apprehensions of the entire conquest of South Carolina and Georgia, at least; and in this state of things it was feared that the urgency of the " armed neutrality" in Europe, which had suddenly risen to great power and influence under the auspices of Catharine II. of Russia, would force a peace on the belligerents upon the basis of the *uti possidetis*, — involving a permanent alienation of the States which should be in possession of the enemy at the close of the war. To avert such a catastrophe, it was thought to be an object of especial importance to obtain without delay the aid and coöperation of Spain in the contest, and to pay for it, if necessary, the price of a surrender of our claim

[1] See Secret Journals, vol. II. pp. 348, 358, 373, and 402.

to the navigation of the Mississippi through her limits into the sea.

We learn from the correspondence of Mr. Madison that in little more than a month after the unanimous adoption of the instructions to Mr. Jay and Dr. Franklin, of which we have just given an account, the delegates of Georgia and South Carolina moved a reconsideration of those instructions. Of this proceeding, the following statement is made by him in a letter of the 25th of November, 1780, addressed to his colleague, Mr. Jones, who was still attending a session of the State legislature at Richmond :—

"The delegates from Georgia and South Carolina, apprehensive that a *uti possidetis* may be obtruded on the belligerent powers by the armed neutrality in Europe, and hoping that the accession of Spain to the alliance will give greater concert and success to the military operations that may be pursued for the recovery of their States, and likewise add weight to the means that may be used to obviate a *uti possidetis*, have moved for a reconsideration of the instructions, in order to empower Mr. Jay, in case of necessity, to yield to the claims of Spain, in consideration of her guaranteeing our independence and affording us a handsome subsidy. The expediency of such a motion is further urged from the dangerous negotiations now on foot by British emissaries for detaching Spain from the war. Wednesday last was assigned for the considera-

21*

tion of this motion, and it has continued the order of the day ever since, without being taken up." [1]

The letter of Mr. Madison, from which this extract is taken, shows how deeply opposed he was, by principle and conviction, to any modification of the instructions already given. He was justly distrustful of the policy of Spain; and believed that the proposed concession to her was a gratuitous and unnecessary, as it might be also an unavailing, sacrifice. What added to his mortification and embarrassment was to find his only colleague then present with him in Congress, Colonel Bland, differing in sentiment from him on so vital a question. Colonel Bland, a gentleman, doubtless, of patriotism and intelligence, seems, nevertheless, to have been eccentric both in his character and opinions. He had been educated abroad to the profession of medicine; after the commencement of the war, he entered the army; had charge, for some time, of the Saratoga prisoners of war, in their cantonments in Virginia; then resigned his military commission; and was recently appointed one of the delegates of the State in Congress. Having, Mr. Madison says, taken up the opinion with regard to the navigation of the Mississippi that we had " no just claim to the subject in controversy with Spain, and that it is the interest of Virginia not to adhere to it," he drew up a letter

1 See Madison's Debates and Correspondence, vol. L pp. 64-68.

to the legislature, recommending to them a revision of their former instructions on the subject.[1]

The remonstrances of Mr. Madison appear to have prevailed with him, for a time, to withhold his letter. But the pressure of the delegates of Georgia and South Carolina, and the solicitude of Congress, increasing with the untoward events of the war in the Southern department; and the moral force of the instructions previously given by Virginia being, in a great degree, invalidated by representations that, under existing circumstances, she would not insist on those instructions; Mr. Madison at length came to the conclusion that, for the removal of all doubts, and in order to produce harmony of action in the delegation, it was most expedient to refer the subject to the legislature for "their precise, full, and ultimate sense" with regard to it.[2]

The party of concession prevailed in the legislature; and on the 2d of January, 1781, new

---

[1] It appears from a letter of the 20th of November, 1786, addressed by Colonel Bland to Mr. Arthur Lee, (see Life of Arthur Lee, vol. II. pp. 384, 385,) that Colonel Bland had, at that time, entirely changed his first opinions with regard to the rights and interests of the United States in the navigation of the Mississippi. At the period mentioned, Mr. Jay, then secretary of foreign affairs, proposed to Congress that the United States should cede to Spain, for a term of years, their right to the free navigation of the Mississippi; and to this proposal Colonel Bland declared himself opposed. He and Mr. Jay, it seems, had each changed their original opinions, but conversely, — the one from concession to resistance, the other from resistance to concession.

[2] See Madison's Debates and Correspondence, vol. I. pp. 65–69, 70, 71, 72, 73, 74, and 75.

instructions were given, to the effect that the navigation of the Mississippi should be claimed only as coextensive with our own territory, and "that every further or other demand of the said navigation be ceded, if insisting on the same is deemed an impediment to a treaty with Spain." On turning to, the Journals of Congress, it appears that on the 15th of February, 1781,—a period of great public anxiety, if not of dismay, when General Greene, with his whole army, was in full retreat before Lord Cornwallis through the State of North Carolina,—new instructions were given by that body to Mr. Jay, authorizing him "to recede from his former instructions, so far as they insist on the free navigation of that part of the river Mississippi which lies below the 31st degree of north latitude, &c., *provided* such cession shall be *unalterably insisted on* by Spain, and provided the free navigation of the said river above the said degree of north latitude shall be acknowledged and guaranteed by his Catholic Majesty to the citizens of the United States in common with his own subjects." [1]

The imperfect character of the Journals of the old Congress (which record the results, without any account of the origin and progress of measures,) has led certain historical writers into error with regard to the nature of the agency of Virginia in this retrograde movement on a great question of national policy. Confining them-

[1] Secret Journals of Congress, vol. II. pp. 393–395.

selves to the isolated entry above referred to,—where the new instructions to Mr. Jay are represented "as moved by the delegates of Virginia, in pursuance of instructions from their constituents,"—they have concluded that the measure had its origin with the State of Virginia.[1] This, we have seen, was not the fact. Mr. Madison, with his well known loyalty to historical truth, felt himself called on, after his final retirement from the public scene, to rectify this misconception; and in a communication of the 8th of June, 1822, to Niles's Register,[2] (a work designed to serve as an authentic repository of the materials of American history,) he gave a detailed and lucid statement of the whole transaction, verified by contemporary documents, and corresponding with the narrative we have given above. To that communication the candid and inquisitive reader is referred for a full elucidation of a matter, which is still occasionally perverted by the spirit of party.

It is an honorable proof of Mr. Madison's love of truth and justice, that he should have taken the pains thus to explain, and set in its proper light before posterity, a momentary change of position by the public authorities of his State, made in opposition to his opinions, and by which

---

[1] Ramsay, History of the United States, vol. II. pp. 300, 301, and Pitkin, Civil and Political History of the United States, vol. II. p. 97

[2] It will be found also in the Appendix, pp. xix.–xxii., to the first volume of the Madison Debates.

his public action was, in no small degree, countervailed and compromised. How much he felt this change of position on public grounds, (for personal considerations were never allowed to influence him,) appears from a letter addressed by him several months afterwards, in the freedom of confidential intercourse, to his friend, Judge Pendleton. The eager expectations of the country, with regard to naval succours, had been already doomed to a long series of disappointments, when intelligence was at last received that the French and Spanish fleets had formed a junction for the investment of Gibraltar, and also to attempt some enterprise against Minorca, —objects, both of them, exclusively of Spanish policy. On this occasion, Mr. Madison gave vent to his feelings in the following indignant reflections : —

"Thus the selfish projects of Spain not only withhold from us the coöperation of her own armaments, but divert, in part, that of our ally; and yet we are to reward her with a cession of what constitutes the value of the finest part of America!"[1]

It happened, fortunately for the country, that our minister in Spain, at that time, took the same wise and sagacious views of our national interests connected with the navigation of the Mississippi, that had so deeply impressed themselves upon the mind of Mr. Madison. Mr. Jay

[1] Manuscript letter of 18th of September, 1781.

had been steadily opposed to any concession to the demands of Spain on this point. In a letter of the 3d of October, 1781, to the President of Congress, after receiving the new instructions of that body, he went so far as to say: " The cession of this navigation will, in my opinion, render a future war with Spain unavoidable; and I shall look upon my subscribing the one, as fixing the certainty of the other." [1] With these impressions, in the execution of his instructions he most properly accompanied the proposed concession with a formal declaration that the United States would not consider themselves bound by the offer in future, if not now frankly accepted and with suitable equivalents rendered for it.[2] The fatuity and all-absorbing selfishness of Spain made the negotiation unavailing; and the ill-advised concession, happily, led to no result.

It appeared from Mr. Pendleton's answer to the letter of Mr. Madison cited above, that he had never before been informed that the proposed concession had been sanctioned by a resolution of the legislature of Virginia; but, on the contrary, had heard insinuations that it originated with the American minister, Mr. Jay. This gave Mr. Madison another occasion of rendering that homage to truth and justice which he never failed to pay, whether an individual or a public body was concerned; at the same time that he

---

[1] Diplomatic Correspondence of the Revolution, vol. VII. p. 464.
[2] Idem, pp. 498, 499.

renewed the expression of the deep regret with which he could not but regard the proceedings that had taken place in the legislature of his own State. He thus writes to Mr. Pendleton : —

"When you get a sight of the resolution of the General Assembly referred to in your favor of the 8th instant, you will readily judge from the tenor of it what steps would be taken by the delegates. It necessarily submitted the fate of the object in question to the discretion and prospects of the gentleman," (the American minister, Mr. Jay,) "whom reports, it seems, have arraigned to you; but who, I am bound in justice to testify, has entirely supported the character which he formerly held with you. I am somewhat surprised that you had never before known of the resolution just mentioned," (that of the 2d of January, 1781,) "especially as, what is indeed much more surprising, it was both debated and passed with open doors and a full gallery. This circumstance alone must have defeated any reservations attached to it."[1]

The reader will be gratified to learn that as soon as the menacing crisis was over, both the new instructions of Virginia to her delegates in Congress, and those of Congress to the minister in Spain, were revoked; and that this great question remained open, to be settled, in more tranquil times, upon its own grave merits, and

[1] Manuscript letter of 16th of October, 1781.

a deliberate consideration of all the vast interests connected with it.

While Congress was thus earnestly bent on strengthening the country by means of foreign connections, it did not overlook the vital sources of internal harmony and strength. Among the measures necessary for an efficient and successful prosecution of the contest, the completion of the Articles of Confederation, which still remained without legal obligation upon any of the parties in consequence of the persevering refusal of a single State to close the compact, was justly deemed an object of paramount importance. It was not so much on account of any intrinsic energy in the powers conferred on Congress by that instrument, that its final consummation was now earnestly desired, as because the enemies of the country, both foreign and domestic, would be encouraged to entertain hopes, however illusory, of detaching some of the States from the common cause, so long as there was no acknowledged obligatory bond of union between them; and also because the absence of such a bond caused a certain distrust to be cast upon all the national engagements entered into by Congress.

These considerations were, with great force and eloquence, urged upon the States in the circular address of Congress with which the Articles of Confederation were accompanied, when those articles, after much embarrassment and delay, were finally agreed upon by that body in November, 1777.

"This business," they say, "equally intricate and important, has, in its progress, been attended with uncommon embarrassment and delay, which the most anxious solicitude and persevering diligence could not prevent. To form a permanent union, accommodated to the opinions and wishes of the delegates of so many States differing in habits, produce, commerce, and internal police, was found to be a work which nothing but time and reflection, conspiring with a disposition to conciliate, could mature and accomplish.

.   .   .   .

"We have reason to regret the time which has elapsed in preparing this plan for consideration. With additional solicitude, we look forward to that which must be necessarily spent, before it can be ratified. Every motive loudly calls upon us to hasten its conclusion. More than any other consideration, it will confound our foreign enemies, defeat the flagitious practices of the disaffected, strengthen and confirm our friends, support our public credit, restore the value of our money, enable us to maintain our fleets and armies, and add weight and respect to our councils at home and to our treaties abroad."[1]

Virginia was the first of the States to respond to this urgent and patriotic appeal. The Articles of Confederation were laid before her legislature

[1] See Address in Secret Journals of Congress, vol. I. pp. 362-365.

on the 9th day of December, 1777, and on the 15th. of that month, a resolution was unanimously adopted approving the plan, and authorizing the delegates of the State in Congress to ratify it, "in the name and on behalf of this Commonwealth;" for which purpose they were required to attend in their places in Congress on or before the 10th day of March next.[1] Nine other States in succession, in the early part of the ensuing year, severally empowered their delegates to ratify the confederation on their behalf.

The subject was again taken up in Congress in June, 1778, when various amendments, proposed by some of the States, were considered, and all of them rejected. On the 9th day of the following month, the articles were formally ratified and signed in Congress by the delegates of eight States. The delegates of North Carolina and Georgia, who had been duly empowered by their constituents to sign, not being present on that occasion, attended in their places a few days afterwards, and added their signatures.

New Jersey, Delaware, and Maryland still withheld their ratifications. Congress, in a special address of the 10th of July, 1778, renewed their appeal to the non-acceding States.

"Intent," say they, "upon the present and future security of these United States, Congress has never ceased to consider a confederacy as

---

[1] See Journal of House of Delegates, October session, 1777, p. 80.

the great principle of union, which can alone establish the liberty of America, and exclude forever the hopes of its enemies. Influenced by considerations so powerful, and duly weighing the difficulties which oppose the expectations of any plan being formed that can exactly meet the wishes and obtain the approbation of so many States, differing essentially in various points, Congress have, after mature deliberation, agreed to adopt without amendments the confederation transmitted to the several States for their approbation. . . . . It now remains only with you to conclude the glorious compact, which, by uniting the wealth, strength, and councils of the whole, may bid defiance to external violence and internal dissensions, whilst it secures the public credit both at home and abroad." [1]

New Jersey, yielding to this renewed appeal of Congress, on the 20th of November, 1778, authorized her delegates to ratify the confederation on her behalf; and on the 1st day of February, 1779, the State of Delaware followed the example.

Maryland alone now stood out in opposition to the compact. Her legislature, on the 15th day of December, 1778, adopted a formal declaration, and accompanied it with elaborate instructions to their delegates in Congress, announcing their inflexible purpose not to accede to the confederation, until a certain amendment, which had

---

[1] Secret Journals of Congress, vol. I. pp. 419, 420.

already been proposed by them to Congress and rejected by that body, should be first obtained.[1] The dissatisfaction of Maryland, which placed her in this attitude of recalcitrant opposition to the confederacy, had its source in the large extent of unappropriated Western lands that fell within the territorial limits of some of the States. The articles of confederation, in declaring that "no State shall be deprived of territory for the benefit of the United States," as well as by the general reservation of the rights of sovereignty to each State, were supposed to guarantee these lands to the several States within whose limits they lay; and the object of the amendment insisted on by Maryland was to vest the entire disposition and control of them in Congress for the common benefit of all the States.

Virginia, by the greater extent of her chartered limits, as well as by the progress of her settlements in the interior, and also by conquest, was the principal claimant of Western territory; and it was against her that the jealousy of the States, not possessing like advantages with herself, was chiefly directed. In the proceedings of the legislature of Maryland, and especially in the language of the instructions to her delegates in Congress, the spirit of hostility and recrimination against Virginia was so strongly manifested that we are compelled to seek the explanation of these feelings in other circumstances than the

[1] See these papers in Hen. Stat. vol. x. pp. 549–556.

22 *

particular topic of debate. The old controversy which had grown, naturally enough, out of the fact of Maryland owing her existence, as a separate Colony, to an infraction of the original chartered limits of Virginia, and yet more, perhaps, the unpleasant altercation which had taken place between the representative assemblies of the two Colonies, only a few years before this period, on the subject of Governor Eden,[1] evidently infused their bitter memories into the tone and temper with which the public authorities of Maryland now discussed a grave question of public policy and constitutional right.

As a matter of legal and constitutional right, Virginia had a firm and unshaken confidence in the validity of her claim to the unappropriated lands within her original chartered limits, except so far as those limits had been modified by subsequent grants of the crown, or by the stipulations of the treaty of peace between England and France in 1763. It was a clear consequence of the Revolution, and of the system of federative association between independent States which followed it, that the public lands, previously held by the crown in the several Colonies, devolved by that event upon the respective States within whose limits they were situated, and with whom abided all the rights of sovereignty that were

[1] See Journal of the Virginia Convention of 1776, p. 30, under date of the 31st of May; and also American Archives, (4th series,) vol. vi. pp. 732-738, 806, 807, and 1505, 1506.

not expressly delegated to Congress. It was, also, a well understood canon of American public law, established by invariable usage both before and after the Revolution, that no legal title could be acquired by the purchase of lands from the Indians, unless with the consent or by the act of the territorial sovereign, or government holding the political dominion over them.[1] It was upon these broad and palpable principles, which have been since repeatedly recognized by the highest tribunals of the country, that the territorial claim of Virginia rested.

But while she defended that claim, as an unquestionable legal right, against those who wantonly or perversely assailed it, she never sought to make use of it in any selfish and unsocial spirit. On the contrary, she had already offered to admit the other States to a free participation of her Western lands as a fund to provide bounties to their soldiers on continental establishment, equally with her own; and in the very remonstrance, which she had been driven to address to Congress against the encouragement given to the pretensions of certain land companies in violation of her rights, she emphatically repeated her willingness to make sacrifices to the common interest in any just and reasonable manner, so as to remove the " ostensible " causes of delay to the final ratification and completion of the

[1] See Decision of Supreme Court of the United States in Johnson v. M'Intosh, 8 Wheat.

articles of confederation. She protested the more earnestly against the patronage extended to the illegal claims of these land companies, because such patronage was plainly inconsistent with the specious object, professed by her adversaries, of making the Western lands a common fund for the benefit of the States. "It was, moreover, notorious," she alleged, "that several men of great influence in some of the neighbouring States were concerned in partnerships with Lord Dunmore and others"; and that their object, in opposing the territorial rights of Virginia, was only to secure for themselves, under pretended purchases from the Indians, valuable and extensive tracts of country lying on the Ohio, and between the Ohio and Mississippi.[1]

Although the ungenerous assaults made upon the title of Virginia to her Western lands were certainly not well calculated to produce in her a temper of concession, her zeal for the common cause rose superior to her just resentments. All her leading statesmen united in recommending a liberal cession of her territorial claims, in order to promote a more cordial harmony and concord among the States, and to hasten the final ratification of the confederation. Mr. Madison, in his correspondence of that day, constantly and persuasively advocated the policy of conciliation and abnegation. Writing, on the 17th of Octo-

---

[1] See Remonstrance of General Assembly of Virginia, in Hen. Stat. vol. x. pp. 557–559.

ber, 1780, to his colleague Mr. Jones, who was then in attendance on the legislature of the State, after communicating to him an unfavorable decision which had just taken place in Congress on a proposition made by the delegates of Virginia with regard to a cession of the Western lands, he adds: "I hope this incident in Congress will not discourage any measures of the Assembly which would otherwise have been taken for the object of ratifying the confederation. Under the cautions I have suggested, they may still be taken with perfect security."[1]

Among the most distinguished and influential of Mr. Madison's correspondents of that period was Judge Edmund Pendleton, whose high position and career we have had frequent occasion to mention. That wise and eminent man, in replying to a letter he had received from Mr. Madison on this same subject, expressed himself in the following terms, which illustrate the elevated principles on which Virginia was disposed to act in the sacrifices she was called on to make for the general good, and, at the same time, the force of the impediments that had been raised in the way of that disposition by unreasonable and intemperate attacks on her rights.

"I have thought long ago," said Mr. Pendleton, "that 'twas high time the confederation was completed, and feared some foreign powers might entertain, from its delay, suspicions of some se-

[1] Madison Debates and Correspondence, vol. I. p. 54.

cret disunion among the States, or a latent intention in Congress to keep it open for purposes unworthy of them. I am happy to hear it is resumed, and think it becoming, and indeed an indispensable duty in this, as in all other social compacts, for the contracting members to yield points to each other, in order to meet as near the centre of the general good as the jarring interests can be brought; and did it depend upon my opinion, I would not hesitate to yield a very large portion of our back lands to accomplish this purpose, except for the reason which Shakspeare has put into the mouth of Hotspur.[1] In reason and justice, the title of Virginia to her Western territory can no more be questioned than to any other spot in it. The point was fully and warmly agitated in Congress, and determined in her favor. Twelve States were satisfied, and agreed to confederate; and yet one stops the whole business, setting up her judgment in opposition to so many! Yield to her in this, and may she not play the same game to gain any future point of interest?"

After some other remarks respecting the course pursued by Maryland in this affair, he adds:—

"With the Assembly, it must rest to determine what they will yield to harmonize and

---

[1] Judge Pendleton, doubtless, here refers to what Hotspur says to Glendower, in the *territorial* dispute which arose between them:—

I do not care; I'll give thrice so much land,
To any well-deserving friend:
But, in the way of bargain, mark ye me,
I'll cavil on the ninth part of a hair.

cement the union; and it must be acknowledged that in other respects, particularly in the field, Maryland has maintained a very worthy character in the contest." He concludes: " It is time for me to leave the subject to those whose province it is to decide on it. It shall be mine to acquiesce." [1]

On the 6th of September, 1780, Congress, again setting forth with impressive solemnity the weighty considerations which demanded an immediate completion of the confederation, appealed to the States having claims to Western territory to make a " liberal surrender of a portion of those claims " for the sake of general harmony and union; and, at the same time, called earnestly on the legislature of Maryland to authorize their delegates in Congress to subscribe the articles, which now wanted only their signature to clothe them with an unanimous and obligatory sanction. The legislature of New York had already passed an act authorizing their delegates in Congress to fix and define the western boundary of that State; which, though involving no surrender of any substantial territorial claim, was yet considered a step in the path of conciliation.

[1] Manuscript letter of Judge Pendleton to Mr. Madison, 25th of September, 1780. Among the distinguished statesmen of Virginia, who recommended a liberal spirit of concession with regard to her Western lands, was George Mason. See his able letter to Mr. Jones in the Bland Papers, vol. II. pp. 125–130, which was probably the first digested outline of the conditions of the cession afterwards made.

The General Assembly of Virginia, which met some few weeks after the above-mentioned proceedings of Congress, "preferring," as they declared, "the good of their country to every object of smaller importance," yielded up to Congress, for the benefit of the United States, the whole of that immense territory claimed and possessed by her northwest of the Ohio, and extending thence to the Mississippi and the lakes.[1] To the cession of this magnificent domain were annexed certain conditions of equity and justice, both with regard to herself and the confederacy, which, although they furnished the ground of much captious opposition for a year or two, as we shall hereafter see, were yet finally accepted by Congress, with slight modifications, as reasonable and satisfactory.

The proffered cession of Virginia was passed by her legislature on the 2d of January, 1781. On the 2d day of February following, the legislature of Maryland passed an act, — apparently in a grudging spirit, and placing her compliance to the credit of the wishes and opinions of "our illustrious ally," — which empowered her delegates in Congress to subscribe and ratify the articles of confederation. Her long and persevering resistance to the wishes and example of her sister States had caused two of them, Virginia and Connecticut, to give their delegates the necessary powers, and even to propose for-

[1] See Hen. Stat., vol. x. pp. 564-567.

mally in Congress, to close the Confederacy without her;[1] and a distinguished authority has expressed the opinion that it was the apprehension of being excluded from the Union, which formed, at last, her motive to give a reluctant consent to the Confederation.[2] Her accession, however, was joyfully welcomed by Congress and the country as consummating the original bond of federal union, and blighting thenceforward the malignant hopes and intrigues of the enemies of American liberty.

Thursday, the 1st of March, 1781, was fixed as the day for completing the Confederation by the signature of the delegates of Maryland; and a committee, consisting of Mr. Walton, Mr. Madison, and Mr. Matthews, was appointed to consider and report a mode for announcing the event to the public. According to their report, the Board of War and the Board of Admiralty were directed to take order for the public proclamation of the fact, as soon as it was consummated: it was, moreover, to be officially and specially communicated to the executives of the several States; to the American ministers abroad, who were instructed to notify it to the courts at which they resided; to the minister of France in America; and to the commander-in-chief of the American army, with a request to announce the same to the troops under

---

[1] Secret Journals of Congress, vol. I. pp. 431–433, and 438, 439.

[2] Judge Marshall, in his Life of Washington, vol. I. p. 430.

his command. These unwonted ceremonies sufficiently attest the deep sense which was then
felt, both in Congress and by the nation, of the
supreme importance of closing, on the eve of
the decisive crisis of the great contest, the articles of plighted faith by which the States were
held together in a common and vital struggle.

CHAPTER IX.

As the period approached for the opening of another campaign, the attention of the States, as well as of Congress, was anxiously turned to the plan of military operations to be adopted. The

Southern States had now become the principal theatre of the war, and naturally expected, therefore, that arrangements of suitable efficiency would be made for their protection and defence. The commander-in-chief, while his presence and that of the main body of the army were still required at the North by considerations of general and overruling importance, was keenly alive to the necessity of vigorous and enlarged provisions for the safety of the South. In a confidential letter to his friend and military companion, Colonel John Laurens, even as early as the spring of the last year, when the fate of Charleston was trembling in the balance, he intimated how agreeable it would be to him to go in person to the South, if the exigencies of the common service should, in the view of Congress, permit it, though obvious scruples forbade such a suggestion emanating from himself.[1]

In Congress, on the 5th of August, 1780, at the instance of the delegates of South Carolina and Georgia, a resolution was adopted, but in very guarded terms, communicating to the commander-in-chief, as the sense of that body, that a portion of the land and naval forces, both of our ally and of the United States, should be employed, when it shall appear to him most convenient, for the expulsion of the enemy from those two States; . . . . "so, however, as not to interfere with any plan of operation already

[1] See Sparks's Washington, vol. VII. p. 23, 24.

formed, as the more immediate object of the campaign." This restriction evidently referred to the combined movement then contemplated against the British army occupying the city and environs of New York, and rendered inoperative the rest of the resolution.

Virginia was the pivot State on which the preparations for the defence of the South mainly turned. As such, on the 24th of May, 1780, she addressed an earnest representation to Congress, calling their attention to the systematic and concentrated efforts then made by the enemy for the conquest of the Southern States, the inadequacy of the local means of defence, and the necessity of speedy and powerful reinforcements of continental troops, as well as of additional supplies of arms and munitions.[1] The tempest of war, driven on by a victorious general who had overrun both of the Carolinas, soon approached her own borders; and, on the 2d of December, 1780, the Assembly adopted the following resolution: —

"*Resolved*, That the General Assembly will appoint some proper person to lay before Congress a clear state of the war in this quarter, the resources of this State in men, money, provisions, clothing, and other necessaries, and to solicit the necessary aids either from our sister States or European allies, and to concert with Congress, the minister of France, and General Washington,

---

[1] See Journal of House of Delegates, May session, 1780, p..20.

the proceedings necessary in the present conjuncture of affairs in the South."[1]

The matters embraced by this resolution were
most proper subjects of representation to the
central authority charged with the common defence; but the unusual expedient of appointing
a special envoy, for the purpose of making the
representation, does not appear to have been
conceived with a very scrupulous delicacy and
regard to the delegates of the State in Congress,
by whom the duty would doubtless have been
discharged with equal fidelity and effect. The
proposition originated with Mr. Henry.[2] On the
choice of the envoy, there was an equal vote
between Mr. Benjamin Harrison, Speaker of the
House of Delegates, and Mr. Richard Henry Lee.
The latter withdrawing his name, Mr. Harrison
was declared elected.

Letters of Mr. Madison to his colleague Mr.
Jones, and to his friend Judge Pendleton, written at the time, show that he was not insensible
to the apparent slight implied, if not intended,
by this proceeding.[3] No personal susceptibility,
however, was permitted to derogate from the
conscientious zeal and manly dignity with which
he discharged his representative trust. The secret journals of Congress show that, on the 1st
of January, 1781, he brought to the notice of

[1] See Journal of House of Delegates, October session, 1780, p.
85.

[2] See manuscript letter of Mr.

Joseph Jones to Mr. Madison, dated the 2d of January, 1781.

[3] See Madison Debates and Correspondence, vol. I. pp. 72 and 81.

the body a despatch of Mr. Adams containing the intelligence that the operations of the enemy were to be directed, during the ensuing campaign, against the South; a copy of which, he moved, should be transmitted to the commander-in-chief, and that "he be informed it is the desire of Congress he should immediately make such distribution of the forces under his command, including those of our allies under Count Rochambeau, as will most effectually counteract the views of the enemy and support the Southern States." The motion was adopted; but not until it had undergone a modification, which changed its character and materially impaired its directness and value by simply asking the opinion of the commander-in-chief on the naked question of transferring the French forces from their position in Rhode Island to some post in Virginia.[1]

Mr. Madison was one of the committee appointed to confer with Colonel Harrison on the subjects of his mission. How earnestly he labored to promote its success, is vouched as well by the spirit of the motion previously made by him, to which we have just referred, as by the nature of the resolutions which Congress, upon the recommendation of that committee, finally adopted. By those resolutions, which were passed on the 20th of February, 1781, the Southern army was henceforward to be composed of all the regular troops from Pennsylvania to Georgia inclusive;

[1] Secret Journals of Congress, vol. i. pp. 179–181.

the Pennsylvania line was ordered to join the army in Virginia without loss of time, by detachments as they may be in readiness to march; and transportation and supplies of every description, clothing, tents, arms, and ammunition were to be promptly furnished, for the purchase of which *specie* funds were to be at once placed at the disposal of the Board of War.[1]

The immediate moral effect of these resolutions was to abate the strong feeling of dissatisfaction which was beginning to be manifested in Virginia under the seeming abandonment in which she had been left by Congress and her sister States of the North, in the dangers which now surrounded her. In every stage of the war, she felt that she had exerted herself to the utmost of her ability for the common cause, both in the North and in the South. Since the fall of Charleston, which had enabled the enemy to direct his operations almost exclusively against the States of South and North Carolina, she had poured out all her resources of men, money, and supplies with unstinted liberality, on the call of Congress and the commander-in-chief, for the defence of that portion of the Confederacy. This she had done, to the entire neglect of her own safety.

When, in the winter and spring of 1781, she found herself suddenly invaded by a hostile armament, — which, having the undisputed com-

1 Journals of Congress, vol. III. p. 379.

mand of the water, was able in a few days to penetrate, by her bays and rivers, to the very heart of her territory,— she was so exhausted by the efforts she had made in other and distant fields,— her magazines, her arsenals, her coffers, her military stations all emptied,— that she was for the moment incapable of organizing any effective resistance. The painful sacrifice which this cost her, both in her pride of character and her local interests, she had been exhorted to bear for the paramount interests of the general cause.

"As the evils you have to apprehend from these predatory incursions," wrote General Washington on the 6th of February, 1781, to the governor of the State, "are not to be compared to the injury to the common cause, and with the danger to your State in particular, from the conquest of the States to the southward of you, I am persuaded the attention to your immediate safety will not divert you from the measures intended to reinforce the Southern army, and put it in a condition to stop the progress of the enemy in that quarter." [1]

The exhortation was faithfully heeded. The presence of the detestable Arnold in his entrenchments at Portsmouth, though requiring a large body of militia to watch and restrain his parricidal enterprises, did not prevent the sending of timely reinforcements to General Greene; which

[1] See Sparks's Washington, vol. VII. p. 402.

enabled him to recross the Dan, and in turn to pursue and offer battle to the adversary before whom he had lately been compelled to retreat.

But Virginia herself was now the doomed and selected theatre of the war. The British general, Cornwallis, wrote to Sir Henry Clinton at New York, —

"I cannot help expressing my wishes that the Chesapeake Bay may become the seat of the war. Until Virginia is, in a manner, subdued, our hold upon the Carolinas must be difficult, if not precarious." [1] In pursuance of this policy, after reposing his troops a few days at Wilmington in North Carolina, whither he had repaired after the battle of Guilford Court-House, he renewed his advance upon Virginia.

In the mean time, Greene had determined to push on to Camden, in the hope of drawing Cornwallis after him, or, if he did not succeed in that, of recovering the posts in South Carolina which were held by the forces under Lord Rawdon. The result of this strategic movement as it turned out, was to leave Virginia, naked and unsupported, to the double invasion of Cornwallis from the South, and Arnold and Phillips from the North.

Even before the arrival of the victorious legions of Cornwallis, the governor of the State had repeatedly urged upon Congress, through letters to its President, the necessity of prompt aids, of

[1] Cited in note to Sparks's Washington, vol. VII. p. 458.

both men and arms, in the position of actual as well as impending danger in which the State was placed. "An enemy three thousand strong," he said, "not a regular in the State, nor arms to put in the hands of the militia, are indeed discouraging circumstances."[1]

While Congress, and the other States, continued inattentive to these representations, it is not surprising that Virginia, with the consciousness of what she had done and suffered for the common cause, should exhibit a keen sensibility to the injustice of such neglect. It was under these circumstances, and before information had been received of the result of Colonel Harrison's mission, that it was proposed in the General Assembly to address a remonstrance to Congress upon the subject. Among the papers of Mr. Madison, we find the draught of such a remonstrance by a member, which Judge Pendleton sent to Mr. Madison as indicating the deep, and, as he considered them, just and well-founded complaints, which the antecedent neglect of Congress and apparent indifference of the other States, had excited.[2] Although the answer finally given to Colonel Harrison's mission prevented this paper

[1] See letter of the 31st of March, 1781, to President of Congress, in Jefferson's Writings, vol. I. 215, 216.

[2] See manuscript letter of Judge Pendleton to Mr. Madison, of the 26th of March, 1781. The paper transmitted was supposed by Mr. Madison to be the production of John Taylor of Caroline, the relative and *protégé* of Judge Pendleton, and at that time a member of the General Assembly.

from receiving an official character, yet as a justification of Virginia from illiberal insinuations which are sometimes, even now, brought against her revolutionary fame; and as a condensed and eloquent presentation of public transactions in the light in which they appeared to an intelligent observer, it seems properly to belong to the history of the times. As such, we insert it here, omitting only the formal introductory part.

Speaking in the name of the General Assembly of Virginia, it says, —

"'Tis not from an impulse of vanity that they would remember past transactions, but it is necessary in order to wrest Virginia from that load of obloquy with which she hath been oppressed by those who rashly judge from detached facts, and not from a collective view of public transactions. Ere the war began, we heard the cries of our brethren at Boston, and paid the tax due to distress. We accompanied our Northern allies during almost every progressive stride it made, where danger seemed to solicit our ardor. We bled with them at Quebec, at Boston, at Harlæm, at White Plains, at Fort Washington, at Brandywine, at Germantown, at Mud Island, at White Marsh, at Saratoga, at Monmouth, and at Stony Point. We almost stood alone at Trenton and Princeton, and during the winter campaign which followed.

"But when we came to look for our Northern allies, after we had thus exhausted our powers in their defence, when Carolina and Georgia became the theatre of war, they were not to be found. We felt that they were absent at Stono, at Savannah, at Charleston, at Monk's Corner, at Buford's defeat, at Lanneau's Ferry, at Camden, at King's Mountain, at the Cowpens, and at Georgetown. Whilst we are continuing our utmost exertions to repair the mighty losses sustained in defending almost every State in the Union, we at length find ourselves invaded, and threatened with the whole weight of the American war. When the Northern States were attacked, the sluices of paper credit were not only opened, but the force of all America concentred to the point of danger. Now, Northern and Southern departments are formed, calculated more to starve the only active war, than for the purpose of common defence.

"Let it be remembered that Georgia and South Carolina are lost, that North Carolina, in a state of uncertainty from continual alarms, cannot furnish supplies, and that Maryland hath only sent those of men. Virginia, then, impoverished by defending the Northern department, exhausted by the Southern war, now finds the whole weight of it on her shoulders. Even after these departments were formed, Congress called for, and, by a great exertion on our part, actually received half a million for the Northern army. The war having converted its rage from the Northern to the Southern States, the former, thus exonerated from the immediate obligations of the Union, might have seized the opportunity of completing their levies, which would have enabled them to return with accumulated vigor to our assistance. But they were employed in availing themselves of resolutions of Congress, by which they got rid of their State paper at the expense of the Union; whilst Virginia was left struggling under that unwieldy load from which no exertions could disengage her, during the continuation of those enormous expenses she was forced to yield to or leave the Southern war to expire through famine.

"Thus situated, our only resource is the wretched one of more paper money, in addition to enormous taxes, which are the more peculiarly distressing as they must be collected whilst near ten thousand of our citizens, exclusive of our regular troops, are in the field. A tax of four and a fourth per cent. on a specie valuation of property; a tax of thirty pounds of tobacco and two bushels of corn on each tithable; a tax of three thousand beeves; a tax of three thousand suits of clothes; a tax of seventy-four wagons and teams, besides many occasional seizures and other collateral dues, all paid or to be paid in the present year, do, when added to the emissions of twenty-one millions of pounds in three months, prove that Virginia hath not been unmindful of the extraordinary efforts expected from her.

"Thus exhausted with our former exertions,

thus straining every nerve in present defence, — pressed with a great hostile army, and threatened with a greater, — beset with enemies both savage and disciplined, — the Assembly of Virginia do, in behalf of their State and in behalf of the common cause, in the most solemn manner summon the other States to their assistance. They demand aids of men, money, and every warlike munition. If they are denied, the consequences be on the heads of those who refuse them. The Assembly of Virginia call the world and future generations to witness that they have done their duty, that they have prosecuted the war with earnestness, and they are still ready so to act, in conjunction with the other States, as to prosecute it to a happy and glorious period."[1]

[1] That the tone of this paper was not without much to call for and justify it, in the delays of Congress and the unconcern of the Northern States, is shown by the testimony and opinions of men remarkable for the calmness of their tempers and the cautious sobriety of their judgments.

Judge Pendleton, in writing to Mr. Madison on the 7th of April, 1781, twelve days after he had transmitted the paper given above, uses this language : —

"Do Congress mean to leave the weight of this Southern war entirely upon Virginia? Or suffer our main army to remain idle spectators of repeated drafts from New York to recruit the enemy in this quarter, without any corresponding assistance to us? Surely not; as it must produce the worst consequences. I am happy to find our people willing to exert themselves on this great occasion, but know they are not alone able to support this burden, nor do I believe they will submit to be duped."

Mr. Sparks, an historian of scrupulous research and candor, and a citizen himself of the North, says, in his Life of Washington : —

"The Eastern and Middle States in particular, after the French troops had arrived in the country, and the theatre of the war had been transferred by the enemy to

At length, the Marquis Lafayette was sent with a detachment of twelve hundred men to the relief of Virginia. This expedition had been planned by the ever watchful providence of the commander-in-chief early in February, and in anticipation of any action of Congress on the subject. It was originally projected with the view of cutting off Arnold, and depended for its success on the coöperation of the French fleet from Rhode Island. When that coöperation was arrested midway by an engagement between the two hostile fleets off the capes of the Chesapeake, the expedition under Lafayette, which had already reached Annapolis on its Southern destination, returned to the head of the bay. There he was met by new orders from the commander-in-chief, which, to his great delight, committed to him, with the detachment under his command, the general direction of the operations for the defence of Virginia.

He hastened to the scene of his important military trust, and, by a forced march, arrived with his troops at Richmond just in time to

the South, relapsed into a state of comparative inactivity and indifference, the more observable on account of the contrast it presented with the ardor, energy, and promptitude which had previously characterized them." And afterwards, when at last the army was on its march to the South, he says, " The soldiers, being mostly from the Eastern and Middle States, marched with reluctance to the southward, and showed strong symptoms of discontent when they passed through Philadelphia. This had been foreseen by General Washington, and he urged the superintendent of finance to advance to them a month's pay in hard money."

prevent, with the assistance of the militia collected there, another occupation of the capital of the State by the enemy's forces under General Phillips. The arrival a few days afterwards of Lord Cornwallis, with his imposing and triumphant army, reduced the youthful general, charged with the defence of Virginia, to so great an inferiority of force as to put in requisition all his vigilance and conduct to avert the accomplishment of the haughty boast of his adversary — "The boy shall not escape me." He effected, with admirable self-possession and skill, a retrograde movement before, and almost in the presence of, an advancing foe with largely superior numbers, until he reached the northern bank of the Rapidan; where he awaited the expected reinforcement of the Pennsylvania troops under General Wayne.

During this interval, the territory of the State lay open to the enterprises of the invader. Expeditions were pushed in various directions; some to obtain possession of military stores; others to seize and destroy private property; and one in particular under the noted partisan, Tarlton, to capture or disperse the legislature, with the governor, then at or near Charlottesville, a quiet and retired village in the midland region of Virginia. The legislature, on the approach of the enemy, adjourned in haste, to meet again in Staunton. Several of its members fell into the hands of the bold marauder; and Mr. Jefferson, who, upon the expiration, three days before, of his second year in the office of governor, had declined a reëlection, narrowly escaped capture at his private residence in the neighbourhood.[1]

For the moment, there seemed to be a general disorganization, both civil and military; and it would certainly not appear an incredible cir-

[1] Many charges, more or less envenomed by the spirit of party hostility, have been brought against the conduct of Mr. Jefferson at this crisis. They have been fully and ably answered by his biographers, Mr. Tucker and Mr. Randall. Any notice of them here would be as superfluous as it is extraneous to the object of this work. But so extraordinary an attempt has been recently made to sustain the most reckless of all these imputations, — that of personal timidity, — by the testimony of one of Mr. Jefferson's most intimate friends, that, having in our possession the document which has been thus strangely applied, we feel called on to produce it, and let it speak for itself.

In the publication referred to, (Hamilton's History of the American Republic, see vol. II. p. 168, and also table of contents to chap. xxiv.,) Judge Pendleton is represented as "charging Mr. Jefferson with cowardice," in the sense of unmanly fear before the enemy; and in support of this representation, the author, after stating that "the near presence of British troops was irksome to the governor," introduces an isolated remark from a letter of Judge Pendleton, in these words: "It is also said the governor intends to resign. It is a little cowardly to quit our posts in a bustling time."

This excerpt is taken from a manuscript letter of Judge Pendleton to Mr. Madison of the 6th of November, 1780, now before us, and is separated from its context, essential to its true meaning. The whole passage is as follows: "We had no House of Delegates on Saturday last, which, with an empty treasury, are circumstances unfavorable at this juncture. Mr. Henry has resigned his seat in Congress; and I hear Mr. Jones intends it. It is also said the governor intends to resign. It is a little cowardly to quit our posts in a bustling time." The remark of Mr. Pendleton, it is seen, refers exclusively to a question of *civil* courage in times of public difficulty, and includes Mr. Henry and Mr. Madison's own colleague, Mr. Jones, equally with Mr. Jefferson, in its friendly and gentle expostulation.

cumstance if, in the midst of such pressing dangers, and in the absence of regular and efficient means of warding them off, the expedient of a temporary dictatorship should, as has been alleged, have been suggested, on the reassembling of the legislature in Staunton. The wisdom and propriety of the suggestion will probably be judged by posterity, more with reference to the personage who was in contemplation for so great a trust, than upon general principles applied to an exceptional proposition in highly exceptional times. There was but one man who, by surpassing weight of character, universal confidence, and multiplied proofs of virtue and wisdom in the field and the council,— by deeds, not words, — could have merited such a trust at the hands of a free people; and he would have declined it.

The records of our public bodies afford no trace whatever of the formal presentation of such a proposition. The fact has, nevertheless, passed into history upon the positive averment of an eminent contemporary actor,[1] uncontradicted by any of his associates in the public service, and supported by tradition. The favored individual, upon whom it was believed the advocates of the scheme designed to confer this supreme and extra-constitutional magistracy, had already been governor of the State, and at the time, too, of an invasion, (that of General Matthew in the

[1] Mr. Jefferson, in his Notes on Virginia.

spring of 1779,) which had not been met with more of success than the present.[1]

While we are left, for the most part, to conjecture and the uncertain lights of tradition with regard to what was contemplated in the

[1] The project of appointing a dictator was twice agitated in the legislature of Virginia, according to Mr. Jefferson, during the war of the Revolution, — first in the autumn of 1776, and again in the summer of 1781. On both occasions, Mr. Henry is represented by the traditional accounts, which have been preserved by historians, as the person contemplated for this dangerous eminence by the patrons of the project. The biographer of Mr. Henry (Mr. Wirt) records a tradition that "the project was crushed," on the first occasion, by a desperate vow of tyrannicide vengeance uttered to Mr. Henry's step-brother by Colonel Archibald Cary, — a stern and jealous friend of republican freedom, who then occupied the post of Speaker of the Senate. On the second occasion, Mr. Jefferson (in Notes on Virginia) says "the proposition wanted a few votes only of being passed;" and Girardin, probably upon his authority, affirms that, "as in the previous instance of a similar attempt, the apprehension of personal danger produced a relinquishment of the scheme." See Burk's History of Virginia, vol. IV. appendix 12.

Mr. Wirt is very earnest in exculpating Mr. Henry from any participation in the project of a dictatorship, and thinks it could not have "received any countenance" from him. A different inference, however, so far, at least, as the principle of the measure is concerned, might not unreasonably be drawn from the language of Mr. Henry, seven years afterwards, in the convention of Virginia on the ratification of the Federal Constitution. Replying to the argument of danger to the public liberty from a probable resort to dictatorial power, amid the civil confusions which, it was alleged, a rejection of the constitution would produce, he there said: "In making a dictator, we follow the example of the most glorious, magnanimous, and skilful nations. In great dangers, this power had been given. Rome had furnished us with an illustrious example. America found a person worthy of the trust. She looked to Virginia for him. We gave a dictatorial power to hands that used it gloriously, and which were rendered more glorious by surrendering it up. Where is there a breed of such dictators? Shall we find a set of American Presidents of such a breed?" See Robertson's Debates of Virginia Convention of 1788.

legislature of the State, the files of Mr. Madison's correspondence at the time afford authentic and indisputable evidence of a similar suggestion emanating from another distinguished source, but looking to a different and yet more exalted character as the object of the proposed trust. Richard Henry Lee, who, when not a delegate to Congress, had hitherto been a member of the legislature of the State, and was Speaker of the last House of Delegates, happened now to be in retirement at his residence in the county of Westmoreland. Hearing of the rapid and unresisted progress of Cornwallis, and of the recent occurrences at Charlottesville, which led to the dispersion of the legislature and the interregnum in the office of governor, he addressed a letter to the delegates of Virginia in Congress, communicating freely and earnestly his thoughts on what the crisis demanded for the public safety.

This letter remained in the hands of Mr. Madison as one of the delegates to whom it was addressed, and is now among his papers. The following extracts will disclose what were the views then entertained by Mr. Lee of both the danger and the remedy. The letter is dated at "Chantilly, June 12th, 1781," and begins:—

"DEAR GENTLEMEN: I am not informed who of our delegates remain at Congress, and, therefore, this letter is addressed to you, who I have good reason to suppose are yet there. The unhappy crisis of our country's fate demands the closest attention of all her sons, and calls for the united wisdom and the strongest exertions of all others who may be affected by our ruin."

After recapitulating, in an impressive manner, the movements of the enemy and the events at Charlottesville, the writer proceeds:—

"Upon the principle, therefore, of duty to my country, and deep affection for the liberties of America, I have ventured to give you this intelligence of our true state, and mean to close it with my opinion of the remedy best fitted and most likely to baffle the designs of our enemies, and to secure the liberty of this country. In the popularity, the judgment, and experience of General Washington, we can alone find the remedy. Let Congress send him immediately to Virginia; and, as the head of the Federal Union, let them possess the General with dictatorial power, until the General Assembly can be convened and have determined upon his powers; and let it be recommended to the Assembly, when met, to continue this power for six, eight, or ten months, as the case may require. The General should be desired, on his arrival here, to call a full meeting of the legislature, where he shall appoint, to consider of the above plan.

"Both ancient and modern times furnish precedents to justify this procedure; but if they did not, the present necessity not only justifies, but absolutely demands the measure. In the winter of 1776, Congress placed such powers in the General, and repeated the same thing (if I mistake not) with regard to Pennsylvania in 1777, after its new government was formed and organized.   .   .   .   .

"The inferiority of our army here to that of the enemy renders it very necessary that two or three thousand regulars be sent with the General, or at least to follow him quickly, and, if they are to be got, accoutrements for a thousand horse, with a good supply of arms and ammunition for infantry.   The better to distract us, and keep our force divided, the armed vessels of the enemy are pushing vigorously into the rivers, and committing depredations on the shores both of bay and rivers.   Is it not possible, by any solicitation, to procure a superior marine force for these Southern waters?

"It is reported here that General Wayne has objections to act under the Marquis' command. If there should be any disagreement, or any objection of this kind, the consequences are too obvious to escape your notice, and will furnish an auxiliary reason for the commander-in-chief coming here, if any additional reason can be requisite, when the very being of the State demands it.

"I am, dear gentlemen,

"Sincerely and affectionately yours,

"RICHARD HENRY LEE."

On the very day that this letter was written, the legislature, being then reassembled at Staunton, elected General Thomas Nelson, who had for several years been in command of the militia of the State, to the office of governor. On the same day, also, Lafayette, having already effected a junction with the Pennsylvania troops under Wayne, was at Boswell's Ordinary, in Louisa County,[1] retracing his steps and making cautious approaches towards the enemy, who still retained a decided numerical superiority. Notwithstanding this advantage, the British general decided to retreat slowly to the lower country; and Lafayette, additionally reinforced by a body of riflemen from the western part of the State, followed his adversary at a heedful distance, without as yet offering battle.

This order of march of the two armies continued, with little variation, till the 6th of July, when Cornwallis prepared to pass with his army, at Jamestown, to the south side of the river. Lafayette then departed momentarily from the Fabian policy he had been hitherto pursuing; and brought on an action, which proving to be a very unequal one, (from having the main body of the enemy to engage, instead of his rear, as he had been led to suppose,) he very adroitly extricated himself without any serious loss.

The hostile army pursued its way to its intrenchments at Portsmouth. Lafayette reposed

[1] See Memoires de Lafayette, vol. i. p. 478.

his troops, for some time, at Malvern Hill, on the northern bank of James River; and afterwards took up a position between the two branches of the York, near their confluence. Lord Cornwallis, after many apparent fluctuations of council, and in order, it was supposed, to obtain a post on the Chesapeake more accessible, at all times, to line-of-battle ships, finally transferred the whole force under his command from Portsmouth to Yorktown. As soon as this change of position was made by the enemy, Lafayette broke up his encampment on the Pamunkey, and gradually concentrated his forces at Williamsburg.[1]

[1] The masterly manner in which Lafayette conducted the campaign in Virginia, down to the time of the arrival of the allied army under Washington and Rochambeau, forms the most brilliant, as well as the most successful, part of his whole public career, whether in Europe or America. Mr. Madison, writing to Judge Pendleton on the 18th of November, 1781, says: " Will not the Assembly pay some handsome compliment to the Marquis for his judicious and zealous services, while the protection of the country was entrusted to him? His having baffled, and finally reduced to the defensive, so powerful an army as we now know he had to contend with, and with so disproportionate a force, would have done honor to the most veteran officer, and, added to his other merits and services, constitutes a claim on their gratitude which, I hope, will not be unattended to."

It was not unattended to. On the 17th of December, 1781, the General Assembly of Virginia passed a resolution, conceived in the warmest terms of affection and applause, tendering to him, " for his many great and important services, to this Commonwealth in particular, and through it to the United States in general, the grateful thanks of the free representatives of a free people." They also directed a marble bust of him to be made by one of the best artists of Paris, " as a lasting monument of his merit and of their gratitude." [Journal of House of Delegates, October session, 1781, p. 43.] Other and touching testimonials of gratitude and affection were

Here, aided by the energetic coöperation of Governor Nelson, he received from day to day reinforcements of volunteers and militia; and here, too, he was soon to be joined by the whole body of the allied forces under Washington and Rochambeau. The earnest representations made to the French court through Colonel Laurens had led to the resolution not only of granting additional and indispensable succours of money, but of sending out a powerful naval armament to support the operations of the joint land forces in America. Information was received by General Washington, on the 14th day of August,[1] that Count de Grasse would arrive in the Chesapeake about the close of the month, with the whole French West India fleet, prepared to unite in any system of military operations which should

again offered to him by the legislature of Virginia in 1784 and 1786. See Hen. Stat. vol. XI. p. 553, and vol XII. p. 30.

How entirely this appreciation of the great ability shown by the youthful general in the Virginia campaign of 1781 was sanctioned by the enlightened judgment of Washington, of Vergennes, and of the French minister of war, Segur, is attested by their recorded opinions at the time. See Sparks's Washington, vol. VIII. pp. 118 and 208, and Memoires de Lafayette, vol. I. 473.

The comparative nullity of General Lafayette's busy and checkered career in his own country, (interspersed, however, with some noble acts of vigor and self-devotion,) contrasted with the unquestionable splendor of his American services and deeds, forms one of the most singular phenomena in the history of the human mind; and proves how fruitless and vain are the highest virtues without a congenial theatre for their display, and unsupported by practical discernment in their application. See a philosophical and not unfriendly estimate of his character by one of the most illustrious of his countrymen in Memoires de Monsieur Guizot, vol. I. pp. 238, 239.

[1] Sparks's Washington, vol. VIII. pp. 127 and 134.

promise the best result in a necessarily limited time. This opportune information, combined with the slowness of the Northern States in responding to the requisitions that had been made upon them for troops to aid in the contemplated operation against New York, and the large reinforcements recently received by the enemy there, determined the mind of the commander-in-chief at once to direct his efforts against the British post and army in Virginia.

The American and French forces already assembled around New York were put in motion without delay. On the 3d day of September a large portion of the allied army passed through Philadelphia, when Mr. Madison wrote to his friend Judge Pendleton in the following buoyant terms: —

"This letter will be the most agreeable of any I have long had the pleasure of writing. I begin with informing you that the commander-in-chief and the Count Rochambeau, — the former with a part of the American army, and the latter with the whole of the French, — are thus far on their way for the Southern department. The American troops passed through the town yesterday: the first division of the French, to-day. The second will pass to-morrow. Nothing can exceed the appearance of this specimen which our ally has sent us of his army, whether we regard the figure of the men, or the exactness of their discipline."

Count de Grasse arrived in the Chesapeake with his fleet of twenty-eight line-of-battle ships, and a proportionate number of frigates, on the 30th of August. With one portion of them he blocked up the mouth of York River; and with another he occupied the James, in order to cut off the retreat of Lord Cornwallis to the Carolinas, should he meditate such an attempt; while the land troops brought from the West Indies, under the Marquis de Saint Simon, were sent forward to join Lafayette at Williamsburg. De Grasse had been but a few days in the Chesapeake, when the whole British naval force from New York, under Admirals Graves and Hood, appeared off Cape Henry, and offered him battle. The gage was not declined by the French admiral, but the action which ensued was not decisive. The two hostile fleets remained in sight of each other, for several successive days, without renewing the engagement. In the mean time, Count de Barras, with the French squadron from Rhode Island, consisting of eight line-of-battle ships, entered the Chesapeake in spite of the efforts of the British admirals to intercept him. The latter then returned to New York; whence Sir Henry Clinton continued to hold out hopes of speedy relief to Cornwallis.

But events hastened to their consummation. Washington and Rochambeau, as soon as they arrived with the allied army at Williamsburg, went on board the Ville de Paris, the flag ship of the French admiral, to concert with him the necessary measures for the immediate and active commencement of the siege. Thus was opened,—in the presence of a magnificent fleet of our ally, covering the waters of the Chesapeake, and coming together, as if by magic, from remote and opposite points of the compass,—that great scene of combined operation between the arms of France and the United States, fraternal yet emulous, which dashed and reversed all the boasts of a haughty invader, and sealed the independence of America with the humiliating surrender of an army that had threatened and denounced its conquest. History has rarely presented a scene more dramatic and imposing in its accessories, more august in its associations, or more transcendent and eventful in its consequences, than the siege and surrender of Yorktown.

NOTE. We have already referred to some proofs of the contemporary appreciation of the able generalship displayed by Lafayette in his operations for the defence of Virginia previous to the arrival of the allied army. To these, we are pleased to have it in our power to add the just estimate of his military character formed by Washington, before the campaign in Virginia had given evidence to the world of the correctness of that estimate. It is extracted from a manuscript letter, now before us, addressed by General Washington, on the 10th of July, 1781, to the Hon. Joseph Jones, one of the delegates of Virginia in Congress.

"The complaints against the Baron de Steuben are not more distressing than unexpected; for I always viewed him in the light of a good officer. If he has formed a junction with the Marquis, he will be no longer master of his own conduct. Of course, the clamors against him will cease with his command. From General Greene's letters, I had little doubt but that he would have been in Virginia ere this. Powerful causes may have detained him: but I am persuaded he will be there as soon as possible, as it is within his command, and now the principal theatre of action. In the mean time, I am afraid to give any order in that quarter, lest it should clash with his views, and produce confusion.

"I shall, however, write fully to him, in the course of a few days, upon the several matters contained in your letter; and until his arrival, it is my opinion the command of the troops in that State cannot be in better hands than the Marquis's. He possesses uncommon military talents; is of a quick and sound judgment; persevering, and enterprising without rashness; and besides these, he is of a very conciliating temper and perfectly sober;—which are qualities that rarely combine in the same person. And were I to add that some men will gain as much experience in the course of three or four years as some others will in ten or a dozen, you cannot deny the fact, and attack me upon that ground."

CHAPTER X.

CONGRESS, on the 24th of October, 1781, received official intelligence of the capitulation of
Yorktown, in a letter from the commander-in-
chief; and, at two o'clock of the same day, went
in procession to the Dutch Lutheran Church,
"to return thanks to Almighty God for crowning the allied arms of the United States and
France with success by the surrender of the
whole British army under Earl Cornwallis." A

few days afterwards, upon the report of a committee appointed to consider the most proper mode of doing honor to the actors in so splendid an achievement, the thanks of Congress were voted, in the warmest terms, to General Washington, Count Rochambeau, and Count de Grasse, not omitting the officers and soldiers under their command.

It was further resolved that "the United States in Congress assembled will cause to be erected at York, in Virginia, a marble column, adorned with emblems of the alliance between the United States and his Most Christian Majesty, and inscribed with a succinct narrative" of the great event; an event which must render that spot forever memorable on the pages of history. But no monumental structure has yet risen to mark it to the eyes of the inquiring patriot or stranger; and a solemn pledge of the national faith to the glorious past of our annals,—a debt which no change or lapse of time can cancel,—remains still unfulfilled.

General Washington, in writing to Congress on the 26th of October, for the purpose of transmitting complete returns of the prisoners, arms, and stores surrendered at York, and also of informing them what disposition of his forces he had determined to make for the remainder of the season, availed himself of the occasion to express to that body, with great earnestness, his opinion of the course which wisdom and prudence demanded in preparing for another campaign.

"Unacquainted," said he, "with the state of politics between Congress and the courts of Europe respecting future negotiations, whatever our prospects from that quarter may be, I cannot justify myself to my own mind without urging Congress, in the warmest terms, to make every arrangement for an early and efficacious campaign, the ensuing year, that may be found necessary. Arguments, I flatter myself, need not be adduced to impress on Congress the high importance of this idea. Whatever may be the events of the coming winter or ensuing summer, an effectual and early preparation for military operations will put us upon the most respectable footing either for war or negotiation; while relaxation will place us in a disreputable situation in point of peaceful prospects, and will certainly expose us to the most disgraceful disasters in case of the continuance of the hostile disposition of our enemies."

Returning to reassume his position in the North, the commander-in-chief arrived in Philadelphia the evening of the 26th of November. On the 28th, he was formally received by Congress; and in the address of the President on that occasion, congratulating him on the glorious success of the allied arms in Virginia, he was assured that "it was the fixed purpose of Congress to draw every advantage from the event by exhorting the States, in the strongest terms, to the most vigorous and timely exertions."

Mr. Madison, in writing to Judge Pendleton the day preceding this public reception of the General by Congress, says:—

"Your favor of the 19th instant came to hand yesterday. On the same evening arrived our illustrious General, returning to his position on the North River. We shall probably, however, have his company here for some days at least, where he will be able to give Congress very seasonable aid in settling the military establishment for the next year; about which there is some diversity of opinion. Whatever the total requisition of men may be on the States, I cannot but wish that Virginia may take effectual measures for bringing into the field her proportion of men."

Writing to the same friend as early as the 2d of October, 1781, in anticipation of the auspicious close of the operation then pending against the enemy at York, he evinced how deeply his mind was penetrated with the necessity of unrelaxed military preparations, on the part of America, to secure the great boon of peace and national independence.

"We have received," said he, "some communications from Europe, relative to the general state of its affairs. They all centre in three important points. The first is, the obstinacy of Great Britain, the second, the fidelity of our ally, and the third, the absolute necessity of vigorous and systematic preparations for war on our part, in order to insure a speedy, as well as favorable peace. The wisdom of the legislature of Virginia will, I flatter myself, not only prevent an illusion from the present brilliant prospects, but take advantage of the military ardor and sanguine hopes of the people to recruit their line for the war."

These views finally prevailed in the deliberations of Congress. On the 10th of December, it was resolved, with a view to the exigencies of another campaign, to complete the different corps of the army to the full extent of the establishment fixed for the service of the past year; and " the legislatures of the several States were to be called upon, in the most pressing manner, to have their respective quotas of the land forces in the field by the first day of March next," and to provide for vacancies, which might thereafter occur, by new enlistments for three years or during the war.[1] It had already been resolved to call upon the States for the sum of eight millions of dollars in specie, for the fiscal service of the ensuing year, to be paid in equal quarterly instalments, — the first payment to be made into the treasury on the first day of April next.[2]

Experience, however, had unfortunately shown that the requisitions of Congress and the com-

[1] Journals of Congress, vol. III. p. 700.

[2] Idem, under dates of October 30 and November 2, 1781.

pliance of the States were not always equivalent terms. While some of the States responded to the calls made upon them with a noble promptitude and self-devotion, others either failed to comply at all, or complied only tardily and in part. The embarrassments to the common service, and the injustice of the unequal burdens borne by the different members of the Confederacy, arising from the delinquency of some of the States, constituted, at this critical period of the war, a crying evil, for which some remedy was loudly demanded. The nature and extent of the evil are nowhere, perhaps, more impressively set forth, in words of truth and soberness, than in a letter addressed by Washington, in the early part of the year,[1] to his young connection and friend, John Parke Custis, then a member of the Virginia legislature.

"The great business of war," he says, "can never be well conducted, if it can be conducted at all, while the powers of Congress are only recommendatory. While one State yields obedience, and another refuses it; while a third mutilates and adopts the measure in part only; and all vary in time and manner, it is scarcely possible that our affairs should prosper, or that anything but disappointments can follow the best concerted plans. The willing States are almost ruined by their exertions; distrust and jealousy ensue. Hence proceed neglect and ill-

[1] February 28th, 1781.

timed compliances; one State waiting to see what another will do. This thwarts all our measures, after a heavy, though ineffectual, expense is incurred."

With regard to the remedy, and the pressing necessity for some immediate change, he proceeds: —

"Our independence, our respectability and consequence in Europe, our greatness as a nation hereafter, depend upon it. The fear of giving sufficient powers to Congress, for the purposes I have mentioned, is futile. A nominal head, which is, at present, but another name for Congress, will no longer do. That honorable body, after hearing the interests and views of the several States fairly discussed and explained by their representatives, must dictate, and not merely recommend and leave it to the States to do afterwards as they please; which, as I have observed before, is in many cases to do nothing at all." [1]

[1] See Sparks's Washington, vol. VII. pp. 440–444.

Among the papers of Mr. Madison printed in 1840 by order of Congress, is a remarkable letter of unknown origin, expressing opinions in striking coincidence with those cited above. The letter appears to have been addressed to Messrs. Pendleton, Wythe, and Jefferson. The copy of it in the possession of Mr. Madison was in the handwriting of his colleague, Mr. Jones. From an indorsement upon it by Mr. Madison, it seems to have been supposed by him that General Washington was the writer. This conjecture, however, is not confirmed by an examination of General Washington's files. It is most probable, from certain allusions in the letter, that it was written by a member of the legislature of Virginia; and one, too, of the first order for wisdom, patriotism, and experience. The following ex-

The conviction became general in the country that Congress should, in some mode or other, be armed with the practical means of enforcing a compliance of the States with the lawful requisitions of the central authority. The legislature of New York, in a very able paper presented to Congress, declared their opinion that it resulted from the very nature of the powers granted to that body by the articles of confederation, as well as the obligations expressly contracted by the States in the same instrument, that Congress was already invested with full authority to compel, with the whole military force of the nation, if necessary, refractory States to conform to the

tracts will serve to show its general drift and tone.

"The States appear to have yielded to Congress the right of ascertaining the sum necessary for the public expense, and oblige themselves to furnish their proportions agreeably to the mode prescribed; they also yield the right of fixing the quotas of men for the common defence, which shall be binding; but no mode is stated how a disobedient or delinquent State is to be compelled to furnish the one or the other, and for want of this controlling power in Congress over the States, when refractory, war cannot be prosecuted with vigor, and the safety of the whole is endangered, besides the hardship and injustice to those that comply, and the prolongation of the war by such delinquencies. If, in surrendering the right of fixing the proportions, the power of compelling obedience is implied, how or by what mode ought the refractory to be punished; by shutting the ports, marching an army into the State, or in what other mode?"

The writer then adds: "It would give me concern should it be thought of me that I am desirous of enlarging the powers of Congress unnecessarily, as I declare to God my only aim is the general good, and which, in time of war, does appear to me to be involved in the exercise of this or some controlling power adequate to drawing out, in due proportion, the abilities and resources of the States." See Madison Debates and Correspondence, vol. i. pp. 81–84.

federal requisitions. Such was understood to be the acknowledged common law of confederacies, both ancient and modern.[1]

Mr. Madison, deeply impressed with the ruinous and destructive consequences threatened by the wanton delinquency of some of the States, but habitually jealous of the exercise of constructive powers, appears to have favored, at this time, a specific amendment of the articles of confederation, which should expressly grant to Congress authority to employ the force of the Union against the trade or property of contumacious States, in such manner as to constrain them to fulfil their federal engagements. In a

---

[1] Mr. Jefferson, in a letter addressed to Colonel Edward Carrington some years after this period, [4th of August, 1787,] says:

"It has been so often said, as to be generally believed, that Congress have no power by the confederation to enforce anything; for example, contributions of money. It was not necessary to give them that power expressly; they have it by the law of nature. When two parties make a compact, there results to each a power of compelling the other to execute it. Compulsion was never so easy as in our case, where a single frigate would soon levy on the commerce of any State the deficiency of its contributions; nor more safe than in the hands of Congress, which has always shown that it would wait, as it ought to do, to

the last extremities, before it would exercise any of its powers which are disagreeable." Jefferson's Writings, vol. II. p. 203.

In 1784, the legislature of Virginia passed a resolution declaring that Congress ought to *enforce* the payment of balances due from any of the States by *distress* on the property of the defaulting States or of their citizens. See Journal of House of Delegates, May session, 1784, pp. 11, 12. — In the debates of the Virginia convention on the ratification of the federal constitution, this resolution was referred to; and Mr. George Nicholas, appealing to Mr. Henry, said, "I am sure that the gentleman recognizes his child;" and it was not disowned. See Robertson's Debates of Virginia Convention of 1788.

letter to Mr. Jefferson of the 16th of April, 1781, he thus expressed himself:—

"The necessity of arming Congress with *coercive* powers arises from the shameful deficiency of some of the States, which are most capable of yielding their apportioned supplies, and the military exactions to which others, already exhausted by the enemy and our own troops, are in consequence exposed. Without such powers, too, in the general government, the whole confederacy may be insulted, and the most salutary measures frustrated by the most inconsiderable State in the Union. At a time when all the other States were submitting to the loss and inconvenience of an embargo on their exports, Delaware absolutely declined coming into the measure, and not only defeated the general object of it, but enriched herself at the expense of those who did their duty. . . . . .

"It may be asked, perhaps, by what means Congress could exercise such a power, if the States were to invest them with it. As long as there is a regular army on foot, a small detachment from it, acting under civil authority, would at any time render a voluntary contribution of supplies due from a State an eligible alternative. But there is a still more easy and efficacious mode. The situation of most of the States is such that two or three vessels of force, employed against their trade, will make it their interest to yield prompt obedience to all just requisitions on them. With respect to those States that have little or no foreign trade of their own, it is provided that all inland trade with such States as supply them with foreign merchandise may be interdicted, and the concurrence of the latter may be enforced, in case of refusal, by operations on their foreign trade."[1]

A proposition of this kind was embodied in the report of a committee of Congress; and although it undoubtedly met the approbation of that body, it seems not to have been pressed to a final decision. Those who favored the measure believed that the mere grant of the proposed power to Congress would obviate all occasion for its exercise, as the States prone to disregard their federal duties, knowing beforehand the penalty of disobedience, would not choose to expose themselves to its visitation. But the lively jealousy of congressional authority, which prevailed in some of the States, rendered it sufficiently evident that no application for additional power, however urgent its apparent necessity, could at that time receive the unanimous assent of all the States, necessary to make it a part of the federal compact.

Among the many projects of reform in the federal system, suggested by individuals or public bodies about this period, much attention has, of late years, been drawn to a letter addressed by Colonel Alexander Hamilton to Mr. Duane, a

[1] Madison Debates and Correspondence, vol. i. pp. 86, 87.

26*

member of Congress from the State of New York. The letter bears date the 3d of September, 1780. Colonel Hamilton was, at that time, one of the aids of the commander-in-chief, and had already won much distinction by his generous ardor in the cause of the Revolution, and by the proofs he had given of superior abilities, both civil and military. His position in the military family of General Washington, and his own active and intelligent spirit, had made him thoroughly conversant with the general course and actual condition of public affairs. The views of such a mind, on the wants and exigencies of the country, could not but possess a high degree both of interest and instruction. But when the letter of a young man of twenty-three years of age is gravely represented as "the ablest and truest production on the state of the Union which appeared during the Revolution," and "as containing in embryo the existing Federal Constitution,"[1] formed seven years afterwards by the joint councils of the most experienced statesmen of America, — when we find this key-note of adulation and applause followed by a numerous school of political writers, who trace up everything of value in our institutions to the precocious wisdom or lucky inspiration of this boasted letter, — we are summoned to study it with a closer scrutiny and attention.

Freely assenting to the many and unquestion-

[1] See Life of Alexander Hamilton in "National Portrait Gallery."

able merits of the letter, in its lucid and vigorous exposition of various subjects, which the melancholy experience of the times had made but too familiar to minds of far less inherent power than that of the writer, we are yet at a loss, — looking at it in the only light in which we are now called to regard it, as a project of constitutional reform, — to understand how it can be considered as "containing in embryo" the Federal Constitution of 1787.

Unlike that constitution, and contrary to the example of the several State constitutions, as well as to the general principles of political science, instead of organizing the proposed new government into separate and independent departments, legislative, executive, and judicial, as all these authorities and examples inculcate, it sets out by vesting all power in a single body, the Congress of the United States. This feature, it is true, belonged also to the old system; but that system was repudiated by the writer as "a futile and senseless confederation."[1] Though the scheme proposed an "Executive Ministry," yet the members of that ministry were to be chosen by the Congress, and to act under its habitual direction. It invested Congress with "a complete sovereignty"; not even leaving intact to the States that control over their "internal police," which has been considered the invariable principle of all confederate governments, and is

[1] See his letter to Robert Morris.

the acknowledged law of the existing Federal Constitution.

How, too, was this "sovereign" government over the people and States of America to be introduced and established? By the absolute *fiat* of a convention appointed by the State legislatures; which convention was to have "full and plenipotentiary authority to conclude *finally*" upon the plan of government, without referring it back for the sanction of the constituent bodies. That is, the State legislatures,—for all conventions of the kind proposed were understood to proceed from them, and this especially must have been so, for it was to assemble in less than two months from the date of the proposal,—though possessing themselves but a limited and delegated authority, were to delegate to their delegates a final authority to establish a government of sovereign powers over the country, without submitting the plan to the approbation either of the people or of the State legislatures themselves. A more absolute ignoring of the only recognized source of political power in a free country it would be difficult to conceive.

These are some of the obvious criticisms to which the scheme of the letter of the 3d of September, 1780, lies open. The defects, or rather crudities, they indicate might well be excused in so young a man, however gifted, writing in the hurry of a camp, and under the bias of the summary habits of thinking and acting which an exclusive military life of some years' continuance would naturally generate. But when the speculations of the writer are held up as the oracles of the highest wisdom, which, it is asserted, ultimately shaped, and were justly entitled to shape, the institutions of the country, we have no choice but to judge them upon their intrinsic merits.

The time had not yet come for superseding the articles of confederation by a new system; even though that system had been freer from objection than the one proposed by Colonel Hamilton in the letter to Mr. Duane. When that letter was written, the accession of but one State was wanting to complete the federal bond, which united all the States in a close and indissoluble community of obligations, as well as interests. The consummation of that bond was invoked by the most reflecting minds of the nation as the "one thing needful" to place the cause of American independence beyond the danger of fatal divisions and reactions. That once completed, conjunctures, as they arose, could be improved to strengthen the bond, or to replace it, in the fulness of time, with a new and more perfect system.

An eminent statesman belonging to the same political school with Colonel Hamilton, and the selected historiographer of the struggles and vicissitudes of the Revolution, speaking of the importance of the final ratification of the articles of confederation, gives expression to the following enlightened and mature reflections:—

"Had peace been made before any agreement for a permanent union was formed, it is far from being improbable that the different parts might have fallen asunder, and a dismemberment have taken place. If the confederation really preserved the idea of union, until the good sense of the nation adopted a more efficient system, this service alone entitles that instrument to the respectful recollection of the American people, and its framers to their gratitude."[1]

The urgent necessity of some independent source of revenue, at the command of Congress, to enable them to provide for a faithful fulfilment of the national engagements, led, at an early period, to an application to the States to vest in Congress a power to levy, for the use of the United States, a duty of five per cent. on foreign merchandise imported into any of the States. A resolution to that effect was passed by Congress on the 3d day of February, 1781; and it was declared, at the same time, that "the moneys arising from the proposed duty were to be appropriated to the discharge of the principal and interest of the debts already contracted, or which may be contracted, on the faith of the United States for supporting the present war, and that the duty be continued until the said debts shall be fully and finally discharged."[2]

[1] Judge Marshall, in Life of Washington, vol. I. pp. 429, 430.
[2] Journals of Congress, vol. III. p. 573.

Mr. Madison, in his correspondence with his friends in Virginia, exerted all his influence to induce the State to comply with this application of Congress.[1] The legislature, in its hurried and agitated session at Staunton in the month of June, did not overlook this call upon its patriotism and national spirit. An act was passed granting, in the fullest manner, the power asked by Congress, with authority also to appoint collectors in the Commonwealth to demand and receive the duty. At the ensuing session in the autumn, however, it appearing that many of the States had failed to comply with the application of Congress, a new act was passed, suspending the operation of the former one until the governor should issue his proclamation announcing that the different States have passed similar laws.[2]

This proceeding of the legislature brought great annoyance and mortification to Mr. Madison, who recognized so fully the vital importance of a system of adequate and independent revenue under the control of the Union. His sentiments on the occasion were freely and strongly expressed in a letter of the 22d of January, 1782, to Mr. Edmund Randolph, now one of his colleagues in Congress, but temporarily absent on a visit to Richmond. We insert here the

[1] See particularly his letter of the 29th of May, 1781, to Judge Pendleton, in Madison Debates and Correspondence, vol. i. pp. 94–96.

[2] See Hen. Stat. vol. x. p. 451. Also idem, pp. 409, 410.

whole letter, not merely as a fit introduction to the leading part he was soon to take in pressing this great measure on the attention of Congress and the nation, but as announcing a fruitful principle, whose consequences reached farther and deeper than any measure of present policy.

"The repeal of the impost act by Virginia," he said, "is still considered as covered with some degree of mystery. Colonel Bland's representations do not remove the veil. Indeed, he seems as much astonished at it, and as unable to penetrate it, as any of us. Many have surmised that the enmity of Dr. Lee against Morris is at the bottom of it. But had that been the case, it can scarcely be supposed that the repeal would have passed so quietly. By this time, I presume you will be able to furnish me with its true history, and I ask the favor of you to do it. Virginia could never have cut off this source of public relief at a more unlucky crisis than when she is protesting her inability to comply with the continental requisitions. She will, I hope, be yet made sensible of the impropriety of the step she has taken, and make amends by a more liberal grant.

"Congress cannot abandon the plan, as long as there is a spark of hope. Nay, other plans on a like principle must be added. Justice, gratitude, our reputation abroad, and our tranquillity at home, require provision for a debt of not less than fifty millions of dollars, and I presume that this provision will not be adequately met by separate acts of the States. If there are not revenue laws, which operate at the same time through all the States, and are exempt from the control of each, the mutual jealousies, which begin already to appear among them, will assuredly defraud both our foreign and domestic creditors of their just claims.

"The deputies of the army are still here, urging the objects of their mission. Congress are thoroughly impressed with the justice of them, and are disposed to do everything which depends on them. But what can a Virginia delegate say to them, whose constituents declare that they are unable to make the necessary contributions, and unwilling to establish funds for obtaining them elsewhere?"

We shall hereafter have occasion to show the bold and manly line of statesmanship which Mr. Madison pursued on this subject. For the present, having recounted the measures adopted by Congress for the prosecution of the war, it becomes necessary to consider what had been done by them to fix the terms and conditions of peace, should negotiations be renewed for that object.

CHAPTER XI.

●

Proceedings of Congress for settling Conditions of Peace — Instructions agreed upon and Minister appointed in 1779, with Reference to Negotiations under Mediation of Spain — That Mediation proves abortive — Spain becomes a Party to the War, and Empress of Russia and Emperor of Austria offer their Mediation in 1781 — New Instructions given, and additional Ministers appointed — Motives and Policy of Instructions in submitting American Ministers to Counsels of France — Statement of Mr. Madison — England, persisting in treating United States as Subjects in a State of Rebellion, declines Preliminaries of mediating Powers — France accedes in first Instance, but, apprised of Ground taken by England, declares Inutility of proceeding till that Ground is abandoned — Debates in British Parliament upon receiving News of Surrender of Army at Yorktown — Resignation of Lord North and Dissolution of his Ministry — Administration of Lord Rockingham make vague Overtures for Peace through Sir Guy Carleton in America, and secret Agents at Paris — Mr. Madison's Views of those Overtures — Renewed Attempt to separate United States and France, indignantly repelled by both — Division in English Cabinet — Death of Lord Rockingham — New Administration under Lord Shelburne disclose Views adverse to Recognition of American Independence — Firm Declaration of Congress — Responsive Resolutions of Legislature of Virginia — Spirit of the Times as manifested in their Proceedings against Arthur Lee, Delegate in Congress, suspected of Disaffection to French Alliance.

As early as February, 1779, when the mediation of Spain, which we have already noticed, was officially communicated to Congress, a committee was appointed to consider and report on what terms the United States would be willing to terminate the war. The committee, consisting of Gouverneur Morris of New York, Mr. Burke of North Carolina, Mr. Witherspoon of New Jersey, Mr. Samuel Adams of Massachusetts, and Mr. Meriwether Smith of Virginia, reported two classes of conditions: the first admitting of no compromise, and to be considered an *ultimatum*; the other discretionary, and to be insisted on, or yielded for equivalents, according to circumstances.

In the first class were included the territorial boundaries of the United States, which were to be fixed by the ancient limits of Canada and Nova Scotia, by the River Mississippi, and the thirty-first parallel of north latitude; the right of the citizens of the United States, equally with the subjects of France and Great Britain, to take and cure fish on the banks and coast of Newfoundland; and the free navigation of the Mississippi, together with a free port on that river below the southern boundary of the United States.

These terms, affecting, in different ways and degrees, the interests of different portions of the confederacy, naturally gave rise, when brought forward as *sine qua non* and inflexible conditions of peace, to much difference of opinion; and were the subject of warm and protracted debates in Congress from the 27th of February to the 14th of August, 1779.[1] On this last day, a final draught of instructions to the minister, who should be appointed to treat of peace, was agreed upon. According to these instructions, the minister was to make it "a preliminary article to any negotiation, that Great Britain shall agree to treat with the United States as free, sovereign, and independent States": he was also to "take especial care that the independence of the said States be effectually assured and confirmed by the treaty or treaties of peace, according to the form and effect of the treaty of alliance with his Most Christian Majesty": and the territorial boundaries were to be established in substantial conformity to the demarcation laid down in the report of the committee.

These three articles were to form the ultimatum of the United States in any negotiation for peace with England. While the common right of the citizens of the United States to participate in the American fisheries was affirmed in the strongest terms, it was not made a part of the ultimatum for peace. It was referred to a commercial treaty, which the same minister was authorized to conclude, if it should be found practicable to do so, and in which an express stipulation was to be inserted that Great Britain

[1] See Secret Journals, vol. II. pp. 137-236.

should not molest or disturb the inhabitants of the United States in the rights of fishery claimed by them; with a formal declaration that any such molestation would be considered a breach of the peace, be made a common cause of all the States, and the force of the Union be exerted to obtain redress for the parties injured.

The question of the navigation of the Mississippi was, about the same time, as we have seen, made the subject of special negotiation with Spain. With regard to all other matters, the minister was instructed "to govern himself by the alliance between his Most Christian Majesty and these States, by the advice of our allies, by his knowledge of our interests, and by his own discretion, in which we repose the fullest confidence."

On the 27th day of September, six weeks after the adoption of these instructions, Mr. John Adams was appointed — not without opposition — the minister for negotiating both a treaty of peace and a treaty of commerce with Great Britain. The haughty impracticability of her councils, with regard to the remotest suggestion of the independence of her "revolted colonies" under the patronage of a foreign power, having put an end to this effort of Spain to restore peace among the belligerents, no negotiation ever took place upon the basis of the foregoing instructions.

It was not long, however, before another and

27 *

powerful mediation was proposed to bring about
the general return of peace. Spain, after the
failure of her mediation, became a party to the
war on the side of her ancient ally, France; and
in another year, the imperious conduct of England, and her open denunciation of hostilities,
added Holland also to the embattled list of her
adversaries. The flames of war thus rapidly
spreading in Europe, the "armed neutrality" of
the northern powers, headed by the Empress
Catherine,[1] and interested in the protection of
their commerce from belligerent interruptions,
determined to make one more effort for the reestablishment of peace. For that purpose, the two
imperial courts of St. Petersburg and Vienna
offered their formal mediation to the belligerents.

This mediation was officially announced to
Congress by the minister of France on the 26th
day of May, 1781. His communication was referred to a committee consisting of Mr. Carroll
of Maryland, Mr. Jones of Virginia, Mr. Witherspoon of New Jersey, Mr. Sullivan of New Hampshire, and Mr. Matthews of South Carolina. Upon
the report of the committee, various propositions
were submitted and debated with regard to the
terms on which the United States would be willing to conclude a peace under the mediation
now offered. Finally, on the 15th of June, 1781,

---

[1] By a resolution of the 5th of October, 1780, Congress formally
declared its adhesion to the principles of the "armed neutrality."

new instructions were agreed upon in Congress, by which the American minister was authorized to concur, on behalf of the United States, with his Most Christian Majesty in accepting the mediation proposed by the Empress of Russia and the Emperor of Germany; but he was expressly enjoined to accede to no treaty which should not, first, effectually secure the independence and sovereignty of the United States, according to the tenor of the treaties subsisting with France, and, secondly, in which the alliance formed by those treaties shall not be left in full force and obligation.

With regard to boundaries, and all other questions than the two above mentioned, the minister was referred to the former instructions of the 14th of August, 1779, and to certain supplemental instructions (in answer to specific inquiries) of the 18th of October, 1780, as embodying "the desires and expectations of Congress"; but it was thought unsafe, at so great a distance from the scene of negotiation, "to tie up the hands of the minister by absolute and peremptory directions upon any other subject than the two essential articles mentioned above." In the conduct of the negotiation generally, he was "to make the most candid and confidential communications upon all subjects to the ministers of our generous ally, the King of France; to undertake nothing in the negotiations for peace or truce without their knowledge and concurrence;

and ultimately to govern himself by their advice and opinion, endeavouring in his whole conduct to make them sensible how much we rely on his Majesty's influence for effectual support in everything that may be necessary to the present security or future prosperity of the United States of America."[1]

This latter clause of the instructions has been not unfrequently criticized as departing from a just sense of national dignity and self-respect, in putting the American minister in undue subjection to the wishes and advice of our ally. The persevering and insidious endeavours of the British government to undermine the fidelity of the allies to each other by proposals addressed to the separate interests, first of one and then of the other, had not unnaturally produced a certain uneasiness in the mind of the French monarch as to the possible effect of these oft repeated intrigues. It was deemed expedient to allay every jealousy of this kind by the frank and unreserved language of the instructions to the American minister; which were ordered to be communicated to the representative of France in the United States.

It is, moreover, quite certain that these instructions, with regard to the duty imposed of habitual consultations with the French government, were rendered more stringent on account of the

[1] For these proceedings, see Secret Journals of Congress, vol. II. from pp. 412–449.

unconciliating temper manifested by Mr. Adams, the sole minister then charged with the negotiations for peace on the part of the United States, and whose conduct, on one or two occasions, had given rise to much dissatisfaction in France. It was after the failure of a motion to associate other persons in the management of the negotiation with him, that the original draught of the instructions was reconsidered, and its phraseology strengthened in the clause of restriction on the minister. In the sequel, it was determined to join four other persons, — Dr. Franklin, Mr. Jay, Mr. Henry Laurens, and Mr. Jefferson, — in the commission with Mr. Adams; but the superadded restriction having then been already incorporated in the instructions, and made known to the French minister, it became awkward and embarrassing to strike it out, and a motion to do so was consequently rejected.[1]

The animadversions on this passage of our diplomatic history have, doubtless, been much tinged by a spirit of party prejudice and recrimination, engendered in subsequent political strifes. It is but a debt of justice to the body whose act, sanctioned by the votes of twenty out of twenty-eight of its members, has been thus freely arraigned, to insert here an authentic statement of the considerations which led to it, as recorded at the time by a calm observer and actor. In the diary of the proceedings and debates of

[1] See Secret Journals, *ubi supra.*

Congress kept, at that period, by Mr. Madison, he gives the following account of the adoption of the instructions, by which the negotiations for peace were submitted to the counsels of France.

"At the juncture when that measure took place, affairs were in the most deplorable situation, the Southern States being overrun and exhausted by the enemy, and the others more inclined to repose after their own fatigues, than to exert their resources for the relief of those which were the seat of war; the old paper currency had failed, and with it public credit itself, to such a degree that no new currency could be substituted; and there was then no prospect of introducing specie for the purpose, our trade being in the most ruinous condition, and the intercourse with the Havannah, in particular, unopened. In the midst of these distresses, the mediation of the two imperial courts was announced. The general idea was that the two most respectable powers of Europe would not interpose without a serious desire of peace, and without the energy requisite to effect it. The hope of peace was, therefore, mingled with an apprehension that considerable concessions might be exacted from America by the mediators, as a compensation for the essential one which Great Britain was to submit to.

"Congress, on a trial, found it impossible, from the diversity of opinions and interests, to define

any other claims than those of independence and
the alliance.   A discretionary power, therefore,
was to be delegated with regard to all other
claims.   Mr. Adams was the sole minister for
peace; he was personally at variance with the
French ministry; his judgment had not the confidence of some, nor his impartiality, in case of
an interference of claims espoused by different
quarters of the United States, the confidence of
others; a motion to associate with him two colleagues, to wit, Mr. Franklin and Mr. Jay, had
been disagreed to by Congress, the former of
these being interested, as one of the land companies,[1] in territorial claims, which had less chance
of being made good in any other way than by
a repossession of the vacant country by the British crown; the latter belonging to a State interested in such arrangements as would deprive the
United States of the navigation of the Mississippi,
and turn the Western trade through New York
— and neither of them being connected with the
Southern States.

   " The idea of having five ministers taken from
the whole Union was not suggested until the
measure had been adopted, and communicated to
the Chevalier de la Luzerne, to be forwarded to
France, when it was too late to revoke it.   It
was supposed also that Mr. Laurens, then in the
Tower, would not be out, and that Mr. Jefferson

---

[1] Dr. Franklin was one of the principal proprietors of the " Wal-
pole Grant," which was the origin of the Vandalia Land Company.

would not go, and that the greater the number
of ministers, the greater the danger of discords
and indiscretions. It was added that, as it was
expected nothing would be yielded by Great
Britain which was not extorted by the address
of France in managing the mediators, and as it
was the intention of Congress that their minister
should not oppose a peace, recommended by
them and approved by France, it would be good
policy to make the declaration to France, and,
by such a mark of confidence, to render her
friendship the more responsible for the issue." [1]

This mediation, imposing as it was, was destined to the same abortive issue which had attended the previous essay, under the auspices of Spain,
and from the same obstinate cause. The pride
and resentment of England refused to admit any
foreign intervention in the quarrel with her
"rebellious subjects"; and on that ground she
withheld her assent from the preliminary articles
which were propounded by the mediators to the
belligerent powers as the basis for opening negotiations. Though she had herself invited the
mediation, — at least that of the Emperor, — she
used the following haughty language in declining
the preliminaries: —

"On every occasion, in which there has been
a question of negotiation since the commencement of the war with France, the King has constantly declared that he could never admit, in

[1] Madison Debates, vol. I. pp. 240-243.

any manner whatever, nor under any form, that there should be any interference between foreign powers and his rebellious subjects. . . . . . This resolution is as immutable as the foundation on which it rests. From the application of this principle to the different points of the first, second, and third articles, results the melancholy but indispensable necessity of declining all that is proposed in these different articles relative to the rebellious subjects of his Majesty."

France, on the other hand, promptly gave her adhesion to the general principles of the preliminaries laid down by the mediators; but while doing so, insisted with frankness and decision upon the necessity of such an explicit understanding beforehand as to leave no doubt whatever as to the equal footing on which the American minister should be received, in the contemplated conferences, as the representative of a "free and independent nation." When apprised of the answer given by the court of London, the King of France caused his ministers to announce to the mediators that the determination of the British cabinet, still "to regard and treat the Americans as its subjects, rendered abortive every exertion for obtaining peace," and would convert the proposed deliberations, if they should proceed under such circumstances, "into a vain pretence." They then, in language of which the dignity is enhanced by its apparent sincerity, declare on behalf of their sovereign: —

"The King is truly sorry to see that things have taken a direction so contrary to his wishes, and to the expectations of their imperial Majesties; and if it were in his power to change it, he would do it with an eagerness which would show to them the purity of his intentions: but his Majesty thinks it his duty to observe that he has allies with whom he has inviolable engagements, that he should betray them by abandoning the American cause, and that he should betray this cause if he consented to negotiate a peace separate from and independent of the United States." [1]

In communicating to Congress, through Monsieur de la Luzerne, the difficulties which had arisen in the progress of the mediation, Count de Vergennes had said that the most effectual reply to the objections of the British cabinet, with regard to treating with the Colonies as an independent power, would be "a decisive victory over its armies in the ensuing campaign." The efficacious virtue of that reply, already given at Yorktown, was now to be tested. On the 27th of November, 1781, the British Parliament again assembled. The King's speech, while announcing with deep "concern" the disaster which had befallen his arms in Virginia, still appealed with earnestness to Parliament for "its firm concurrence and assistance" in the prosecution of the

---

[1] See Diplomatic Correspondence of the Revolution, vol. II. pp. 35–51. Also Secret Journals, vol. III. pp. 26–31.

contest. In the debates, however, which followed, it soon appeared from the declarations both of the prime minister, and of his second, the lord advocate for Scotland (Dundas), that a change was intended in the mode of conducting the war in America, and that the operations of the next campaign were to be limited to the retention and defence of the posts already held by them in the United States.

This first symptom of ministerial relenting gave confidence to the efforts of the opposition; and after several assaults, with varying success, a resolution moved by General Conway, "against the further prosecution of offensive war on the continent of North America," was finally carried in the House of Commons by a majority of 19, on the 27th of February, 1782. This resolution was followed up by repeated motions expressive of a want of confidence in ministers; which, though not actually carried, yet received such large and increasing votes, on each renewed trial, that at length, on the 20th of March, Lord North announced to the House the determination of himself and his colleagues to retire. Thus fell, under the rebound of the victory of Yorktown, an administration which, for twelve long years, had kept possession of power; and which, against the wishes and convictions of its ostensible head, as is now revealed, was the passive instrument of the obstinate and infatuated policy of the King towards America.

Before the dissolution of the late ministry, and apparently as a last expedient to maintain themselves in office, a bill was introduced by the attorney-general "to enable his Majesty to conclude a truce or peace with the revolted Colonies in America."[1] A new administration was formed under the auspices of the Marquis of Rockingham, he being made first Lord of the Treasury; the Earl of Shelburne and Mr. Fox, Secretaries of State; and Lord Camden, Lord John Cavendish, the Duke of Grafton, the Duke of Richmond, General Conway, Mr. Burke, and Colonel Barré, all hitherto avowed friends and champions of colonial rights, assigned distinguished places in it. One of the leading objects to which the new government was understood to be pledged was peace with America, to which the acknowledgment of its independence, if found necessary, was to be no bar.[2] Upon this last point, however, there was reason to apprehend a want of harmony in the cabinet; as it was known that Lord Shelburne, who was the representative of that portion of the Whig party which, of late years, had more particularly acknowledged the lead of Lord Chatham, sympathized in the dying protest of that great statesman against the dismemberment of the British Empire.

One of the first measures of the new adminis-

[1] Belsham's History of Great Britain, vol. VII. pp. 283-285.
[2] See Annual Register for 1782, p. 177.

tration was to give to Sir Guy Carleton, who had been appointed by the late ministry[1] to succeed Sir Henry Clinton in the command of the British army in America, and to Admiral Digby, powers to treat with Congress for the restoration of peace; and, at the same time, communications were opened with the American ministers in Europe. In this state of things, Mr. Madison, on the 14th of May, 1782, wrote from Philadelphia to his colleague Mr. Randolph, who was still in attendance on the legislature at Richmond, as follows:—

"The Ceres man-of-war, we are informed by a New York paper, arrived there in twenty-five days on the 5th instant, having on board his excellency Sir Guy Carleton, commander-in-chief, &c., and commissioner for making peace or war in North America. The intelligence brought by this conveyance is that the vibrations of power between the ministry and their rivals had terminated in the complete dissolution of the former, and organization of the latter. What change of measures will follow this change of men is yet concealed from us.

"The bill for empowering the King to conclude a peace or truce with the revolted Colonies in North America had been brought into Parliament on the 27th of March. The language of it is, at the same time, cautious and comprehensive; and seems to make eventual provision

---

[1] Annual Register for 1782, p. 167.

28 *

for our independence, without betraying any purpose of acknowledging it. The terms, peace and truce, are scarcely applicable to any other conventions than national ones; and the King is authorized to annul or suspend all acts of Parliament whatever, as far as they speak of the Colonies. He can, therefore, clearly remove any parliamentary bar to his recognition of our independence; and I know of no other bar to his treating with America on that ground

"All this, however, is very different from a real peace. The King will assuredly prefer war, as long as his ministry will stand by him; and the sentiments of his present ministry, particularly of Shelburne, are as peremptory against the dismemberment of the empire as those of any of their predecessors. They will, at least, try a campaign of negotiation against the United States, and of war against their other enemies,. before they submit to it. It is probable that the arrival of Sir Guy Carleton will not long precede an opening of the first campaign. Congress will, I am persuaded, give a proper verbal answer to any overtures with which he may insult them; but the best answer will come from the States, in such supplies of men and money as will expel him and all our other enemies from the United States."

The language of Mr. Madison was well justified by the nature of Sir Guy Carleton's commission, so far as it was disclosed in the communication addressed by that officer to General Washington, immediately after his arrival in the United States. In announcing his arrival, and appointment to the command of the British army in America, he simply transmitted copies of the resolution of the House of Commons of the 27th of February, of the address to the King in pursuance of it, and of the King's answer; together with the bill for a truce or peace, which was brought in, but had not then been passed by either House of Parliament. In these papers, the United States were still denominated "revolted Colonies"; and while a vague and indeterminate wish was intimated for a restoration of harmony with them, the motive of the proffered reconciliation was expressly avowed to be to enable England to direct her efforts with less distraction and more effect against her European enemies, — in other words, against an ally of the United States, to whom they owed the most solemn obligations of justice, honor, and gratitude, as well as of plighted faith. Overtures of such a character, studiously framed, too, in the vaguest possible language, as to the terms of reconciliation, were nothing less than insulting; and it is not surprising, therefore, that General Washington declined granting a passport for the messenger of Sir Guy Carleton to convey them to Congress, nor that Congress, when the application was made known to them by the commander-in-chief, directed him positively to refuse it.[1]

[1] Journals of Congress, vol. iv. p. 31.

It was now evident that the attempt, which had been so unblushingly made by the English commissioners in 1778, to debauch the United States from the alliance with France, and to entrap them by insidious manœuvres for a separate peace, was to be renewed. Advances of this kind had already been made to the American ministers in Europe, and repelled by them, as they deserved to be. At the same time, efforts were used to detach France from the United States by offers involving the highest advantage to her interests; but she spurned the allurement in a spirit of loyalty to her engagements which entitled her to a manly and faithful return. Every dictate of prudence and safety, as well as every sentiment of honor, forbade a separation from France in this pregnant and decisive moment. "Our business," said Mr. Madison, in writing to a friend then in communication with the legislature of Virginia, "is plain. Fidelity to our allies, and vigor in military preparations — these, and these alone, will secure us against all political devices." [1]

The legislature of Virginia very promptly announced its sentiments in a series of resolutions, unanimously adopted, of which one declared that "a proposition from the enemy to all or any of these United States for peace or truce, separate from their allies, is insidious and inadmissible"; and another pledged "the Assembly to exert the

[1] Madison Debates and Correspondence, vol. i. p. 125.

utmost power of the State to carry on the war with vigor and effect, until peace shall be obtained in a manner consistent with our national faith and federal union." [1]

Resolutions in the same unbending tone were passed, and with like promptitude and unanimity, by the legislatures of Pennsylvania, Maryland, and New Jersey; and such was soon the declared sense of the representative assemblies of almost all the States. The British commissioners, however, still continued their endeavours to operate on the sentiments of the mass of the nation. On the 2d of August, 1782, they addressed another letter to General Washington, communicating to him, by authority, intelligence of the opening of negotiations at Paris, and that Mr. Grenville, on behalf of the English government, had been directed " to propose the independence of the thirteen Colonies, in the first instance"; with the understanding, however, they added, that the loyalists should be restored by the several States to their possessions, or receive a full compensation for the confiscation of their estates.[2] This letter they caused to be immediately published.

Congress, fearing that the publication might exert an unfavorable influence on the firmness of the public mind, as well as upon the military preparations of the States, met it by the adoption

[1] Hen. Stat., vol. xi. p. 545.
[2] Sparks's Washington, vol. viii. pp. 540, 541.

of a resolution declaring that "the letter of the commissioners, as mere matter of information, was inexplicit as to the nature and extent of the independency directed to be proposed by the British plenipotentiary," and furnished no ground "on which any public measure can or ought to be taken." They therefore recommended "to the several States in the Union not to remit of their exertions for carrying on the war with vigor, as the only effectual means of securing the settlement of a safe and honorable peace."[1]

With regard to the proposal of independence by the British agent at Paris, it was soon discovered that a marked divergence of opinion had manifested itself in the councils of Lord Rockingham's administration. Mr. Fox, and those members of the cabinet who were most intimately connected with the head of the administration, were undoubtedly in favor of a frank and unequivocal acknowledgment of American independence. But Lord Shelburne and his friends, belonging to that section of the Whig party which was led by the late Earl of Chatham, could not reconcile themselves, without a long and painful struggle, to the loss of so rich and magnificent a heritage of the British crown; and in this, they represented the personal feelings and unwavering policy of the King.

Mr. Fox and Lord Shelburne, as we have seen, were the two secretaries of state in the Rocking-

[1] Journals of Congress, vol. IV. p. 60.

ham administration; one for the northern, the other for the southern department. Each of them sent an agent to Paris to enter into communication with Dr. Franklin and the Count de Vergennes on the subject of peace. Mr. Oswald was the organ of Lord Shelburne, and exceedingly guarded in his communications. Mr. Thomas Grenville appeared as the representative of Mr. Fox; and in an interview with Dr. Franklin, while yet unfurnished with his full powers to treat, said he was instructed to acknowledge the independence of the United States in the first instance, and previous to the commencement of the treaty. About this time, news was received in England of the brilliant and decisive victory achieved by Sir George Rodney over the French fleet in the West Indies under the Count de Grasse. Diplomatic delays ensued on the part of the British government, which were attributed to the effect of this unlooked-for belligerent success.

Soon after, the administration of Lord Rockingham was dissolved by the sudden death of the virtuous and high-minded nobleman at the head of it. Lord Shelburne then became first lord of the treasury; upon which Mr. Fox, Lord John Cavendish, Mr. Burke, and others of the Rockingham connection immediately resigned. In the new ministry, the younger Pitt commenced his long and brilliant official career, with the appointment of chancellor of the exchequer,

and Lord Grantham and Mr. Thomas Townsend
were made secretaries of state; while Lord Camden, General Conway, Colonel Barré, the Dukes
of Grafton and Richmond, Lord Keppel, and
others of the old Whigs, continued to hold their
places in the government. In the debates and
explanations which followed the change of administration, the new premier made no secret of
his repugnance to the acknowledgment of American independence. "His opinion still was," he
said, "as it ever had been, that whenever that
acknowledgment should be made by the British
Parliament, the sun of England's glory was set
forever."[1] It may well be conceived what sentiments, both of astonishment and distrust, were
excited in America by this declaration of the
minister, after the authorized communication made
by Sir Guy Carleton and Admiral Digby to General Washington, and the diplomatic assurances
of Mr. Grenville to Dr. Franklin at Paris.

The course of policy embraced by the new
administration seems to have been to bring
about a reunion of the Colonies with the parent
country by allowing them a wholly independent
legislature, to the entire exclusion of any authority of the British Parliament, as had been recently done in the case of Ireland, but retaining
the sovereignty of the King as the common head

[1] Belsham's History of Great
Britain, vol. VII. p. 325. See the
same declaration of Lord Shelburne cited in a letter of General
Washington written at the time.
Sparks's Washington, vol. VIII.
p. 344.

of the whole empire. The outline of this plan had been given forth by General Conway, as well as by the first lord of the treasury;[1] and hopes were entertained that, by a system of blandishment and conciliation, the people of America might be finally won over to it. All the arts of Sir Guy Carleton, with the aid of private emissaries in the different States, were employed to dispose the public mind for such a compromise; which was but a new device to break through the treaty of alliance with France, of which "the direct and essential end" was, upon its face, declared to be "the liberty, sovereignty, and independence, absolute and unlimited, of the United States."[2]

In this state of things, Congress again thought proper to interpose its warning voice; and upon the report of a committee, of which Mr. Madison was a member, (as in every proceeding, connected with the assertion of the national honor and independence, he now took a leading and most active part,) the following declaration was, on the 4th of October, 1782, unanimously adopted and published to the world: —

"It appears that the British court still flatters itself with the vain hope of prevailing on the United States to agree to some terms of dependence upon Great Britain, or at least to a separate

[1] See Diplomatic Correspondence of the American Revolution, vol. III. pp. 373–375 and 483, 484, and vol. VIII. pp. 116, 117. See also Sparks's Washington, vol. VIII. p. 328.

[2] See Article 2d of Treaty of Alliance.

of the whole empire. It ...
had been given ...
well as in the ...
hopes were entertain in ...
blandishment, in conclu... ... ed
America might ... ... by
the arts of ... ... great
private ... ...ndeav-
employed to ... ... States
compromise: ... ...create in
break through ... their pres-
of which ... ... system now
upon its face ... ...istry, whereby
eignty, and indepen... ... ...ch the force of
of the United States ...complish, they di-

In this state of ... ...is utmost vigilance
proper to inter... ... ...n he might suspect
the report of ... of the enemy, from
was a member ... ...wealth; and they in-
nected with ... of the State in Congress
and independ... opening of communications
most active ... ...minister of the English gov-
on the ... ...he subject of a peace separate
and pu... ...lly, the King of France, nor un-
It appears ... ...endence of America be, in the most
self with ... ...er, acknowledged as a preliminary
States ...
upon ...

...o resolved that all demands or appli-
the British court for the restitution

peace; and there is reason to believe that commissioners may be sent to America to offer propositions of that nature to the United States, or that secret emissaries may be employed to delude and deceive. In order, therefore, to extinguish ill-founded hopes, to frustrate insidious attempts, and to manifest to the whole world the purity of the intentions, and the fixed and unalterable determination of the United States, —

"*Resolved*, unanimously, that Congress are sincerely desirous of an honorable and permanent peace; that, as the only means of obtaining it, they will inviolably adhere to the treaty of alliance with his Most Christian Majesty, and conclude neither a separate peace nor truce with Great Britain; that they will prosecute the war with vigor until, by the blessing of God on the united arms, a peace shall be happily accomplished, by which, the full and absolute sovereignty and independence of these United States having been duly assured, their rights and interests, as well as those of their allies, shall be effectually provided for and secured."[1]

At the same time, it was declared that Congress would enter into no discussion of any overtures for peace but "in confidence and in concert with his Most Christian Majesty";[2] and, "to guard against the secret artifices and machina-

---

[1] Journals of Congress, vol. IV. pp. 84, 85.

[2] A declaration, in the same terms, had been made in the preceding month of May. See Secret Journals.

tions of the enemy," it was recommended to the respective States "to be vigilant and active in detecting and seizing British emissaries and spies," and, in general, to prohibit all intercourse between the enemy and the inhabitants of the country.

The legislature of Virginia, which assembled soon after the adoption of these resolutions by Congress, responded to them in a spirit of great energy and firmness. Declaring that an endeavour to sow dissensions between the United States and their generous ally, as well as to create in the minds of the people a dislike to their present government and rulers, was the system now plainly pursued by the British ministry, whereby it was hoped to effect that which the force of arms had not been able to accomplish, they directed the governor to use his utmost vigilance to prevent all persons, whom he might suspect of being secret emissaries of the enemy, from coming into the Commonwealth; and they instructed the delegates of the State in Congress not to consent to the opening of communications with any agent or minister of the English government, "upon the subject of a peace separate from our great ally, the King of France, nor unless the independence of America be, in the most ample manner, acknowledged as a preliminary thereto."

They also resolved that all demands or applications of the British court for the restitution of the property of the loyalists, which had been confiscated by the laws of the State, were wholly inadmissible; and they made it the duty of their delegates in Congress to move a positive instruction to the ministers, charged with the negotiations for peace, not to agree to any such restitution, nor "to submit that the laws made by any independent State of the Union be subjected to the adjudication of any power or powers on earth." These proceedings were all passed by an unanimous vote.[1]

There was another proceeding of this Assembly, so characteristic of the times and of the spirit which animated the body, that it is impossible to pass it by unnoticed. Mr. Arthur Lee was at this time one of the delegates of the State in Congress. He had been educated in England, and fixed his residence, previous to the Revolution, in London. He was among the earliest and most spirited opponents of the unconstitutional measures of the British Parliament towards America, and was the agent both of Virginia and Massachusetts in their colonial intercourse with the mother country. After the occurrence of the rupture, he was appointed by Congress a joint commissioner with Dr. Franklin and Silas Deane to negotiate treaties with the powers of Europe, and with them concluded and signed the treaties of alliance and commerce with France in 1778.

[1] See Journal of House of Delegates, October session, 1782, pp. 69, 70.

Afterwards at issue with Deane, the infirmities of his temper betrayed him into unpleasant controversies also with Dr. Franklin; and his conduct rendered him at the same time unacceptable to the French government. He returned to America in 1780, and was soon chosen a member of the legislature of Virginia. By that body he was elected, in December, 1781, one of the delegates of the State in Congress. His talents were of a high order; but notwithstanding the many and undoubted proofs he had given of his attachment to the interests and liberties of America, his unfriendliness to Dr. Franklin, and his resentment of the want of confidence in him manifested by the French government, were supposed to have produced in his mind a sentiment of disaffection to the alliance itself. The relations, moreover, of particular intimacy which he was known to have held with Lord Shelburne, and other persons of rank and consideration in England, naturally made his conduct and opinions an object of jealousy at the present moment.

A letter addressed by him to Mr. Mann Page, a member of the House of Delegates of Virginia, of which body Mr. Lee himself was also a member, (there being at that period no legal incompatibility between a seat in Congress and one in the State legislature,) was spoken of as containing highly obnoxious opinions. This led to the adoption of the following resolution:—

29 *

"That the committee of privileges and elections do inquire into the subject-matter of a letter said to have been written by Arthur Lee, Esq., a delegate of this State in Congress, to Mann Page, Esq., a member of this House, containing matter injurious to the public interests; and that the said committee do call for persons and papers for their information."

A report was made by the committee exculpating Mr. Lee, on the ground of his letter being a private and confidential one, not intended for the public eye, and because his former services placed him above the suspicion of designs inimical to the State, or America in general. A substitute, moved by Mr. Henry Tazewell, — to the effect that the sentiments contained in the letter were such as, exposed to the public eye, "might create in our allies a distrust of our representatives," and the writing of it, therefore, was not to be justified, — received the votes of a considerable number of most respectable members; but the report of the committee was finally adopted by a majority of the House. This result, however, did not produce acquiescence. A few days afterwards, a formal motion was made that Mr. Lee be. recalled from Congress; and, at the same time, information, subscribed by distinguished and responsible names, was laid before the House by a leading member in his place,' casting farther

---

[1] This member was Colonel John Francis Mercer, just chosen a delegate to Congress in the place of Mr. Edmund Randolph, resigned. See Journal of House of Delegates, October session, 1782, pp. 71, 72.

suspicions upon his political conduct and sentiments.

The sequel of the motion is thus given in a letter from Mr. Edmund Randolph to Mr. Madison of the 27th of December, 1782: —

"The attack which I hinted at in my last, as being made upon Mr. Lee, was pushed with great vigor. Upon the motion for his recall, the ayes were 39, and the noes 41. His defence was pathetic. It called upon the Assembly to remember his services, to protect his honor, and not to put it out of his power to profit his country by his labors. The failure of some of his enemies to attend alone saved him. Should Henry come to the next session, it seems impossible he should be again elected."

Nothing, perhaps, could mark more strongly the inflexible determination of the legislature of Virginia to maintain the national faith and honor, and to set at defiance every contrary device of British policy and intrigue, than this narrow escape from the stigma of its condemnation of one of its most honored servants and members, pleading, with pathetic effect, the merit of former and unquestionable services, and sustained by the all-prevailing eloquence of a brother, Richard Henry Lee, who stood at his side, and covered him with the ægis of his popularity and fame.

CHAPTER XII.

THE firm attitude and language of the public
bodies in the United States, strengthening the
hands of their representatives in Europe, at length
brought home to the British ministry the absolute conviction that, if they desired peace with
America, it was not to be had by any attempt,
open or covert, to separate her from her ally,
or upon any terms short of unqualified independence. In little more than two months after the

formation of the new ministry, a commission was issued to Mr. Oswald, empowering him to treat with any commissioners who should be appointed on behalf of "the thirteen United States of America." Mr. Fitzherbert[1] had been already sent to Paris, in the place of Mr. Grenville, with powers to treat for a general peace with France, Spain, and Holland.

The negotiations now proceeded with activity. Mr. Jay, one of the American commissioners, had arrived in Paris from Madrid several months before, and been busily engaged, in conjunction with Dr. Franklin, in discussing, both with the French government and the agents of Great Britain, some important preliminary questions connected with the treaty. Mr. Adams did not arrive from Holland,—where he had been employed in protracted negotiations, which he had just brought to a successful termination,—until the latter part of October; but was thenceforward earnestly and unremittingly associated in the labors of his colleagues. Mr. Laurens, who had been released but a few months from his confinement in the Tower, appeared yet later, and only in time to unite in the last scenes of the negotiation.[2]

---

[1] Afterwards Lord St. Helena.

[2] Mr. Laurens had, in the first instance, declined the appointment of commissioner to treat of peace; but Congress, when apprised of his non-acceptance, was induced to pass a resolution directing the secretary of foreign affairs to inform him that the motives which led to his appointment still existed, and that his services in the execution of the commission could not be dispensed with. Secret Journals, vol. III. p. 213. A day or two after the passage of this resolution, a number of the Parliamentary Register

The independence of America being now, in some sort, an agreed question, the principal matters which remained to be adjusted, were, on the part of the United States, the settlement of exterior boundaries, and the right to participate in the fisheries on the banks of Newfoundland and other banks in the North American seas. On the part of Great Britain, the question which seemed most to interest the feelings, if not the policy, of her government, was the restitution of the confiscated estates of the loyalists, or compensation for their loss; and after that, the recovery of debts due to her subjects from American citizens.

With regard to the boundaries claimed by the United States, as well as the fisheries, we have seen that neither of them was formally made a

---

was received, containing a petition which had been addressed by Mr. Laurens to the House of Commons, praying to be discharged from his confinement, and couched in terms studiously framed to propitiate the favor of those to whom it was addressed. Mr. Madison, jealous of the dignity of his country, as soon as he became satisfied of the genuineness of this paper, — the tone of which appeared to him so unbecoming the position of a representative of the United States abroad,— moved that the resolution previously adopted should not be transmitted till the further order of Congress. A disposition with many to discredit the authenticity of the paper, at the time, seems alone to have prevented the adoption of the motion.

We add with pleasure that the patriotism and vigilance which Mr. Laurens manifested after his liberation, in guarding the rights of his country against the insidious policy of the English cabinet, atoned, in Mr. Madison's estimation, for this momentary departure from the elevated bearing of an American representative — the unhappy effect, doubtless, of a long and debilitating confinement, and the derangement of health, mental and bodily, which it superinduced. See Madison Debates and Correspondence, vol. i. pp. 175–178.

part of the *ultimatum* of peace laid down in the general instructions of the 15th of June, 1781.[1] Both were; nevertheless, deemed objects of vital importance to the United States, and invariably so treated by Congress in all their deliberations.

In the original instructions of the 14th of August, 1779, the recognition of the boundaries claimed by the United States was, as we have heretofore stated, made a *sine qua non* of peace, while the fisheries were not. The latter were to be included, however, in a distinct commercial negotiation, in which the American minister was instructed "not to agree to any treaty of commerce with Great Britain, without an explicit stipulation on her part not to molest or disturb the inhabitants of the United States in the rights of fishery claimed by them."[2]

The settlement of boundaries having, against the wishes of the Southern States who were more particularly interested in that question, been pretermitted in the ultimatum for peace as fixed by the instructions of June, 1781; and the fisheries being still a *sine qua non* of a treaty of commerce under the commercial instructions given in August, 1779; which remained unrevoked; Mr. Madison, in order to restore an equitable balance between these two great sectional interests, moved, on the 29th of June, 1781, that no treaty of commerce should be made with Great

[1] Ante, pp. 256, 257.
[2] Ante, pp. 254, 255, and Secret Journals, vol. II. pp. 229-231.

Britain unless, in addition to the required stipulation in favor of the fisheries, there were stipulations also in favor of all the objects embraced in the ultimatum for peace established in August, 1779.[1]

This motion was negatived by the votes of six States out of eleven present; and the fisheries, the peculiar object of solicitude to the Northern States, were thus left in possession of the preferential footing they held under the instructions for a treaty of commerce. As the only means, then, of arriving at that impartiality which a just national sentiment demanded, Mr. Madison, a few days afterwards, (12th of July, 1781,) submitted a motion that "the commission and instructions for negotiating a treaty of commerce between these United States and Great Britain, given to the Hon. John Adams on the 29th of September, 1779, be and they are hereby revoked." This proposition was agreed to by eight out of eleven States, New Hampshire, Massachusetts, and Connecticut alone dissenting.[2]

A rightful equality being thus reëstablished, Mr. Madison had soon an opportunity of evincing the spirit of comprehensive nationality with which he was animated. He was one of a committee to which an urgent representation of the legislature of Massachusetts, pressing upon Congress

[1] See Secret Journals, vol. II. p. 458.

[2] Idem, pp. 463, 464. The date (29th of September. 1779) mentioned in the resolution was the date of the commission, but not of the instructions, which were agreed to on the 14th of August, 1779.

the expediency of embracing the fisheries in a settlement of the terms of peace, was referred. In the report of that committee, made on the 8th of January, 1782, and bearing undoubted traces of Mr. Madison's luminous pen, is a powerful argument in favor of the right of the inhabitants of the United States to participate in the fisheries, standing side by side with a conclusive vindication of the boundaries claimed by them; and the committee recommend that the American negotiators be instructed " to contend for that right as equally desired and expected by Congress with any of the other claims heretofore declared to be objects of the 'desires and expectations' of Congress." [1]

In a representation to the minister of France, prepared by another committee, of which Mr. Madison was also a leading member, and adopted by Congress on the 3d of October, 1782, the fisheries again assumed their equal rank in an enumeration of the rights claimed by the United States. In that imposing paper, the declaration is emphatically repeated that " Congress consider the territorial claims of the United States as heretofore made, their participation of the fisheries, and the free navigation of the Mississippi, not only as their indubitable rights, but as essential to their prosperity." [2]

With such repeated and unequivocal expressions of the intentions and wishes of Congress in

[1] See Secret Journals, vol. III. pp. 150–161. [2] Idem, pp. 241–243.

regard to these great objects of national interest, — enforced, too, as they had been at an
early day, by a most able letter of instructions
from the secretary of foreign affairs to one of
the negotiators for peace,[1] — the American ministers could be at no loss to understand with
what earnestness and perseverance they were to
be insisted on; although, for certain political considerations operating at the time, they had not
been formally made a part of the ultimatum for
peace. They were at length yielded by the British commissioners, and acknowledged in the provisional articles of peace agreed upon; but at
the price of a stipulation that "Congress should
earnestly recommend to the legislatures of the
respective States to provide for the restitution
of the confiscated estates of the loyalists."

This concession was in direct conflict with the
feelings and remonstrances of the States in which
such confiscations were made; and had also been
strongly deprecated by the instructions which,
from time to time, were addressed by Congress
to its plenipotentiaries. But as some stipulation
on the subject was made by the British government an indispensable condition of peace, and
the American negotiators had frankly declared
there was no power in Congress to act authoritatively in the matter, a simple recommen-

[1] Letter of Mr. R. R. Livingston to Dr. Franklin of the 7th of January, 1782, in Diplomatic Corre-
spondence of the American Revolution, vol. III. pp. 268-281.

dation of the measure by Congress to the States was finally agreed upon. There was a stipulation also that "creditors on either side should meet with no lawful impediment" to the recovery of the full value of their debts.

These provisional articles were signed by the American and British commissioners on the 30th of November, 1782, "to be inserted in and constitute a treaty of peace between the crown of Great Britain and the United States of America, when the terms of a peace should be agreed upon between Great Britain and France." They were not made known to the French government until after they had been concluded and actually signed by the negotiators; nor had the American commissioners apprised the Count de Vergennes of the successive steps and progress of the negotiation, while it was pending.

This reserve, and apparent distrust, were so contrary to the spirit which had hitherto characterized the intercourse of the two governments, and were so directly opposed to the repeated and solemn assurances of Congress that "they would hearken to no propositions for peace but in confidence and in concert with his Most Christian Majesty,"[1] that the mortification felt at a seeming departure from the pledges of the national faith was no small abatement from the general satisfaction given by the substance of the provis-

[1] See Declarations of the 31st of May and 3d of October, 1782, before referred to.

ional articles. The unpleasant sentiment thus excited was increased by the fact that a *secret* article was agreed to by the American commissioners, stipulating a more favorable northern boundary for Florida in the event of its conquest by the arms of Great Britain, than if it should remain in the possession of Spain at the termination of the war. This stipulation was not admitted into the body of the provisional articles, but formed a separate and additional article, was separately signed by the commissioners, and was concealed from the French government, even when the other articles were communicated to it.

The despatches of the American commissioners, containing the history and results of their negotiations, were received in the United States on the 11th day of March, 1783. They were laid before Congress on the 12th; and four days were occupied in reading them. The impressions produced by them in Congress are thus described by Mr. Madison in his diary of the proceedings of that body, under date of the 12th, 13th, 14th, and 15th of March:—

"These days were employed in reading the despatches brought on Wednesday morning by Captain Barney, commanding the Washington packet. They were dated from December the 4th to the 24th, from the ministers plenipotentiary for peace, with journals of preceding transactions, and were accompanied by the preliminary articles signed on the 30th of November, between the said ministers and Mr. Oswald, the British minister.

"The terms granted to America appeared to Congress, on the whole, extremely liberal. It was observed by several, however, that the stipulation obliging Congress to recommend to the States a restitution of confiscated property, although it could scarcely be understood that the States would comply, had the appearance of sacrificing the dignity of Congress to the pride of the British King.

"The separate and secret manner in which our ministers had proceeded with respect to France, and the confidential manner with respect to the British ministers, affected different members of Congress differently. Many of the most judicious members thought they had all been in some measure ensnared by the dexterity of the British minister, and particularly disapproved of the conduct of Mr. Jay in submitting to the enemy his jealousy of the French, without even the knowledge of Dr. Franklin, and of the unguarded manner in which he, Mr. Adams, and Dr. Franklin had given, in writing, sentiments unfriendly to our ally, and serving as weapons for the insidious policy of the enemy. The separate article was most offensive, being considered as obtained by Great Britain, not for the sake of the territory ceded to her, but as a means of disuniting the United States and France, as inconsistent with the spirit of the alliance, and a dishonorable departure from the candor, rectitude, and plain dealing professed by Congress.

"The dilemma in which Congress were placed was sorely felt. If they should communicate to the French minister everything, they exposed their own ministers; destroyed all confidence in them on the part of France; and might engage them in dangerous factions against Congress, which was the more to be apprehended, as the terms obtained by their management were popular in their nature. If Congress should conceal everything, and the French court should, either from the enemy or otherwise, come to the knowledge of it, all confidence would be at an end between the allies; the enemy might be encouraged to make fresh experiments, and the public safety, as well as the national honor, be endangered.

"Upon the whole, it was thought and observed by many that our ministers, particularly Mr. Jay, instead of making allowances for and affording facilities to France, in her delicate situation between Spain and the United States, had joined with the enemy in taking advantage of it to increase her perplexity; and that they had made the safety of their country depend on the sincerity of Lord Shelburne, which was suspected by all the world besides, and even by most of themselves. [See Mr. Laurens's letter, December the twenty-fourth.]

"The displeasure of the French court at the neglect of our ministers to maintain a confidential intercourse, and particularly to communicate the preliminary articles before they were signed, was not only signified to the secretary of foreign affairs, but to sundry members, by the Chevalier de la Luzerne. To the former he showed a letter from the Count de Vergennes[1] directing him to remonstrate to Congress against the conduct of the American ministers, (which a subsequent letter countermanded, alleging that Dr. Franklin had given some explanations that had been admitted); and he told Mr. Livingston that the American ministers had deceived the Count de Vergennes by telling him, a few days before the preliminary articles were signed, that the agreement on them was at a distance; that when he carried the articles signed into council, the King expressed great indignation, and asked, if the Americans served him thus before peace was made, and whilst they were begging for aids,

---

[1] A copy of this letter, dated the 19th of December, 1782, was obtained by Mr. Sparks from the French archives, and will be found in his edition of Franklin's Works, vol. IX. pp. 452-458. It is written with nobleness and dignity, and, in its whole tone and spirit, affords convincing proof of the injustice of the suspicions entertained by some of the American commissioners. It begins by saying to the minister: " You will surely be gratified, as well as myself, with the extensive advantages which our allies, the Americans, are to receive from the peace; but you certainly will not be less surprised than I have been at the conduct of the commissioners." In another part of the letter, the Count de Vergennes says if he had been willing to act as the American ministers had done, he could long ago have concluded a treaty between France and England; but he adds: " The King has been resolved that all his allies should be satisfied, being determined to continue the war, whatever advantages may be offered to him, if England is disposed to wrong any one of them."

what was to be expected after peace, &c. To several members he mentioned that the King had been surprised and displeased, and that he said he did not think he had such allies to deal with. To one of them who asked whether the court of France meant to complain to Congress, Monsieur Marbois answered that great powers never complained, but that they felt and remembered. It did not appear from any circumstances that the separate article was known to the court of France, or to the Chevalier de la Luzerne."

The part played by Mr. Jay in this diplomatic drama seems to have been a very prominent one, and exhibited strong suspicions of the integrity of the French councils. It appears from a letter addressed by him to the secretary of foreign affairs on the 18th of September, 1782, and received in the United States several months before the despatches announcing the result of the negotiation, that, viewing the conduct and conversations of the Count de Vergennes through a discoloring medium, he early took up the impression that the policy of the French government was adverse to a prompt and frank acknowledgment of the independence of the United States on the part of Great Britain. He attributed to them the Machiavelian design "of postponing an acknowledgment of our independence by England to the conclusion of a general peace, in order to keep us under their direction until not only their and our objects are attained, but also until Spain shall be gratified in her demands to exclude everybody from the Gulf of Mexico." [1]

He had had, also, some informal communications with Monsieur Rayneval, the principal secretary of Count de Vergennes, in which the secretary, expressing, as he professed to do, his "personal ideas," sought to moderate the claims of the United States with regard to Western territory. This was done, doubtless, in order to remove, as speedily as possible, all obstacles to an amicable adjustment with Spain, as well as Great Britain, and thereby to facilitate the reëstablishment of a general peace. But these communications were interpreted by Mr. Jay into a conclusive proof that the French government was hostile to, and would with all its influence oppose, the extension of the United States to the Mississippi. In like manner, an intercepted letter of Monsieur Marbois, secretary of the French legation in the United States, containing some loose speculations of the writer on the fisheries, which was placed in the hands of Mr. Jay by the British agents in Paris, was considered by him as revealing, beyond dispute, the secret but determined hostility of the French government to the American claims on that subject.

In the United States, the constant and undisguised language held by the French minister to Congress was directed to inculcate moderation in

[1] Diplomatic Correspondence of the American Revolution, vol. VIII. p. 126. See also Mr. Jay's long and elaborate letter of the 17th of November, 1782, in same volume, pp. 129-208.

our demands on all these questions; but this was
well understood to proceed from the great anxiety of France for peace, — now rendered doubly
necessary to her by her financial distresses, — as
well as from her natural desire to preserve harmony and good relations with her ancient ally,
Spain, whose pretensions, in several particulars,
unfortunately came into conflict with the just
claims of the United States. But Mr. Jay, in
the turn which his sentiments had taken, could
not view these things in the same charitable and
philosophical light.

His mind, constantly wrought upon from within
and without, saw in the most natural and ordinary occurrences "confirmation strong as proof
of holy writ" of the truth of his preconceived
suspicions. Monsieur Rayneval, about this time,
was sent over to London to ascertain, by personal communication with the British ministers,
how far the sincerity of their pacific professions
was to be relied on, and to smooth the way to
a restoration of peace by a frank understanding,
if possible, on certain points of fundamental importance. Mr. Jay was immediately "persuaded"
that the object of Monsieur Rayneval's mission
was to prejudice the American claims with the
British cabinet, to prevail upon Lord Shelburne
not to do anything which should amount to a
preliminary acknowledgment of American independence, but to enter into a compact with
France to divide the fisheries with her, and the

Western territory with Spain, to the entire exclusion of the United States from both![1] With these irritant suspicions festering·into morbid activity, he adopted the extraordinary expedient of making one of Lord Shelburne's emissaries in Paris the depositary of his confidence, and of sending him over to London, without the knowledge of his colleague, Dr. Franklin, charged with representations from himself to Lord Shelburne to countervail the suspected treachery of the French government.

An historical inquirer, whose candor and love of truth are worthy of his superior industry and judgment, and who has had free access to the diplomatic archives of both the French and British governments, and especially the confidential correspondence of Count de Vergennes and Monsieur Rayneval during the period of the suspected mission of the latter, has, in his investigations, found every one of Mr. Jay's suspicions not merely unsustained, but contradicted, by the record.[2] How monitory this lesson of the delusions

---

[1] See his letter of the 17th of November, 1782, in Diplomatic Correspondence of the American Revolution, vol. VIII. pp. 163, 164.

[2] See the note of Mr. Sparks on the letter of Mr. Jay, just referred to, Idem, 208–212. See also the strong opinion of the integrity of France, in her relations with the United States at this time, expressed by the same judicious writer, in his Life of Franklin, p. 495.

Monsieur Rayneval himself, being apprised in 1795, by Mr. Monroe, (then American minister at Paris,) of the suspicions and insinuations of which the conduct of the French government in the negotiations for peace, and especially his own mission to London in 1782, had been the subject, addressed a letter of refutation to that gentleman, which is distinguished by the apparent frankness and fulness of

to which the highest intellect is exposed, when swayed by suspicion and prejudice; and how much more to be relied on are the conclusions of a calm and dispassionate reason in the absence of all proofs, — for such was the situation of the American Congress when called to sit in judgment on these transactions, — than the rash deductions of an honest but excited mind in the full blaze of light, by which it is heated rather than illuminated, and seeing through the *mirage* of its prepossessions the objects and facts that pass under its immediate observation.

Mr. Adams's former unpleasant relations with the French government but too well disposed him to enter, heart and hand, into all the suspicions and denunciations of Mr. Jay. Dr. Franklin, while uniting with his two colleagues in the line of conduct which was ultimately pursued, did not share in the remotest degree the distrust by which they were actuated. In a letter of the 23d of July, 1783, to the secretary of foreign affairs, Mr. Livingston, he makes the following explicit disclaimer : —

"I will only add that, with respect to myself, neither the letter from Monsieur Marbois, handed us through the British negotiators, (a suspicious channel,) nor the conversations concerning the

its statements. Mr. Monroe sent a copy of the letter, shortly after its date, to Mr. Madison, among whose files it has been preserved. As still farther elucidating a most interesting passage in the early relations of France and the United States, which must continue to challenge the attention of history by its bearing on the honor of both nations, we have inserted it in the Appendix, D.

fishery, the boundaries, the royalists, &c., recommending moderation in our demands, are of weight sufficient in my mind to fix an opinion that this court wished to restrain us in obtaining any degree of advantage we could prevail on our enemies to accord; since these discourses are fairly resolvable by supposing a very natural apprehension that we, relying too much on the ability of France to continue the war in our favor, might insist on more advantages than the English would be willing to grant, and thereby lose the opportunity of making peace, so necessary to all our friends." [1]

Mr. Laurens has left, in the letter referred to in the extract before quoted from Mr. Madison's diary, an unequivocal testimony of what he thought of the relative claims of France and England, at that time, to the confidence of America. In that letter, written little more than three weeks after the signature of the provisional articles, he says : —

"It is the incessant endeavour of the British government to detach us from our ally, and it is given out in London that they have outmanoeuvred the court of France. God forbid that any future act or future supineness, on the part of the United States of America, should give the smallest degree of countenance to so dishonorable an insinuation. Every engine has been,

---

[1] See Diplomatic Correspondence of the American Revolution, vol. IV. pp. 188, 189.

every degree of craft under the mask of returning affection will be, practised for creating jealousies between the States and their good and
great ally. Through their ally's assistance and
their own virtuous perseverance, they attained to
those preliminaries; they will virtuously perse-
vere until they shall have performed every tittle of
their engagements with that ally, — against whom,
I must declare, for my own part, I see no cause
for entertaining more particular jealousies than
ought to be kept upon guard against every negotiating court in the world, nor half so much as
should, at this moment, be upon the watch against
every motion arising from our new half-friends." [1]

We must here leave Mr. Madison again to
give his appreciation of this diplomatic imbroglio.
No one was less inclined to censoriousness than
he; but in the unreserved freedom of a private
communication to a friend, he thus sententiously
summed up the parts of the different actors, as
they appeared to him.

"In this business, Jay has taken the lead, and
proceeded to a length of which you can form
little idea. Adams has followed with cordiality.
Franklin has been dragged into it. Laurens, in
his separate letter, professes a violent suspicion
of Great Britain, and good-will and confidence
towards France." [2]

The secretary of foreign affairs, to whom the

[1] Diplomatic Correspondence of
the American Revolution, vol. II.
pp. 485, 486.

[2] Letter of the 18th of March,

1783, to Edmund Randolph in
Madison Debates and Correspondence, vol. I. p. 518.

despatches received from the American ministers
had been referred, made a communication to
Congress on the 18th of March, which, — after
describing the painful dilemma to which Congress
was reduced by the secret article relative to
Florida, either of dishonoring themselves by becoming a party to the concealment, or of wound-
ing the feelings and destroying the influence of
their ministers by disclosing the article to the
French court, — recommended as the least disad-
vantageous alternative, that he be authorized to
communicate it to the French resident minister
in such manner as may best tend to obviate unfavorable impressions.[1]

In the debates which this proposition gave rise
to, Mr. Wolcott of Connecticut, Mr. Clark of New
Jersey, Mr. Arthur Lee and Mr. Bland of Virginia, Mr. Williamson of North Carolina, and Mr.
Rutledge of South Carolina, appeared as the
apologists of the ministers. In opposing the recommendation of the secretary, while none of
them absolutely justified the conduct of the ministers, all of them evinced, more or less, (Mr.
Lee, Mr. Bland, and Mr. Rutledge especially,) a
participation in the jealousies and suspicions of
France, under the influence of which Messrs. Jay
and Adams had avowedly acted.

Among those who sustained the recommendation of the secretary, Colonel Mercer of Virginia
expressed his disapprobation of the conduct of

[1] Diplomatic Correspondence of the American Revolution, vol. XI.
pp. 309–315.

364 LIFE AND TIMES OF MADISON.

the ministers in terms of strong and unqualified
censure. Colonel Alexander Hamilton, who had
taken his seat in Congress only a few months
before, as one of the delegates of New York,
urged the propriety of proceeding with coolness
and circumspection. While admitting the plausi-
bility of some of the reasons assigned for imput-
ing to France the policy of procrastinating the
definite acknowledgment of our independence by
Great Britain, the arguments in his judgment,
though strong, were not conclusive.

"Caution and vigilance," he said, "were justified by the appearance, and that alone. But
compare this policy with that of Great Britain;
survey the past cruelty and present duplicity of
her councils; behold her watching every occasion
and trying every project for dissolving the honorable ties which bind the United States to their
ally; and then say on which side our resentments
and jealousies ought to lie. With respect to the
instruction submitting our ministers to the advice of France, he had disapproved it uniformly
since it had come to his knowledge; but he had
always judged it improper to repeal it. He disapproved highly of the conduct of our ministers
in not showing the preliminary articles to our
ally before they signed them, and still more so,
of their agreeing to the separate article. This
conduct gave an advantage to the enemy, which
they would not fail to improve for the purpose
of inspiring France with indignation and distrust
of the United States."

After some other observations, he concluded that "a middle course, with respect to our ministers, was best; that they ought to be commended in general; but that the communication of the separate article ought to take place. He observed that our ministers were divided as to the policy of France, but that they all were agreed as to the necessity of being on the watch against Great Britain. He apprehended that if the ministers were to be recalled or reprehended, they would be disgusted, and head and foment parties in this country. He observed particularly, with respect to Mr. Jay, that, although he was a man of profound sagacity and pure integrity, yet he was of a suspicious temper, and that this trait might explain the extraordinary jealousies which he professed."

Mr. Wilson of Pennsylvania, whose moderation and impartiality, added to his high character for abilities and experience, gave great weight to his opinions, also took part in the discussion. Alluding to the instruction of the 15th of June, 1781, which submitted our ministers to the advice of France, he said : —

"However objectionable this step may have been in Congress, the magnanimity of our ally in declining to obtrude his advice on our ministers ought to have been a fresh motive to their confidence and respect. Although they deserve commendation in general for their services, in this respect they do not. He was of opinion

31 *

that the spirit of the treaty with France forbade the signing of the preliminary articles without her consent, and that the separate article ought to be disclosed; but as the merits of our ministers entitled them to the mildest and most delicate mode in which it could be done, he wished the communication to be left to themselves, as they would be the best judges of the explanation which ought to be made for the concealment, and their feelings would be less wounded than if it were made without their intervention."

The debate on the recommendation of the secretary of foreign affairs was closed by Mr. Madison in the following comprehensive remarks, which, in consideration of the high interest and delicacy of the questions involved, as well as of the manly frankness with which they were treated, we insert here without the omission of any part.

"He expressed his surprise at the attempts made to fix the blame of all our embarrassments on the instruction of June 15, 1781, when it appeared that no use had been made of the power given by it to the court of France; that our ministers had construed it in such a way as to leave them at full liberty; and that no one in Congress pretended to blame them on that account. For himself, he was persuaded their construction was just; the advice of France having been made a guide to them only in cases where the question respected the concessions of the United States to Great Britain necessary and proper for obtaining peace and an acknowledgment of independence, not where it respected concessions to other powers and for other purposes. He reminded Congress of the change which had taken place in our affairs since that instruction was passed, and remarked the probability that many who were now, perhaps, the loudest in disclaiming, would, under the circumstances of that period, have been the foremost to adopt it.[1] He admitted that the change of circumstances had rendered it inapplicable; but thought an express repeal of it might, at this crisis at least, have a bad effect.

"The instructions," he observed, "for disregarding which our ministers had been blamed, and which, if obeyed, would have prevented the dilemma now felt, were those which required them to act 'in concert and in confidence with our ally'; and these instructions," he said, "had been repeatedly confirmed in every stage of the Revolution, by *unanimous* votes of Congress; several of the gentlemen present,[2] who now justified our ministers, having concurred in them; and one of them[3] having penned two of the acts, in one of

---

[1] "The committee who reported the instruction were Mr. Carroll, Mr. Jones, Mr. Witherspoon, Mr. Sullivan, and Mr. Matthews. Mr. Witherspoon was particularly prominent throughout."

[2] "Messrs. Bland, Lee, and Rutledge."

[3] "Mr. Rutledge, who framed in the committee the first draught of the declaration made in September last, and the instructions about the same time. This was considerably altered, but not in that respect." [The acts here referred to are, doubtless, those of the 3d and 4th of October, 1782, which see in Secret Journals of Congress, vol. III. pp. 241 and 248. See also *supra*, p. 271.]

which Congress went farther than they had done in any preceding act, by declaring that they would not make peace until the interests of our allies and friends, as well as of the United States, should be provided for.

"As to the propriety of communicating to our ally the separate article, he thought it resulted clearly from considerations both of national honor and national security. He said that Congress, having repeatedly assured their ally that they would take no step in a negotiation but in concert and in confidence with him, and having even published to the world solemn declarations to the same effect, would, if they abetted this concealment of their ministers, be considered by all nations as devoid of all constancy and good faith, unless a breach of these assurances and declarations could be justified by an absolute necessity, or some perfidy on the part of France. It was manifest no such necessity could be pleaded.

"As to perfidy on the part of France, nothing but suspicious and equivocal circumstances had been quoted in evidence of it, and even in these it appeared that our ministers were divided; that the embarrassment in which France was placed by the interfering claims of Spain with the United States must have been foreseen by our ministers, and that the impartial public would expect that, instead of coöperating with Great Britain in taking advantage of this embarrassment, they ought to have made every allowance and given every facility to it, consistent with a regard to the rights of their country; that admitting every fact alleged by our ministers to be true, it could, by no means, be inferred that the opposition made by France to our claims was the effect of any hostile or ambitious designs against them, or any other design than that of reconciling them with those of Spain.

"The hostile aspect which the separate article, as well as the concealment of it, bore to Spain, would· be regarded by the impartial world as a dishonorable alliance with our enemies against the interests of our friends; that notwithstanding the disappointments and even indignities which the United States had received from Spain, it could neither be denied nor concealed that the former had derived many substantial advantages from her taking part in the war, and had even obtained some pecuniary aids; that the United States had made professions corresponding with those obligations; that they had testified the important light in which they considered the support resulting to their cause from the arms of Spain, by the importunity with which they had courted her alliance, by the concessions with which they had offered tó purchase it, and by the anxiety which they expressed at every appearance of her separate negotiations for a peace with the common enemy.

"That our national safety would be endan-

gered by Congress making themselves a party
to the concealment of the separate article, he
thought could be questioned by no one. No
definitive treaty of peace, he observed, had as
yet taken place; the important articles between
some of the belligerent parties had not even
been adjusted; our insidious enemy was evidently
laboring to sow dissensions among them; the in-
caution of our ministers had but too much facil-
itated them between the United States and
France; a renewal of war, therefore, in some
form or other, was still to be apprehended; and
what would be our situation if France and Spain
had no confidence in us; and what confidence
could they have, if we did not disclaim the policy
which had been followed by our ministers.

"He took notice of the intimation given by
the British minister to Mr. Adams, of an intended
expedition from New York against West Florida
as a proof of the illicit confidence into which
our ministers had been drawn, and urged the indispensable duty of Congress to communicate it
to those concerned in it. He hoped that if a
committee should be appointed — for which, however, he saw no necessity — this would be included in their report, and that their report
would be made with as little delay as possible."

The letter of the secretary of foreign affairs,
together with the despatches of the American
commissioners, and the several propositions which
had been made in the course of the debate, was

finally referred to a committee consisting of Mr. Wilson of Pennsylvania, Mr. Gorham of Massachusetts, Mr. Rutledge of South Carolina, Mr. Clark of New Jersey, and Mr. Hamilton of New York. On the 22d of, March, the committee made their report, recommending that the ministers be thanked for their zeal in negotiating the preliminary articles, that they be instructed to communicate the separate article to the court of France in such way as would best get over the concealment, and that they be informed by the secretary of foreign affairs of the wish of Congress that they had communicated the preliminary articles to the court of France before those articles had been executed.[1]

The report of the committee led to a renewal of the discussion on the conduct of the ministers in withholding a knowledge of their negotiations from the French government; and efforts were made, by motions of recommitment and postponement, to prevent any action of Congress on the subject. The receipt of intelligence, on the following day, that the preliminaries of a general peace among all the belligerents had been signed at Paris on the 20th of January preceding, favored the designs of those who were desirous of preventing any expression of opinion by Congress with regard to the conduct of the American negotiators; and so it happened in the end that there was no positive action of Congress on the report of the committee.

[1] See Madison Debates, vol. i. p. 405.

But on the 25th of March a letter was addressed by the secretary of foreign affairs to the commissioners, which may be fairly presumed to embody the deliberate sentiments of a majority of Congress on the several questions which had arisen out of the negotiation, — it being in close conformity to the report of the committee. He informs them that the preliminary articles had met with the warmest approbation of Congress, and been generally seen by the people in the most favorable point of view; that the stipulations with regard to independence, to boundaries, and the fisheries, were entirely satisfactory; so likewise was the provision for the recovery of British debts; and although the article respecting the confiscated estates of the loyalists was not likely to receive the sanction of the separate States, on whose free will its execution was expressly made to depend, yet, in agreeing to it, under the circumstances of the case and with the declaration by which they had accompanied it, there was no fault on their part, but the folly was that of the British commissioners, as well in asking as in accepting such a stipulation.

He then proceeds: "But, gentlemen, though the issue of your treaty has been successful, though I am satisfied that we are much indebted to your firmness and perseverance, to your accurate knowledge of our situation and of our wants, for this success, yet I feel no little pain at the distrust manifested in the management of it, particularly in signing the treaty without communicating it to the court of Versailles till after the signature, and in concealing the separate article from it, even when signed. I have examined with the most minute attention all the reasons assigned in your several letters to justify these suspicions. I confess they do not strike me so forcibly as they appear to have done you; and it gives me pain that the character for candor and fidelity to its engagements, which should always characterize a great people, should have been impeached thereby. The concealment was, in my opinion, absolutely unnecessary; for had the court of France disapproved the terms you had made, — after they had been agreed upon, they could not have acted so absurdly as to counteract you at that late day, and thereby put themselves in the power of an enemy who would certainly betray them, and perhaps justify you in making terms for yourselves." [1]

Such was the language of truth and candor uttered by one who was in a position to form the most competent as well as impartial judgment. The sober voice of a dispassionate posterity ratifies and confirms it. The sentiment of distrust indulged by a portion of the American negotiators was unjust alike to France and to America.[2]

[1] See Diplomatic Correspondence of the American Revolution, vol. x. pp. 129–133.

[2] A singular anachronism is sometimes committed in the discussions of this question by citing, from the interested revelations afterwards made by order of the

We look in vain through the records of history for the example of an international compact so manly and generous in its terms, so loyal and steadfast in its fulfilment, so fruitful and glorious in its consequences, as the alliance of 1778 between the ancient monarchy of the Franks and the infant republic of the Anglo-Saxon colonists of America. If the policy of weakening a powerful and haughty rival entered into the motives of France, as naturally it would do, where shall we find the instance of such important protection and support given to a State just struggling into existence, without the slightest advantage being taken, in the conditions of the alliance, of the necessities and dependence of the feebler party?

We shall certainly not find it in the case of England, who, for the support she gave to the United Provinces in their noble struggle for independence against the bloody and ferocious despotism of Spain, stipulated that all her expenses should be repaid at the conclusion of the war, and in the mean time required several of the

French Convention, certain declarations of a minister of Louis XVI., Count Montmorin, unfavorable to the consolidation and development of the power of the United States. These declarations, whatever may have been their true import, it must be recollected, were several years posterior to the time of which we are now speaking. They were probably produced, in no small degree, by the remembrance of the conduct of our ministers in the negotiations for peace, which, there is reason to believe, had made so deep an impression even upon the steady mind of Count de Vergennes as to have modified materially, after the close of the war, his long-cherished political system with regard to the relations of France and America. See Histoire de la Louisiane, par M. Marbois, p. 164.

towns and fortresses of Holland to be placed in her hands as security for the payment. France, on the contrary, in the war for American independence, — which she boldly guaranteed from the outset, along with the territorial integrity of the States, — not only bore the whole charge of her military and naval armaments, immense as they were, but in several instances made gratuitous advances for the support of the army of her ally.

Of the value and vital importance of the coöperation of France in the achievement of American independence, it would be unmanly to attempt to disguise, either from ourselves or the world, the multiplied proofs with which the authentic records of the struggle abound. Those records all conspire to show there were two things which were the indispensable conditions of success: money to supply the exhaustion of the national finances, and a naval ascendency to insure the command of the water. Both of these resources were, at the critical moment, derived from the friendship and policy of France.

Nor, in a review of the interesting relations of the two countries at so eventful an epoch in the history of both, ought we to confine ourselves to the ordinary calculations of an official state policy. However great the influence which such considerations doubtless had in ultimately determining the course of the French government, it is an unquestionable fact that in the French

nation itself there was an enthusiastic and generous sympathy with America, — bravely contending against oppression, — which reacted upon and
infused itself into the cabinet and the court.

With these recollections present to the mind,
one cannot but subscribe to the sentiment expressed at the close of the war, by the gallant
Lafayette, who bore a filial relation to both
countries. "As a Frenchman," he said, "whose
heart beats with patriotism, I am proud of the
part which France has acted, and of the alliance
she made. As an American, I freely acknowledge the obligation due to her; and in that I·
believe consists true dignity." [1]

[1] Comme un Français, dont le cœur brûle de patriotisme, je me réjouis du rôle que la France a joué, et de l'alliance qu'elle a fait. Comme Americain, je reconnais l'obligation, et je crois qu'en cela consiste la vraie dignité." Lett. to W. Carmichael in Mémoires de Lafayette, vol. II. pp. 51, 52.

Among the French contemporary writers, witnesses of the enthusiasm of their countrymen inspired by the American Revolution, Count de Segur is perhaps the one who has furnished us the most striking details. He has given particularly a lively and graphic picture of the interest and admiration which everywhere followed Franklin and his colleagues on their arrival in France. "Il serait difficile," he says, "d'exprimer avec quel empressement, avec quelle faveur furent accueillis en France, au sein d'une vieille monarchie, ces envoyés d'un peuple en insurrection contre son monarque." Their simplicity of dress, and unaffected but dignified demeanour, contrasted with the magnificence and artificial forms of Versailles and Paris, gave them, he says, "cet air antique qui semblait transporter tout-à-coup dans nos murs, au milieu de la civilisation amollie et servile du dix-huitième siécle, quelques sages contemporains de Platon, ou des républicains du temps de Caton et de Fabius"; and even before their official recognition by the government, "on voyait chaque jour accourir dans leurs maisons, avec empressement, les hommes les plus distingués de la capitale et de la cour, ainsi que tous les philosophes, les savans et les littérateurs les plus célèbres." Mémoires de Segur, vol. I. pp. 108–110.

CHAPTER XIII.

On the receipt of the intelligence that the preliminaries of a general peace had been signed between all the belligerents at Paris, — an event

32 *

on which the effect of the provisional articles between the United States and Great Britain was generally understood to be suspended, — great impatience was manifested by Congress to realize the pacific results of the arrangement. On the 24th of March, 1783, the day after the arrival of the intelligence, a resolution was passed, directing the agent of the marine to recall all armed vessels cruising under commissions from the United States. A letter was also addressed by the secretary of foreign affairs to Sir Guy Carleton and Admiral Digby, communicating to them, by authority of Congress, a copy of this resolution, and inviting corresponding measures on their part for arresting further hostilities at sea as well as on land.[1]

Congress was soon made sensible of the precipitation with which they had moved in this matter by letters from the British commanders, declining to act upon the communication made to them, until they had received official accounts and orders from home. On the 10th of April, other letters of General Carleton and Admiral Digby were laid before Congress, announcing the receipt by them of instructions from their own government for a cessation of arms, both by sea and land.[2] At the same time, a communication came from Dr. Franklin and Mr. Adams, inclos-

[1] See Madison Debates, vol. I. pp. 427, 428.

[2] For all the letters above referred to between the secretary of foreign affairs and the British commanders, see Diplomatic Correspondence of the American Revolution, vol. II. pp. 319–329.

ing a declaration which had been entered into
between them and the British minister. at Paris,
for applying to the United States the same epochs
for the suspension of hostilities that had been
agreed upon between Great Britain and France.[1]
Congress, on the following day, proclaimed in
due form a cessation of hostilities, to take effect
in conformity to that declaration.

After these proceedings, other embarrassing
questions arose, as to the true construction of
the provisional articles with regard to the time
for a mutual release of prisoners of war, and
also as to the necessity and propriety of a formal
ratification of those articles by Congress. These
questions were referred to a committee consisting of Mr. Madison, Mr. Peters of Pennsylvania,
and Colonel Hamilton. Mr. Madison and Mr.
Peters, forming a majority of the committee, were
of opinion that as there was no express provision
in the articles for their ratification, and as they
constituted merely a basis upon which a future
definitive treaty was to be concluded, which
treaty, when concluded, would require to be ratified, there was neither propriety nor necessity
for a ratification of the provisional articles. Such
a ratification, they thought also, was positively
objectionable, as it would be considered as obliging Congress to an immediate fulfilment of all
the stipulations contained in the articles, before

---

[1] See Diplomatic Correspondence of the American Revolution, vol.
x. pp. 121, 122. Also Madison Debates, vol. ı. pp. 437, 438.

there was any evidence that a corresponding obligation would be assumed by the other party.

A release of the prisoners of war held by the United States would, under these circumstances, they thought, be premature and inexpedient, and surrender an important security for the fulfilment of the stipulations entered into on the part of Great Britain.

These wise conclusions were presented to Congress in a lucid report drawn by Mr. Madison,[1] but were overruled by the prevailing impatience of the body to consummate, at once and at all hazards, the arrangements entered into for the return of peace. On the 15th of April, 1783, resolutions were passed in favor of a formal ratification of the provisional articles, and directing the agent of marine to cause the naval prisoners to be set at liberty, and the secretary of war, in conjunction with the commander-in-chief, to take measures for setting at liberty all land prisoners.[2]

Colonel Hamilton, who had dissented from the report of the committee, upon farther reflection changed his opinion as to the construction of the provisional articles respecting the release of prisoners of war, and moved on the following day a modification of the resolution which had been adopted on that subject, by varying the direction

[1] See the report, and discussion upon it, in Madison Debates, vol. L. pp. 440–443.

[2] See Journals of Congress, vol. IV. pp. 187, 188, and Secret Journals, vol. III. pp. 327–338.

to the commander-in-chief from positive and unconditional measures for setting the prisoners at liberty to "*preparatory* arrangements relative to the 7th article of the treaty."[1] The motion received the votes of a majority of the States in Congress, but not the requisite number, under the articles of confederation, to give it effect. The consequences of the improvident action of Congress, which was deprecated at the time by the good sense and sagacity of Washington,[2] were soon shown in delays and evasions in the execution of the articles on the side of Great Britain; and months yet elapsed, as we shall see,

[1] See Madison Debates, vol. I. p. 444, and Journals of Congress, vol. IV. p. 188.

[2] In a letter to Colonel Hamilton, dated the 22d of April, 1783, he says: —

"I did not receive your letter of 15th instant until after my return from Ringwood, where I had a meeting with the secretary of war, for the purpose of making arrangements for the release of our prisoners, agreeably to the resolve of Congress of the fifteenth instant. Finding a diversity of opinion respecting the treaty, and the line of conduct we ought to observe with the prisoners, I requested, in precise terms, to know from General Lincoln, (before I entered on the business,) whether we were to exercise our own judgment as to the *time*, as well as *mode*, of releasing them, or were to be confined to the latter. Being informed that we had no option in the first, Congress wishing to be eased of the expense as soon as possible, I acted solely on that ground. At the same time, I scruple not to confess to you that, if this measure was not dictated by necessity, it is, in my opinion, an impolitic one, as we place ourselves in the power of the British before the treaty is definitive." See letter in Ham. Hist. Am. Rep. vol. II. p. 510. The result was, that the British, having obtained an immediate and unconditional release of all their prisoners in the hands of the Americans, became totally careless in the execution of other stipulations on their part, and violated one of them particularly in a manner so open as to lead to a very pointed and vigorous protest from Gen. Washington to Sir Guy Carleton. See Sparks's Washington, vol. VIII. pp. 431, 432.

before the uncertainties of an armistice were terminated by a definitive treaty of peace.

The transition from war to peace, in civil convulsions especially, is often attended with as many dangers to the public liberty and safety as that from peace to war. In the case of the United States, it was rendered peculiarly difficult and critical by the distresses and unrequited sufferings of the army. We have seen the extremities of destitution and almost of famine to which, on more than one occasion, they were reduced by the want of adequate means at the disposal of Congress for their support. They had often been compelled to accept their pay in depreciated paper-money, which the necessities of their families, or their own, obliged them to part with at any sacrifice, however ruinous; and large arrearages were now due to them, for which they had received no satisfaction whatever, real or nominal.

The half-pay for life, promised to the officers by a solemn resolution of Congress, seemed likely to prove illusory, from the want of any permanent and adequate national fund to secure its payment; and the grant itself was becoming odious to many, as constituting its recipients, in their estimation, a sort of privileged class. There had always been in Congress a party morbidly jealous of the army, not even excepting from their distrust the illustrious commander-in-chief; and this party had its ramifications in some of the most powerful and influential of the States.

The suspension of all active military operations, since the first news of the opening of negotiations for peace at Paris, had given the army leisure to reflect upon its situation, and produced a corresponding uneasiness as to the destitute and impoverished condition in which it might be left at the period of its disbandment.

Under these circumstances, a meeting was held by the officers in their cantonments at Newburgh, in December, 1782, and an "address and petition," on behalf of the soldiers and themselves, was agreed upon and signed. This paper, distinguished alike by its deferential and its dignified tone, exhibited the erect spirit of freemen, conscious both of their sufferings and their deserts. It summed up, in the following impressive terms, the grounds and motives of their appeal:—

"At this period of the war, it is with peculiar pain we find ourselves constrained to address your august body on matters of a pecuniary nature. We have struggled with our difficulties year after year, under the hopes that each would be the last; but we have been disappointed. We find our embarrassments thicken so fast, and have become so complex, that many of us are unable to go further. In this exigence, we apply to Congress for relief as our head and sovereign.

"To prove that our hardships are exceedingly disproportionate to those of any other citizens of America, let a recurrence be had to the paymaster's accounts for the last four years. If to

this it should be objected that the respective
States have made settlements and given securities for the pay due for part of that time, let
the present value of those nominal obligations
be ascertained by the moneyed men, and they
will be found little indeed; and yet, trifling as
they are, many have been under the sad necessity of parting with them, to prevent their families from actually starving. We complain that
shadows have been offered to us, while the substance has been gleaned by others. Our situation compels us to search for the cause of our
extreme poverty. The citizens murmur at the
greatness of their taxes, and are astonished that
no part reaches the army. The numerous demands which are between the first collectors and
the soldiers swallow up the whole.

"Our distresses are now brought to a point.
We have borne all that men can bear,— our
property is expended, our private resources are
at an end, and our friends are wearied and disgusted with our incessant applications. We therefore most seriously and earnestly beg that a
supply of money may be forwarded to the army
as soon as possible. The uneasiness of the soldiers for the want of pay is great and dangerous; any further experiment upon their patience
may have fatal effects."

The memorialists, after mentioning the large
arrearages due to the army for deficiencies in
clothing and provisions, as well as for pay, proceed:—

"Whenever there has been a real want of means, any defect in system, or neglect in execution in the departments of the army, we have invariably been the sufferers, by hunger and nakedness and by languishing in a hospital. We beg leave to urge an immediate adjustment of all dues; that as great a part as possible be paid, and the remainder put on such a footing as will restore cheerfulness to the army, revive confidence in the justice and generosity of its constituents, and contribute to the very desirable effect of reëstablishing public credit."

With regard to the half-pay for life promised by Congress, they say: "We see with chagrin the odious point of view in which the citizens of too many of the States endeavour to place the men entitled to it. We hope, for the honor of human nature, that there are none so hardened in the sin of ingratitude as to deny the justice of the reward. We have reason to believe that the objection generally is against the mode of the reward. To prevent, therefore, any altercations and distinctions which may tend to injure that harmony which we ardently desire may reign throughout the community, we are willing to commute the half-pay pledged for full pay for a certain number of years, or for a sum in gross, as shall be agreed to by the committee sent with this address."

They then conclude their appeal in these words: "To the representation now made, the army have not a doubt that Congress will pay all that attention which the serious nature of it requires. It would be criminal in the officers to conceal the general dissatisfaction which prevails, and is gaining ground in the army, from the pressure of evils and injuries which, in the course of seven long years, have made their condition in many instances wretched. They therefore entreat that Congress, to convince the army and the world that the independence of America shall not be placed on the ruin of any particular class of her citizens, will point out a mode for immediate redress."[1]

General McDougall, Colonel Ogden, and Colonel Brooks were appointed by the meeting of officers a committee to take charge of their memorial, to present it to Congress, and to support it by their personal representations and influence. The memorial was presented on the 6th of January, 1783; and as a mark of the consideration due to both the source and the subject of it, it was referred to a grand committee, consisting of one member for each State. The grand committee appointed an early day for giving audience to the deputies of the army; when they severally entered into explanations and details with regard to the feelings and grievances of their constituents, which could not but add to the sense already felt of the extreme gravity of the con-

[1] See the memorial at length in Journals of Congress, vol. IV. pp. 206–208.

juncture.[1] A sub-committee of three members was appointed to consider and report to the grand committee the measures which it would be proper to recommend to Congress for their adoption.

Of this sub-committee, as well as of the grand committee, Mr. Madison was a member. The report made was taken up for consideration in Congress on the 24th of January; and on that and the following day resolutions were adopted, in pursuance of the recommendation of the committee, for making an immediate advance of one month's pay to the army, and declaring, in reference to the arrearages which should be found due on a settlement of accounts, that the troops, in common with the other creditors of the United States, have an undoubted right to expect that adequate and substantial funds will be obtained by Congress from the respective States, as a security for their ultimate payment.

With regard to half-pay, the committee recommended that it be left to the option of the officers to preserve their claim to half-pay for life, as provided by previous resolutions of Congress, or to accept, in lieu of it, full pay for a determinate number of years; the amount so ascertained to be paid one year after the conclusion of the war in money, or placed upon good funded security, bearing six per cent. interest. In acting upon this recommendation of the

[1] See Madison Debates, vol. I. pp. 256-259.

committee, (a difference of opinion occurring as to what number of years' full pay is the fair equivalent of half-pay for life,) the subject was referred to a special committee, upon whose report it was proposed, on the 4th of February, to fix the number of years' full pay at five and a half, — that rate of commutation being deduced from Dr. Price's Table of Annuities. This proposition was negatived; as were others indicating, severally, different rates of commutation.

It appeared that the Eastern States and New Jersey were hostile, in principle, to the promise which had been made of half-pay for life; and the validity of the act itself was even questioned, as, having passed before the completion of the articles of confederation, it was carried by a vote of less than seven States. This objection was warmly replied to by Mr. Madison, who said, —

"The act was valid, because it was decided according to the rule then in force; and that, as the officers had served under it, justice corroborated it; and he was astonished to hear those principles controverted. He was also astonished to hear objections against a commutation come from States, in compliance with whose objections against half-pay itself this expedient had been substituted."[1]

In this discordance of opinions, it was thought best to let the subject lie over for farther consideration.

[1] See Madison Debates, vol. i. p. 320.

In the mean time, the discontents of the army were daily heightened by the opposition and delays which a claim, so indisputably just in their estimation, met with in Congress. Mr. Madison records a conversation of great interest and importance which took place among half a dozen members of Congress, assembled at the house of one of them, on the 20th of February, 1783, to exchange views on some matters of critical moment then depending before Congress, and especially the situation of the army.

"Mr. Hamilton and Mr. Peters," he says, "who [having been themselves officers] had the best knowledge of the temper, transactions, and views of the army, informed the company that it was certain that the army had secretly determined not to lay down their arms until due provision and a satisfactory prospect should be afforded on the subject of their pay; that there was reason to expect a public declaration to this effect would soon be made; that plans had been agitated, if not formed, for subsisting themselves after such declaration; that, as a proof of their earnestness on this subject, the commander was already become extremely unpopular among almost all ranks, from his known dislike to every unlawful proceeding; that this unpopularity was daily increasing, and industriously promoted by many leading characters; that his choice of unfit and indiscreet persons into his family was the pretext, and with some the motive, but the substantial one a desire to displace him from the respect and confidence of the army, in order to substitute General ———— as the conductor of their efforts to obtain justice." [1]

On the 25th of February, the report of the committee on the subject of half-pay for life and the proposed commutation for it was taken up; when a motion was made by Mr. Gilman of New Hampshire, seconded by Mr. Condict of New Jersey, to refer the officers of the army to their respective States for a settlement of their claims under the provision of Congress. The proposition, though favored by the same States which had heretofore shown their hostility to the half-pay establishment, was negatived by a majority of States. On the following day, the rate of the proposed commutation was, on the question for filling the blank in the report, fixed at five years' full pay.[2] The consideration of the subject was resumed on the 28th of February; when, after another abortive effort to refer the several lines of the army to their respective States for the adjustment of the claim to half-pay, the question was finally put on agreeing to the report in favor of a commutation of five years' full pay. Seven States only voted in the affirmative; and as the articles of confederation required the as-

[1] See Madison Debates, vol. I. pp. 358, 359, and Journals of Congress, vol. IV. pp. 166, 167, and pp. 350, 351.
[2] See Madison Debates, vol. I. 168.

sent of nine, in all cases of pecuniary charge or appropriation, the question was lost.[1]

On the receipt of a communication from its deputies in Philadelphia, giving an account of these proceedings, the dissatisfaction of the army rose to a pitch of great excitement; and there were not wanting those who stood ready and eager to fan the flame. On the 10th of March, an anonymous call was circulated for a general meeting of the officers the following day, "to consider the late letter from our representatives in Philadelphia, and what measures, if any, should be adopted to obtain that redress of grievances, which they seem to have solicited in vain."

At the same time, an anonymous address was issued to the officers of the army, professing to come from a "fellow-soldier," who had shared their sufferings and was involved in a common fortune with them; presenting a highly wrought and glowing picture of their wrongs, and of the neglect and injustice with which they had been treated; calling upon them to carry their appeal from the justice to the fears of the government, and to suspect the man who would advise to more moderation and longer forbearance; — in the event of peace, not to separate from their arms until justice was done them; and should war continue, it concluded, "courting the auspices and inviting the direction of your illustrious

---

[1] Madison Debates, vol. I. pp. 365, 366, and 368, 369, and Journals, vol. IV. pp. 168, 169.

leader, you will retire to some unsettled country, smile in your turn, and 'mock when their fear cometh on.'"

There was unfortunately too much of foundation for many of the representations of fact contained in this address; and far too keen a sense of suffering and neglect in the army to render it either prudent or just for the commander-in-chief to oppose himself to any regular and proper method of setting forth their complaints. While, therefore, in general orders issued the following day, he expressed his disapprobation of the call which had been made as irregular and disorderly, he himself convened a general meeting of the officers to take place a few days later, to receive the report of their deputies to Congress, to deliberate maturely on the measures "most rational and best calculated to attain the just and important object in view," and to report, through the senior officer in rank, (who was requested to preside on the occasion,) the result of their deliberations to him.

The meeting took place on the 15th of March. General Gates, as the senior officer in rank, presided. The commander-in-chief, who had not failed to avail himself of the precious interval of four days, between the date of his general orders and the assemblage of the officers, to breathe into them individually, as far as possible, his own patriotic and magnanimous spirit, attended the meeting; and upon its opening, begged permission to address it.

After animadverting with just severity upon the arrogant and reckless tone of the anonymous address, which had denounced as an object of suspicion the man who should counsel moderation and forbearance, he spoke of his long and intimate and endearing relations to the army.

"If my conduct heretofore," he said, "has not evinced to you that I have been a faithful friend to the army, my declaration of it at this time would be equally unavailing and improper. But as I was among the first who embarked in the cause of our common country; as I have never left your side one moment, but when called from you on public business; as I have been the constant companion and witness of your distresses, and not among the last to feel and acknowledge your merits; as I have ever considered my own military reputation as inseparably connected with that of the army; as my heart has ever expanded with joy when I have heard its praises, and my indignation has arisen when the mouth of detraction has been opened against it, it can scarcely be supposed, at this last stage of the war, that I can be indifferent to its interests."

He then proceeded to demand with earnestness, "But how are those interests to be promoted? The way is plain, says the anonymous addresser. 'If war continues, remove into the unsettled country; there establish yourselves, and leave an ungrateful country to defend itself.'

But whom are they to defend? our wives, our children, our farms and other property, which we leave behind us? Or, in this state of hostile separation, are we to take the first two, (the latter cannot be removed,) to perish in a wilderness with hunger, cold and nakedness?

"'If peace takes place, never sheathe your swords,' says he, 'until you have obtained full and ample justice.' This dreadful alternative of either deserting our country in the extremest hour of her distress, or of turning our arms against her, (which is the apparent object, unless Congress can be compelled into instant compliance,) has something so shocking in it that humanity revolts at the idea. My God! what can this writer have in view by recommending such measures? Can he be a friend to the army? Can he be a friend to this country? Rather, is he not an insidious foe?—some emissary, perhaps, from New York, plotting the ruin of both by sowing the seeds of discord and separation between the civil and military powers of the continent?"

He expressed his entire conviction that it was the intention of Congress to do full justice to the claims of the army, and that they would not cease in their endeavours to provide proper funds for that object, until they had successfully accomplished it; and for himself, he solemnly and affectionately declared to the army, which he had so long had the honor to command, that " in the attainment of complete justice for all your toils and dangers, and in the gratification of every wish, so far as may be done consistently with the great duty I owe my country and those powers we are bound to respect, you may freely command my services to the utmost extent of my abilities."

He closed his address with these noble and impressive counsels : —

"Let me request you to rely on the plighted faith of your country, and to place a full confidence in the purity of the intentions of Congress that, previous to your dissolution as an army, they will cause all your accounts to be finally liquidated, as directed in the resolutions which were published to you two days ago, and that they will adopt the most effectual measures in their power to render ample justice to you for your faithful and meritorious services. And let me conjure you, in the name of our common country, as you value your own sacred honor, as you respect the rights of humanity, and as you regard the military and national character of America, to express your utmost horror and detestation of the man who wishes, under any specious pretences, to overturn the liberties of your country, and who wickedly attempts to open the floodgates of civil discord, and deluge our rising empire in blood."

Never was there presented a spectacle of greater moral sublimity than this: the war-worn chief and father of his country, casting behind him every suggestion of ambition; burying every resentment; and forgetting every wrong either to himself or his army; in the noble attitude of pleading before his discontented, but to him devoted, followers, — with the eloquent sincerity of virtue and patriotism, — the cause of civil obedience, of social order, and republican liberty! The effect was immediate and electrical.

No sooner had Washington withdrawn, than resolutions were unanimously adopted by the meeting, first returning him their thanks for his excellent address, and assuring him that "the officers reciprocate his affectionate expressions with the greatest sincerity of which the human mind is capable"; then expressing their unshaken confidence in the ultimate justice of Congress, and requesting the commander-in-chief to write to that body, earnestly entreating its most speedy decision on the subject of their claims; and finally declaring that "the officers of the American army view with abhorrence, and reject with disdain, the infamous propositions contained in the late anonymous paper addressed to them."[1]

It is difficult to decide whether this unparalleled civic victory achieved by Washington furnished the greater proof of his virtue or of his abilities. In contemplating it, the mind is irresistibly drawn to the precisely similar circumstances in the history of the parent country,

[1] See Journals of Congress, vol. IV. pp 213–215.

which, differently employed and taken advantage of, led a successful usurper to absolute power. A philosophical historian,[1] in estimating the abilities and intellectual character of the usurper, justly remarks that "to incite such an army as his to rebellion against the parliament required no uncommon art or industry. To have kept them in obedience had been the more difficult enterprise." It was this more difficult enterprise which the abilities of Washington, guided and nerved by his virtues, so gloriously accomplished.

Mr. Madison, in his diary of the proceedings of Congress, has recorded the profound impression made upon that body by the able and magnanimous conduct of the commander-in-chief. "The steps taken by the General," he says, "to avert the gathering storm, and his professions of adherence to his duty to Congress and to his country, excited the most affectionate sentiments towards him."[2] In a letter to a friend, written at the same time, he says, "the conduct of Washington does equal honor to his prudence and his virtue."[3]

On the very day, the 22d of March, that his communication transmitting the result of the meeting of the officers was received by Congress, and immediately after it was read, the report of the committee in favor of the commu-

[1] Hume.
[2] Madison Debates and Correspondence, vol. I. p. 384.
[3] Idem, p. 519.

tation of five years' full pay in lieu of half-pay
for life was taken up, and agreed to by the
requisite number of nine States.[1] The lively satisfaction of the army at this decision was a few
days afterwards communicated to Congress by
the General.[2]

Thus was dissipated, for the present, one of
the darkest and most portentous clouds that had
ever lowered over the destinies of the country.
The anxieties which it and like critical questions, pending at the same moment, produced in
the minds of Congress, are vividly portrayed in
the contemporary correspondence, and other memorials of the time. Mr. Madison, writing on
the day when the news arrived of the commo-
tions in the army, says: "This alarming intelligence from the army, added to the critical situation to which our affairs in Europe were reduced
by the variance of our ministers with our ally,
and to the difficulty of establishing the means
of fulfilling the engagements and securing the
harmony of the United States, and to the confusions apprehended from the approaching resignation of the superintendent of finance, gave
peculiar awe and solemnity to the present moment, and oppressed the minds of Congress with
an anxiety and distress, which had been scarcely
felt in any period of the Revolution."[3]

[1] Journals of Congress, vol. IV. pp. 178, 179.

[2] See Sparks's Washington, vol. VIII. p. 409.

[3] Madison Debates, vol. L pp.

384, 385. See also letter of Colonel Hamilton to General Washington, of the 17th of March, 1783.
Hist. Am. Rep. vol. II. p. 338.

In looking back to this crisis of danger and alarm, which seemed at one moment to threaten the country with the most fearful convulsions, we are led to inquire whether it had arisen naturally and spontaneously in the course of affairs, or whether factitious influences had been employed to bring it on and inflame it. Notwithstanding the hardships and sufferings of the army, and the painful delays which had taken place in the adjustment of their claims, they had hitherto shown no unreasonable distrust of Congress, but awaited with patience, and not without hope and confidence, its final action on their memorial.

But there were other parties, having large pecuniary claims against the government, who were eagerly intent to obtain from Congress and the States some definite pledge of tangible funds, to enhance the value of the evidences of public debt which they held. These parties, not possessing so much of the public sympathy, were supposed to lend themselves to the dangerous scheme of enlisting and exaggerating the discontents of the army, with the view of bringing the influence of fear, — more potent, as they thought, than that of justice, — to operate on the deliberations of Congress and of the States, in favor of a general system of funding the public debt.

Mr. Madison, in his diary of Congress, under the date of the 17th of March, 1783, the day when General Washington's letter communicating the seditious appeal to the army was received, records that, "By private letters from the army, and other circumstances, there appeared good ground for suspecting that the civil creditors were intriguing, in order to inflame the army into such desperation as would produce a general provision for the public debts."[1]

But the most important testimony on this subject is that of the commander-in-chief, whose opportunities of personal information, added to his well-known caution, must give the greatest weight to the following statement, made by him in a letter addressed on the 12th of March, 1783, to Mr. Jones, one of the delegates of Virginia in Congress : —

"My official letter to Congress of this date will inform you of what has happened in this quarter; in addition to which it may be necessary that it should be known to you and to such others as you may think proper, that the army, though very irritable on account of their long-protracted sufferings, have been apparently extremely quiet while their business was depending before Congress, until four days past. In the mean time, it should seem reports have been propagated in Philadelphia that dangerous combinations were forming in the army; and this at a time when there was not a syllable of the kind in agitation in camp.

"It also appears that upon the arrival of a

[1] Madison Debates, vol. I. p. 384.

certain gentleman from Philadelphia in camp, whose name, at present, I do not incline to mention, such sentiments as these were immediately and industriously circulated — that it was universally expected the army would not disband until they had obtained justice; that the public creditors looked up to them for redress of their grievances, would afford them every aid, and even join them in the field, if necessary; that some members of Congress wished the measure might take effect, in order to compel the public, particularly the delinquent States, to do justice; with many other suggestions of a similar nature.

"From whence, and a variety of other considerations, it is generally believed that the scheme was not only planned, but also digested and matured in Philadelphia, and that some people have been playing a double game, spreading at the camp and in Philadelphia reports, and raising jealousies, equally void of foundation until called into being by their vile artifices; for as soon as the minds of the army were thought to be prepared for the transaction, anonymous invitations were circulated, requesting a general meeting of the officers the next day. At the same time, many copies of the address to the officers of the army were scattered in every State line of it." [1]

It is not to be supposed that General Washington, — whose habitual respect for the public authorities of the country, Congress especially,

[1] Sparks's Washington, vol. VIII. pp. 393, 394.

34 *

was pushed even to a scrupulous deference,— would have hazarded statements of this kind, involving the conduct of members of Congress among others, without the most absolute conviction of their correctness. That there were members of that body who entered into the policy of bringing the discontents of the army in aid of the civil creditors of the United States, is established by contemporary proofs of unquestionable authenticity.

Colonel Alexander Hamilton, then a delegate in Congress from New York, wrote, as early as the 7th of February, 1783, to General Washington, *confidentially*, to the following effect: —

"If the war continues, it would seem that the army must, in June, subsist itself, to defend the country; if peace should take place, it will subsist itself, to do justice to itself. It appears to be a prevailing opinion in the army that the disposition to recompense their services will cease with the necessity for them, and that, if they once lay down their arms, they part with the means of obtaining justice. It is to be lamented that appearances afford too much ground for their distrust.

"It becomes a serious question, what is the true line of policy? The claims of the army, urged with moderation, but with firmness, may operate on those weak minds which are influenced by their apprehensions more than by their judgments, so as to produce a concurrence in the measures which the exigencies of affairs demand. They may add weight to the applications of Congress to the several States. So far a useful turn may be given to them. But the difficulty will be to keep a complaining and suffering army within the bounds of moderation.

"This your Excellency's influence must effect. In order to it, it will be desirable not to discountenance their endeavours to procure redress, but rather by the intervention of confidential and prudent persons, to take the direction of them. This, however, must not appear. It is of moment to the public tranquillity that your Excellency should preserve the confidence of the army, without losing that of the people. This will enable you, in case of extremity, to guide the torrent, and to bring order, perhaps even good, out of confusion. 'Tis a part which requires address, but 'tis one which your own situation, as well as the welfare of the community, points out."

In a subsequent part of the letter is the following paragraph : —

"The great desideratum, at present, is the establishment of general funds, which alone can do justice to the creditors of the United States, (of whom the army forms the most meritorious class,) restore public credit, and supply the future wants of government. This is the object of all men of sense; in this, the influence of the army, properly directed, may coöperate."[1]

[1] See letter in Ham. Hist. Am. Rep. vol. II. pp. 365-367.

To the suggestion contained in this letter, General Washington, on the 4th of March, replied with dignity and wisdom, in the following terms: —

"The just claims of the army ought, and, it is to be hoped, will have their weight with every sensible legislature in the Union, if Congress point to their demands, show (if the case be so) the reasonableness of them, and the impracticability of complying without their aid. In any other point of view, it would, in my opinion, be impolitic to introduce the army on the *tapis*, lest it should excite jealousy and bring on its concomitants."[1]

On the 12th day of March, he again wrote to Colonel Hamilton, repeating, with regard to the occurrences which had taken place in camp, all the statements contained in his letter of the same date to Mr. Jones, with the added remark, "There is something very mysterious in this business."[2]

Colonel Hamilton replied to this letter on the 17th of March, and in a postscript makes the following observations: —

"Your Excellency mentions that it has been surmised the plan in agitation was formed in Philadelphia; that combinations have been talked of between the public creditors and the army; and that members of Congress had encouraged

[1] See letter in Ham. Hist. Am. Rep. vol. II. p. 381.
[2] Idem, p. 385.

the idea. This is partly true. I have myself urged in Congress the propriety of uniting the influence of the public creditors, and the army as a part of them, to prevail upon the States to enter into their views. I have expressed the same sentiments out of doors. Several other members of Congress have done the same. The meaning, however, of all this was simply that Congress should adopt such a plan as would embrace the relief of all the public creditors, including the army, in order that the personal influence of some, the connections of others, and a sense of justice to the army, as well as the apprehension of ill consequences, might form a mass of influence in each State in favor of the measures of Congress. In this view, as I mentioned to your Excellency in a former letter, I thought the discontents of the army might be turned to good account. I am still of opinion that their earnest but respectful applications for redress will have a good effect. As to any combination of force, it would only be productive of the horrors of a civil war, might end in the ruin of the country, and would certainly end in the ruin of the army." [1]

In a subsequent letter of the 25th of March to General Washington, Colonel Hamilton farther explained his ideas as to the inexpediency and hopelessness of the army's seeking redress by force, and then adds —

[1] See letter in Ham. Hist. Am. Rep. vol. II. p. 390.

"I make these observations, not that I imagine your Excellency can want motives to continue your influence in the path of moderation; but merely to show why I cannot myself enter into the views of coercion which some gentlemen entertain; for I confess, could force avail, I should almost wish to see it employed. I have an indifferent opinion of the honesty of this country, and ill forebodings of its future system."[1]

General Washington, in a letter to Colonel Hamilton of the 4th of April, gives the *coup de grâce*, in the following emphatic terms, to every idea of making the army an instrument, in the hands of the civil creditors and their patrons, to carry through a favorite scheme of finance:—

"I will now, in strict confidence, mention a matter which may be useful for you to be informed of. It is that some men (and leading ones too) in this army are beginning to entertain suspicions that Congress, or some members of it, regardless of their past sufferings and present distress,—maugre the justice which is due to them, and the returns which a grateful people should make to men who certainly have contributed more than any other class to the establishment of national independency,—[wish to make] use of them as puppets to establish continental funds; and that rather than not succeed in this measure, or weaken their ground, they would make a sacrifice of the army and all its interests.

[1] See letter in Ham. Hist. Am. Rep. vol. II. p. 498.

"I have two reasons for mentioning this matter to you. The one is, that the army (considering the irritable state it is in, its sufferings, and composition) is a dangerous instrument to play with; the other, that every possible means consistent with their own views, (which are certainly moderate,) should be essayed to get it disbanded without delay. I might add a third; it is that the financier is suspected to be at the bottom of the scheme."[1]

By the inflexible firmness and stern integrity of Washington, proof alike against seduction and surprise, the country and the army were delivered from the dangers which impended over both.

It is deeply to be regretted that even a shade of dissatisfaction, at such a moment, should have rested upon the conduct of one who had rendered such important services to the cause of American independence as Robert Morris, the superintendent of finance. A letter of conditional resignation, which had been recently addressed by him to Congress, was interpreted by many as a menace to intimidate that body and the States into the adoption of certain plans for the benefit of the public creditors; and it detracted, for a time, from the consideration he had so justly enjoyed.

Mr. Madison was one of those who had, in the main, zealously sustained Mr. Morris's administra-

[1] See letter in Ham. Hist. Am. Rep. vol. II. pp. 449, 450.

tion; and warmly vindicated him from the assaults of two of his colleagues, Mr. Lee and Mr. Bland.[1] But when, on the reading of his conditional resignation in Congress, a motion was made, first to commit it, and then to assign a day for its consideration, as if with the wish of inducing Mr. Morris to withdraw it, Mr. Madison firmly declared that, " however anxious might be their wishes, or alarming their apprehensions, Congress could not *condescend* to solicit Mr. Morris, even if there were a prospect of the solicitation being successful."[2] Happily for his fame, no less than for the interests of the country, circumstances occurred which prevented his resignation from then taking effect.[3]

[1] Madison Debates, vol. L pp. 137, 138.

[2] Idem, pp. 274, 275.

[3] See report of interview between him and committee of Congress, on the 28th of April, 1783, in Journals of Congress, vol. IV. p. 216.

CHAPTER XIV.

It now remained for Congress to devise and mature some reliable system of revenue that would enable them to meet the national engagements, as well as to provide for the current wants of the public service. This had become an object of the highest importance, not merely to the honor, but to the very existence of the nation. Requisitions upon the States having long since proved a wholly unreliable resource, Congress, by their resolution of the 3d of February, 1781, which we have already had occasion to refer to, appealed to the several States to grant them the power to levy, for the use of the United States, a uniform duty of five per cent. upon all foreign merchandise imported into the country.

This application had been acceded to by all of the States except Rhode Island, who persisted in refusing, and Georgia, who had not yet definitively acted upon the subject. Virginia, who had promptly passed an act in full conformity with the application of Congress, afterwards suspended the operation of her act, until all the other States should notify their compliance. While Congress was endeavouring, by renewed remonstrances, to urge their application upon the non-complying States, Rhode Island especially, information was received that Virginia had at length wholly repealed her act of compliance.

There was no person to whom this intelligence could have been more painful than Mr. Madison. We have seen how early, and with how much earnestness of duty and conviction, he espoused the cause of obtaining more adequate and certain revenues for the support of the war and the faithful discharge of all the public engagements. It was an object which, in his estimation, "justice, gratitude, our reputation abroad, and our tranquillity at home," imperiously called for; and in a letter to his colleague, Mr. Randolph, of the 28th of January, 1782, when informed merely of the provisional suspension by the legislature of Virginia of their first act, he emphatically declared, "Congress cannot abandon the plan, as long as there is a spark of hope: nay, other plans, on a like principle, must be added." [1]

An elaborate answer had been prepared by a committee, of which Colonel Hamilton was chairman, to the objections brought by Rhode Island against the grant of the proposed impost; and a deputation of members was appointed by Congress to take charge of it, and, by their personal representations, to enforce upon the legislature of that State the strong motives, deduced from the public safety and honor, for her compliance. The answer was marked, in several of its features, by the peculiar and uncompromising views of its author; but it nevertheless passed without opposition. The deputation had already set out upon their mission, and had accomplished one day's journey, when, hearing of the unfavorable decision of Virginia, they returned to ask farther instructions. Notwithstanding the discouragement

[1] Ante, pp. 311-313.

produced by this new phase of the question, it was determined that they should proceed on their errand.[1]

The resolution of the 25th of January, 1783, upon the memorial of the army, having recognized their right in common with the other creditors of the United States to expect a substantial security for the payment of the debts due them, and pledged Congress to use its best efforts to obtain from the States adequate funds for that object, it was made the order of the day for the 27th to take into consideration the nature of those funds and the means of obtaining them. On that day, a wide and interesting debate took place; and a resolution was proposed in the following words — that "complete justice cannot be done to the creditors of the United States, nor the restoration of public credit be effected, nor the further exigencies of the war be provided for, but by the establishment of *general* funds to be collected by Congress."[2]

On the same day, and immediately after this proposition was made, an official notification was laid before Congress of the act of the legislature of Virginia, repealing the former act by which they granted the five per cent. impost. Among the circumstances which influenced the conduct of Virginia at this time, were, undoubt-

[1] See Madison Debates, vol. I. pp. 238, 239, and Journals of Congress, vol. IV. p. 120.

[2] Madison Debates, vol. I. pp. 284, 285.

edly, the persevering refusal of Rhode Island to concur in the grant, and also the belief gener-ally entertained by the people of Virginia that they· had already contributed more than their fair proportionate share of the expenses of the war. But the preamble to the act of repeal set forth reasons of a more comprehensive and sig-nificant character, which furnish a striking illus-tration of the jealousy of federal power then beginning to prevail, and the extreme reluctance of the States to enlarge the sphere of congres-sional authority.

It affirmed that, " Whereas, the permitting any power, other than the General Assembly of this Commonwealth, to levy duties or taxes upon the citizens of this State within the same, is injuri-ous to its sovereignty, may prove destructive of the rights and liberties of the people, and, so far as Congress might exercise the same, is contra-vening the spirit of the confederation in the eighth article thereof," — therefore the former act shall be and is repealed.[1]

The legislature here announced principles, not only opposed to the grant of a power to Con-gress to levy a five per cent. impost duty, but directly at war with any plan of general reve-nue under the control of Congress. Mr. Madi-son could not but feel how delicate his position, as a delegate of Virginia, was rendered by so sweeping a declaration of the adverse sentiments

[1] Hen. Stat. vol. XI. p. 171.

35 *

of his constituents; but his sense of the national dangers and embarrassments, and of the duty he owed to the whole country, overruled every personal consideration. In a letter to Mr. Edmund Randolph, of the 28th of January, 1783, he says:

"Such of the Virginia delegates as concur in the opinion [of the necessity and expediency of some system of general revenue] are put in a delicate situation by the preamble to the late repeal of the impost by Virginia. Persuaded as I am, however, of the truth of the proposition, and believing as I do, that, with the same knowledge of facts which my station commands, my constituents would never have passed that act, and would now rescind it, my assent will be hazarded. For many reasons, which I have not time to explain in cypher, it is my decided opinion that unless such funds be established, the foundations of our independence will be laid in injustice and dishonor, and that the advantages of the Revolution, dependent upon the federal compact, will be of short duration."

On the very day that this letter was written, Mr. Madison, in execution of his patriotic determination, delivered his sentiments in Congress at much length, and with great earnestness and ability, in support of the propriety and necessity of a system of continental revenue.

He commenced by observing that "it was needless to go into proofs of the necessity of paying the public debts. The idea of erecting our national independence on the ruins of public faith and national honor must be horrid to every mind which retained either honesty or pride." The only question was, which of the plans suggested for the ultimate discharge of the public engagements, and the support of public credit, is sufficient and reliable. He then proceeded to show that the old method of periodical requisitions on the States had been tried, and had signally failed; that there were insuperable difficulties in the way of the establishment of permanent funds by the States separately, to be applied regularly to the liquidation of the public debt; and that the only expedient that remained was some plan " of general revenue operating throughout the United States under the superintendence of Congress.

"The consequences with respect to the Union of omitting such a provision for the debts of the United States," he said, "claimed particular attention. The tenor of the memorial from Pennsylvania, and of the information just given on the floor by one of its delegates, (Mr. Fitzsimmons,) renders it extremely probable that that State would, as soon as it should be known that Congress had declined such provision, or the States rejected it, appropriate the revenue required by Congress to the payment of its own citizens and troops, creditors of the United States. The irregular conduct of other States on this subject, enforced by such an example, could not fail to

spread the evil throughout the whole continent.
What, then, would become of the confederation?
What would be the authority of Congress? What
the tie by which the States would be held together? What the source by which the army
could be subsisted and clothed? What the mode
of dividing and discharging our foreign debt?
What the rule of settling the internal accounts?
What the tribunal by which controversies among
the States could be adjudicated?

"It ought to be carefully remembered that
this subject was brought before Congress by a
very solemn appeal from the army to the justice
and gratitude of the country. Besides immediate
pay, they ask for permanent security for the arrears. Is not this request a reasonable one?
Will it be just and politic to pass over the only
adequate security that can be devised, and, instead of fulfilling the stipulations of the United
States to them, to leave them to seek their rewards from the States to which they respectively
belong? The patience of the army has been
equal to their bravery; but that patience must
have its limits, and the result of despair cannot
be foreseen, nor ought to be risked."

After adverting to the several objections alleged by the legislature of Virginia against a
system of general revenue under the control of
Congress, and answering each of those objections
in succession, Mr. Madison concluded with the
following remarks in reference to his own position,

which deserve to be borne in remembrance for
the elevated conception they convey of both the
responsibility and the self-respect belonging to
the representative character.

"The State of Virginia," he said, " as appears
by an act yesterday laid before Congress, has
withdrawn its assent once given to the impost.
This circumstance could not but produce some
embarrassment in a representative of that State
advocating the scheme — one, too, whose principles were extremely unfavorable to a disregard
of the sense of constituents. But it should not
deter him from listening to considerations which,
in the present instance, ought to prevail over it.

" One of these considerations was that, although
the delegates who compose Congress more immediately represent, and were amenable to, the
States from which they respectively come, yet in
another view they owed a fidelity to the collective interests of the whole. Secondly, although
not only the express instructions, but the declared sense of constituents, as in the present
case, were to be a law in general to their representative, still there were occasions on which
the latter ought to hazard personal consequences,
from a respect to what his clear conviction de-
termines to be the true interest of the former;
and the present he conceived to fall under this
exception. Lastly, the part he took on the present occasion was the more justifiable to his own
mind by his thorough persuasion that, with the

same knowledge of public affairs which his station commanded, the legislature of Virginia would not have repealed the law in favor of the impost, and would even now rescind the repeal."

Having thus made up his mind to meet whatever consequences might arise to himself personally from a conscientious discharge of his duty to the country, he addressed himself, with all the energies both of his understanding and his will, to perfecting' such a plan of general revenue as, while providing for the obligations of the national faith and honor, would have a reasonable prospect of obtaining the necessary assent of the States. The urgency of the crisis demanded something *practicable*, if not in every particular conformable to the rigid exactness of theoretical speculation.

The proposition which had been offered declared the "establishment of general funds, to be collected by Congress," to be indispensably necessary. Mr. Madison moved to modify it by substituting a more precise declaration, that "the establishment of permanent and adequate funds, to operate generally throughout the United States," was indispensably necessary; and in order to obtain first the sanction of Congress to the general principle, without encumbering it with a question of detail, which would probably give rise to great difference of opinion, he proposed to omit, for the present, the cumulative clause, "to be collected by Congress;" leaving that for separate and ulterior consideration.

The proposition so modified was passed in committee of the whole the following day, without opposition,[1] and on the 12th of February, was agreed to in the House by the votes of eight States; none of the States giving a collective negative, but three of them being divided in their votes.[2] Virginia was one of the divided States; Mr. Arthur Lee and Colonel Mercer voting against the proposition, and assailing it in every stage of its progress. Against their united assaults, Mr. Madison sometimes stood alone to defend it, and was made to feel, on more than one occasion, that "a man's enemies are the men of his own house."

After the adoption of the general proposition, Congress spent several days, in committee of the whole, in considering and discussing the details of some practical measure to give effect to it. The first question discussed was the expediency of submitting to the States, in a new form, the application for authority to levy imposts. This being determined in the affirmative, the sense of the body was taken, by separate and direct votes, on the mode of collecting the proposed duties, whether by officers of state or federal appointment, and also on the duration of the term for which the authority should be asked.

On the first, it was decided by a large major-

[1] See Madison Debates, vol. I. p. 304.   [2] Journals of Congress, vol. IV. p. 160.

ity of the States, (New York and Pennsylvania alone dissenting,) that the appointment of collectors should be left to the States, but when appointed, to be amenable to, and under the control of Congress; and on the second, that the power asked should be for a term of twenty-five years.[1]

Many other suggestions were thrown out and discussed in committee of the whole, pointing to other sources of revenue and modes of taxation; when the whole subject was at length, on the 21st of February, referred to a select committee, consisting of Mr. Gorham of Massachusetts, Colonel Hamilton of New York, Mr. Madison of Virginia, Mr. Fitzsimmons of Pennsylvania, and Mr. Rutledge of South Carolina.[2]

The committee was closely occupied with their difficult and important duty for several weeks. Mr. Madison desired that the plan presented by them should be a broad and comprehensive one, embracing the equitable claims and interests of all the States, so as to add to the probability of a general concurrence in the scheme which should be finally recommended. He was, therefore, in favor of including in their report, together with the best practicable arrangements for a general revenue, provisions for an equitable abatement of the quotas of such of the States as had been in possession of the enemy during any con-

[1] See Madison Debates, vol. L. pp. 333, 334, 342–7, and 347–9.   [2] Idem, p. 357, and Journals of Congress, vol. IV. pp. 165 and 174.

siderable period of the war; a reasonable allowance to others for expenses incurred by them
without the previous sanction of Congress, in
their own defence against invasion, or in military
enterprises for the common benefit; a renewed
recommendation of a liberal cession of public
lands by the individual States claiming them;
and the substitution, under certain qualifications,
of the number of inhabitants, as a rule for apportioning pecuniary burdens among the States,
in lieu of the unsatisfactory and impracticable
standard established by the articles of confederation in a valuation of the appropriated lands
within each State, and of the improvements
thereon.

Accompanying Mr. Madison's diary of the proceedings and debates of Congress, is a remarkable
paper drawn up by him at the time, exhibiting
a financial and political chart of the several
States, and showing how the interests and dispositions of each would be affected by the various
parts of his extensive and well-adjusted *projet*.[1]
This paper affords a striking illustration of the
largeness of the author's views, of his habit of
surveying a subject on every side and in all its
relations, and of his eminent talent for political
organization and construction.

On the 6th of March, the committee made
their report, embracing all the principles and
provisions above mentioned. It underwent re-

[1] See Madison Debates, vol. I. pp. 361–364.

peated discussions in Congress; parts of it were, from time to time, recommitted to the committee which brought it in; some modifications and alterations were made; and finally, on the 18th of April, 1783, the report received the sanction of Congress in all its essential and fundamental provisions, omitting only the abatements, and allowances proposed in favor of certain classes of States, which, however just and equitable in themselves, were too obnoxious to the operation of local and sectional jealousies to admit of an impartial judgment upon their merits.

The plan, thus carefully digested, and adopted upon mature deliberation, embraced the following objects: First, the grant by the States to Congress of a power to levy, for a term of twenty-five years, certain specific rates of duty on a few enumerated articles of general consumption imported from abroad, and upon all other imports a uniform duty of five per cent. These duties were to be set apart inviolably for the purpose of paying the interest or principal of the debt contracted, on the faith of the United States, for the support of the war; but as their present proceeds, it was computed, would not exceed a million of dollars,—leaving a million and a half of the annual interest of the debt to be provided for by other means,—it was proposed that the States should establish within themselves, for a term of twenty-five years also, substantial and effectual revenues of such nature as they should judge most convenient, in order to pay their respective proportions of this additional sum, which was to be faithfully applied, in like manner, to the debt contracted for the support of the war.

The officers for the collection of both descriptions of revenue, were to be appointed by the States, but to be amenable to and removable by Congress.

In farther aid of these funds, the States, claiming large bodies of unappropriated lands, were to be called on to complete the "liberal cessions" already recommended; and which, it was hoped, with the progressive increase of the revenue from imposts, and the usual requisitions upon the States, would furnish the means of extinguishing the principal of the debt at no distant day.

Finally, as the rule prescribed by the articles of confederation for apportioning the common charge among the States, according to the estimated value of all the appropriated lands within each, was scarcely susceptible of execution, or, if it were, would be productive of mutual distrust and dissatisfaction among the States, it was proposed to substitute in lieu of it a periodical census of the population, which should include the whole number of white and free inhabitants, and three fifths of all other persons. This was the origin of the compromise afterwards incorporated into the constitution of the United

States.[1] Both it and the renewed recommendation of "liberal cessions" of the public lands by

[1] The history of this question is somewhat curious, and deserves to be recalled. In the articles of confederation as originally reported by a committee to Congress, in July, 1776, the rule of apportionment proposed was the "number of inhabitants of every age, sex, and quality, except Indians not paying taxes." This rule was objected to by the Southern States as including slaves, equally with freemen, in estimating the tax-paying ability of the several States; whereas, they contended that, the labor of slaves being less productive than that of freemen, in the ratio of at least two to one, not more than one half of the slaves ought to be included in the census of inhabitants, by which the common charge was to be apportioned among all the States. This the Northern States would not consent to; and the disagreement led to the substitution, in the articles of confederation, of the value of land in lieu of the number of inhabitants, as the rule of apportionment. [See particularly what is said by Mr. Wilson of Pennsylvania, and Mr. Clark of New Jersey, in Madison Debates, vol. I. p. 422.]

During this Congress, (1783,) much time had been spent in endeavouring to devise some satisfactory mode of making a valuation of the appropriated lands in the several States, as required by the articles of confederation; but the mode at last agreed upon being liable to many and insuperable objections, the committee, charged with the preparation of a plan of revenue, determined to recommend to the States to rescind altogether the existing rule established by the confederation, and to substitute the standard of numbers, including only slaves within certain designated ages. [See Madison Debates, vol. I. pp. 376, 377.]

When the report of the committee was taken up for consideration, it was generally agreed that, instead of fixing the number of slaves to be included in the census by ages, it would be better to fix it by some certain specific ratio. It was proposed, on the 28th of March, by the committee, that two blacks should be rated as one freeman. Mr. Rutledge of South Carolina said that, in his opinion, it would be more just to rate three blacks as one freeman, though he would, in a spirit of compromise, agree to the ratio proposed by the committee. Mr. Arthur Lee declared that, in his judgment, two slaves were not equal to one freeman. Mr. Carroll of Maryland was for rating them as four to one. The representatives of the Northern States generally were for rating them as four to three. A motion was at length made to rate them as three to two, but was rejected.

Mr. Madison, then, in order to bring about a compromise among these various opinions, rose and proposed that the slaves should be

individual States, though proper adjuncts of a financial system for the confederacy, were yet more important as political provisions tending to promote the future harmony and union of the States.

Immediately after the adoption of the plan, a committee, consisting of Mr. Madison, Mr. Ellsworth, and Mr. Hamilton, was appointed to prepare an address to the States, to accompany and recommend it to their acceptance. The address was drawn by Mr. Madison. For lucid exposition, pregnant conciseness and precision, dignity, eloquence, and force, it will ever stand among the model State papers of America. After developing and explaining the various parts of the plan, with the cogent considerations of justice and policy on which they were severally founded, the address proceeds: —

rated as five to three. This proposition was carried by the votes of all the Southern States, together with Pennsylvania, New Jersey, and New Hampshire, and the blank in the report was accordingly filled with the rate of three fifths. But after the blank was so filled, a motion was made by Mr. Bland of Virginia to strike out the clause as amended, and was carried, in consequence of the loss of the vote of New York by the absence of Colonel Hamilton. This being the case, Colonel Hamilton, three days afterwards, (1st April,) moved a reconsideration of the vote of the 28th of March on Mr. Bland's motion; and upon the reconsideration, the clause which had been struck out was reinstated, with the rate of three fifths for slaves, as proposed by Mr. Madison, and in that form was finally adopted by the votes of eight States. It will be seen, therefore, that the compromise of this question, which now forms a part of the constitution of the United States, had its origin with Mr. Madison in the Congress of 1783, and not, as it has been recently attempted to show, with Colonel Hamilton. [See Madison Debates, vol. I. pp. 422–425, and 430, and Journals of Congress, vol. IV. pp. 180, and 182, 183.]

"The plan thus communicated and explained by Congress must now receive its fate from their constituents. All the objects comprised in it are conceived to be of great importance to the happiness of this confederate republic, are necessary to render the fruits of the Revolution a full reward for the blood, the toils, the cares, and the calamities which have purchased it. But the object, of which the necessity will be peculiarly felt, and which it is peculiarly the duty of Congress to inculcate, is the provision recommended for the national debt. Although this debt is greater than could have been wished, it is still less, on the whole, than could have been expected; and when referred to the cause in which it has been incurred, and compared with the burdens which wars of ambition and vainglory have entailed on other nations, it ought to be borne not only with cheerfulness, but pride."

An appeal is then made to those generous and elevated sentiments which enter into the policy of great States, no less than into the motives and conduct of wise and honorable men.

"If other motives," it says, "than that of justice could be requisite on this occasion, no nation could ever feel stronger; for to whom are the debts to be paid?

"To an ally, in the first place, who, to the exertion of his arms in support of our cause, has added the succours of his treasure; who, to his important loans, has added liberal donations;

and whose loans themselves carry the impression of his magnanimity and friendship. . . . . .

"To individuals in a foreign country, in the next place, who were the first to give so precious a token of their confidence in our justice, and of their friendship for our cause, and who are members of a republic which was second in espousing our rank among nations. . . . . .

"Another class of creditors is that illustrious and patriotic band of fellow-citizens, whose blood and whose bravery have defended the liberties of their country; who have patiently borne, among other distresses, the privation of their stipends, while the distresses of their country disabled it from bestowing them; and who, even now, ask for no more than such a portion of their dues as will enable them to retire from the field of victory and glory into the bosom of peace and private citizenship, and for such effectual security for the residue of their claims as their country is now unquestionably able to provide. For a full view of their sentiments and wishes on this subject, we transmit the paper No. 7; and as a fresh proof and lively instance of their superiority to every species of seduction from the paths of virtue and honor, we add the paper No. 8.

"The remaining class of creditors is composed partly of such of our fellow-citizens as originally lent to the public the use of their funds, or have since manifested most confidence in their country by receiving transfers from the lenders, and partly of those whose property has been either advanced or assumed for the public service. To discriminate the merits of these several descriptions of creditors would be a task equally unnecessary and invidious. If the voice of humanity plead more loudly in favor of some than of others, the voice of policy, no less than of justice, pleads in favor of all. A wise nation will never permit those who relieve the wants of their country, or who rely most on its faith, its firmness, and its resources, when either of them is distrusted, to suffer by the event."

The address concludes with the following reflections, worthy alike of the patriot, the statesman, and the enlightened friend of freedom and of mankind.

"Let it be remembered, finally, that it has ever been the pride and boast of America that the rights for which she contended were the rights of human nature. By the blessing of the Author of these rights on the means exerted for their defence, they have prevailed against all opposition, and form the basis of thirteen independent States. No instance has heretofore occurred, nor can any instance be expected hereafter to occur, in which the unadulterated forms of republican government can pretend to so fair an opportunity of justifying themselves by their fruits. In this view, the citizens of the United States are responsible for the greatest trust ever confided to a political society.

"If justice, good faith, honor, gratitude, and all the other qualities that ennoble the character of a nation, and fulfil the ends of governments, be the fruits of our establishments, the cause of liberty will acquire a dignity and lustre which it has never yet enjoyed; and an example will be set which cannot but have the most favorable influence on the rights of mankind. If, on the other side, our government should be unfortunately blotted with the reverse of these cardinal and essential virtues, the great cause which we have engaged to vindicate will be dishonored and betrayed; the last and fairest experiment in favor of the rights of human nature will be turned against them, and their patrons and friends exposed to be insulted and silenced by the votaries of tyranny and usurpation."

This great measure, carried through Congress mainly by the persevering exertions of Mr. Madison, and presented to the States by his lucid and eloquent pen, had encountered the steady, and at last almost solitary opposition of Colonel Hamilton. His objections to the plan rested chiefly on the agency assigned to the States in the appointment of the officers to be charged with the collection of the proposed revenues, and the limitation of the grant to a specific term of years. He also desired to include, with the other revenues provided for, both a land tax and a house tax to be imposed directly by the federal authority. On several of these points, his opinions were overruled by repeated votes of Congress; and when the plan, progressively matured, was finally submitted as a whole to the House, his vote was the only one, besides that of one of the delegates of Massachusetts, (Mr. Higginson,) recorded with the stereotyped negative of the Rhode Island representatives against it.[1]

The political disciples and admirers of Colonel Hamilton have made a merit of his conduct on this occasion, as marking superior wisdom and sagacity; and have, in the same degree, censured the course of Mr. Madison for concurring in measures deemed by them inconsistent with the complete efficiency of a perfect national system. Without entering into any discussion here of the relative merits of different systems, in an abstract point of view, it is sufficient, in the present connection, to recall the remark — as just as it is striking — of a celebrated and practised English statesman. "The true point of political wisdom," he says, "consists in distinguishing justly between what is absolutely best in speculation, and what is best of the things practicable in particular conjunctures."[2] The plan which received the sanction of Mr. Madison was the utmost that the prevailing jealousies of federal authority, at the time, gave any, the slightest hope of obtaining from the States; and the urgent and vital necessities of the republic demanded that something

[1] Journals of Congress, vol. IV. pp. 190, 191.   [2] Bolingbroke, Dissertation on Parties, Lett. VII.

practicable, — " the best of the things practicable " in the existing conjuncture of public affairs and public sentiment, — should be presented for adoption.[1]

Mr. Fitzsimmons, a leading delegate of Pennsylvania, a high authority on all questions of finance, and generally concurring with Colonel Hamilton's views of national policy, separated from him on this occasion; and on the 20th of March, 1783, in recording his vote against the substitute proposed by Hamilton for the plan of the committee, he declared that, " on mature reflection, he was convinced that a *complete* general revenue was unattainable from the States, was impracticable in the hands of Congress, and that the modified provision reported by the committee, if established by the States, would restore

[1] Mr. Madison himself, in the following remarks made by him in the debates on this subject, clearly defined and announced the principles of political action by which he was governed.

"For his part," he said, " although for various reasons he had wished for such a plan " (that is, as he had before said, the establishment of a permanent revenue, to be collected and applied by Congress) " as most eligible, he had never been sanguine that it was *practicable*; and the discussions which had taken place had finally satisfied him that it would be necessary to limit the call for a general revenue to duties on commerce, and to call for the deficiency in the most permanent way that could be reconciled with a revenue established within each State separately, and appropriated to the common treasury. He said the rule which he had laid down to himself in this business was, to concur in every arrangement that should appear necessary for an honorable and just fulfilment of the public engagements, and in no measure tending to augment the power of Congress, which should appear unnecessary; and particularly disclaimed the idea of perpetuating a public debt." See Madison Debates, vol. I. pp. 354, 355.

public credit among ourselves. He apprehended, however, that no limited funds would procure loans abroad, which would require funds commensurate to their duration."[1]

Washington, who had followed the deliberations of Congress on this subject with the deepest anxiety and closest attention, gave the plan finally adopted by Congress his warmest approval. In that noble circular letter which he addressed about this time to the governors and legislatures of the several States, on the occasion of the provisional disbandment of the army, (8th of June, 1783,) and which he desired should be considered as his "legacy" to the country he had so long and faithfully served, he speaks of the measure itself, and of the address by which it was explained and recommended to the States, in the following terms of cordial and emphatic praise.

"As to the second article," said he, "which respects the performance of public justice, Congress have, in their late address to the United States, almost exhausted the subject. They have explained their ideas so fully, and have enforced the obligations the States are under to render complete justice to all the public creditors with so much dignity and energy that, in my opinion, no real friend of the honor and independence of America can hesitate a single moment respecting the propriety of complying with the just and

[1] See Madison Debates, vol. I. p. 403.

honorable measures proposed. If their arguments do not produce conviction, I know of nothing that will have greater influence; especially when we recollect that the system referred to, being the result of the collective wisdom of the continent, must be esteemed, if not perfect, the least objectionable of any that could be devised; and that, if it shall not be carried into immediate execution, a national bankruptcy, with all its deplorable consequences, will take place, before any different plan can possibly be proposed and adopted. So pressing are the present circumstances, and such is the alternative now offered to the States."

Although relations of entire cordiality existed at this time between Colonel Hamilton and Mr. Madison, and continued many years afterwards, yet the characteristic differences of their political systems, both in principle and temper, began to disclose themselves to the eye of the attentive observer. The two most remarkable official papers of this critical epoch in our history proceeded from their respective pens: the answer to the Rhode Island objections to the impost, of the 16th of December, 1782, from that of Colonel Hamilton; and the address to the States, in recommendation of the revenue system of the 18th of April, 1783, as we have seen, from that of Mr. Madison.

In the former paper, we meet with high-toned and uncompromising notions of federal power, —

broad and startling doctrines of implication from powers expressly granted,—and a fond and constant recurrence to the necessity of a single directing will, with the favorite doctrines of the author respecting the beneficial influences of a public debt, and of funding systems. In the address to the States, on the other hand, we recognize the enlightened caution of a comprehensive and practical statesmanship, dealing with the conflicting elements of a mixed political system, in which the jealousies of State pride and sovereignty were to be reconciled with the necessary efficiency of a general, but not unlimited, pervading power; striving after that harmonious union and coöperation of distinct wills, which is of the essence of such a system, instead of the absolute and exclusive ascendency of a single will; and animated, in general, with that "spirit of mutual deference and concession which" the august and enlightened body that finally gave a stable constitution to the country, declared "the peculiarity of our political situation rendered indispensable."

How repugnant to the prevailing sentiment of the country were the tone and doctrines of the political creed embodied in the answer to the legislature of Rhode Island, was exemplified, in a singular manner, in the influence they exerted on the fate of the proposition of Congress before the legislature of Virginia. The answer to Rhode Island was, with other documents referred to, placed in an appendix to the address of Congress recommending their plan to the consideration of the States.   On the arrival of the address in Virginia, the sentiments of the legislature, then in session, were exceedingly favorable to the acceptance of the proposed plan; and its speedy adoption was confidently anticipated.   As time and opportunity were given, however, for the examination of the various documents which accompanied the address, a strong spirit of opposition soon manifested itself; and finally, the proposition was rejected by the votes of a large majority of the legislature.   Mr. Madison's colleague, Mr. Jones, who was a member of the body, and then attending its session in Richmond, thus announced to him the result, and the causes which led to it, in a letter bearing date the 14th of June, 1783: —

"The plan of revenue recommended by Congress has been considered in a committee of the whole; and the result is contained in the inclosed resolutions, which were agreed to without a division, the number appearing in support of the plan of Congress being so few as not to require it. Mr. Braxton and young Mr. Nelson [afterwards Judge William Nelson] only supported it. In the course of the debate, Mr. Richard Henry Lee and Mr. Charles Mynn Thruston spoke of Congress as *lusting* for power. The idea in the letter to Rhode Island, that Congress, having a right to borrow and make requisitions that were binding on the States, had a right also to concert the means for accomplishing the end, was reprobated in general as alarming and of dangerous tendency. In short, some of the sentiments in the letter to Rhode Island, though argumentative only, operated so powerfully on people's minds here that nothing could induce them to adopt the manner recommended by Congress for obtaining revenue."

In a subsequent part of the letter, recurring to the same subject, after speaking of the probable success of another measure, he says: "I entertain, however, no sanguine expectation of anything I hear in conversation, since the great majority against the plan of revenue, which, from conversations when I first arrived, I was led to believe would be adopted. Many now say the reading of the pamphlet of Congress determined them against the measure, disapproving the sentiments conveyed in the letter to Rhode Island."[1]

This result could not but be attended with deep mortification to Mr. Madison, who, in all his correspondence with his friends in Virginia, evinced the profound interest he felt in the reception of the propositions of Congress by the legislature of his own State. His feelings, on being informed of the result, were briefly expressed in a letter of the 24th of June to his friend and former colleague, Mr. Edmund Randolph.

[1] Manuscript letter of Hon. Joseph Jones to Mr. Madison, June 14, 1783.

"I was prepared," he said, "by Mr. Jones's late letters, for the fate to which the budget of Congress has been consigned; but the circumstances under which it arrived here gave peculiar pungency to the information. I wish that those who abuse Congress and baffle their measures may as much promote the public good as they profess to intend. I am sure they will not do it more effectually than is intended by some, at least, of those who promote the measures of Congress."

But this mortification and disappointment were happily of short duration. The legislature, when they reassembled a few months afterwards, had recovered from the unfavorable impressions which had their origin mainly in collateral and extrinsic circumstances; and promptly passed an act for giving effect to the most important part of the recommendations of Congress.[1] They thus signalized their loyalty to the obligations of national faith and honor, and at the same time justified the manly independence of their representative, who had so boldly and nobly risked himself for the right in opposition to temporary prejudice and delusion.

NOTE.

In a late publication, entitled, "History of the American Republic, &c., by J. C. Hamilton," (see vol. II. pp. 398, 399,) a reckless charge is made against Mr. Madison, of falsifying his reports of the proceedings of the Congress of 1782–3, with the special view of misrepresenting the votes and opinions of Colonel Hamilton in that body. Could even the most prejudiced and embittered mind suppose Mr.

[1] Hen. Stat. vol. XI. pp. 350–352.

Madison capable of so great a baseness, it could hardly be imagined that he would perpetrate the low and paltry crime without an adequate motive. But at the time when the reports in question were taken, and many years afterwards, as is shown by their correspondence, the most friendly personal relations, and, on some points, a cordial political coöperation, existed between Mr. Madison and Colonel Hamilton. It cannot fail to be remarked also that, in most of the instances in which these falsifications, with the intent to misrepresent Colonel Hamilton, are charged, nothing is imputed to him but what would render his conduct more meritorious, according to the views and opinions entertained by the reporter, and where, too, by the evidence furnished by the reporter, no credit could be gained to himself at the expense of Colonel Hamilton.

Take, for example, Mr. Madison's report of the proceedings on the proposition for the establishment of permanent and adequate general funds, in which he is accused of designing, by a false report, to place himself in *priority* of time to Colonel Hamilton in the suggestion of that proposition. It will be seen that Mr. Madison, in his " Debates," records the fact that the *principle* of the proposition was embodied in a report on the claims of the army made by Colonel Hamilton, and adopted by Congress three days before his own motion [Madison Debates, vol. I. pp. 275-280]; and again, the " Debates " show the declaration of Mr. Wilson, the mover of the proposition which was modified by Mr. Madison, that he had been led to bring forward his proposition by the previous action of Congress in favor of Colonel Hamilton's report. [Idem, p. 299.]

That Mr. Madison has given a most faithful and accurate account of the successive phases and modifications through which the proposition was developed into the form in which it was finally adopted by Congress, is abundantly proved by the very minuteness of his report, day after day, of the proceedings upon it; if, indeed, the intrinsic voucher of his own high and unassailable character could be supposed to stand in need of collateral support.

It is nothing to the purpose to say, as the writer in question does, that the journals show no such resolution as that either of Mr. Wilson or Mr. Madison. It is well known that the general rule pursued in keeping the journals of the old Congress was not to record propositions until they were definitively acted upon in the House, and to take no note whatever of proceedings in committee of the whole. The journals show, in conformity to Mr. Madison's statement, that on the 29th of January, 1783, Congress resolved itself into a committee of the whole to consider the most effectual means of restoring and supporting public credit, and that the motion then before the House was referred to the committee. [Journals of Congress, vol. IV. p. 153.] It was in that committee that the proposition of Mr. Wilson, as new modelled by Mr. Madison, was acted upon and adopted [see Madison Debates, vol. I. pp. 302–304]; and on the 12th day of February following, it was taken up for consideration in the House, and there passed, as the journals show, in the precise form in which it is reported by Mr. Madison as having been agreed to in committee of the whole on the 29th of January. [Journals of Congress, vol. IV. p. 160.]

The writer referred to alleges, in contradiction of Mr. Madison's contemporaneous report, that the motion attributed by Mr. Madison to Mr. Wilson was, in fact, offered by Colonel Hamilton, without any other proof of his assertion than a copy of a resolution taken, he says, from an autograph of Colonel Hamilton in the archives of the department of state. Even if the resolution in the handwriting of Colonel Hamilton corresponded exactly with the proposition which, Mr. Madison positively states, was introduced by Mr. Wilson, it would, by no means, prove that Colonel Hamilton, and not Mr. Wilson, *offered* it; but the resolution produced is shown by comparison not to be identical, either with the proposition of Mr. Wilson or that finally adopted by Congress. It differs from the motion of Mr. Wilson by the introduction of a clause which, according to Mr. Madison's report, was added on the motion of Mr. Gorham, [Madison Debates, vol. I. pp. 285, 286,] and from the resolution as adopted by Congress in other and various respects.

These are in themselves matters of small importance, and would be altogether unworthy of the notice we have bestowed upon them, but for the use that has been attempted to be made of them to bolster up a charge of falsehood and misrepresentation against Mr. Madison.

With regard to the proceedings of Congress in endeavouring to devise some satisfactory mode of arriving at a valuation of lands in the respective States as a basis of federal assessments, (the subject of another charge against Mr. Madison of misrepresenting Colonel Hamilton in his reports of the debates of Congress,) it is shown by incontrovertible facts that Colonel Hamilton and Mr. Madison agreed in their opinions of the futility of those proceedings. They voted together against the abortive project that was adopted by a majority of Congress; and they also united in support of a new and different rule of apportionment which was very soon afterwards recommended to the States. [See Journals of Congress, vol. IV. pp. 163, 164, and 182,

183.] If both he and Colonel Hamilton threw out tentative propositions, neither of which was adopted, what possible motive could Mr.
Madison have had for attributing to Colonel Hamilton any suggestion
of that kind which he did not in reality make ? On the main point of
the impracticability of establishing a reliable valuation of lands in the
several States, let the reader refer to the strong language of Colonel
Hamilton's letter to the governor of New York on the subject, [see it
in History of the American Republic, vol. II. pp. 369–376,] and then
say what ground there is for the charge brought against Mr. Madison
of misrepresenting and misstating the opinions of Colonel Hamilton in
that regard.

There is one other instance in which this charge of falsification is
brought against Mr. Madison, which we will briefly notice, and then
dismiss the revolting theme. It relates to the proceedings of a grand
committee of Congress, on the 7th of December, 1782, on the subject
of compounding with the holders of the old depreciated continental
paper money. It appears that all the members of the committee, with
the exception of Mr. Carroll of Maryland, were agreed on the principle of some indemnification ; and that the only question was, as to
the rate of depreciation at which the emissions should be redeemed.

Various rates were proposed ; among others, 1 for 40, that being
the rate at which Congress, by their resolution of the 18th of March,
1780, allowed the States to pay in their quotas to the federal treasury.
That resolution, which was itself denounced at the time as a gross
breach of the public faith, was insisted upon by some as pledging the
public faith, in all future time, to redemption at the specified rate. On
the other hand, it was regarded simply as recognising and fixing the
actual rate of depreciation at which, about the period of the resolution,
the money had passed in ordinary transactions of business. But since
that time, it had passed at far lower rates of depreciation, till it had
ceased to circulate, and finally sunk almost to nothing. Under this
view of the subject, but a single vote was given in favor of 1 for 40.

Other rates were then put to the vote,—1 for 75, 1 for 100, and 1
for 150. Mr. Madison, in reporting the votes given in grand committee on these several rates, represents Colonel Hamilton and Mr. Fitzsimmons as voting in favor of 1 for 100,—he himself not voting for
any of the rates proposed, as " in many cases the money had changed
hands at a value far below any rate that had been named." [Madison
Debates, vol. I. pp. 226–228.]

This writer, so lavish in his criminations of Mr. Madison, boldly pro-
nounces the foregoing statement of the proceedings of the grand com-

mittee to be "incorrect in all its parts," though he produces no statement of what those proceedings were; and he charges that the "object" of the statement was "to represent Hamilton as voting in favor of a breach of faith." [History of the American Republic, vol. II. pp. 353–356.] Now, it is obvious to remark that, in the view of the reporter, there was no breach of faith in the vote imputed to Hamilton; and the greater the rate of depreciation for which Hamilton had voted, the more praiseworthy the reporter would have considered the vote, as protecting the public from the effect of unconscionable, if not fraudulent, speculations.

The writer, finding from the journals that Congress acted on the subject of depreciation on the 7th of January, 1783, arbitrarily and gratuitously confounds the proceedings of the House with the proceedings of the grand committee, and then accuses Mr. Madison of "altering" the date of those proceedings from the 7th of January to the 7th of December, and of representing the proceedings as having taken place in grand committee instead of the House, in order "to give color to his alteration of the date," and to escape the danger of contradiction by the journals, as he elsewhere says. [History of the American Republic, vol. II. p. 399.]

It certainly does not follow as a matter of course, because the House acted on the report of the grand committee on the 7th of January, as the journals show, that the grand committee did not meet and deliberate on the subject of their report on the 7th of December preceding, as Mr. Madison states. The grand committee met also on the 24th of December; and all the various rates of depreciation proposed at their previous meeting having then successively failed, it was finally agreed, at the last meeting, to report in favor of 1 for 40. [See Madison Debates, vol. I. p. 239.]

But upon the coming in of the report, Mr. Madison states, the chair decided that, according to rule, the blank should not have been filled up by the committee; and so the rate was expunged. This, doubtless, led to the motion made by Colonel Hamilton in the House, when the report of the committee was taken up for consideration on the 7th of January, to fill the blank with the word "forty," that having been the final vote of the committee. The motion received the votes of only three States out of the twelve present, Colonel Hamilton's own State being divided [Journals of Congress, vol. IV. p. 142]; and if the rejection of 1 for 40 was a breach of public faith, as the writer alleges, it certainly met with a very large sanction for an act of national dishonor.

But the final and conclusive argument triumphantly brought forward by the writer against the truth of Mr. Madison's report is, that "Colonel Hamilton was not a member of the committee, and consequently could not have given the vote imputed to him by Madison, or any other vote." In support of this assertion, the writer refers to the Journal of Congress, which, in giving an account of the action of the body on the report of the grand committee on the 7th of January, professes to enumerate the names of the members of whom the committee consisted, and does not include among them that of Colonel Hamilton.

The journal, in this enumeration, is evidently governed by the list of those who originally composed the committee, which had been raised during the preceding Congress. That Colonel Hamilton was subsequently put upon the committee, and was a member of it at the time to which Mr. Madison's statement relates, is sufficiently shown by other facts appearing upon the journal, as well as by the positive averment of Mr. Madison. A grand committee consisted, as its title imports, of a member from each State. Mr. Duane was the member of the committee originally taken from New York, and his name appears as such among those given in the journal. The journal, however, shows that he and his colleague, Mr. L'Hommedieu, obtained formal leave of absence from Congress on the 27th of November, 1782, and that he did not resume his seat until the 16th day of July, 1783. [See Journals of Congress, vol. IV. pp. 110 and 239.]

Some one must have been taken from New York to supply the place left vacant in the grand committee by his absence; and who so likely to be chosen for the vacancy as Colonel Hamilton? He came in, with a distinguished reputation, as a member of the new Congress that commenced its term the first Monday in November, 1782, and took his seat in the body on the 25th of that month. Mr. Floyd, who took his seat two days later, was the only other member from New York present for several months after the departure of Messrs. Duane and L'Hommedieu.

It is in the same manner that Mr. Madison became a member of the grand committee. His name does not appear among those enumerated in the journal, any more than that of Colonel Hamilton. The member there mentioned as being upon the grand committee from Virginia was Mr. Arthur Lee. But it is shown by the journal that he obtained leave of absence on the 4th of October, 1782, and did not return until the 16th day of July, 1783, the day of Mr. Duane's return. Mr. Madison was, doubtless, put in his place, though no entry either of his appointment or of that of Colonel Hamilton, appears upon the journal;

which was kept, as is well known to all who have had occasion to look into our early congressional history, in a very loose and imperfect manner. If the silence of the journal is to be regarded as of any weight, it proves that no persons whatever were appointed to supply the places of Mr. Lee and Mr. Duane on the grand committee, for there is mention of none : but that is a supposition wholly inadmissible.

We have thus, once for all, and with a revulsion of feeling which it is difficult to describe, noticed charges of the grossest and most offensive nature against one of the purest and most elevated characters that ever adorned humanity, — one " whose pure and spotless virtue," a great contemporary, who knew him well, has said, " no calumny has ever attempted to sully." We would fain indulge the hope that we might have spared ourselves this unwelcome task ; for who that cherishes the national reputation, who that has the slightest faith in the principles of truth and honor in the human breast, can seriously believe that one who had so long and so conspicuously enjoyed the respect and veneration of his countrymen in places of the highest trust, could ever have been capable of the acts of baseness and falsehood with which he is now charged by a solitary accuser ?

CHAPTER XV.

Questions in Congress growing out of Cession of Northwest Territory by Virginia — Influence of Land Companies — Geographical and political Combinations against the Claims of Virginia — Letters of Mr. Madison with Regard to them — Proceedings and Report of the Committee to which the Subject was referred — Attempt to set up adverse Title in New York — Researches and Labors of Mr. Madison in Defence of Virginia Title — Alliance between Adversaries of the territorial Rights of Virginia and Partisans of the Independence of Vermont — Mr. Madison's Account of the State of Parties in Congress on these two Questions — He predicts the ultimate Acceptance of the Terms of Virginia, if the State remain firm and prudent — Mr. Witherspoon's Resolutions — New Committee appointed to consider Cession of Virginia — Remonstrance of New Jersey — Design of Adversaries of Virginia to limit her Western Boundary, if possible, to the Alleghany Mountains — Final Compromise, and Acceptance of the Cession by Congress — Influence of Mr. Madison in accomplishing the Result — History of Vermont Question — Proceedings of Congress upon it — New York and New Hampshire resist Claim of Vermont to be considered an independent State — Views of Mr. Madison on the Subject — Powerful Combination of Interests in Congress favorable to Independence of Vermont, and her Admission as a State into the Confederacy — Acts of Violence committed by her Authorities prevent Consummation of the Plan — Compelled to await the regular Exercise of the Power granted by the Constitution of 1788, before she is finally admitted into the Union.

AMONG the important subjects which occupied the attention of Congress at this time, few were attended with more complications, or exercised a more sensible influence on the reciprocal interests and relations of the States than the questions which grew out of the cession of her northwestern territory by Virginia. We have seen what jealousies had been excited in many of the States by the great extent of the limits of Virginia, as defined by her charter; and that, to quiet those jealousies, and to promote harmony and union, she had, on the 2d day of January, 1781, proffered to Congress a cession of the whole of the territory claimed by her northwest of the river Ohio, embracing what are now five of the most prosperous and powerful States of the Union.

To this munificent donation were annexed such conditions as appeared to her plainly just and equitable. Among them were the following: that she should be reimbursed the expenses incurred by her in conquering and defending the ceded territory during the war; that the French and other inhabitants, who had professed themselves citizens of Virginia, should be protected in the enjoyment of their rights and property; that Colonel George Rogers Clarke, and the officers and soldiers who accompanied him in the expedition by which the British posts in that country were reduced, should have a certain quantity of land laid off for them, in fulfilment of the promises made to them by Virginia; and also, if the quantity of good lands on the southeast side of the Ohio, which had been set apart by Virginia for her troops on continental and State establishment, should prove insufficient to satisfy their legal bounties, the deficiency was to be made up to them in good lands to be laid off between the Scioto and the Miami on the northwest side of the Ohio.

To these provisions of a special nature, were added stipulations of a more general character, which equally concerned the interests of all the States; to wit, that the ceded territory should, in due time, be formed "into republican States"; that all the unappropriated and ungranted lands within the same should be considered as "a common fund for the use and benefit" of all the members of the confederacy, to be "faithfully and *bonâ fide* disposed of for that purpose, and for no other use or purpose whatsoever;" and, "consequently, that all purchases and deeds obtained from Indians, for the use and benefit of any private person or persons whatsoever, and royal grants, within the ceded territory, inconsistent with the chartered rights, laws, and customs of Virginia, be deemed and declared absolutely void and of no effect." Finally, in consideration of the immense extent and value of this cession, Virginia asked that her remaining territory should be guaranteed to her by the United States.

It was to have been hoped that, whatever dissatisfaction and jealousy had been previously

raised in the minds of many of the other States
by the superior territorial dimensions of Virginia,
would have been at once allayed by this generous offer to surrender so large a portion of her
inheritance for the common good, and that the
offer would have been promptly and cordially
accepted by Congress. Such, unhappily, was not
the spirit in which the proffered cession was met.
The unfriendly jealousy of some of the other
States exacted a yet larger sacrifice of her domain; and hopes were entertained that by vex-
atious delays, and devices of one kind or another,
her limits might be ultimately restricted to the
narrow boundary of the Alleghanies, which form
the dividing ridge between the Eastern and
Western waters.

Coöperating with these feelings of State jealousy and envy, were the interests of certain large
and powerful land companies, embracing in their
associations numerous and influential individuals
in several of the States. The claims of these
companies lay within the chartered limits of Virginia, and had been acquired in open violation
of her laws and territorial rights, as well as in
opposition to the established usages and maxims
of American public law respecting transactions
with the aborigines. Forming as they would, if
allowed, a very large subtraction from what was
intended as a common and public fund for the
benefit of the confederacy and the discharge of
the national engagements, Virginia made it one

of the articles of her proffered cession that these claims should be considered, as they were in law, absolutely null and of no effect. Such a stipulation, of course, arrayed against the cession the interested hostility of the land companies and all who were connected with them.

On the 31st of January, 1781, the cession of Virginia, together with cessions tendered by New York and Connecticut, was referred to a committee of seven members. At a later day, it seems that these territorial cessions were recommitted to another committee of five,[1] to which were also committed memorials from the land companies. The new committee consisted of members taken from States, all of which, with a single exception, had signalized themselves by their vehement opposition to the territorial rights of Virginia; to wit, New Jersey, represented in the committee by Mr. Boudinot, Rhode Island by Mr. Varnum, Maryland by Mr. Jenifer, Pennsylvania by Mr. Smith, and New Hampshire by Mr. Livermore. The hostile composition of the committee, as well as the ominous reference of the memorials of the land companies, significantly prefigured the character of the report that was to be expected from it.

[1] The original appointment of this committee is nowhere noted on the journals of Congress. The first notice of its existence we meet with in the journals is on the 16th of October, 1781; and the first mention of the members who composed it, is on the 1st of May, 1782, when the report was taken up for consideration. Journals of Congress, vol. IV. pp. 20-25.

Mr. Madison, writing to Judge Pendleton on the 30th of October, 1781, gives the following account of the spirit of Congress and of the committee on the subject: —

"You are not mistaken in your apprehension for our Western interests. An agrarian law is as much coveted by the little members of the Union as ever it was by the indigent citizens of Rome. The conditions annexed by Virginia to her territorial cession have furnished a committee of Congress a handle for taking up questions of right, both with respect to the ceding States and the great land companies, which they have not before ventured to touch. We have made every opposition and remonstrance to the conduct of the committee which the forms of proceeding will admit. When a report is made, we shall renew our efforts upon more eligible ground, but with little hope of arresting any aggression upon Virginia, which depends solely on the inclination of Congress." [1]

It appears that the committee had given notice to the delegates of Virginia that, on a certain day, they should proceed to hear the agents of the land companies in support of their claims, and consequently in opposition to the title of the State. The delegates, considering that, under the articles of confederation, neither the committee nor Congress itself had any jurisdiction to pass upon the title by which a State holds and

[1] Madison Debates and Correspondence, vol. I. pp. 99, 100.

claims the territory lying within her declared limits, — a position which she had impregnably assumed, as we have already seen,[1] by her remonstrance to Congress of the 10th of December, 1779, — and feeling, moreover, that it was a manifest "derogation from the sovereignty of a State to be drawn into a contest by an individual or company of individuals," very properly declined to appear before the committee upon the summons addressed to them. They then appealed to Congress to arrest these irregular proceedings of the committee by an authoritative declaration of the legitimate extent of their powers; but the appeal was made in vain.[2]

At length the committee, on the 3d day of November, 1781, made their report, which bore, to the fullest extent, all those features of intense jealousy and hostility towards Virginia which had been foreshadowed. They declare that "all the lands ceded, or *pretended* to be ceded, to the United States by the State of Virginia," are a part of the lands belonging to the Six Nations of Indians and their tributaries, the jurisdiction of which is appendant to the government of New York. They, therefore, recommend the acceptance of the cession of New York, as thereby "the jurisdiction of the whole Western territory, belonging to the Six Nations of Indians and their tributaries, will be vested in the United States,

---

[1] Ante, pp. 207, 208.
[2] Journals of Congress, vol. III. pp. 676, 677, and 681.

greatly to the advantage of the Union." At the same time, they emphatically counsel the rejection of the proffered cession of Virginia.

They proceed to say, in regard to the lands reserved by Virginia on the southeast of the Ohio, that even they are "within the claim of New York, being a part of the country of the said Six Nations and their tributaries." In this connection, they disclose the bold but fondly cherished project of limiting the western extension of Virginia by the Alleghany ridge of mountains; declaring that "a large part of the lands last aforesaid are to the west of the west boundary line of the late colony of Virginia as established by the King of Great Britain in council, previous to the present Revolution," and that "in 1763 a very large part thereof was separated and appointed for a distinct government and Colony by the King, with the knowledge and approbation of the government of Virginia."

A sweeping condemnation is then pronounced on the conditions annexed to the cession of Virginia, as "incompatible with the honor, interests, and peace of the United States, and therefore, in the opinion of the committee, altogether inadmissible." Finally, Virginia is arrogantly called on, "as she values the peace, welfare, and increase of the United States," to reconsider her act of cession, and, by "a proper act for that purpose, cede to the United States all claims and pretensions of claims beyond a reasonable western boundary, consistent with her former acts while a Colony under the power of Great Britain," and "free from any conditions and restrictions whatever."[1]

With regard to the land companies, they recommend the absolute confirmation of the claims of one of them, (the Indiana Company,) although those claims, lying exclusively within the limits of Virginia, had been declared "utterly void and of no effect" by a solemn decision of the legislature of that State, after a deliberate hearing of several days in the presence of both Houses;[2] and in relation to another of the companies, (the Vandalia,) whose claim amounted to a thorough territorial dismemberment of the same State, the committee, while declining, on account of the overshadowing magnitude of the claim, to recommend its formal confirmation, yet treated it as an equitable one, and proposed to grant to such of the claimants as are citizens of the United States, "a full and ample reimbursement" out of the very lands which were the subject of the claim.

The attempt to set up a claim of territorial jurisdiction for the State of New York beyond her chartered limits, founded upon the alleged patronage of certain nomad tribes of Indians, and a claim of ownership and dominion for those Indians over lands comprehended within the char-

[1] Journals of Congress, vol. IV. pp. 21–24.   [2] Journal of House of Delegates, May session, 1779, pp. 39, 40.

tered limits of another State, was so entirely contrary not only to reason, but to principles of jurisprudence well settled before, as since, the Revolution,[1] that it can be attributed only to a predetermination to oust Virginia, at all hazards, of her territorial rights.[2]

[1] See Chalmers's Annals, p. 677, and case of Johnson v. McIntosh.

[2] The grounds on which the territorial rights of Virginia had been hitherto assailed, were, 1. The alleged vagueness and uncertainty in the description of limits in the charter of 1609, under which she claimed; 2. The subsequent annulment of that charter in the controversy between the London Company and the crown; 3. The virtual establishment of a new boundary to the west by the royal proclamation of 1763; and 4. The devolution of the rights of the crown to vacant territory upon the United States collectively, and not upon the individual States, after the Declaration of Independence. It was upon these several propositions that Paine, the author of "Common Sense," undertook in 1780, previous to the cession of Virginia, to controvert her claims in a pamphlet, which he entitled the "Public Good."

On the other hand, Virginia insisted, 1. That her chartered limits were plainly and sufficiently defined by designated parallels of latitude, and lines of sea-coast to the east and the west; 2. That the annulment of the charter of 1609 affected only the rights of the London Company, and not those of the beneficiary party, the Colonists; 3. That the proclamation of 1763 had no other object or effect than to suspend, for a time, grants of land on the Western waters, leaving the chartered rights and limits of the colony untouched; and 4. That it was an incontestable principle of American public law that the territorial sovereignty, within the chartered limits of the different Colonies, devolved, after the Revolution, upon the States severally, and not upon the confederacy.

Upon all these points, judicial decisions, since pronounced by the highest tribunals of the country, as well as the ultimate acceptance of her cession by Congress in the form (essentially) in which she tendered it, have fully sustained and justified the claims of Virginia. The conjured-up title of New York, after it had served the purposes of its momentary apparition, seems never to have been thought of seriously since. It is a painful evidence, however, of the tenacity of old political prejudices and controversies, that a committee of Congress, as late as 1842, should have undertaken to call in question the original title of Virginia, upon the

Mr. Madison, in writing to Mr. Jefferson, then a member of the legislature of Virginia, a few days after the coming in of this report, speaks of it in the following terms:—

"By the conveyance through which you will receive this, the delegates have communicated to the State the proceedings in Congress to which the territorial cessions have given birth. The complexion of them will, I suppose, be somewhat unexpected, and produce no small irritation. They clearly speak the hostile machinations of some of the States against our territorial claims, and afford suspicions that the predominant temper of Congress may coincide with them. It is proper to recollect, however, that, the report of the committee having not yet been taken into consideration, no certain inference can be drawn as to its issue; and that the report itself is not founded on the obnoxious doctrine of an inherent right in the United States to the territory in question, but on the expediency of clothing them with the title of New York, which is supposed to be maintainable against all others. . . . . . The committee was composed of a member from Maryland, Pennsylvania, New Jersey, Rhode Island, and New Hampshire, all of which States, except the last, are systematically

exploded grounds of Paine's pamphlet. See Report of Select Committee of the House of Representatives, 2d session, 27th Congress, Rep. No. 1063. An able and victorious answer to this report was made by the committee on public lands, in the 1st session of 28th Congress, Rep. No. 457.

and notoriously adverse to the claims of Western territory, and particularly those of Virginia." [1]

Mr. Madison, feeling that, however little hope there might be of arresting these aggressions upon her rights, Virginia owed it to her own character and the opinion of the world to set forth the evidence of her title, with the clearness of which it was susceptible, invoked the coöperation of Mr. Jefferson and other able professional friends at home, in searching for and collecting the various legal and historical documents on which it rested. The severe domestic affliction which soon after fell upon Mr. Jefferson prevented his aid; and other causes interfering with the contributions of the other learned friends to whom he had appealed, Mr. Madison was left almost wholly to his own resources of industry and intrinsic force of mind, (for he was then no lawyer,) to sustain the rights of Virginia against the host of her assailants. His correspondence of that period shows how successfully he had mastered all the difficulties of a question belonging essentially to the department of technical and professional knowledge; and how, under the modest guise of seeking information from others, he supplied them with every element, both of principle and fact, necessary for its solution.[2]

[1] Madison Debates and Correspondence, vol. I. pp. 102, 103.

[2] See particularly his letters of 15th of January and 16th of April, 1782, to Mr. Jefferson, in Madison Debates and Correspondence, vol. I. pp. 106–109 and 119–122; and to Mr. Edmund Randolph of the 9th of April and 18th of August, 1782, in Idem, pp. 118, 159, 160.

The report of the committee was not taken up for consideration in Congress until the 1st of May, 1782. The delegates of Virginia determined then to press for a final decision upon the cession proffered by the State; but sensible how much that decision might be influenced by the interests of the land companies, they moved, as a preliminary question, that, previous to any determination in Congress relative to the cessions of the Western lands, each member do declare upon his honor whether he is or is not personally interested, directly or indirectly, in the claims of any of the land companies; and that his declaration be entered on the Journal. This motion was parried; and finally, on the 6th day of May, the farther consideration of the report was, upon the motion of a delegate from Pennsylvania, and against the remonstrances of the delegates from Virginia, postponed.[1]

The General Assembly of the State met soon after these proceedings in Congress; and then, for the first time, the report of the committee, with the proceedings of Congress upon it, was laid before them. It naturally excited a warm and indignant feeling. Among other measures adopted, a committee was appointed, consisting of Mr. George Mason, Mr. Jefferson, Mr. Arthur Lee, Mr. Edmund Randolph, and Dr. Thomas Walker, to prepare a full and detailed vindication of the claims of Virginia to her Western

[1] See Journals of Congress, vol. iv. pp. 20 and 26.

territory;[1] but it does not appear that the task was ever executed by the committee. Mr. Madison still continued to give his earnest and persevering attention to the subject. In some instructive "observations" recorded by him at the time, (1st of May, 1782,) he has shown how large an influence this question, together with the kindred one of Vermont, to which we shall presently have occasion to advert, exerted on the state of parties in Congress at that period.

The following extract from that paper will indicate how powerful was the combination against the cause, which it devolved upon him to sustain.

"The territorial claims, particularly those of Virginia," he there says, "are opposed by Rhode Island, New Jersey, Pensylvania, Delaware, and Maryland. Rhode Island is influenced in her opposition by, first, a lucrative desire of sharing in the vacant territory as a fund of revenue; secondly, by the envy and jealousy naturally excited by superior resources and importance. New Jersey, Pennsylvania, Delaware, and Maryland are influenced partly by the same considerations; but principally by the intrigues of their citizens, who are interested in the land companies. The decisive influence of this last consideration is manifest from the peculiar and persevering opposition made against Virginia, within whose limits those claims lie."

[1] Manuscript letter of E. Randolph to J. Madison, 21st of June, 1782.

The paper then proceeds to show how Massachusetts and Connecticut, — mainly by the interest they felt in the Vermont question, — were joined to this compact phalanx against the territorial claims of Virginia, and of some of the other States; and concludes with the following survey of the comparatively feeble forces, in number at least, arrayed on the other side.

"The Western claims are espoused by Virginia, North and South Carolina, Georgia, and New York, all of these States being interested therein. South Carolina is the least so. The claim of New York is very extensive, but her title very flimsy. She urges it more with the hope of obtaining some advantage or credit by its cession, than of ever maintaining it. If this cession should be accepted, and the affair of Vermont terminated, as these are the only ties which unite her with the Southern States, she will immediately connect her policy with that of the Eastern States; so far, at least, as the remains of former prejudice will permit."[1]

Notwithstanding the fearful odds against Virginia in this geographical array of parties, Mr. Madison did not despair of ultimate success. "If the State is firm and prudent," he said in a letter to a friend, written about the same time, "I have little doubt that she will be again courted."[2]

[1] See Madison Debates and Correspondence, vol. I. pp. 123, 124.

[2] Letter to E. Randolph, in Madison Debates and Correspondence, vol. I. p. 126.

The subject next came up in Congress, on the 5th and 6th of September, 1782, upon the report of a grand committee, declaring that "the Western lands, if ceded to the United States, might contribute towards a fund for paying the debt of these States."[1] One of the delegates of Virginia, Mr. Bland, moved, as an amendment and corollary to this proposition, that the cessions already tendered be accepted by Congress, with the conditions therein named. This gave rise to a wide discussion on the whole range of topics connected with the question.[2]

Finally, Mr. Witherspoon of New Jersey moved a set of resolutions, recommending to the States which had made no cessions, now to act upon the subject, and to those, whose cessions were not fully conformable to the wishes of Congress, to reconsider their acts; and declaring that, "in case of a compliance with the above recommendation, no determinations of the particular States, relating to private property of lands within those cessions, shall be reversed or altered without their consent, unless in such cases as the ninth article of the confederation shall render it necessary." This last resolution related to the obnoxious claims of the land companies, and was plainly a concession held out to the demands of Virginia. The proposition of Mr. Witherspoon was immediately taken into consideration, and

[1] Journals of Congress, vol. IV. pp. 68, 69.

[2] Madison Debates, vol. I. pp. 166-168.

referred to a committee consisting of himself,
Mr. Madison, Mr. Rutledge of South Carolina,
Mr. Osgood of Massachusetts, and Mr. Montgom-
ery of Pennsylvania.

It would seem that the intimate relations of
Mr. Madison with his venerable and distinguished
preceptor, the mover of the proposition and the
chairman of the committee, must have influenced
the latter to engage in this work of conciliation;
for no State in the confederacy was more vio-
lently opposed to all the views of Virginia on
the subject of Western territory than that which
Dr. Witherspoon represented. However this may
be, it was a touching and noble spectacle to see
the pupil and the preceptor, representing discordant interests and views as they did, thus closely
associated, as members of the same committee, in
the sublime office of national peacemakers. On
the 25th of September, 1782, the committee
made their report, recommending the adoption
of Dr. Witherspoon's proposition in the very words
in which he had offered it. The temper of Congress, however, was not yet ripe for compromise,
and the proposition was rejected.[1]

The next step in the history of this thorny
and complicated question was the naked acceptance by Congress, on the 29th of October, 1782,
upon the motion of the delegates of Maryland,
of " all the right, title, interest, jurisdiction, and
claim of the State of New York, as ceded by

[1] Journals of Congress, vol. IV. pp. 82, 83.

and contained in an instrument of writing executed by her agents for that purpose."[1]

The matter seems then to have rested, with regard to the cession of Virginia, until the 4th of June, 1783, when the consideration of the report of the committee of the 3d of November, 1781, was resumed; and so much of it as related to the cession of Virginia was referred to another committee, consisting of Mr. Rutledge of South Carolina, Mr. Bedford of Delaware, Mr. Carroll of Maryland, Mr. Higginson of Massachusetts, and Mr. Wilson of Pennsylvania.[2]

This committee made a report, favorable in the main to the acceptance of the cession tendered by Virginia,[3] which was taken up for consideration on the 10th of June, 1783. After a debate, which disclosed two changes in the state of parties, which Mr. Madison had anticipated, (to wit, the opposition of New York,[4] and the accession of Massachusetts and Connecticut,) the farther consideration of the report was postponed until the 20th of the same month. On that day, a violent remonstrance was presented and read from the legislature of New Jersey, denouncing the cession of Virginia "as partial, unjust, and illiberal," accusing her of an unworthy attempt to "aggrandize herself by the detention of prop-

[1] Journals of Congress, vol. IV. p. 100.

[2] Idem, pp. 226, 227.

[3] See Madison Debates and Correspondence, vol. I. p. 543.

[4] On this occasion, Col. Hamilton "asserted the right of the United States" to the vacant territory. Madison Debates, vol. I. pp. 458, 459.

erty which had been procured by the common blood and treasure of all the States," and earnestly calling upon Congress to reject the cession.[1]

In the course of the discussion, one of the delegates of New Jersey, Mr. Clark, vehemently declared that "the time would yet come when Congress would draw a line limiting the States to the westward, and saying thus far shall ye go, and no farther." Mr. Madison also records that, "from several circumstances, there was reason to believe that Rhode Island, New Jersey, Pennsylvania, and Delaware, if not Maryland likewise, retained latent views of confining Virginia to the Alleghany Mountains." He adds that, "there being seven States only present, and the spirit of compromise decreasing," no vote was taken on the subject.[2] The next day, Congress, which, for two days past, had been sitting in the midst of a mutinous demonstration of a band of soldiers, adjourned from Philadelphia to Princeton.

On the 13th day of September, 1783, at the latter place, the cession of Virginia was again brought before Congress, on the report of a committee consisting of Mr. Rutledge of South Carolina, Mr. Ellsworth of Connecticut, Mr. Bedford of Delaware, Mr. Gorham of Massachusetts, and Mr. Madison. Of the eight conditions annexed by Virginia to her cession, they reported that

[1] See Journals of Congress, vol. IV. p. 231.   [2] Madison Debates, vol. I. pp. 463–465.

the first six were, in their opinion, just and reasonable, in the precise form in which they were
proposed, and ought to be agreed to by Congress.

With regard to the seventh condition, which
appealed to Congress to declare the claims of
the land companies to be "absolutely void and
of no effect," they reported that it would not, in
their judgment, be proper for Congress to make
such a declaration; but that the sixth condition,
the acceptance of which they had recommended,
in providing that the ceded lands were to be "a
common fund for the benefit of the confederacy,"
and that "they should be faithfully and *bonâ fide*
disposed of for that purpose, and for no other
use or purpose whatever," was a sufficient compliance with the demands of Virginia on that
point.

As to the eighth and last condition, by which
Virginia proposed a guarantee of her remaining
territory, the committee were of opinion that
such a guarantee presupposed a discussion of the
question of title, which the acts of Congress on
the subject expressly disclaimed; and that the
territorial rights of a State, whatever they were,
were effectually guaranteed by the articles of
confederation. With these modifications alone, if
assented to by the legislature of Virginia, the
committee recommended that her cession be accepted, in all other respects, upon the terms on
which she had offered it.[1]

[1] Journals of Congress, vol. IV. pp. 265–267.

On the question to agree to the report of the committee, the delegates of Maryland, resisting to the last, moved a substitute which affirmed the sovereign right of the United States as one undivided and independent nation, succeeding to the rights of the British crown, to possess the whole of the Western territory; and farther proposed that the said territory be laid off into one or more convenient States, and that a federal land-office be established for the disposal of the soil. Maryland and New Jersey alone voted in favor of the substitute; and the report of the committee was finally agreed to by the votes of eight States out of the eleven present.[1]

Thus was closed, at last, the tedious and exciting controversy which had so long distracted the councils of Congress, and the burden and responsibilities of which had weighed so heavily upon Mr. Madison during the whole period of his service in that body. That it was finally brought to a consummation, consistent alike with the honor and rights of the ceding State and the general good of the confederacy, through so many opposing barriers of local and political prejudice, and of powerful private interests, was due, in an especial manner, to the firmness, prudence, vigilance, and ability he displayed in every stage of the protracted struggle.

In announcing the result to his friends, Mr. Jefferson and Mr. Randolph, which he did by let-

[1] See Journals of Congress, vol. IV. pp. 263–265, and 267.

ters addressed to both on the same day, (the 20th of September, 1783,) he confined himself to a brief expression of "his sincere hope that it would meet the ultimatum of Virginia."[1] That sanction — the object of his solicitude and the reward of his labors — it received in an act of the legislature passed in the ensuing month, which authorized a deed to be made for the territory northwest of the Ohio, in pursuance of the terms of cession agreed upon; and that deed was, on the 1st day of March, 1784, signed, sealed, and delivered in Congress by Thomas Jefferson, Samuel Hardy, Arthur Lee, and James Monroe, then the representatives of the State in the national council.[2]

It is now proper to give our attention to the question of Vermont, — a question which, for a lengthened period, occupied the deliberations of Congress, was connected, by various relations, with the territorial claims of Virginia, and, for a time, exercised an important influence upon their progress and reception.

The bold mountain region west of the river Connecticut, and stretching thence to the borders of Lake Champlain, had become known to the hardy yeomanry of New England in the war of 1756 with France; and immediately after the close of that war, it began to be settled by

[1] Madison Debates and Correspondence, vol. I. pp. 572 and 574.
[2] See Act of Assembly in Hen. Stat. vol. XI. pp. 326–328, and Deed of Cession, Idem, pp. 571–575.

adventurers from the neighbouring States. The original settlements were made under grants obtained from the Colony of New Hampshire, from which circumstance the district itself bore, for many years, the name of the "New Hampshire Grants."

The Colony of New York, at the same time, claimed the ownership and dominion over it, as being included within the limits of the royal grant to the Duke of York, and, in 1764, obtained an order of the king and council, placing the country, as far east as Connecticut River, under its jurisdiction. This was done, however, without the consent, and in opposition to the wishes of the inhabitants of the district, a majority of whom steadily refused to acknowledge the authority of New York. The conflicting claims of the two adjacent Colonies giving them a good excuse for rejecting the pretensions of both, they finally set up as a separate and distinct community. At the Revolution, they declared themselves independent; and in 1777 they organized a *de facto* government of their own.

In this state of things, the subject seems to have been first brought to the notice of Congress on the 22d of May, 1779, by certain resolutions moved by the delegates of New York, invoking the interposition of Congress, and affirming that " no part or district of one or more of the States shall be permitted to separate therefrom, or become independent thereon, without the express consent and approbation of such State or States respectively."[1] These resolutions were not acted on; but on the 2d of June, 1779, a committee was appointed to repair to the New Hampshire Grants, and "inquire into the reasons why the inhabitants refuse to continue citizens of the respective States, which heretofore exercised jurisdiction over them."[2]

A majority of the committee not having met to perform the duty assigned to them, they were discharged from its farther prosecution by a resolution adopted on the 24th of September, 1779. On that day, a series of resolutions was unanimously adopted by Congress, which,—after reciting that "the animosities aforesaid have lately proceeded so far, and risen so high, as to endanger the internal peace of the confederacy, and to render it indispensably necessary for Congress to interpose for the restoration of quiet and good order," and that in the disputes subsisting between the adjacent States on the one hand, and the people of the disturbed district on the other, "each of the said States claim the said district against each other, as well as against the people of the district,"—recommend that the States in question pass laws expressly authorizing Congress to hear and determine all differences, as well between themselves as between them and the said district, and pledge the faith of Congress "to carry into execution, and support whatever

[1] Journals of Congress, vol. III. pp. 285, 286. [2] Idem, p. 297.

determination" they may come to in the premises, and for whichsoever of the parties it may
be pronounced.

In the mean time, they declare it to be the
" duty of the people of the district to abstain from
exercising any power over any of the inhabitants
who profess themselves to be citizens of, or to
owe allegiance to, any or either of the said
States;" and also that these States, in like manner, ought "to suspend executing their laws"
over any of the inhabitants of the district, except
such as acknowledge their jurisdiction; and, finally, they declare that "Congress will consider
any violences committed against the tenor of
these resolutions as a breach of the peace of the
confederacy, which they are determined to keep
and maintain." [1]

On the 19th of September, 1780, a hearing
took place before Congress, for the first time, on
the disputes between the inhabitants of the "New
Hampshire Grants" on the one hand, and the
States of New York and New Hampshire on the
other, as well as between those two States respectively on the subject of their mutually interfering claims. Two persons attended on behalf
of the people of the district in controversy, exhibiting a commission signed by the acting governor or president, and under a seal, styled the
"Seal of the State of Vermont." [2]

Mr. Madison, writing to his colleague, Mr. Jones,

[1] Journals of Congress, vol. III. pp. 365–367. [2] Idem, pp. 520, 521.

on the same day, speaks of these proceedings in the following manner: —

"The Vermont business has been two days under agitation, and nothing done in it, except rejecting a proposition for postponing the determination of Congress till commissioners should inquire into the titles and boundaries of New Hampshire and New York. Congress have bound themselves so strongly by their own act to bring it to an issue at this time, and are pressed by New York so closely with this engagement, that it is not possible any longer to try evasive expedients. For my own part, if a final decision must take place, I am clearly of opinion that it ought to be made on principles that will effectually discountenance the erection of new governments without the sanction of proper authority, and in a style marking a due firmness and decision in Congress." [1]

After a continued hearing of several days, from which, however, the agents of Vermont at last withdrew,[2] Congress postponed the farther consideration of the subject, without coming to any decision. At the time when the foregoing letter was written, it expressed, it is probable, not only Mr. Madison's personal opinions, but the prevailing sentiment in Congress. The agents and partisans of Vermont, however, still continued to push their interests, more or less openly,

---

[1] Madison Debates and Correspondence, vol. I. pp. 52, 53.

[2] See Journals of Congress, vol. III. p. 526.

in that body. There was too obvious a bond of
sympathy between them and the opponents of
the territorial claims of Virginia to be overlooked.
Mr. Madison, in a letter to Mr. Edmund Randolph of the 1st of May, 1781, says: "The subject of Vermont has not yet been called up.
Their agents, and those of the land-mongers
are playing, with great adroitness, into each
others' hands. Mr. Jones will explain this game
to you."[1]

There were yet other and more pressing considerations which added strength to their cause.
The frequent and violent conflicts between the
rival authorities in the disputed territory could
not but attract the attention and excite the
hopes and intrigues of the common enemy. Insidious overtures were made to the inhabitants
of the district, which some of their leaders, it was
believed, were disposed to incline too favorable
an ear to. Under these circumstances, a number
of persons, both in and out of Congress, began
to think that the best security against this source
of division and danger was to acknowledge the
claims of the district to a separate and independent existence, and to admit it as a new State
into the confederacy.

On the 7th of August, 1781, a committee consisting of Mr. Sherman of Connecticut, Mr. McKean
of Pennsylvania, Mr. Carroll of Maryland, Mr.
Varnum of Rhode Island, and Mr. Madison, (it is

[1] Madison Debates and Correspondence, vol. I. p. 92.

obvious, from the composition of the committee, that Mr. Madison's voice must have been wholly drowned in it,) made a report, which, — after briefly mentioning that the States of New York and New Hampshire had been already heard before Congress on their respective claims to jurisdiction over "the people inhabiting the New Hampshire Grants," and that "the people aforesaid claim and exercise the powers of a sovereign, independent State, and desire to be admitted into the federal Union of the United States of America," — recommends, "in order thereto, and that they may have an opportunity of being heard in vindication of their claim," that a committee of five be appointed to confer with such persons as may be chosen by the people of that district, or by their representative body, respecting their claim to be an independent State, and on what terms they should be admitted into the confederacy, in case Congress should recognize their independence.

This report was adopted; and on the following day a committee, precisely similar in its elements to the preceding one, but not composed of the same individuals,[1] was appointed to hold the proposed conference with such persons as may be deputed by the people or representatives of Vermont. It then appeared that agents, duly com-

[1] The new committee consisted of Mr. Boudinot of New Jersey, Mr. Vandyke of Delaware, Mr. Carroll of Maryland, Mr. Montgomery of Pennsylvania, and Mr. Randolph of Virginia. Journals of Congress, vol. III. p. 656.

missioned on the part of Vermont, were already in attendance. After a conference with these agents, the committee, on the 20th of August, delivered in their report; upon which Congress adopted a resolution declaring that "it be an indispensable preliminary to the recognition of the independence of the people inhabiting the territory called Vermont, and their admission into the Federal Union, that they explicitly renounce all demands of lands on the east side of Connecticut River, and on the west side of a line running from the northwest corner of the State of Massachusetts" to the southern extremity of Lake Champlain; and that the United States will guarantee to the States of New Hampshire and New York all the adjacent lands, lying on the east and west side of the aforesaid limits respectively, against any claims or encroachments of the inhabitants of Vermont.

These proceedings plainly indicated the "foregone conclusion" of Congress to admit the inhabitants of Vermont as a separate State into the confederacy, on the terms specified. They furnish abundant confirmation, at the same time, of the curious state of parties in Congress described by Mr. Madison in his memorandum of the 1st of May, 1782, to which reference has already been made,—showing that it was the same alliance between the Eastern and Middle States, founded on temporary and accidental causes, which stood opposed to the territorial rights of

Virginia and which patronized the claims of Vermont.[1]

Facile and liberal as were the terms offered by Congress to the inhabitants of Vermont, they were at first unceremoniously rejected by these " turbulent sons of freedom," — so called by one of the noblest of their own kindred.[2]   The fol-

[1] The array of parties here alluded to is thus described by Mr. Madison, in his memorandum of the 1st of May, 1782: —

" The independence of Vermont, and its admission into the confederacy, are patronized by the Eastern States, (New Hampshire excepted,) 1. From ancient prejudice against New York; 2. The interest which the citizens of those States have in lands granted by Vermont; 3. But principally from the accession of weight they will derive from it in Congress. New Hampshire, having gained its main object by the exclusion of its territory east of Connecticut River from the claims of Vermont, is already indifferent to its independence, and will probably soon combine with other Eastern States in its favor.

" The same patronage is yielded to the pretensions of Vermont by Pennsylvania and Maryland, with the sole view of .reinforcing the opposition to claims of Western territory, particularly those of Virginia; and by New Jersey and Delaware, with the additional view of strengthening the influence of the little States. Both of these

considerations operate also on Rhode Island, in addition to the above mentioned.

" The independence of Vermont, and its admission into the Union, are opposed by New York for reasons obvious and well known. The like opposition is made by Virginia, North Carolina, South Carolina, and Georgia. The grounds of this opposition are, 1. An habitual jealousy of the predominance of Eastern interest; 2. The opposition expected from Vermont to Western claims; 3. The inexpediency of admitting so unimportant a State to an equal vote in deciding on peace, and all the other grand interests of the Union now depending; 4. The influence of the example on a premature dismemberment of the other States. These considerations influence the four States last mentioned in different degrees. The second and third, to say nothing of the fourth, ought to be decisive with Virginia." See Madison Debates and Correspondence, vol. I. pp. 122, 123.

[2] See letter of General Stark to Washington, in Sparks's Washington, vol. VIII. p. 83.

lowing history of the matter is given in a letter
of Mr. Madison to Judge Pendleton of the 22d
of January, 1782.

"Congress are much occupied and perplexed
at present with the case of Vermont. The pretensions of that settlement to the character of
an independent State, with the grounds on which
they are made, and the countenance given them
by Congress, are, I presume, pretty well known
to you. It has long been contended that an explicit acknowledgment of that character, and an
admission of them into the Federal Union, was
an act both of justice and policy. The discovery
made through several channels, and particularly
the intercepted letters of Lord George Germain,
added such force to the latter of these considerations that, in the course of the last summer,
preliminary overtures were made, on the part of
Congress, for taking them into the confederation,
containing, as one condition on the part of Vermont, that they should contract their claims
within the bounds to which they were originally
confined, and guaranteeing to New York and
New Hampshire all the territory without those
bounds, to which their encroachments had been
extended.

"Instead of complying with this condition, they
have gone on in their encroachments both on
the New York and New Hampshire sides; and
there is, at this moment, every symptom of approaching hostility with each of them. In this

delicate crisis, the interposition of Congress is again called for, and, indeed, seems to be indispensable; but whether in the way of military coercion, or a renewal of former overtures, or by making the first a consequence of the refusal of the last, is not so unanimously decided.

"Indeed, with several members, and I may say States, in Congress, a power either to decide on their independence, or to open the door of the confederacy to them, is utterly disclaimed; besides which, the danger of the precedent, and the preponderancy it would give to the Eastern scale, deserve serious consideration. These reasons, nevertheless, can only prevail when the alternative contains fewer evils. It is very unhappy that such plausible pretexts, if not necessary occasions, of assuming power should occur. Nothing is more distressing to those who have a true respect for the constitutional modifications of power, than to be obliged to decide on them."[1]

[1] Under the articles of confederation, it seems quite clear that Congress possessed no power to admit Vermont as a new State into the confederacy. There was a special provision in those articles that Canada, by acceding to the confederation and joining in the measures of Congress, should, *ipso facto*, be admitted into and entitled to all the advantages of the Union, — accompanied with an express declaration that no other Colony, (by which was evidently meant *British* Colony, exterior to the then existing territorial limits of the United States,) should be admitted into the same, unless agreed to by nine States. The ablest commentators of the time assert that the eventual establishment of new States, within the original limits of the United States, was overlooked by the framers of the confederation; and that the provision which was afterwards made by Congress, in the ordinance respecting the Northwestern Territory, for the ultimate

Although the terms offered by Congress were thus heedlessly declined by the people of Vermont at first, the subject was subsequently reconsidered by their representative Assembly, when a formal assent was given to the boundaries prescribed for the new State. Congress might well have thought themselves released from the obligation of accepting a compliance which was so tardy and ungracious; but they referred the question to a committee, which, composed, as all the preceding committees had been, of sympathizing elements, made a report on the 17th of April, 1782, recommending that "the district or territory called Vermont be recognized as a free, sovereign, and independent State," and that measures be taken for its admission into the federal Union.[1]

Before this report was taken into consideration

introduction of new States out of that territory, was "the assumption of an *excrescent* power," growing out of circumstances which imposed upon Congress the "task of overleaping their constitutional boundaries." [See Federalist, No. 38 and No. 43.]

It was to supply this defect of power, and to guard against the dangers of usurpation under the plea of necessity, that an express authority was given to Congress, in the constitution of 1788, to "admit new States into the Union," but under limitations which forbid the formation of a new State within the jurisdiction of another State, or by the junction of two or more States, or parts of States, without the consent of the legislatures of the States concerned, as well as of Congress. These limitations are a precise fulfilment of the idea we have seen expressed by Mr. Madison in his letter to Mr. Jones of the 19th of September, 1780. [See ante, p. 469.]

[1] See Journals of Congress, vol. iv. pp. 11, 12. The committee consisted of Mr. Clymer of Pennsylvania, Mr. Carroll of Maryland, Mr. Clark of New Jersey, Mr. Livermore of New Hampshire, and Mr. Law of Connecticut.

by Congress, the authorities of Vermont committed fresh acts of violence on persons professing allegiance to the State of New York, by which some of them were condemned to banishment, "not to return on pain of death, and confiscation of estate," and others were fined in large sums, and deprived of their property. These facts were brought to the knowledge of Congress by a representation from the governor of New York ; whereupon resolutions, moved by Mr. McKean of Pennsylvania, were adopted, declaring the aforesaid acts to be in direct violation of the resolutions of Congress passed on the 24th of September, 1779,[1] to be highly derogatory to the authority of the United States, and dangerous to the confederacy, — requiring the people of the district (now again called the "New Hampshire Grants,") to make full and ample restitution, without delay, to the parties injured, — and "pledging the United States to take effectual measures to enforce a compliance with the aforesaid resolutions, in case the same be disobeyed by the people of the said district."[2]

These resolutions, moved by the delegate of a State which had always hitherto been counted among the patrons of Vermont, were sustained by the votes of several other States alike committed to her cause, and finally passed, with the dissent only of Rhode Island and New Jersey.

[1] See ante, pp. 467, 468.
[2] See Journals of Congress, vol. IV. pp. 112–114.

Thus did these "turbulent sons of freedom" dash
from their lips, by their own rashness, the cup
of independence and admission into the Union,
at the moment that it was held out to them by
the generous hand of Congress. Instead of compliance, the resolutions last adopted by Congress
produced only a tart and unbecoming remonstrance to the national council from the acting
authorities of Vermont; and fears began to be
seriously entertained, and nowhere with more
painful anxiety than in the paternal bosom of
the commander-in-chief,[1] that brethren might be
called to shed each others' blood in the closing,
and otherwise triumphant, scenes of a contest
commenced and prosecuted for the common liberty and happiness of all. The good genius of
America forbade; and Vermont had to bide her
time till, in the manner and form prescribed by
the general provisions of the constitution of 1788,
she was regularly admitted into the sisterhood
of States.

[1] See his letter to Mr. Jones, one of the delegates of Virginia in
Congress, in Sparks's Washington, vol. VIII. pp. 382-384.

CHAPTER XVI.

IN our last chapter, mention was incidentally
made of the adjournment of Congress from Phil-

adelphia to Princeton, in consequence of the freedom of their deliberations at the former place being interrupted by the mutiny of a band of soldiers. A circumstance so unusual, and at the same time admonitory, in the civil history of the United States demands a fuller development.

The uncertain and equivocal state of things produced by the long interval between the provisional articles of peace and a definitive treaty, gave rise to much embarrassment in Congress as to the disposal to be made of the army. Instead of a final disbandment, which was earnestly pressed by some, it was determined, on the 26th of May, 1783, that the commander-in-chief be authorized to grant furloughs to the men enlisted to serve during the war;[1] so that, if the provisional articles should not be followed by a definitive treaty, the soldiers thus engaged might be promptly recalled to the standard of the country, without the necessity of a new enlistment. This measure even, without the means of paying the arrears due to the army, was not very easy of execution. Mr. Madison, in writing to a friend some months before, had said: "Without money, there is some reason to surmise that it may be as difficult to disband an army as it has been to raise one."[2]

But the great influence which the commander-

---

[1] See Journals of Congress, vol. IV. p. 224. The furloughed men were allowed to take their arms with them.

[2] See Madison Debates and Correspondence, vol. I. pp. 174, 175.

in-chief possessed over the hearts and minds of the army, combined with their own exemplary civic virtue and patriotism, enabled him to carry it into effect to the satisfaction of both the army and Congress, not only with an empty military chest, but even before any settlement of their accounts was made. In writing to the president of Congress on the 7th of June, 1783, he says: "The two subjects of complaint with the army appear to be the delay of the three months' payment, which had been expected, and the want of a settlement of accounts. I have thought myself authorized to assure them that Congress had attended and would attend particularly to their grievances, and have made some little variations respecting furloughs from what was at first proposed." He then warmly commends "the temperate and orderly conduct of the whole army," on the occasion of the execution of a measure so delicate and trying, and concludes with these words of touching and affectionate fidelity to his veteran followers: "Permit me to recall to mind all their former sufferings and merits, and to recommend their reasonable request to the early and favorable notice of Congress."[1]

But while such was the admirable conduct of the whole army under the immediate command and influence of Washington, a different spirit was manifested by one or two detachments at a distance. On the 13th of June, the troops in

[1] See Sparks's Washington, vol. VIII. pp. 438, 439.

the barracks at Philadelphia sent in a memorial
to Congress, signed by the non-commissioned officers in behalf of the whole, setting forth their
claims, and demanding a satisfactory answer in
the course of the day, with a threat, otherwise,
of taking measures to right themselves.[1]

Hardly was this demonstration quieted, when
information was laid before Congress on the 19th
of June, by the executive council of Pennsylvania, that eighty soldiers, who would probably be
joined by the discharged soldiers of Armand's
legion, were on their way from Lancaster to
Philadelphia, in spite of the expostulations of
their officers, declaring that they would proceed
to the hall of Congress and demand justice, and
intimating designs against the bank. On the following day, these mutineers, under the guidance
of their sergeants, came into the city, professing
then to have no other object than a settlement
of accounts, which they supposed "they had a
better chance for at Philadelphia than Lancaster."

The scenes which took place the day after,
(21st of June,) are thus described by Mr. Madison in his diary of the proceedings of Congress:

"The mutinous soldiers presented themselves,
drawn up in the street before the state house,
where Congress had assembled. The executive
council of the State, sitting under the same roof,
was called on for the proper interposition. President Dickenson came in, and explained the diffi-

culty, under actual circumstances, of bringing out
the militia of the place for the suppression of
the mutiny. He thought that, without some outrages on persons or property, the militia could
not be relied on. General St. Clair, then in Philadelphia, was sent for, and desired to use his interposition in order to prevail on the troops to
return to the barracks. His report gave no encouragement.

"In this posture of things, it was proposed
by Mr. Izard that Congress should adjourn. It
was proposed by Mr. Hamilton that General St.
Clair, in concert with the executive council of
the State, should take order for terminating the
mutiny. Mr. Reed moved that the General
should endeavour to withdraw the troops by assuring them of the disposition of Congress to do
them justice.

"It was finally agreed that Congress should
remain till the usual hour of adjournment, but
without taking any step in relation to the alleged
grievances of the soldiers, or any other business
whatever. In the mean time, the soldiers remained in their position without offering any
violence; individuals only occasionally uttering
offensive words, and wantonly pointing their mus-
kets to the windows of the hall of Congress.
No danger from premeditated violence was apprehended; but it was observed that spirituous
drink, from the tippling-houses adjoining, began
to be liberally served out to the soldiers, and

might lead to hasty excesses. None were committed, however; and about three o'clock, the usual hour, Congress adjourned, — the soldiers (though in some instances offering a mock obstruction) permitting the members to pass through their ranks. They soon afterwards retired themselves to the barracks." [1]

In the evening of the same day, Congress reassembled in their hall, and passed resolutions for formally communicating to the president and executive council of Pennsylvania "the gross insult which had been offered to the authority of the United States by the disorderly and menacing appearance of a body of armed soldiers about the place within which Congress was assembled," and appointing a committee, consisting of Colonel Hamilton, Mr. Ellsworth, and Mr. Peters, to confer with those authorities, and to represent to them the necessity "of effectual measures being immediately taken for suppressing the revolt, and maintaining the dignity and authority of the United States."

In case the committee, after their conference with the State authorities, should be of opinion that "there was not a satisfactory ground for expecting adequate and prompt exertions of the State for supporting the dignity of the federal government," the president of Congress was, on their advice to that effect, to summon the body to meet, on the 26th of the month, at Trenton

1 Madison Debates, vol. I. pp. 465, 466.

or Princeton, in the State of New Jersey.[1] The
answer of the executive council giving no assurance of any prompt and effectual interposition
on their part, but on the contrary avowing that
the coöperation of the militia of the city was
not to be counted on, except "in case of further
outrage, and actual violence to person or property," the president of Congress, upon the advice
of the committee, proclaimed an adjournment to
the State of New Jersey, as directed by the resolutions already adopted.

A resolution had been passed, at the same
time, directing the secretary of war to communicate to the commander-in-chief the occurrences
which had taken place, in order that he might
despatch to the city such force as he should
judge expedient for suppressing the disturbances.
The communication was received by General
Washington at Newburgh on the 24th of the
month, when he immediately wrote to the president of Congress as follows: —

"It was not until three o'clock this afternoon
that I had the first information of the infamous
and outrageous mutiny of a part of the Pennsylvania troops. It was then I received your
Excellency's letter of the 21st, by your express;
and, agreeably to your request contained in it,
I instantly ordered three complete regiments of
infantry and a detachment of artillery to be put
in motion as soon as possible. This corps, which,

[1] Journals of Congress, vol. iv. pp. 231, 232.

you will observe by the return, is a large proportion of our whole force, will consist of fifteen
hundred effectives. As all the troops who composed this gallant little army, as well those who
are furloughed as those who remain in service,
are men of tried fidelity, I could not have occasion to make any choice of corps."

Filled with indignation and horror at the dis-
loyal proceedings of this band of mutineers,
and anxious that the reproach of their conduct
should not, in any manner, be visited upon the
character of the army which had followed him
through so many trials, and which he loved so
well, he proceeded :—

"While I suffer the most poignant distress in
observing that a handful of men, contemptible in
numbers, and equally so in point of service, (if
the veteran troops from the southward have not
been seduced by their example,) and who are
not worthy to be called soldiers, should disgrace
themselves and their country, as the Pennsylvania mutineers have done, by insulting the sovereign authority of the United States, and that
of their own, I feel an inexpressible satisfaction
that even their behaviour cannot stain the name
of the American soldiery. . . . . For when
we consider that these Pennsylvania levies, who
have now mutinied, are recruits and soldiers of
a day, who have not borne the heat and burden
of the war, and who can have, in reality, very
few hardships to complain of; and when we, at

the same time, recollect that those soldiers who have lately been furloughed from this army are the veterans who have patiently borne hunger, nakedness, and cold; who have suffered and bled without a murmur, and who, with perfect good order, have retired to their homes without a settlement of their accounts, or a farthing of money in their pockets; we shall be as much astonished at the virtues of the latter, as we are struck with horror and detestation at the proceedings of the former; and every candid mind, without indulging ill-grounded prejudices, will undoubtedly make the proper discrimination."

Congress assembled at Princeton at the time appointed, and was welcomed by a patriotic letter from the governor of the State, assuring that body of the loyal attachment and support of the citizens of New Jersey. The trustees and masters of the college immediately placed at the disposal of Congress the use of "its hall, library, and every other convenience which the edifice could afford." The offer was thankfully accepted; and in those walls where, eleven years before, Madison was a quiet and peaceful student from a distant province of the British crown, we now see him the active and busy representative of that same province, become a sovereign and independent State, and in conjunction with assembled representatives from twelve other widely separated provinces, which had in like manner thrown off their subjection to the British crown, making laws for united and independent America, and freely deliberating on the terms of peace with their former sovereign, now an alien and belligerent power. Human life has few more remarkable contrasts than this.

One of the first measures of Congress in their new residence was to order Major-General Howe, who had been placed in command of the detachment of fifteen hundred men sent by Washington for the suppression of the disorders in Philadelphia, to march into Pennsylvania with such part of his force as he should deem necessary to put an effectual end to the late mutiny, and to apprehend and bring to trial all such persons, belonging to the army, as had been principally active in it. This service was promptly and satisfactorily performed. The mutineers immediately submitted. Two of the sergeants were tried by a court-martial, and condemned to death; but it appearing that they had been seduced by two of their subaltern officers of very bad character, who had made their escape on the approach of General Howe's detachment, they were finally pardoned by Congress.

Although this affair was thus speedily terminated, it served to evince the necessity of Congress possessing an independent jurisdiction in the place of their sittings. Much time was spent in discussing the nature and extent of the local jurisdiction they should be invested with, in order to insure the freedom and dignity of their deliberations, and also in fixing upon a permanent seat for their future residence. This last question brought into competition so many geographical interests and aspirations that it was exceedingly difficult to arrive at any solution.

The competition was at length narrowed down to the banks of the Delaware and the banks of the Potomac. After a decision in favor of the former, which was not satisfactory to the Southern States, a representative of Massachusetts, Mr. Gerry, brought forward a proposition for the alternate residence of Congress in two places, as better calculated "to promote the mutual confidence and affection of the States," and with that view, moved that suitable buildings for the accommodation of Congress be erected on the banks of the Potomac, near the lower falls, as well as on the banks of the Delaware, near its falls, as had already been determined upon by a previous vote.[1] The proposition, which was certainly conceived in a generous and enlarged spirit, met the acceptance of Congress; but the practical inconveniences of such an arrangement, under the immense accumulation of public business to be expected in so extensive a country, became too obvious to permit a serious attempt to carry it into execution.[2]

[1] See Journals of Congress, vol. IV. pp. 297, 300, and 307, 308.

[2] This arrangement, destined to a very brief duration, was brought about by a temporary coalition between the Eastern and Southern States against the Middle; which seemed a retributive offset to the coalition we have already seen entered into between the Middle and

With regard to the jurisdiction over the proposed federal towns, Congress, not having been able·to determine the precise nature and extent of it to their own satisfaction, provided in general that "an exclusive jurisdiction, or such other as Congress may direct, should be vested in the United States." Mr. Madison, always alive to the importance of every question which respected the constitutional boundaries of power, expressed his views on this subject, in a letter of July 28th, 1783, to his friend Judge Pendleton, as follows:

"In order to prepare the way to their permanent residence, Congress have appointed a com-

---

Eastern States against the Southern, with regard to the territorial question. A letter addressed, in January, 1784, by Mr. Higginson, one of the delegates of Massachusetts, to Colonel Bland, lately a delegate from Virginia, shows both the fact of the coalition, and the strong feelings of dissatisfaction which then existed among the Eastern delegates towards Pennsylvania in particular, the chief of the Middle States. We subjoin the following extract from that letter as a curious piece of contemporary history.

"You returned home, I imagine, with much greater satisfaction, having given your voice in favor of the alternate residence of Congress. That decision of Congress was, in my opinion, founded on the best of policy. It has long been my wish to see the Southern and Eastern States united. Their common safety and interest must be increased by that decision; for the Middle States had certainly laid such plans, and acquired such an influence, as would have given them the entire direction of the national concerns. Pennsylvania, or rather a junto of ambitious individuals in it, had conceived the idea of lording it over the other States; and nothing but a coalition of the extremities could have prevented their succeeding. They always exerted themselves to keep up a high degree of jealousy between the Southern and Eastern States; and while their attention was engaged in watching each other, these would-be despots were ever concerting and executing their plans for the subjugation of both." See the Bland Papers, vol. II. p. 113.

mittee to define the jurisdiction proper for them to be invested with. Williamsburg has asked an explanation on this point. The nearer the subject is viewed, the less easy it is to mark the just boundary between the authority of Congress and that of the State on one side, and, on the other, between the former and the privileges of the inhabitants. May it not also be made a question whether, in constitutional strictness, the gift of any State, without the concurrence of all the rest, can authorize Congress to exercise any power not delegated by the confederation, — as Congress, it would seem, are incompetent to every act not warranted by that instrument, or some other flowing from the same source."

Thus did the thoughtful and comprehensive mind of Mr. Madison foreshadow the difficulties of a question, which it was reserved for the convention of 1787 to solve by an express provision in the new constitution. It is remarkable that, in the same letter, he suggested the expedient by which the permanent and sole seat of Congress and of the federal government was ultimately assigned to the banks of the Potomac.

"Williamsburg," he says, "seems to have a very slender chance, as far as I can discover. Annapolis, I apprehend, would have a greater number of advocates. But the best chance, both for Maryland and Virginia, will be to unite in offering a double jurisdiction on the Potomac." [1]

[1] See Madison Debates and Correspondence, vol. I. pp. 558, 559.

After Congress had disposed of the question of their permanent residence in the manner above mentioned, they settled that of their temporary abode, in the same spirit of geographical compromise, by directing that, until the buildings to be erected on the banks of the Delaware and the Potomac should be prepared for the reception of Congress, their residence shall be alternately, at equal periods of not more than one year and not less than six months, in Trenton and Annapolis, and that Congress be adjourned on the 4th day of November, to meet at Annapolis on the 26th of the same month.[1]

Until the day fixed for their adjournment, they continued their sessions in Princeton. Two events of an imposing character occurred to illustrate the period of their sojournment in that quiet, academic retreat. Upon the invitation of Congress, the commander-in-chief transferred his residence to Princeton from his head-quarters on the Hudson. The ostensible motive of the invitation was the desire to consult him upon the details of a proper peace establishment; but the yearnings of the hearts of the representatives of the nation towards their great chief, and the comfort of leaning upon his mighty arm, in peace as in war, doubtless entered largely into the feelings which prompted it.

He arrived on the 25th of August, and was on the following day received by Congress in a

[1] Journals of Congress, vol. IV. pp. 302 and 315, 316.

public audience. To the affectionate welcome and congratulations of the president, he replied by assuring Congress of his readiness "to contribute his best endeavours towards the establishment of the national security, in whatever manner the sovereign power may think proper to direct, until the definitive treaty of peace or the evacuation of the country by the British forces; after either of which events, he should ask permission to retire to the peaceful shades of private life." Accommodations were provided for him at Rocky Hill, a pleasant country residence ·in the immediate vicinity of Princeton; where he continued for more than two months, and until a few days before the evacuation of the city of New York by the British army under the command of Sir Guy Carleton.

The other event to which we have alluded was the public reception of the Chevalier Van Berckel, minister of the United Netherlands, — the second foreign minister ever accredited to the United States, and the representative of an illustrious republic, which was next to our great ally among the powers of Europe in the recognition of our national independence. Congress was naturally desirous of marking the occasion with every circumstance of public honor and respect which their present situation admitted. The office of secretary of foreign affairs being vacant by the resignation of Mr. Livingston, Mr. Robert Morris, superintendent of finance, and General Lincoln, secretary of war, were charged with the direction of the ceremonial; and the commander-in-chief, the executives of New Jersey and Pennsylvania, the minister of France, and "such civil and military gentlemen as were in or near Princeton," were invited to attend. It was also ordered that "an entertainment be given to the minister at the public expense."

The audience took place in the room occupied by Congress in the college building, on the 31st of October. The striking historical parallel in the heroic struggles through which the two republics had passed in order to achieve their national independence, could not but be called to mind on both sides.

The minister, in addressing Congress, said: "While all Europe kept its eyes fixed on your exploits, their High Mightinesses, the States-General, could not refrain from very seriously interesting themselves therein, recollecting, as they always did, the dangers and difficulties to which their forefathers were subjected before they could free themselves from the yoke in which they were enthralled. They knew, better than any other, the worth of independence; and they knew better to set a just value on the greatness of your designs. They applauded your generous enterprise, which was inspired by a love of your country, conducted with prudence and supported with heroic courage; and they rejoiced at the happy success which crowned your labors."

To these allusions, the president of Congress replied: "In a contest for the rights of human nature, the citizens of the United States of America could not but be impressed with the glorious example of those illustrious patriots, who, triumphing over every difficulty and danger, established the liberties of the United Netherlands on the most honorable and permanent basis. Congress, at an early period of the war, sought the friendship of their High Mightinesses, convinced that the same inviolable regard for liberty, and the same wisdom, justice, and magnanimity which led their forefathers to glory were handed down unimpaired to their posterity; and our satisfaction was great in accomplishing with them a treaty of amity and commerce on terms so acceptable to both nations."

He added the following cordial and glowing anticipation of the future intercourse of the two republics, which happily their relations, to the present day, have not failed to justify.

"Governed by the same ardent love of freedom, and the same maxims of policy, cemented by a liberal system of commerce, and earnestly disposed to advance our mutual prosperity by a reciprocity of good offices, we persuade ourselves that the most friendly and beneficial connection between the two republics will be preserved inviolate to the latest ages."

Almost a year had now elapsed since the signature of the provisional articles of peace at

Paris; and although military operations had ceased on both sides, the main body of the British army still occupied the city of New York, awaiting, no doubt, the farther progress of the negotiations for a definitive treaty. The nature and causes of the delay which had taken place in those negotiations are to be sought chiefly in the complications and vicissitudes of political parties in England.

A few days after the conclusion of the provisional articles with the United States, the British Parliament assembled; and in the speech from the throne, the reluctant concession of American independence was mentioned as still in some degree contingent upon the settlement of the terms of peace with France.[1] A motion, made by Mr. Fox, for the production of the provisional articles, was negatived; and, soon after, Parliament adjourned to the 21st of the following month. In the mean time, preliminary articles of peace were concluded with the other powers at Paris; and on the 27th of January, 1783, all

[1] In taking leave of his transatlantic subjects, the king expressed a paternal solicitude lest their constitutional liberties should in future be endangered by the privation of monarchical rule, — a sentiment which found an echo, perhaps, in some American minds at that day. "In thus admitting," he said, "their separation from the crown of these kingdoms, I have sacrificed every consideration of my own to the wishes and opinion of my people. I make it my humble and earnest prayer to Almighty God that Great Britain may not feel the evils which might result from so great a dismemberment of the empire, and that America may be free from those calamities which have formerly proved, in the mother country, how essential monarchy is to the enjoyment of constitutional liberty."

the treaties — as well the provisional articles with the United States, as the preliminary articles with France and Spain — were laid before Parliament and ordered to be printed. The 17th of February was assigned for their consideration.

That day was destined to witness one of the most extraordinary and ill-starred political combinations which the history of parties in any country has ever presented, — a coalition between the former champion of American subjugation, and the eloquent advocate of American freedom who had only a year before expelled him from power. These recent antagonists were now closely and openly united in concerted opposition to the terms of peace. While a professed disapprobation of the conditions of peace constituted the ostensible ground of this union between Mr. Fox and Lord North, their known violent resentments against Lord Shelburne, and the prospect of again installing themselves in power upon his ruin, furnished motives so much more obvious and intelligible for a conjunction of political elements otherwise so repulsive and discordant, that the coalition between them revolted the moral sense of the nation. Neither the captivating wit and incomparable address of the one, nor the lofty abilities and generous temper of the other, were ever afterwards able to restore either of them entirely to the public confidence and esteem.

The coalition, nevertheless, had a momentary success. An amendment to the usual address

42 *

having been carried by them, after a long and vehement debate, on the 17th of February, formal resolutions, condemning the terms of peace as making " greater concessions to the adversaries of Great Britain than they were entitled to expect," were introduced on the 21st by Lord John Cavendish, and carried, with a like majority, by the same political combination.[1] The adoption of these resolutions produced the result which was intended, of the resignation of Lord Shelburne and the dissolution of his ministry; but owing to the natural repugnance of the king to the leaders of the coalition, and in consequence of the number of rival pretensions, both personal and political, to be reconciled in a new arrangement, a long ministerial interregnum ensued.

It was not until the 2nd of April that another administration was formed, with the Duke of Portland, first lord of the treasury, Lord North, secretary of state for the home department, and Mr. Fox, secretary for foreign affairs. The other places in the government were distributed be-

[1] In the course of the debate of the 17th of February, very free and pointed animadversions were made upon the coalition, which, it was generally understood, had been concluded the night before. In the House of Commons, Mr. Powys said: —

" The present era was remarkable for strange confederacies; great and arbitrary despots stood forth as the protectors of an infant republic; and in that House, lofty and strenuous asserters of high prerogative had combined with the humble worshippers of the majesty of the people; the most determined advocate of crown influence was seen hand in hand with the great purifier of the constitution."

tween the political friends of the two chiefs of
the coalition; but the larger number, as well as
the most important in character and influence,
fell to the share of Mr. Fox's friends.

In the resolutions of Lord John Cavendish, it
was expressly declared that, in consideration of
the public faith being pledged, the peace agreed
upon by the provisional and preliminary articles
should be inviolably maintained; and it was also
admitted that the acknowledgment of American
independence was in compliance with the necessity of the times and the sense of Parliament.
The criticisms made in debate on the arrangement
with America bore, in a general way, on the
extent of the boundaries, and the large participation in the fisheries yielded by it, but were
directed, with particular stress and earnestness,
against the inadequate and unsatisfactory nature
of the provisions made on behalf of the loyalists.

A few days after the formation of the coalition
ministry, Mr. Hartley was appointed in the place
of Mr. Oswald, to settle with the American
commissioners at Paris the terms of a definitive
treaty, and immediately set out on his mission.
It seemed, at first, to be the desire of the new
ministry to include in the definitive treaty some
arrangement respecting the commercial intercourse between the two countries.

The late administration had evinced on this
subject a spirit of unusual and enlightened liberality. Mr. Pitt, as chancellor of the exchequer,

had introduced into the House of Commons a bill for the temporary regulation of the inter-course, by which the vessels of the United States were to be admitted into all the ports of Great Britain in the same manner as the vessels of "other independent, sovereign States;" and the productions of the United States, imported in their own vessels, were to pay no other or higher duties than the same productions would be liable to, "if they were the property of British subjects and imported in British vessels." The trade of the British West India Islands, and of the other British Colonies and plantations in America, was, by the same bill, to be opened to the citizens of the United States with American produce in American vessels, on an equal footing with the subjects of Great Britain with British merchandise in British vessels.

The wise liberality of this measure exposed it to the vehement attacks of the British navigating interest; and it was withdrawn by the new ministry. What they now desired to obtain, and to make a part of the definitive treaty, was admission into the ports of the United States with the privileges of natives, both for their vessels and cargoes, in exchange for like privileges accorded to American vessels and cargoes, with regard to the ports of Great Britain alone; leaving the trade with the British West Indies and the other colonial possessions of the British crown to the operation of the Navigation Act, which would entirely exclude the citizens of the United States from any participation in that trade. Information, however, was soon received in England that the American ports were already open to British trade without restriction; and Lord Sheffield's "Observations," which appeared about the same time, having satisfied them that no future defensive or retaliatory measures of any efficiency were to be apprehended from the United States, so long as there was no central authority in the confederacy armed with the direct power of regulating the commerce of the States with foreign nations, the ministry grew altogether indifferent to any commercial arrangement.

The American commissioners, on their part, were very anxious to obtain for the citizens and vessels of the United States free admission to the trade with the British West Indies and other Colonies in America, and offered to pay for it the price of the privileges of natives, to be accorded to British subjects and vessels in the ports of the United States.[1] The negotiations

[1] Mr. Madison thought the proposed concession unwise in principle, as disarming the United States of a power of discrimination which might become essential for the protection of the national enterprise and industry, and also very unequal in its effects upon the interests of the producing and the navigating States. In this last view, in a letter addressed to Mr. Edmund Randolph in May, 1788, he remarked:—

"With regard to the concession to be made on the part of the United States, it may be observed that it will affect chiefly, if not solely, those States (producing) which will share least in the advantages purchased by it. So striking, indeed, does this contrast appear, that it may with certainty be inferred that, if Great Britain were negotiating a treaty with the former (navigating) States only, she would reject a mutual communication of

continued to drag on wearily and heavily, amid propositions on the one side and the other; and what was specially remarkable, propositions made by the British negotiator were, in several instances, disallowed and rejected by his own government. At length appeared the royal proclamation of the 2d of July, 1783, virtually interdicting the West India trade to the citizens and vessels of the United States, by allowing it only to "British subjects in British-built ships, owned by his Majesty's subjects, and navigated according to law."[1]

On the 27th of July, the American commissioners wrote to Mr. Livingston, the secretary for foreign affairs, and gave him the following account of the state of the negotiations:—

"The definitive treaties between the late belligerent powers are none of them yet completed. Ours has gone on slowly, owing partly to the necessity Mr. Hartley, successor of Mr. Oswald, thinks himself under of sending every proposition, either his own or ours, to his court for their approbation, and their delay in answering, through negligence perhaps, since they have heard our ports are open, or through indecision, occasioned by ignorance of the subject, or through

the privileges of natives; nor is it clear that her apprehensions on this side will not yet lead her to reject such a stipulation with the whole."

See this letter, for its able and profound views in general on the policy of the United States with regard to commercial treaties, in Madison Debates and Correspondence, vol. I. pp. 533–538.

[1] Diplomatic Correspondence of the American Revolution, vol. VII. pp. 82, 83.

want of union among the ministers. We send you herewith copies of several papers that have passed between us. He has, for some time, assured us that he is in hourly expectation of answers; but they do not arrive."[1]

In the mean time, not a little distrust and uneasiness were beginning to be felt in the United States, in consequence of these delays. We have seen with what promptitude Congress, immediately after the arrival of the provisional articles, had ordered a release of the prisoners of war held by them, in fulfilment of the stipulations of one of those articles; and yet the most important of the posts, which Great Britain was, by that same article, bound to withdraw her armies from "with all convenient speed," were still occupied by her troops; and another of its stipulations, that "no negroes or other property of the American inhabitants should be carried away," was daily and openly violated with the avowed knowledge and connivance of the British commander-in-chief.

There were, nevertheless, those in Congress who thought it expedient, even under these circumstances, to disband the army; and on the 23d of May a committee, consisting of Colonel Hamilton, Mr. Peters, and Mr. Gorham, reported a resolution that the non-commissioned officers and soldiers, enlisted to serve during the war, be

[1] Diplomatic Correspondence of the American Revolution, vol. x. p. 193.

immediately discharged. Mr. Madison moved to recommit the report; and although a decided majority of the members present voted for the motion, (including even the members of the committee, with the exception of Colonel Hamilton,) it was lost for the want of the requisite number of affirmative States.[1]

A proposition was then submitted by Mr. Williamson of North Carolina to furlough, instead of discharging, the troops enlisted for the war. Colonel Mercer of Virginia opposed both propositions in a motion, setting forth, as the grounds of it: "First, that Sir Guy Carleton had not given satisfactory reasons for continuing at New York; secondly, that he had broken the articles of the provisional treaty, relative to the negroes, by sending them off." Mr. Madison, in giving an account of these proceedings, records "that the motion of Colonel Mercer appeared exceptionable to several, particularly to Mr. Hamilton; and rather than it should be entered on the Journals by yeas and nays, it was agreed that the whole subject should lie over." The propositions both to discharge and to furlough the troops were, however, successively negatived.[2]

The subject came up again on the 26th of May, when, upon the motion of Colonel Hamilton, resolutions were unanimously adopted in-

[1] Journals of Congress, vol. IV. pp. 222, 223.

454, 455, and Journals of Congress, vol. IV. p. 222.

[2] Madison Debates, vol. I. pp.

structing our ministers abroad to remonstrate to
the court of Great Britain against the violation
of the provisional articles in the carrying away
the negroes, and to demand reparation for the
same, and directing the commander-in-chief likewise to continue his remonstrances on the subject
to Sir Guy Carleton. The proposition previously
submitted by Mr. Williamson of North Carolina
to furlough the troops enlisted for the war, was
then moved by Colonel Hamilton, and was passed,
as we have already had occasion to mention.[1]

The same party in Congress which favored an
immediate disbandment of the army, and had
carried through the proposition for an immediate
release of the prisoners of war, now proposed
other measures to precipitate the complete execution of the provisional articles on the part of
the United States in advance of the conclusion
of a definitive treaty, and notwithstanding the
disregard which had been shown of those articles
by the British authorities. On the 9th of May,
Mr. Dyer of Connecticut moved " a recommendation to the States to restore confiscated property
according to the provisional articles;" and on the
14th of the same month, Mr. Hamilton and Mr.
Ellsworth moved "a call on the States to fulfil
the recommendation relative to the Tories."[2] A
committee was at length appointed, consisting of
Mr. Hamilton, Mr. Ellsworth, Mr. Izard of South

[1] Journals of Congress, vol. IV.   [2] Madison Debates, vol. I. p.
pp. 223, 224.   451.

Carolina, Mr. Madison, and Mr. Hawkins of North Carolina, to consider and report to Congress "what further steps are proper to be taken by them for carrying into effect the stipulations contained in the articles between the United States and Great Britain, dated the 30th of November last."[1]

The several States in which confiscations of the estates of the Tories or Loyalists had taken place, had strongly remonstrated against any agreement being entered into by the American commissioners for the restitution of those estates; and instructions to the same effect had been given to the commissioners by Congress. Under these circumstances, they did not venture upon any other stipulation in the provisional articles than that Congress would *recommend* to the legislatures of the respective States to provide for the restitution of the confiscated estates. This stipulation was contained in the fifth article. By the fourth article, it was stipulated that creditors should meet with no lawful impediment to the recovery of their debts; and by the sixth, that no *future* confiscations or prosecutions should take place against any persons, on account of the part they may have taken in the war.

The committee above mentioned, of which Colonel Hamilton was chairman, made a report, proposing that,—"Whereas Congress are desirous of giving speedy and full effect to all the stipulations of the provisional articles on the part of

[1] Journals of Congress, vol. IV. p. 224.

the United States, and of accelerating thereby
the blessings of peace, in the confidence that the
conduct of his Britannic Majesty will be governed by a like disposition," — the several States
be *required*, and they are hereby *required*, to remove all obstructions to the full and immediate
execution of the fourth and sixth articles; and
that it be earnestly recommended to them to
take into serious consideration the fifth article,
and "to conform to the several matters therein
contained, with that spirit of moderation and liberality which ought ever to characterize the deliberations and measures of a free and enlightened
nation."

In the midst of the flagrant disregard, exhibited by the representatives and agents of the
British government, of the stipulations contained
in the provisional articles on their side, the over-
zealous anxiety manifested in this report to hurry
on the full execution of the articles by the United
States, in the vain notion of propitiating the temper of an obstinate and infatuated monarch, very
naturally revolted the sentiments of Congress.
On the 30th of May, when the report was taken
up for consideration, a motion was made to commit it, which was carried by the vote of every
member present except Colonel Hamilton, who
stood alone in opposition to the motion.[1]

From this time, no farther attempt appears to

---

[1] Journals of Congress, vol. IV. pp. 225, 226. See also Secret Journals, vol. III. pp. 355-358.

have been made in Congress to press a premature execution of the provisional articles on the part of the United States.

Inexplicable delays still continued at Paris in the negotiations for a definitive treaty; until, at last, — every proposition to modify or enlarge the provisional articles having terminated in illusion or abortion, and the other powers having agreed upon definitive treaties among themselves, and France pressing earnestly for some conclusion between Great Britain and the United States, — it was agreed to convert the provisional articles as they originally stood, without the slightest variation, into a definitive treaty. As such, they were signed and executed over again, by the respective plenipotentiaries at Paris, on the 3d day of September, 1783; and on the same day the definitive treaties between the other powers were consummated, with like solemnity, at Versailles.

The American commissioners, in communicating the result to the president of Congress, make the following remarks: —

"Whether the British court meant to avoid a definitive treaty with us, through a vain hope, from the exaggerated accounts of divisions among our people and want of authority in Congress, that some revolution would soon happen in their favor, or whether their dilatory conduct was caused by the strife of two opposite and nearly equal parties in the cabinet, is hard to decide." [1]

[1] Diplomatic Correspondence of the American Revolution, vol. x. p. 217.

The long drama, diplomatic and military, was now closed. Sir Guy Carleton received instructions to evacuate New York without farther delay; and on the 18th of October, Congress issued a proclamation finally discharging the troops enlisted for the war, and returning to the whole army "the thanks of their country for their long, eminent, and faithful services." In this parting address, Congress paid a well merited tribute to the civic, as well as military, virtues of the defenders of American freedom.

"In the progress of an arduous and difficult war," said they, "the armies of the United States have eminently displayed every military and patriotic virtue, and are not less to be applauded for their fortitude and magnanimity in the most trying scenes of distress, than for a series of heroic and illustrious achievements which exalt them to a high rank among the most zealous and successful defenders of the rights and liberties of mankind."

At the same time, another proclamation was issued, appointing a day of public thanksgiving in humble acknowledgment of the interposition of Divine Providence in bringing a contest apparently so unequal, and through so many perils and difficulties, to an issue so auspicious and glorious. In reviewing the manifestations of divine goodness, this document impressively recalled "that He hath been pleased to conduct us in safety through all the perils and vicissitudes of the

43 *

war; that he hath given us unanimity and resolution to adhere to our just rights; that he hath raised up a powerful ally to assist us in supporting them, and crowned our united efforts with success:" and then looking forward to the mighty and eventful future, it invoked the same goodness "to give wisdom and unanimity to our public councils; to cement all our citizens in the bonds of affection; to inspire them with an earnest regard for the national honor and interest; to enable them to improve the days of prosperity by every good work, and to be lovers of peace and tranquillity; to bless us in our husbandry, our commerce and navigation; to smile upon our seminaries and means of education; to cause pure religion and virtue to flourish; to give peace to all nations, and to fill the world with his glory."[1]

In this noble manner did the Congress of the United States celebrate and proclaim the termination of the protracted conflict of arms, through which the liberty and independence of their country were at last achieved. This, too, was the closing scene of Mr. Madison's service in that illustrious body. He had now served one year more than the triennial term of rotation which had been established by the legislation of his own State, as well as by the articles of confederation; and while Washington was on his way to Annapolis to resign into the hands of Congress

[1] See Journals of Congress, vol. IV. pp. 298, 299.

the military commission he had borne with such unrivalled virtue and glory, Madison was on his return to the State of their common nativity, having, by able and unwearied services in council, sustained the same cause which his immortal countryman crowned with triumph in the field. They were soon to be united again in other labors, not less important to the lasting happiness and glory of their country.

CHAPTER XVII.

THE period of Mr. Madison's service in Congress presented by far the most arduous and complex problems of national policy, internal and external, which the war of the Revolution gave rise to. He came into the body just at the moment when the system of paper credit, by which the war had been hitherto supported, experienced a sudden and fatal collapse; and when it became imperiously necessary to provide other financial resources, at home or abroad. At the same moment, the enemy, despairing of the success of the diplomatic wiles he had for some time been essaying in vain, recommenced his operations in the field with a vigor and formidable array of force, both military and naval, that he had never before displayed, and which was directed to the entire conquest and permanent occupation of the whole of the Southern States.

New and most important relations with the powers of Europe were, also, then inaugurated, not only by the alliance with France, but by the successive mediations offered for the reëstablishment of peace; and especially by the negotiations with Spain, who demanded, as the price of her support, the surrender of the Mississippi and of the Western country. In the midst of these exigencies of war and negotiation, jealousies and discords prevailed, to a great degree, among the States of the Union, mainly in regard to their interests in the territory which Spain was endeavouring to obtain; and owing to those discords, the articles of confederation, by which the national energies were to be firmly united and efficiently directed, still remained uncompleted.

We have seen what an able and leading and successful part Mr. Madison took in all these great and difficult questions, — ever loyal to the rights and dignity of his own State, but animated, at the same time, with a comprehensive

American spirit, which looked upon all the members of the confederacy as one family, bound to mutual concession and harmony among themselves, but to inflexible firmness and perseverance in the maintenance of the common dignity and rights against the rest of the world. It was this just and elevated spirit, combined with his disciplined statesmanship, superior knowledge, and balanced judgment and temper, which placed him, yet a young man, in the very first rank of the distinguished assembly of which he was a member. And when it is recollected that in that assembly he sat with such men as Samuel Adams, Gerry, Gorham, Langdon, Ellery, Ellsworth, Sherman, and Wolcott, from the East; John Dickinson, Witherspoon, Clymer, Wilson, Peters, McKean, Robert R. Livingston, Alexander Hamilton, and Duane, from the Middle States; the Rutledges, Laurens, Middleton, Matthews, Randolph, Lee, Jones, Mercer, Williamson, and Burke, from the South — such a rank in such a body might well have filled the measure of an ambition much greater than his.

The law of Virginia, at the time of Mr. Madison's election to Congress, expressly disqualified a delegate from serving more than three years in any term of six.[1] As he was first elected in the autumn of 1779, he could not, under this limitation, have continued in Congress beyond the autumn of 1782. But when the annual

[1] Hen. Stat. vol. x. p. 74.

election came on, at the May session of 1782, of
delegates to serve in the Congress commencing
with the first Monday of November following, so
important was it felt to be to secure the continuance of his services in the field of patriotic
labor, in which he had so much signalized his
usefulness to the State and to the whole country, that the law which rendered him ineligible
was repealed,[1] and he was chosen for a fourth
year of consecutive service in the national councils.[2]

At the end of the fourth year, there remained,
under the triennial rotation established by the
articles of confederation, but which did not begin
to operate until the 1st of March, 1781, (the
date of the final ratification of those articles,) a
period of four months, from November to March,
during which he was legally capable of serving.
It was even proposed to reëlect him for this brief
fragment of a year. But he felt it proper to discourage the suggestion.[3]

From these signal and most honorable proofs
of the general satisfaction his conduct had given
his constituents, it must not, however, be inferred

[1] Hen. Stat. vol. x. p. 164.

[2] In a manuscript letter of his
colleague, Mr. Joseph Jones, to
Mr. Madison, of the 25th of June,
1782, there is the following allusion
to the motives of the repeal of the
disqualifying law. " I mentioned "
(in a former letter) " the continuation of the old delegates by a vote,
but which I afterwards found to be
a mistake, the vote being postponed until the bill had passed repealing the law which rendered
yourself and J. J. ineligible."

[3] Madison Debates and Correspondence, vol. I. p. 540, and manuscript letter of E. Pendleton to J.
Madison, of the 9th of June, 1783.

that there was absolute unanimity in the sentiments they implied. In the legislature of Virginia there was at that time a party, though not a numerous one, which manifested an habitual jealousy and distrust of the national authorities, and all their leading measures. To those who were actuated by that feeling, Mr. Madison could not have been an acceptable representative; and they were ready enough to avail themselves of the rigors of a statutory ostracism to displace him. Mr. Edmund Randolph, in writing to him on the 20th of June, 1782, gives the following account of the abortive attempt then made to effect his exclusion, under the specious cover of an existing legal disqualification.

"My last and preceding communications which spoke of certain manœuvres, alluded to in your letter of the 11th instant, mentioned, I believe, that a design appeared to be formed against the reëlection of you and myself to Congress. The attack was unexpected; and the secret suggestions, which were intended to injure, had had their fullest operation before it came to the knowledge of our friends. But it may be triumphantly said that the wicked and malignant did not dare to exclude from their most poisonous reports a respect for our characters. You were assailed under the garb of friendship. It was lamented that the rigor of the law should cut off so valuable a servant from public employment. And to say the truth, there was such a fervency of compliment that it was unpleasant to distrust its sincerity.

"I, too, was declared to be ineligible, after a preface overflowing with panegyric; and, indeed, the manifesto of hostility never could wear a milder form. However, Patrick Henry propounded the question respecting my eligibility, for he had been informed of their clandestine operations. No man rose to assert the negative, except Richard Henry Lee. He was fulsome in commendation, as I was informed, and protested against every possibility of exception but from that quarter. He had no other coadjutor than the 'old squire.'[1] The Doctor" (Arthur Lee) "spoke in opposition to his brother, upon pretty much the same principle as that which actuates two Eastern delegates when they divide, namely, an affectation of candor."

During this long and anxious term of public service, Mr. Madison was hardly ever absent from his seat in Congress. While other members, and his own colleagues, were frequently absent, and for months together, it does not appear that he allowed himself even a brief visit to his relatives in Virginia, with whom he continued to keep up an affectionate intercourse by letter. In a communication to his father, dated the 20th of May,

---

[1] This was the title by which Richard Lee, the colleague of Richard Henry Lee in the representation of Westmoreland, was ordinarily known.

1782, he thus expressed his strong and conscientious sense of representative duty.

"It has at no time been more difficult for me to fix my probable return to Virginia. At present all my colleagues have left Congress except Colonel Bland; and it is a crisis which calls for a full representation from every State. Anxious as I am to visit my friends, as long as I sustain a public trust I shall feel a principle which is superior to it [the indulgence of private wishes]."

Nor was this the only sacrifice incident to Mr. Madison's public service at this exigent epoch. The provision made by Virginia for the support of her delegates in Congress, though liberal in theory, was exceedingly precarious, and sometimes, indeed, wholly illusory in practice. As the nature of that provision furnishes an illustration of the manners and customs of the time, and especially of the mode of living and expense which then prevailed in Virginia, it may not be without interest to the reader to give some account of it. The act of Assembly on the subject declared that "the delegates shall be allowed the expense for such part of their families as they may severally incline to keep with them; provisions for necessary servants and horses, not exceeding three servants and four horses for each; pay for house-rent and fuel;" and the farther sum of twenty dollars *per diem*, while in attendance on Congress, and two dollars for every mile

of travel, going and returning; but these last
sums were payable in paper money, subject to
the rates of depreciation of the day.

After this provision, apparently so princely, the
act rather ludicrously proceeds: "In order that
the said delegates may always keep in mind that
economy is expected from them by their country, a general account of all their disbursements
for housekeeping, as aforesaid, shall be transmitted by them quarterly to the auditor of public
accounts, by whom a warrant is to be given on
the treasurer to pay the amount out of the public
moneys in his hands."[1] It often, and indeed generally happened, that when the warrant was
obtained on the treasurer, there was no public
money in his hands to meet it, and the disappointed delegate was left to every variety of
shifts and expedients to raise money from other
quarters to defray his current expenses.

Mr. Madison, being then a bachelor, occasioned
a much lighter charge to the treasury of the
State than most of his colleagues. He did not,
probably, avail himself of the establishment provided by law for the delegates to a greater extent than a single servant, and one or two horses.
And yet, upon this comparatively modest scale
of expense, he found himself often much embarrassed, and compelled to draw largely on his private resources. In a letter to his father of the
12th of February, 1782, he thus describes his
necessities: —

[1] See Hen. Stat. vol. x. p. 168.

"The disappointment in forwarding the money by Mr. Brownlow has been sorely felt by me; and the more so, as the legislature has made no provision for the subsistence of the delegates that can be relied on. I hope some opportunity will soon put it in your power to renew the attempt to transmit it, and that the delay will have made a considerable addition to it. Besides the necessity of this supply for the common occasions, I have frequent opportunities here of purchasing many scarce and necessary books at a fourth of the price which, if to be had at all, they will hereafter cost me."

Although the legislature, at their May session in 1782, made a new and different provision for their delegates, ("a more certain and adequate one," it was declared to be,) by directing that, in lieu of all expenses, they should receive a fixed allowance of eight dollars *per diem*, of the specie standard, "to be paid out of such public money as should thereafter be set apart and appropriated for that use,"[1] it does not appear that the new arrangement brought with it any sensible relief to the pecuniary wants of the delegates. It was through his friend Mr. Edmund Randolph, who resided at Richmond, that Mr. Madison carried on his intercourse with the treasurer of the State for the needed but still unreliable supplies. The following specimens of that correspondence, while painting strongly the distresses of the delegates, impart a dash of humor to the picture.

[1] See Hen. Stat. vol. xi. pp. 31, 32.

On the 27th of August, 1782, he says to his friend: "I cannot, in any way, make you more sensible of the importance of your kind remittances for me than by informing you that I have, for some time past, been a pensioner on the favor of Haym Salomon, a Jew broker." And on the 24th of September he writes: "Your credit with Mr. Cohen, which procured me fifty pounds, with two hundred dollars transmitted by Mr. Ambler, (the treasurer,) have been of much service; but I am relapsing fast into distress. The case of my brethren is equally alarming."

On the 8th of October he writes again: "The remittance to Colonel Bland is a source of hope to his brethren. I am almost ashamed to reiterate my wants so incessantly to you; but they begin to be so urgent that it is impossible to suppress them. The kindness of our little friend in Front Street, near the Coffee-House, is a fund which will preserve me from extremities; but I never resort to it without great mortification, as he obstinately rejects all recompense. The price of money is so usurious that he thinks it ought to be extorted from none but those who aim at profitable speculations. To a necessitous delegate he gratuitously spares a supply out of his private stock."

It was fortunate for the delegates that their public cares and straitened circumstances found some alleviation in social enjoyments among themselves. Of these no one had a keener relish,

44 *

within the bounds of lawful indulgence, than Mr.
Madison. With several of his colleagues from
Virginia, and a few members from other States,
he made an arrangement which admitted them
into the accommodations of a private household.
These gentlemen, with their families and the in-
mates of the house, formed a cultivated and congenial circle, in which Mr. Madison enjoyed a
seasonable and pleasant relaxation from the occupations of his congressional life.

The attractions of this circle were greatly enhanced to him, during the last winter of his residence in Philadelphia, by the presence of Mr.
Jefferson, who, on his suggestion, had been again
and unanimously appointed one of the commissioners to treat of peace, and was now at the
seat of government to inform himself, from the
public archives, of the condition and progress of
the negotiations. To this new source of pleasure
to Mr. Madison was added a yet stronger fascina-
tion, in an attachment to an interesting and accomplished young lady, daughter of an old friend
of Mr. Jefferson, who was a co-signer with him
of the Declaration of Independence.[1] This attachment, which promised at one time the most
auspicious result, terminated at last in disappointment. We cannot forbear to add the following
extract of a letter addressed to him on the occasion by Mr. Jefferson, as connected with an event
which is never without importance in the life of

[1] General William Floyd, one of the delegates of New York.

a man of virtuous sensibilities, and as affording
a touching proof of the intimate and fraternal
sympathies which united the two friends.

"I sincerely lament," he said, "the misadven-
ture which has happened, from whatever cause
it may have happened. Should it be final, however, the world still presents the same and many
other resources of happiness, and you possess
many within yourself. Firmness of mind and
unintermitting occupation will not long leave you
in pain. No event has been more contrary to
my expectations, and these were founded on what
I thought a good knowledge of the ground. But
of all machines, ours is the most complicated and
inexplicable."[1]

Among the qualities which distinguished Mr.
Madison at this period, and indeed through his
whole life, was a vein of quiet humor, which relieved the severity of his public labors, and lighted
up with an inexpressible charm, in his moments
of relaxation, the graver aspects of his character.
Of this, an instance has been already given to
the public in a joint and playful letter addressed
by Ellery of Rhode Island and himself, amid
the deep gloom and anxiety of the spring of
1780, to their three colleagues, — Schuyler of
New York, Matthews of South Carolina, and Peabody of New Hampshire, — then on a mission to
headquarters to concert with the commander-in-
chief a plan of operations for the ensuing cam-

[1] Manuscript letter of the 31st of August, 1783.

paign.[1] It was by his genial disposition and social affinities he acquired that knowledge of the characteristic peculiarities of the different sections of the confederacy, which furnished him the many amusing and illustrative anecdotes he was wont, in after life, to entertain his friends with.

After the close of his congressional service, he spent some weeks in Philadelphia, and arrived at his father's residence in Virginia in December, 1783. This again became his home; and here, at the age of thirty-two years, he resumed those habits of close and systematic study which he formed in early life. His experience in Congress had, doubtless, made him sensible of the great value of legal knowledge to the statesman; and after an interval of social and domestic recreation, which he had so well earned by his public labors, he grappled resolutely with the black-letter terrors of the common law. In a letter to Mr. Edmund Randolph, of the 10th of March, 1784, he thus speaks of his undertaking:—

"On my arrival here, which happened early in December, I entered, as soon as the necessary attentions to my friends admitted, on the course of reading which I have long meditated. Coke-Littleton, in consequence, and a few others from the same shelf, have been my chief society during the winter. My progress, which, in so short a time, could not have been great under the

[1] See Life of Ellery, in Sanderson's Lives of the Signers of Independence.

most favorable circumstances, has been much retarded by the want of some important books, and still more by some living oracle for occasional consultation."

These legal studies, though interrupted, from time to time, by the public duties which were soon again devolved upon him, he continued to pursue for several years, as we learn from. his subsequent correspondence with his friends. In a letter to the Marquis Lafayette, of the 20th of March, 1785, he sportively alludes to his pursuits, in contrast with the more agreeable occupations of some of their common friends.

"I received a letter, a few days ago, from Mr. Mercer, written in the bosom of wedlock at Mr. Spriggs's; another at the same time from Monroe, who was well at New York. I have nothing to say of myself, but that I have exchanged Richmond for Orange, as you will have seen by the above date; that I enjoy a satisfactory share of health; that I spend the chief of my time in reading, and the chief of my reading, on law; that I shall hear, with the greatest pleasure, of your being far better employed; and that I am, with the most affectionate esteem, yours."

As late as the 27th of July, 1785, we find again an allusion to his legal studies, in a letter of that date to Mr. Randolph. "I keep up my attention," he says, "as far as I can command my time, to the course of reading which I have of late pursued; and shall continue to do so.

I am, however, far from being determined ever to make a professional use of it. My wish is, if possible, to provide a decent and independent subsistence, without encountering the difficulties I foresee in that line. Another of my wishes is to depend as little as possible on the labor of slaves. The difficulty of reconciling these views has brought into my mind several projects."

Mr. Madison never did make any professional use of his legal attainments; but on several occasions, in his public career, he gave such proof of the depth and accuracy of those attainments, even in the most abstruse and recondite parts of the law, as to leave no doubt that, if he had made it his profession, he could not have failed to attain the very highest eminence in it.[1]

[1] A remarkable instance of the accuracy and even subtlety of Mr. Madison's legal knowledge, — abiding with him to a late period of his life, — was frequently mentioned by Mr. Jefferson. Both of them were members of the board of commissioners appointed by the legislature of Virginia in 1818, to fix upon a proper location for the University. The board consisted of twenty-one members, including some of the most distinguished judges and lawyers of the State. Of the former, it is sufficient to mention Judges Roane and Cabell, of the court of appeals, and Judges Brockenbrough, Stuart, Holmes, and Dade, of the general court, together with Chancellor Taylor; and of the latter, Mr. Philip C. Pendleton, General Breckenridge, and General John G. Jackson, as well as Mr. Jefferson himself, who, it is known, was a most profound lawyer, and especially versed in all the learning of the law of real property. Among the considerations presented to influence the choice of the commissioners, was the offer of a very valuable body of lands in the neighbourhood of Lexington, for which a deed was tendered. The deed passed through the hands of the judges and lawyers without criticism. When Mr. Madison came to examine it, he modestly suggested a *quære*, found-

The part he had so recently acted in public affairs of the greatest national importance, was altogether too prominent and distinguished to admit of his devoting either his time or his thoughts wholly to professional studies. Questions of great delicacy and difficulty were constantly springing up in the operations of our complex, federative system; and upon these Mr. Madison was appealed to as a sort of oracle, in his retirement. Of this description was a question which had just arisen, affecting Virginia especially in her relations with one of her sister States, and involving the practical construction of the fourth article of the confederation.

That article required of each State the surrender of fugitives from justice,—charged "with treason, felony, or other high misdemeanour" committed within the jurisdiction of another State,—upon the demand of the executive authority of the latter. A citizen of Virginia was charged with having committed in South Carolina a violent and unprovoked assault upon a person who was a justice of the peace, during the sitting of the court of general sessions; and his surrender for trial was demanded, under this provision of the federal compact, of the executive of Virginia by the governor of South Carolina. The demand was re-

ed upon some rather recondite doctrine with regard to the limitations of real estate, whether the deed was good in law. The defect pointed out was finally recognized by the board to be fatal to the validity of the deed, and it was so represented to be in their report to the legislature.

ferred to Mr. Edmund Randolph, the attorney-general of the State, who gave a learned and elaborate opinion in writing against the surrender; mainly on the ground that the vague description of the offence, in the documents transmitted by the executive of South Carolina, did not necessarily constitute it a case of "high misdemeanour." He sent a copy of his opinion to Mr. Madison, to elicit his judgment upon the question.

We give a few extracts from Mr. Madison's answer, dated "Orange, 10th of March, 1784," as showing the careful deliberation and enlarged views with which these questions of state were habitually revolved by him, whether in a private and irresponsible, or a public and official, position.

"If I were to hazard an opinion after yours, it would be that the respect due to the chief magistrate of a confederate State, enforced as it is by the articles of confederation, requires an admission of the fact as it has been represented. If the representation be adjudged incomplete or ambiguous, explanations may certainly be called for; and if, on a final view of the charge, Virginia should hold it not a *casus foederis*, she will be at liberty to withhold her citizen, (at least upon that ground,) as South Carolina will be to appeal to the tribunal provided for all controversies among the States."

Then looking at the subject from the broad and elevated point of view from which he was accustomed to contemplate all such questions, after saying that "his present view would admit few exceptions to the propriety of surrendering fugitive offenders," he declared it as his opinion that the peculiar and intimate relations subsisting between the States of the American confederacy will be found to require an extension of the federal agreement for the mutual surrender of fugitives to numerous cases below the grade of "high misdemeanour."

"In a word," he says, "experience will show, if I mistake not, that the relative situation of the United States calls for a '*droit public*' much more minute than that comprised in the federal articles, and which presupposes much greater mutual confidence and amity among the societies that are to obey it than the law that has grown out of the transactions and intercourse of jealous and hostile nations."

His foresight was, a few years afterwards, justified and fulfilled in the provisions of the new constitution, which, after the specification of "treason" and "felony," as in the articles of confederation, added the general denomination of "other crime" instead of "high misdemeanour," and extended the principle of extradition to a class of *civil* fugitives, for which some provision was rendered indispensably necessary by the varying domestic institutions of the different States.

Among those who were in most intimate communication with Mr. Madison at this time, and who most frequently and largely interchanged views with him on the doubtful questions arising in the operations of the government, was Mr. Jefferson, now a successor, as he had been the predecessor, of Mr. Madison in the national councils. From his correspondence with Mr. Madison, we learn the difficulties and delays that attended the ratification of the definitive treaty of peace by Congress, owing to the non-attendance of the requisite number of States. By some members it was contended that seven States were sufficient for the ratification. Mr. Jefferson and a majority of the members insisted that, without the assent of nine States, the act would be invalid. The attendance of nine States was not obtained until the 14th of January, 1784, when the ratification was immediately consummated, but not in time, it was apprehended, to be exchanged in Europe within the six months fixed by the treaty itself.

During the anxious suspense of these questions, and for the whole period, indeed, that Mr. Jefferson was with Congress at Annapolis, he was in almost constant correspondence with Mr. Madison, and freely sought his opinions and reflections on the political complications which were then so frequently occurring. To these calls, Mr. Madison, from his retirement, responded with promptitude and fulness. Gratifying as it is to remark the general accordance in the conclusions their minds had severally attained on these subjects, it is yet more so to observe the tone of affectionate frankness and cordiality which prevailed in their communications. After disposing of the various and thorny public questions with which their correspondence had been chiefly occupied, Mr. Jefferson, in the close of a long letter of the 20th of February, 1784, devoted mainly to the discussion of some of those questions, fondly reverts to a scheme of personal friendship and happiness he had formed for their future intercourse.

"I hope," he says, "you have found access to my library. I beg you to make free use of it. The steward is living there now, and of course will always be in the way. Monroe is buying land almost adjoining me. Short will do the same. What would I not give could you fall into the circle. With such a society, I could once more venture home, and lay myself up for the residue of life, — quitting all its contentions, which grow daily more and more insupportable.

"Think of it. To render it practicable, only requires you to think it so. Life is of no value but as it brings us gratifications. Among the most valuable of these is rational society. It informs the mind, sweetens the temper, cheers our spirits, and promotes health. There is a little farm of one hundred and forty acres adjoining me, and within two miles, all of good land, though old, with a small, indifferent house on it, — the whole worth not more than £250. Such an one might be a farm of experiment, and support a little table and household. It is on the road to Orange, and so much nearer than I am. It is convenient enough for supplementary supplies from thence. Once more, think of it, and adieu."

Mr. Madison's answer to this letter was dated the 16th of March, 1784. Having first reviewed, elaborately and exhaustively, the several public questions presented for his opinion, he responded as follows to the friendly personal wishes contained in Mr. Jefferson's letter: —

"I know not, my dear sir, what to reply to the affectionate invitation which closes your letter. I subscribe to the justness of your general reflections. I feel the attractions of the particular situation you point out to me. I cannot altogether renounce the prospect. Still less can I as yet embrace it. It is far from being improbable that a few years may prepare me for giving such a destiny to my future life; in which case the same, or some equally convenient spot, may be commanded by a little augmentation of price. But wherever my final lot may fix me, be assured that I shall ever remain, with the sincerest affection and esteem, your friend and servant."

The ingenuous reader cannot but sympathize in the effusions of mutual confidence and affection, and the yearnings for each other's society, by which these great men, amid their public cares, were thus early drawn together. Although

Mr. Madison never acquired the little *Sabine* farm that was set before him in all the charms of Catonian simplicity, yet, as his paternal residence in the county of Orange, where he always lived, was within thirty miles of Monticello, and Mr. Monroe for many years resided with his family on the land 'which he had bought in the immediate neighborhood of the latter place, few day-dreams of human felicity have ever been more nearly fulfilled than that which Mr. Jefferson indulged for himself and his friends.

In this same letter, Mr. Madison gave Mr. Jefferson a commission to purchase books for him, from which it will be seen what was the paramount object of patriotic anxiety and reflection that then, and for several years to come, occupied his thoughts.

"I must leave to your discretion," he said, " the occasional purchase of rare and valuable books, disregarding the risk of duplicates. You know tolerably well the objects of my curiosity. I will only particularize my wish of whatever may throw light on the general constitution and *droit public* of the several confederacies which have existed. I observe in. Boiraud's catalogue several pieces on the Dutch, the German, and the Helvetic. The operations of our own must render all such lights of consequence. Books on the law of nature and nations fall within the same remark."

In another letter, addressed to Mr. Jefferson a

year later, (27th of April, 1785,) when he was minister in Europe, Mr. Madison enlarged his commission for the purchase of books; but the great American question — the right organization of a confederate republic — was still, it will be seen, uppermost in his thoughts and studies.

"I thank you much," he says, "for your attention to my literary wants. All the purchases you have made for me are such as I should have made for myself with the same opportunities. You will oblige me by adding to them the Dictionary, in 13 vols. 4to., by Felice and others;[1] also De Thou, in French. If the utility of Moreri be not superseded by some later work, I should be glad to have him too. I am afraid, if I were to attempt a catalogue of my wants, I should not only trouble you beyond measure, but exceed the limits which other considerations ought to prescribe to me. I cannot, however, abridge the commission you were so kind as to take on yourself in a former letter, of procuring for me, from time to time, such books as may be 'either old and curious, or new and useful.' Under this description will fall those particularized in my former letters, to wit, treatises on the ancient or modern federal republics, on the law of nations, and the history, natural and political, of the New World; to which I will add such of the Greek and Roman authors (where

---

[1] Dictionary of Law, National, Civil, and Political, — otherwise called *Code de l'Humanité.*

they can be got very cheap) as are worth having, and are not on the common list of school classics," &c. &c. &c. &c.

While Mr. Madison was laying this broad foundation of liberal and comprehensive studies to perfect the rare statesmanship, of which the first fruits had already been given to his country, he was summoned from his brief retirement to engage again in the active service of the State. At the annual election of members of the legislature in the month of April, 1784, he was called forth by the people of his native county to represent them in the House of Delegates. It was now eight years since he had been a member of that body; and the theatre of action there presented was altogether unlike that on which, for the last four years, he had been arduously employed.

Not only were the questions to be acted on, for the most part, of a different character, — though sometimes necessarily and closely connected with those of the national forum, — but the manner of treating them, and the agencies by which their decision was controlled, were strikingly contrasted. The more numerous composition of the House of Delegates of Virginia, as well as the temperament of the people, gave far greater scope for the arts of oratory; and this again secured a very decided lead to a few individuals, who, to the reputation of patriotism and long familiarity with public affairs, superadded the seductive power of eloquence.

It so happened that the official service of Mr. Henry in the executive department of the State, and that of Mr. Richard Henry Lee in the Continental Congress, expired in the same year, 1779. Both of them were immediately afterwards chosen, by their respective counties, members of the popular branch of the legislature, in which, with very brief intervals, they had continued to serve ever since. Whether it was the emulation of oratory, or the effect of different original tendencies in their political principles and sympathies, they soon became rival and antagonist leaders in the House of Delegates, and were habitually arrayed against each other on almost all questions of public policy.

On those which related more particularly to the internal policy of the State, while Mr. Henry on several occasions favored paper money, tender laws, stay laws, the postponement or remission of taxes, and a very indulgent, if not lax, system with regard to the enforcement of both public and private engagements and in the administration of justice generally, Mr. Lee was the declared and inflexible opponent of all these measures. Contrary to what might have been expected from the natural tendency of the respective systems pursued by them in State politics, Mr. Henry, down to the period of which we are now speaking, had shown himself much more disposed to sustain and strengthen the federal authority than Mr. Lee, who had manifested a spirit of opposition to Congress and all its most prominent acts, ever since he left that body. Thus they became, for the time, the living and active exponents of two adverse political systems in both state and national questions. Opposing champions,—the rival pretensions of oratory made them, in some sort, the gladiators of the Assembly; and from the homage paid to their age and longer service, as well as from the power and attractions of their eloquence, the privileged *rôle* of leaders was, by general consent, accorded to them.

They were both members of the House of Delegates, with all the eclat and influence of their traditional leadership, when Mr. Madison returned to it in 1784. At the same time were members, John Marshall, future chief justice of the United States, Spencer Roane, future president of the court of appeals of Virginia, Henry Tazewell, William Grayson, John Taylor, and Wilson Cary Nicholas, future senators of the United States, John Breckenridge, future attorney-general of the United States, Joseph Jones, late colleague of Mr. Madison in Congress, and Braxton, Tyler, Stuart, Ronald, Thruston, Corbin, and Page, all men of unquestioned ability. But, for the most part, they were younger statesmen; and deferring to the claims of the great popular and parliamentary leaders, they willingly stood aside when these veteran champions, with their burnished armour, entered the arena.

NOTE.

THE intimate relations of Mr. Lee and Mr. Henry, previous to their return to the legislature in 1779–1780, and their subsequent cordial union in opposition to the federal constitution of 1788, have led some writers into the error of supposing that they had generally harmonized in their political views, and coöperated on all the great public questions of their time. (See Grigsby's Discourse, p. 145, and Life of R. H. Lee, vol. I. pp. 45, 46.) The representation in the text is, however, abundantly sustained by the contemporaneous correspondence on Mr. Madison's files, as well as by other unquestionable testimony.

Mr. Jones, in a letter to Mr. Madison of the 24th of November, 1780, says:—

" We have had a warm debate in the House upon a bill to explain and amend the act of the last session for funding the new bills of credit of Congress under the scheme of the 18th of March. The question agitated, whether those bills, as well as the two millions of State money issued last session, should be a tender in payment of debts; and determined that they should be a legal tender. Henry for the question, Richard Henry Lee against it; and both, aided by their auxiliaries, took up two days or nearly in discussing the question. Indeed, we lose a great deal of time in idle, unnecessary debate."

In another letter to Mr. Madison, dated the 31st of May, 1788, he says:—

" Since my last, the bill for postponing to 20th of November next the making distress for the taxes has passed the House of Delegates by a majority of 13, and was, the day before yesterday, assented to by the Senate. Hurtful and dangerous as this step will, I fear, prove, it was warmly espoused by Mr. Henry, opposed by his *antagonist*, and every effort made to fix the day to an earlier period, but in vain."

Mr. Edmund Randolph, in writing to Mr. Madison on the 1st of June, 1782, says (speaking of Mr. Jefferson):—

" His triumph might certainly be an illustrious one over his former enemies, were he to resume the legislative character; for in the *constant division* between the two *leaders*, Henry and Lee, he might incline the scale to whichever side he would."

To these extracts, taken somewhat at random from Mr. Madison's files, may be added the testimony of another distinguished contemporary witness. Judge Roane, who afterwards married a daughter of Mr. Henry, was, as we have seen, a member of the House of Delegates with him and Mr. Lee in 1783 and 1784. In a letter addressed to Mr. Wirt, (see Life of Henry, p. 249,) he says:—

"I met with Patrick Henry in the Assembly of May, 1783. I also there met with Richard Henry Lee. I lodged with Mr. Lee one or two sessions, and was perfectly acquainted with him, while I was yet a stranger to Mr. Henry. These two gentlemen were the *great leaders* in the House of Delegates, and were *almost constantly opposed.* There were many other great men who belonged to that body; but, as *orators*, they cannot be named with Henry and Lee."

CHAPTER XVIII.

Mr. Madison came into the legislature with no ambition of leadership. Animated with a sincere and unaffected respect for the abilities and services of his seniors, his sole desire was to conciliate their support, as well as to enlist the coöperation of his younger and able associates, in favor of those objects of public interest which his reflections and experience had led him to consider of the highest importance to the welfare both of the State and of the Confederacy. He has himself given to the world an impressive account of the considerations which induced him to yield to the renewed call of his fellow-citizens for his services in the legislature.

"Having served," he says, "as a member of Congress through the period between March, 1780, and the arrival of peace in 1783, I had become intimately acquainted with the public distresses and the causes of them. I had observed the successful opposition to every attempt to procure a remedy by new grants of power to Congress. I had found, moreover, that despair of success hung over the compromising principle of 1783 for the public necessities, which had been so elaborately planned and so impressively recommended to the States.

"Sympathizing, under this aspect of affairs, in the alarm of the friends of free government, at the threatened danger of an abortive result to the great, and perhaps last, experiment in its favor, I could not be insensible to the obligation to aid, as far as I could, in averting the calamity. With this view, I acceded to the desire of my fellow-citizens of the county that I should be one of its representatives in the legislature; hoping that I might there best contribute to inculcate the critical posture to which the revolutionary cause was reduced, and the merit of a leading agency of the State in bringing about a rescue of the Union and the blessings of liberty staked on it from an impending catastrophe." [1]

Never losing sight of this, the great and paramount object of his legislative mission, he devoted himself, with diligence and faithfulness, to every question which concerned the peculiar and domestic interests of Virginia. He was an active member of all the leading committees, and chairman of the committee on commerce. The duty of this last committee was defined to be, "to take into consideration all matters and things relating to the trade, manufactures, and commerce of the Commonwealth, to report their proceedings thereupon to the House, and to recommend such improvements as, in their judgment, may be made therein."

Mr. Madison had given much consideration, as his correspondence attests, even during the period of his service in Congress, to the commercial condition and interests of Virginia. In a letter of the 10th of December, 1783, written immediately after his arrival at home, he makes the following remarks on the subject.

[1] See Madison Debates and Correspondence, vol. II. pp. 693, 694.

"The situation of the commerce of this country, as far as I can learn, is even more deplorable than I had conceived. It cannot pay less to Philadelphia and Baltimore, if one may judge from a comparison of prices here and in Europe, than thirty or forty per cent. on all the exports and imports, — a tribute which, if paid into the treasury of the State, would yield a surplus above all its wants. If the Assembly should take any steps towards its emancipation, you will, no doubt, be apprised of them, as well as of their other proceedings from Richmond."

The natural and most effectual remedy for this state of things, in the opinion of Mr. Madison, was to concentrate the trade of Virginia at one or two of her ports, and thus to establish, within her own limits, commercial marts where her exports and imports would be collected in mass, and afterwards distributed to the ultimate consumer. This regulation was recommended by the farther consideration of breaking up the oppressive monopoly under which the trade of Virginia was conducted by British merchants and their factors, who, profiting of their ancient connections in the country, carried their supplies up its numerous rivers, and entering into direct and isolated negotiations with the planters, and enticing them by the pernicious lure of long credits, controlled at will, and for their own advantage, the prices both of what they sold and what they bought. By restricting them to designated and public marts, where they would be brought into free and equal competition with the rest of the world, resorting to a common market of purchase and sale, it was thought that the system which, on the return of peace, still continued to enslave Virginia to the cupidity of the British trader, would receive an important check.

An act for "restraining foreign vessels to certain ports within the Commonwealth,"[1] was finally passed in pursuance of these views, but not without encountering strenuous opposition. Mr. Madison, writing to Mr. Jefferson, then at Paris, on the 3d of July, 1784, immediately after the adjournment of the legislature, and giving him an account of its proceedings, says:—

"We made a warm struggle for the establishment of Norfolk and Alexandria as our only ports, but were obliged to add York, Tappahannock, and Bermuda Hundred in order to gain anything, and to restrain to these ports foreigners only."

Here, perhaps, is the true explanation of the causes which have contributed to frustrate, and may, for an indefinite time, yet frustrate the establishment of a great mart of foreign commerce in Virginia. It is, apparently, the superabundance of her natural advantages, the number and consequent competition of her fine rivers and harbors, which prevent that centralization of trade and capital, indispensable

---

[1] Hen. Stat. vol. xi. pp. 402–404.

to constitute a great emporium. How different, in this respect, is the situation of the leading commercial State of the Union. Nature, by giving her but a single great river, and but a single maritime port, where that river meets the ocean, has, by a fiat far more powerful than legislative decrees, converged all her resources and connections of trade, embracing the larger portion of the Union, to one grand, absorbing centre. If it shall be found that the multiplied bounties of nature have made diffusion, and not concentration, the commercial lot of Virginia, it is a condition of things not without important compensations in the more equal distribution of local benefits, while its disadvantages, in a general view, are now much lessened by the rapid and cheap intercommunications which exist among all the seats of trade and industry within the Union.

The following extract of a letter addressed by Mr. Madison to Mr. Jefferson, on the 20th of August, 1784, presents so striking a view of the obstacles opposed to the policy of concentration on the one hand, and of the arguments which recommended it on the other, that it seems essential to a proper comprehension of this portion of the legislative and commercial history of the country to lay it before the reader.

"The act which produces most agitation and discussion is that which restrains foreign trade to enumerated ports. Those who meditate a revival of it on the old plan of British monopoly and diffusive credit, or whose mercantile arrangements might be disturbed by the innovation,—with those whose local situations give them, or are thought to give them, an advantage in large vessels coming up the rivers to their usual stations,—are busy in decoying the people into a belief that trade ought, in all cases, to be left to regulate itself; that to confine it to particular ports is to renounce the boon with which nature has favored our country; and that if one set of men are to be importers and exporters, another set to be carriers between the mouths and heads of the rivers, and a third retailers, trade, as it must pass through so many hands, all taking a profit, must in the end come dearer to the people than if the simple plan should be continued which unites these branches in the same hands.

"These and other objections, though unsound, are not altogether unplausible; and being propagated with more zeal and pains by those who have an interest to serve, than proper answers are given by those who regard the general interest only, make it very possible that the measure may be rescinded before it is to take effect. Should it escape such a fate, it will be owing to a few striking and undeniable facts; namely, that goods are much dearer in Virginia than in the States where trade is drawn to a general mart; that even goods brought from Philadelphia and Baltimore to Winchester, and other western and southwestern parts of Virginia, are retailed cheaper than those imported directly from Europe are sold on tide water; that, generous as the present price of our tobacco appears, the same article has currently sold fifteen or twenty per cent., at least, higher in Philadelphia, where, being as far from the ultimate market, it cannot be intrinsically worth more; that scarce a single vessel from any part of Europe, other than the British dominions, comes into our ports, whilst vessels from so many other parts of Europe resort to other parts of America, — almost all of them, too, in pursuit of the staple of Virginia."

As Mr. Madison anticipated, efforts were made to repeal this act at the session of 1785–1786, and again at that of 1786–1787.   Those efforts were defeated by the firmness and perseverance of its original friends, who were not able, however, to prevent successive additions to the list of enumerated ports.   Such was the power of local considerations, combined with the interested views of a foreign mercantile monopoly, in opposition to the plans of a far-seeing and statesman-like policy.[1]

[1] The interest and importance of the subject induce us to subjoin yet another extract from Mr. Madison's correspondence of this period, taken from a letter addressed by him to Mr. Monroe, (then a member of the Continental Congress,) on the 21st of June, 1785.

"I observe in a late newspaper that the commercial discontents of Boston are spreading to New York and Philadelphia.   Whether they will reach Virginia or not, I am unable to say.   If they should, they must proceed from a different interest, — from that of the planters, not that of the merchants.   The present system here is as favorable to the latter, as it is ruinous to the former.   Our trade was never more completely monopo-

Another object, intimately connected with the commercial interests of Virginia, early attracted the attention of Mr. Madison.   The river Potomac was the boundary between Maryland and Virginia.   The charter to Lord Baltimore had defined the boundary to be along the southern shore of the river; and, by the constitution of 1776, Virginia had released to Maryland all the territory embraced within that charter, "with all the rights of property, jurisdiction, and government, and all other rights whatsoever which might at any time heretofore have been claimed

lized by Great Britain, when it was under the direction of the British Parliament, than it is at this moment. But as our merchants are almost all connected with that country, and that only, and as we have neither ships nor seamen of our own, nor likely to have any in the present course of things, no mercantile complaints are heard. The planters are dissatisfied, and with reason; but they enter little into the science of commerce, and rarely, of themselves, combine in defence of their interests."

Then stating some well-known facts to show how much higher were the prices of Virginia produce in Northern markets than in her own, as well as how much cheaper foreign merchandise was to be had there, he proceeds, —

"It is difficult, notwithstanding, to make them [the planters] sensible of the utility of establishing a Philadelphia or a Baltimore* among ourselves, as one indispensable step towards relief; and the difficulty is not a little increased by the pains taken by the merchants to prevent such a reformation, and by the opposition arising from local views. I have been told that Arthur Lee paved the way to his election in Prince William by promising that, among other things, he would overset the port bill. Mr. Jefferson writes me that the port bill has been published in all the gazettes in Europe, with the highest approbation everywhere except in Great Britain. It would, indeed, be as surprising if she should be in favor of it, as it is that any among ourselves should be against it. I see no possibility of engaging other nations in a rivalship with her, without some such regulation of our commerce."

* By concentrating our commerce at Alexandria and Norfolk, the object of the port bill.

by her, except the free navigation and use of the rivers Potomac and Pohomoke." Mr. Madison was apprehensive that the broad and general terms in which this surrender of the rights of jurisdiction and government was made to Maryland, might be .interpreted into a total relinquishment by Virginia of any jurisdiction over the Potomac River, and thus a fatal door be opened for the violation or evasion of her port regulations upon that important channel of commerce.

Mr. Jefferson, being then at Annapolis as one of the delegates of Virginia in Congress, Mr. Madison, in a letter to him of the 16th of March, 1784, called his attention to this subject, that he might sound the sentiments of the Maryland delegates with regard to it, and ascertain what prospect there was of an amicable adjustment of the question.

"I was told," he says, "on my journey along the Potomac, of several flagrant evasions which had been practised with impunity and success by foreign vessels which had loaded at Alexandria. The jurisdiction of half the rivers ought to have been expressly reserved. The terms of the surrender are the more extraordinary, as the patents of the Northern Neck place the whole river Potomac within the government of Virginia; so that we were armed with a title both of prior and posterior date to that of Maryland. What will be the best course to repair the error, — whether to extend our laws upon the river, making Maryland the plaintiff, if she chooses to contest their authority,—to state the case to her at once, and propose a settlement by negotiation,—or to propose a mutual appointment of commissioners for the general purpose of preserving a harmony and efficacy in the regulations on both sides?

"The last mode squares best with my present ideas. It can give no irritation to Maryland; it can weaken no plea of Virginia; it will give Maryland an opportunity of stirring the question, if she chooses; and will not be fruitless if Maryland should admit our jurisdiction. If I see the subject in its true light, no time should be lost in fixing the interest of Virginia. The good humor into which the cession of the back lands must have put Maryland, forms an apt crisis for any negotiations which may be necessary. You will be able probably to look into her charter and laws, and to collect the leading sentiments relative to the matter."

Mr. Jefferson replied to this letter on the 25th of April. "I like," he said, "the method you propose of settling ·at once with Maryland all matters relative to the Potomac. To introduce this the more easily, I have conversed with Mr. Stone [one of their delegates] on the subject, and finding him of the same opinion, have told him I would by letters bring the subject forward on our part. They will consider it, therefore, as originated by this conversation."

The matter being thus put in train by Mr. Madison previous to the meeting of the legislature, he pursued it when that body assembled. The following resolution introduced by him (in blank as to names), was adopted by the House of Delegates on the 28th of June, and was concurred in two days afterwards by the Senate.

"Whereas, great inconveniences are found to result from the want of some concerted regulations between this State and the State of Maryland touching the jurisdiction and navigation of the river Potomac,—

"*Resolved*, That George Mason, Edmund Randolph, James Madison, Jr., and Alexander Henderson, Esquires, be appointed commissioners, and that they or any three of them do meet such commissioners as may be appointed on the part of Maryland, and, in concert with them, frame such liberal and equitable measures concerning the said river as may be mutually advantageous to the two States, and that they make report thereof to the General Assembly.

"*Resolved*, That the executive be requested to notify the above appointment, with the object of it, to the State of Maryland, and desire its concurrence in the proposition."[1]

It was this essay, originated by Mr. Madison, to establish, by mutual concert, common regulations of navigation and trade between two conterminous States, which led, as we shall hereafter

[1] Journal of House of Delegates, May session, 1784, pp. 84 and 89.

see, to the call of the convention at Annapolis for considering the establishment of an uniform system of commercial regulations among all the States; and that produced the general convention of Philadelphia, whose proceedings terminated in the present constitution of the United States. As the first step in a connected series of movements which conducted the country to so happy a consummation, we have thought its history required the development we have here given it.

It had been the intention of Mr. Madison, in connection with this subject, to bring forward a proposition for improving the navigation of the upper parts of the Potomac River, as one of the principal channels by which the trade of the West was to be drawn into Virginia; and he desired especially to associate the name and influence of Washington, in some becoming manner, with an enterprise of so much grandeur. In the letter to Mr. Jefferson of the 3d of July, 1784, already referred to, written after the close of the first session of the legislature for that year, he says: "I found no opportunity of broaching a scheme for opening the navigation of the Potomac, under the auspices of General Washington." But to this object his attention was earnestly given at the ensuing session; and he had then the happiness of carrying through the legislature, with the powerful aid and coöperation of General Washington himself, a comprehensive and well considered system of internal improvements for the whole State.[1]

After disposing of these questions involving the material interests of the State, Mr. Madison turned his attention to ameliorations of her civil and political system. One of the earliest measures adopted by Virginia, after the formation of her republican constitution in 1776, was the appointment of a committee of revisors, of which Mr. Jefferson, Mr. Pendleton, and Mr. Wythe were the acting members, for the purpose of reviewing the entire body of her laws then in

[1] It was in the correspondence of this period between Mr. Jefferson and Mr. Madison that the first suggestion appears of entering upon these great works, under the auspices of General Washington's name and direction. How entirely Mr. Jefferson appreciated their vast importance and consequences in the future, and how earnestly he desired to see General Washington connected with them, as objects worthy his patriotism and fame, is shown by a letter addressed to Mr. Madison as early as the 20th of February, 1784.

"The Ohio and its branches," he says, "which head up against the Potomac, afford the shortest water communication by 500 miles of any which can be got between the Western waters and the Atlantic, and of course promise us almost a monopoly of the Western and Indian trade. I think the opening of this navigation is an object on which no time is to be lost. Pennsylvania is attending to the Western commerce." After mentioning what Pennsylvania was then doing to secure the great prize, he proceeds: "Could not our Assembly be induced to lay a particular tax which should bring in £5,000 or £10,000 a year, to be applied till the navigation of the Ohio and Potomac is opened, then James River, and so on, through the whole successively. General Washington has that of the Potomac much at heart. The superintendence of it would be a noble amusement in his retirement, and leave a monument of him as long as the waters should flow. I am of opinion he would accept of the direction as long as the money should be to be employed on the Potomac; and the popularity of his name would carry it through the Assembly." Manuscript letter.

force,— proposing such changes as should appear
necessary to adapt them to her new institutions,
— and digesting the whole in the form of bills for
the deliberate consideration of a future legislature. The arduous labors of the committee were
completed early in 1779, and were embraced in
one hundred and twenty-six bills, which they reported to the General Assembly at the May session of that year.

No opportunity had been found, amid the dis-
tractions and exigencies of the war, to enter
systematically upon the important work of consummating this revision of the laws. On the
return of peace, it presented itself as one of the
first and most essential objects of the statesman's
care. Mr. Madison took the lead in it. But
deeming it an indispensable preliminary to legislative action on a scheme "which proposed such
various and material changes in our legal code,"
that the fullest opportunity should be afforded
for its examination, and that a knowledge of its
provisions should be "diffused throughout the
community," he offered a resolution, in which
those considerations were set forth, directing a
number of copies of the report to be printed for
distribution in the several counties of the State,
as well as for supplying the members of the legislative, executive, and judiciary departments of
the government. After the adoption of the resolution, the further prosecution of the work was
deferred to the next meeting of the legislature.

Mr. Madison's views of reform extended also
to the constitution of the State; more, it would
seem, with a view to place it on an authentic
and unequivocal basis of popular assent than to
remove mere theoretical defects. The constitution of 1776 had been framed at a crisis of great
public anxiety, and in the midst of national
emergencies of a very pressing character. The
body from which it proceeded, having received
no express power from the people to establish
a permanent form of government,—though such
power was strongly implied from the circumstances under which it was chosen,—the paramount authority of the instrument, as a supreme
law, was constantly exposed to be called in question, and was actually questioned by men of great
weight in the public councils.

The habitual reverence of Mr. Madison for the
public will, as the only legitimate basis on which
republican institutions can rest, made him desirous that the fundamental law of Virginia
should be clothed with that highest sanction, in
a way which should admit of no doubt. He favored, therefore, the call of a convention with
full power from the people to establish a constitution; which convention, when assembled, would
either ratify the existing government as it was,
or use the occasion to make such amendments
in it as to bring its provisions into closer conformity with the theoretical rules of political
science. These appear to have been his leading

views. He was neither an agitator nor a visionary in the cause.

In writing to Mr. Jefferson on the 15th of
May, 1784, a few days after the meeting of the
legislature, and referring to the project of a revision of the State constitution, he says: "Whether
any experiment will be made this session, is uncertain. Several members, with whom I have
casually conversed, give me more encouragement
than I had indulged. As Colonel Mason remains
in private life, the expediency of starting the
idea will depend much on the part to be expected from Richard Henry Lee and Mr. Henry."

In another letter to Mr. Jefferson dated the
3d of July, immediately after the adjournment
of the legislature, he gives the following history
of what was done on the subject, and of his own
part in the proceedings: —

"A trial was made for a State convention; but
in a form not the most lucky. The adverse
temper of the House, and particularly of Mr.
Henry, had determined me to be silent on the
subject. But a petition from Augusta having,
among other things, touched on a reform of the
government, and Richard Henry Lee arriving
with favorable sentiments, we thought it might
not be amiss to stir the matter. Mr. Stuart,
from Augusta, accordingly proposed to the committee of 'propositions and grievances' the resolutions reported to the House, as per Journal.
Unluckily, Mr. Lee was obliged by sickness to

leave us the day before the question came on in committee of the whole; and Mr. Henry showed a more violent opposition than we had expected. The consequence was that, after two days debate, the report was negatived; and the majority, not content with stopping the measure at present, availed themselves of their strength to put a supposed bar on the Journal against a future possibility of carrying it. The members for a convention with full powers were not considerable in number, but included most of the young men of education and talents. A great many would have concurred in a convention for specified amendments; but they were not disposed to be active, even for such a qualified plan."

As the resolutions which were reported by the committee of " propositions and grievances," embody very clearly and succinctly the views of Mr. Madison, and others who favored a convention, we insert them for the information of the reader.

" *Resolved*, That such other part of the said petition as prays for a reformation of the government of this Commonwealth is reasonable; that the ordinance of the convention, commonly called the constitution, does not rest upon an authentic basis, and was no more than a temporary organization of government for preventing anarchy, and pointing our efforts to the two principal objects, of war against our then invaders, and peace and happiness among ourselves; but

47 *

this, like all other acts of legislation, being subject to change by subsequent legislatures, possessing equal power with themselves, should now
receive those amendments which time and trial
have suggested, and be rendered permanent by
a power superior to that of the ordinary legislature.

"*Resolved,* That an ordinance pass, recommending to the good people of this Commonwealth the
choice of delegates to meet in general convention,
with powers to form a constitution of government
to which all laws, present and future, should be
subordinate; provided, that the present government shall remain in every respect as it now is,
until such constitution shall be finally settled
and actually substituted."[1]

These resolutions were committed to a committee of the whole House on the state of the
Commonwealth, where they were the subject of
the two days' animated debate mentioned by
Mr. Madison. That committee made a report,
which was concurred in by the House by a vote
of 57 to 42, and which, by its tone of firmness
and adherence to existing institutions, recalls the
"*nolumus leges Angliæ mutare*" of the old barons in the Parliament of Merton, and is a faithful
and instructive exemplification of the conservative
temper and character of the people of Virginia
of that day. It was in these words: —

[1] See Journal of House of Delegates of Virginia, May session, 1784,
p. 55.

"*Resolved,* That it is the opinion of this committee that so much of the petition from Augusta county as relates to an alteration of the constitution or form of government ought to be rejected, such a measure not being within the province of the House of Delegates to assume; but, on the contrary, it is the express duty of the representatives of the people, at all times and on all occasions, to preserve the same inviolate, until a majority of all the free people of the Commonwealth shall direct a reform thereof." [1]

This decision of the legislature was followed by forty-five years of continued and, in general, contented acquiescence in the constitution of 1776 by the people, and of recognition of its authority by the various departments of the government, which amply supplied any technical defect in its origin. The Commonwealth, under its auspices, enjoyed a reign of public virtue and of practical and well-ordered freedom which, in spite of theoretical criticisms, future times will look back to with gratitude and respect, if not with envy and regret.[2]

[1] See Journal of House of Delegates of Virginia, May session, 1784, p. 70.

[2] Among Mr. Madison's papers we find the notes of the speech made by him on the proposed revision of the constitution. They are very brief and condensed. As a sample of his lucid order in the arrangement of his thoughts for debate, and as exhibiting an outline of the reasons which determined him in favor of the proposition, we subjoin them here, precisely as we find them.

"Nature of Constitution exam⁴. See Mass. p. 7. 8. 15. 16. N. Y. p. 63. Penn p. 85. 86. Del. p. 106. N. C. p. 146. 150. S. C. p. 188. Geo. p. 186.

"Convention of 1776, without due power from people.

"1. passed ordinance for Const⁰ on recommendation of Cong⁰ of 15 May, prior to

The question of religious freedom, with which Mr. Madison had been so much and so earnestly occupied in the earlier stages of his career, met him again on his return into the councils of the State. Petitions were presented to the legislature, alleging a decay of public morals, and proposing, as the most appropriate remedy, a general assessment upon the people for the support of religious teachers. Among the standing commit-

decl⁼ of Independence; as was done in N. H p. 1. and N. J. p. 78. 84.

" 2. passed from impulse of necessity — see last clause of the preamble.

" 3. before independence declared by Cong⁵.

" 4. power from people no where pretended.

" 5. other ordinances of same session deemed alterable, — as relative to senators — oaths — salt.

" 6. provision for case of West Augusta in its nature temporary.

" 7. convention make themselves branch of the Legislature.

" Constitution, if so to be called defective —

" 1. in a union of powers, which is tyranny, Montesqu.

" 2. Executive department dependent on legislature, 1. for salary. 2. for character in triennial expulsion. 3. expensive. 4. may be for life contrary to art. 5. of Declaration of rights.

" 3. Judiciary dependent for amt of salary.

" 4. Privileges and wages of members of Legislature unlimited and undefined.

" 5. Senate badly constituted and improperly barred of the originating of laws.

" 6. equality of representation not provided for — see N. Y. p. 65. S. C. p. 165.

" 7. Impeachments of great moment and on bad footing.

" 8. county courts seem to be fixed, p. 143. 144 — Also General court.

" 9. Habeas corpus omitted.

" 10. No mode of expounding Constitution, and of course, no check to Genl Assembly.

" 11. Right of suffrage not well fixed — quære if popish recusants &c. not disfranchised.

" Constitution rests on acquiescence, a bad basis.

" Revision during war improper — on return of peace, decency requires surrender of power to people.

" No danger in referring to the people, who already exercise an equivalent power.

" If no change be made in the constitution, it is advisable to have it ratified, and secured against the doubts and imputations under which it now labours."

Mr. Madison's opinions on the constitution of Virginia, with regard to the right of suffrage, the mode of appointment and tenure of the judiciary, and other questions of internal organic law, were essentially different from Mr. Jefferson's, — marking not merely the common difference between theory and practice, but important differences as to the theory itself of a well-balanced republic, guarded, on every side, against the danger of oppression and abuse. For his opinions on these questions, expressed about this time, see his letter to Mr. John Brown of Kentucky, dated 23d of August, 1785, and his observations on Mr. Jefferson's " Draught of a Constitution," addressed to the same gentleman in October, 1788.

tees of the House of Delegates, at that time, was a committee charged "with all matters relating to religion and morality," and denominated "the committee of religion." To that committee were referred the above-mentioned petitions; and in a short time they reported that the suggestion of the petitioners was, in their opinion, reasonable and expedient. Mr. Madison, in giving an account, at the time, of the proceedings of the legislature to a correspondent then absent from the country, says, "The friends of this measure did not choose to try their strength in the House." The report of the committee was, therefore, not acted upon during that session of the legislature; but the question was renewed at the succeeding session, and became then, as we shall see, the subject of high and solemn debate.

Petitions were also presented from the Baptist, Presbyterian, and Protestant Episcopal churches, — the two former asking a removal of all remaining distinctions in favor of the Episcopal church, and that "religious freedom be established upon the broad basis of perfect political equality;" and the last demanding the repeal of certain laws which restrained, as they alleged, their power of self-government, and praying for an act of incorporation to enable them to hold their property securely, and to regulate their own spiritual concerns.[1] The committee of re-

[1] See Journal of House of Delegates of Virginia, May session, 1784, pp. 20, 21, and 36.

ligion, to whom these petitions were referred, reported the demands of all of them to be reasonable, and particularly that the applications made by the clergies of both the Episcopal and Presbyterian churches, for the incorporation of their respective societies, were so; and that "like incorporations ought to be extended to all other religious societies within this Commonwealth, which may apply for the same."[1]

It does not appear, however, that a bill was actually brought in for the incorporation of any other church than the Episcopal. This, when reported, was committed to a committee of the whole House, and occasioned warm discussions. Mr. Madison, in the letter cited above, gives the following account of it, and of its reception.

"The Episcopal clergy introduced a notable project for reëstablishing their independence of the laity. The foundation of it was that the whole body should be legally incorporated, invested with the present property of the church, made capable of acquiring indefinitely, empowered to make canon and by-laws not contrary to the laws of the land; and incumbents, when once chosen by the vestries, to be irremovable otherwise than by sentence of the convocation. Extraordinary as such a project was, it was preserved from a dishonorable death by the talents of Mr. Henry. It lies over for another session."

[1] See Journal of House of Delegates of Virginia, May session, 1784, p. 43.

It is shown by the Journal of the House that
this bill, after being debated two days in committee of the whole, was specially assigned to
the second Monday in November, at the ensuing
session, to be again considered in the same committee. The proceedings upon it at that time,
and the part then taken by Mr. Madison with
regard both to it and the proposition of a general assessment, will hereafter demand our attention.

The questions of federal policy brought before
the legislature at this session were, for the most
part, acted upon in a spirit of great liberality,
and with unusual promptitude. The proposed
amendment of the eighth article of the confederation,—which formed a part of the "revenue plan"
adopted by Congress on the 18th of April, 1783,
and by which the whole number of free white
inhabitants and three fifths of all others was to
be substituted for the value of lands and their
improvements as the rule for apportioning federal burdens among the States,—had not hitherto
been acted upon in Virginia. It was now taken
up at an early period of the session, and acceded
to by a general vote. At the same time, as it
was uncertain whether the amendment would be
accepted by all the other States, it was resolved
that immediate measures should be taken to obtain and transmit to Congress the information
they had called for to enable them to fix the
valuation of lands and their improvements in the

several States, required by the existing rule of apportionment under the articles of confederation. Appropriate acts were passed, during the session, for carrying both of these resolutions into effect.[1]

A resolution was then passed, declaring that, until arrangements shall be completed for apportioning among the States the common debts and charges of the confederacy by one or other of the above-mentioned rules, "the preservation of justice and the national character" demand that all requisitions, which may, from time to time, be made upon the States by Congress for discharging the debts incurred during the war or for defraying the ordinary expenses of government, — whether apportioned by either of the said rules, or by such other temporary rule as may be judged more equitable, — should be faithfully complied with. To this was added another resolution of unwonted vigor in favor of the federal authority. It was in the following words:—

"*Resolved*, That the delegates representing this State in Congress ought to be instructed to urge in Congress all measures necessary for accelerating a fair and final settlement of the accounts subsisting between the United States and individual States; and that whenever such settlement shall have been completed, a payment of the balance appearing thereupon to be due" (or estimated by Congress to be due, in case of ob-

---

[1] See Journal of House of Delegates, p. 11, and Hen. Stat. vol. xi. pp. 401, 402, and 415–417.

struction or failure of a definite rule of settlement, as a subsequent resolution provided) "ought to be enforced, if necessary, by such distress on the property of the defaulting States or of their citizens, as by the United States, in Congress assembled, may be deemed adequate and most eligible."[1]

This resolution of the House of Delegates of Virginia, implying and recognizing the preëxistence of a coercive power in Congress with regard to the States, and invoking its exercise, has been considered to be the offspring of Mr. Henry. As the assertion was made to his face, and not contradicted, it may be assumed to be true.[2] It is rendered the more probable by the contemporary evidence which Mr. Madison's correspondence affords of Mr. Henry's general views, at that time, in relation to the federal authority. In writing to Mr. Jefferson on the 15th of May, 1784, four days before the adoption of this resolution, he says: "The latter [Mr. Henry] arrived yesterday; and, from a short conversation, I find him strenuous for invigorating the federal government, though without any precise plan."

A resolution was also adopted, declaring that Congress ought to be invested, for the term of fifteen years, with the power of prohibiting the vessels of any nation with which no commercial treaty had been formed from trading with any

---

[1] Journal of House of Delegates, May session, 1784, pp. 11 and 12.

[2] See Robertson's Debates of Virginia Convention of 1788. Also, *ante*, p. 303.

of the States of the confederacy; and with the
further power of prohibiting foreigners, unless
expressly authorized by treaty to do so, from
importing into the United States any goods,
wares, or merchandise not the produce or man-
ufacture of the country, of which they are citizens or subjects. This resolution was in exact
pursuance and fulfilment of a recommendation
which had been made by Congress on the 30th
of April, 1784, as the most efficient means of
countervailing the illiberal policy manifested by
Great Britain, since the reëstablishment of peace,
in excluding the vessels of the United States
from the trade with her West India islands.[1]
Virginia had, by an act passed in the autumn
of 1783, already taken the initiative in the same
line of action, by authorizing and inviting Congress, so far as depended on her, to prohibit the
importation of the produce of the British West
India islands into the United States in British
vessels.[2] She now gave effect to the recommendation of Congress by passing another act in the
very terms of that recommendation.[3]

Upon the subject of British debts, to which
the recent ratification of the definitive treaty of
peace by Congress gave a very solemn importance, the proceedings of the legislature were
not characterized by an equal spirit of loyalty to
the federal authority. The treaty having ex-

[1] Journals of Congress, vol. IV. p. 393.
[2] Hen. Stat. vol. XI. p. 313.
[3] Idem, pp. 388, 389.

pressly stipulated that there should be " no lawful impediment on either side to the recovery of debts heretofore contracted," and Virginia having, during the war, passed laws, which were still in force, prohibiting the recovery of debts due to British subjects, the repeal of those laws seemed now the necessary consequence of the paramount obligation of a treaty concluded by the United States in virtue of an explicit power granted by the articles of confederation to Congress.

The previous disregard of the provisional articles of peace by the British authorities, in the removal of negroes contrary to the positive stipulation of one of those articles, gave a color for delays on the part of the State, which, concurring with the general pecuniary embarrassments of the people, too easily influenced the deliberations of the Assembly. A special committee was appointed to inquire into and report upon an infraction of the seventh article of the treaty by the agents of Great Britain, " so far as the same respects the detention of slaves and other property belonging to the citizens of this Commonwealth." The report of the committee having verified the infraction, a resolution was brought forward, instructing the delegates of the State in Congress to lay the same before that body, and to ask its interposition to remonstrate to and demand reparation from the British government, with an additional instruction in these words : —

" And that the said delegates be instructed to

inform Congress that the General Assembly have no inclination to interfere with the power of making treaties with foreign nations, which the confederation hath wisely vested in Congress; but it is conceived that a just regard for the national honor, and the interest of the citizens of this Commonwealth, obliges the Assembly to withhold their coöperation in the complete fulfilment of the said treaty, until the success of the aforesaid remonstrance is known, or Congress shall signify their sentiments touching the premises."

To many members of the legislature, of whom Mr. Madison was one, this resolution, while disclaiming any interference with the treaty-making power of Congress, appeared plainly to assume the decision of a question respecting the obligation and fulfilment of treaty stipulations, which necessarily and exclusively belonged to the province of the department constitutionally charged with the treaty-making power. An amendment of the resolution was, therefore, offered by Mr. Madison, which, in lieu of the instruction recited above, proposed the following:—

"In case of refusal or unreasonable delay of due reparation, the said delegates be instructed to urge that the sanction of Congress be given to the just policy of retaining so much of the debts due from the citizens of this Commonwealth to British subjects as will fully repair the losses sustained by the infraction of the treaty aforesaid."[1]

[1] See Journal of House of Delegates, May session, 1784, pp. 74, 75.

The amendment failed, there appearing thirty-three votes for it, and fifty against it; and the original resolution was then agreed to by the House. This was the inauguration of a policy which led to long and serious international embroilments, and gave rise to mutual and bitter recriminations of breaches of public faith. The question will meet us often again in the course of this narrative. We will only remark, for the present, that the accustomed division took place upon it between the two ancient leaders of the public councils of Virginia at that time. Mr. Richard Henry Lee voted in favor of an immediate compliance with the stipulations of the treaty of peace, by the repeal of all laws in Virginia inconsistent with it;[1] while Mr. Henry was the champion of the policy that prevailed in the resolution adopted.[2]

[1] See Journal of House of Delegates, May session, 1784, p. 41.

[2] That the reader may have a full view of the proceedings of the legislature, and of the opinions of Mr. Madison on a subject of so much interest to the national character and the peaceful relations of the country, we here give an outline of a comprehensive proposition which was submitted by him in committee of the whole, both as to the recovery of debts due to British subjects, and the mode of indemnity to be pursued for injuries to American citizens from infraction of the treaty. With regard to the first, he proposed a provision for the progressive recovery of British debts, to be paid in instalments, as under all the circumstances of the case an equitable and proper arrangement; which proposition was introduced with the following preamble:—

"Whereas, by the 4th article of the definitive treaty of peace, ratified and proclaimed by the United States in Congress assembled on the 14th day of January last, 'it is agreed that creditors on either side shall meet with no lawful impediment to the recovery of the full value, in sterling money, of all *bona fide* debts heretofore contracted'; and whereas it is the

The legislature of Virginia, at this its first session since the grand closing scene of the Revolution in the resignation of the commander-in-chief, was not unmindful of the tribute of grati-

duty and determination of this Commonwealth, with a becoming reverence for the faith of treaties, truly and honestly to give to the said article all the effect which circumstances not within its control will now possibly admit; and inasmuch as the debts due from the good people of this Commonwealth to the subjects of Great Britain were contracted under the prospect of gradual payments, and are justly computed to exceed the possibility of full payment at once, more especially under the diminution of their property resulting from the devastations of the late war, and it is therefore conceived that the interest of the British creditors themselves will be favored by fixing certain reasonable periods at which divided payments shall be made."

Then follows a resolution authorizing a progressive recovery of the debts to British subjects, in annual instalments to be determined by the legislature.

With regard to the mode of indemnity for injuries suffered by American citizens, after reciting the stipulations of the treaty which had been violated by the functionaries and agents of the British government, the proposition proceeds:—

" And whereas the good people of this Commonwealth have a clear right to expect that whilst, on one side, they are called upon by the United States in Congress assembled, to whom, by the federal constitution, the powers of war and peace are exclusively delegated, to carry into effect the stipulations in favor of British subjects, an equal observance of the stipulations in their own favor should, on the other side, be duly secured to them under the authority of the confederacy, —

" Resolved, That it is the opinion of this committee that the delegates representing this State in Congress ought to be instructed to urge in Congress peremptory measures for obtaining from Great Britain satisfaction for the infringement of the article aforesaid; and in case of refusal or unreasonable delay of such satisfaction, to urge that the sanction of Congress be given to the just policy of retaining so much of the debts due from citizens of this Commonwealth to British subjects as will fully repair the losses sustained from such infringement; and that, to enable the said delegates to proceed herein with the greater precision and effect, the executive ought to be requested to take immediate measures for obtaining and transmitting to them all just claims of the citizens of this Commonwealth under the 7th article as aforesaid."

tude and affection due to her illustrious son. At
an early day of the session, a committee was
appointed, of which Mr. Madison was a member,
to draw up an address to Washington, conveying
to him the thanks of the legislature "for his unremitted zeal and services in the cause of liberty, and congratulating him on his return to
his native State and the exalted pleasures of
domestic life." The committee was instructed
also to consider and report "what further measures may be necessary for perpetuating the gratitude and veneration of his country."

An address was agreed on by the two Houses, to
be presented by a joint committee of both bodies.
In this address the united representatives of the
Commonwealth, among other grateful and patriotic sentiments, declare : "We shall ever remember, sir, with affection and gratitude, the patriotic
exchange you made of the felicities of private
life for the severe task of conducting the armies
of your country through a conflict with one of
the most powerful nations of the earth. We
shall ever remember with admiration the wisdom
which marked your councils on this arduous occasion ; the firmness and dignity which no trials
of adverse fortune could shake ; the moderation
and equanimity which no scenes of triumph could
disturb ; nor shall we ever forget the exemplary
respect which, in every instance, you have shown
to the rights of the civil authority, or the exalted virtue which on many occasions led you to

commit to danger your fame itself, rather than hazard for a moment the true interest of your country."

With regard to other measures proper to perpetuate the gratitude of the country, it was resolved to cause to be erected a statue of Washington, of the finest marble and best workmanship, with the following inscription upon its pedestal, which is known to have been the composition of Mr. Madison: —

"The General Assembly of Virginia have caused this statue to be erected as a monument of affection and gratitude to George Washington, who, uniting to the endowments of the hero the virtues of the patriot, and exerting both in establishing the liberties of his country, has rendered his name dear to his fellow-citizens, and given to the world an immortal example of true glory": —

Words of sympathetic and virtuous eloquence, worthy to go down, with the spotless marble and the shining fame of its immortal subject, to the latest generations of mankind.[1]

[1] It was proposed by Houdon, the artist, on his return to France from America, to change this noble inscription, which he was unable to appreciate, upon the idle plea that it was too long for the space it was to occupy; and the proposition was seriously entertained by Mr. Jefferson, then American minister at Paris. (See his letter of the 8th of February, 1786, to Mr. Madison, in the first volume of his Writings, p. 442.) The Latin inscription which was offered as a substitute was singularly jejune and pompous, if we may judge from the translation given by Mr. Jefferson; and was almost ludicrous by the bathos of its termination. The translation is as follows: "Behold, reader, the form of George Washington. For his worth, ask history; that will tell it, when this stone shall have

It was a striking manifestation of the nobleness of Washington's character, that, while himself the object of these high honors bestowed by the legislature of his native State, he sought to interest their feelings on behalf of one whose misfortunes, and the merit of whose early services in the cause of American independence, caused his moral obliquities to be overlooked for the time, but who, by his subsequent conduct, and in nothing more than his revilings of his benefactor, showed how unworthy he was of the benevolence he inspired. On the 12th of June, 1784, General Washington wrote to Mr. Madison: —

"Can nothing be done in our Assembly for poor Paine? Must the merit and services of 'Common Sense' continue to glide down the stream of time unrewarded by this country? His writings certainly have had a powerful effect upon the public mind. Ought they not, then, to meet an adequate return? He is poor, he is chagrined, and almost, if not altogether, in despair of relief. His views are moderate; a decent independency is, I believe, all he aims at. Ought he

yielded to the decays of time. His country erects this monument; Houdon makes it." It is difficult to conceive how Mr. Jefferson could have obtained the assent of his mind and taste to entertain or submit the proposition of such a change. The quiet and uncontending manner in which Mr. Madison disposes of the suggestion, in his answer to Mr. Jefferson, is edifying and characteristic. "I am sensible," he says, "of the inferiority in every respect of the original inscription to the proposed substitute; but I am apprehensive that no change can *now* be effected." Manuscript letter to Mr. Jefferson of the 12th of May, 1786.

to be disappointed of this? If you think otherwise, I am sure you will not only move the
matter, but give it your support. For me, it
only remains to feel for his situation, and to assure you of the sincere esteem and regard with
which I have the honor to be, dear sir, yours,
                              "GEORGE WASHINGTON."

Mr. Madison entered warmly into the views
of his illustrious correspondent, and promptly introduced a bill for granting a tract of land to
Paine, the kind of provision he desired. The
proposition, though sustained by powerful advocates, did not receive the sanction of the legislature. Mr. Madison appears to have been much
chagrined at its failure; and in writing to General Washington, on the 2d of July, 1784, he
says: "Should it finally appear that the merits
of the man whose writings have so much contributed to infuse and foster the spirit of independence in the people of America are unable
to inspire them with a just beneficence, the
world, it is to be feared, will give us as little
credit for our policy as for our gratitude in this
particular."

The decision of the legislature, however, stands
justified in the eyes of posterity by the exhibition
which the unhappy subject of this exalted patronage afterwards made of his own unworthiness,[1]

[1] In any period of the republic,   man, in his published letter of
the language which this infatuated   1796, dared to apply to Washing-

and may be classed with other instances to prove that the judgments of collective bodies of men are often truer tests of individual merit than the indulgent estimates of superior minds led away by their own benevolent impulses. With this generous but fruitless endeavour to give effect to a magnanimous intercession closed the present session of the General Assembly of Virginia; and Mr. Madison was allowed, though for a brief season, a respite from his legislative labors.

ton, could not but shock every honest mind; but in the present age, when the calm lights of history have served only to heighten the purity and splendor of his fame, it would not be believed, but for the existence of the dark record, that a sacrilegious license had ever gone so far as to say of Washington, " that, treacherous in private and hypocritical in public life, the world would be puzzled to decide whether he was an apostate or an impostor, — whether he had abandoned good principles, or ever had any."

CHAPTER XIX.

Occupations of Mr. Madison during Recess of the Legislature — Able Letter to Mr. Jefferson on Right to Navigation of the Mississippi — Sets out on a Tour to the North — Meets with the Marquis Lafayette — Accompanies him to an Indian Treaty in the Western Part of New York — Incidents at the Treaty — Impressions of Lafayette's Character — Reassembling of the Legislature — Mr. Madison made Chairman of Committee of Courts of Justice — Reports Plan for establishing Courts of Assize — Advocates successfully the Enactment of a Law by Virginia to repress and punish Enterprises of her Citizens against Nations with which the United States are at Peace — This Act the first Example of American Legislation to punish those Offences against the Law of Nations now known under the Name of *Filibustering* — Renewed Effort for the Execution of the Treaty of Peace respecting British Debts — Proposition made by Mr. Madison at the late Session again brought forward — Improved Sentiments of the Legislature with Regard to it — Finally lost by a singular Accident — General Assessment for Support of Teachers of the Christian Religion again proposed — Warmly sustained by Mr. Henry and other distinguished Members — Mr. Madison firmly, and almost singly in Debate, opposes it — Outline of his powerful Argument, as collected from a Fragment among his Papers — Progress of the Measure in the House — Bill for incorporating the Episcopal Church — Question of Assessment, by the persevering Opposition of Mr. Madison and his Auxiliaries, postponed to the next Session of the Legislature, and in the mean Time referred to the People for an Expression of their Sense upon it.

MR. MADISON, on his release from his legislative duties at Richmond, did not give himself up to vacancy and inaction. A mind so long conversant with the great questions and mighty interests affecting the future destinies of the nation naturally recurred to them in a retirement which afforded leisure for contemplating them in all their various relations, and in the new and important directions they might take on the return of peace.

Among the questions on which the future growth and prosperity of the American empire essentially depended, and which the war had left undecided, was that of the free navigation to the ocean of the noble river placed by nature on our Western borders, as the outlet of their teeming productions. The obstinacy and infatuation of the power which possessed its mouth still sought to withhold this boon of Providence from the equal participation of the citizens of the United States. We have seen the early and sagacious interest shown by Mr. Madison in this important subject. His solicitude respecting it increased as the time approached when it must receive a definitive solution.

An efficacious influence, he thought, was to be exerted by the other powers of Europe, and especially by France, on the narrow and bigoted councils of Spain, with regard to a principle of public law and international justice which more or less concerned them all. His friend Mr. Jefferson was now one of the ministers of the United States at Paris, and in a position to enlist the moral influence, if not the formal intervention, of the governments of Europe on the side of the American claim. A letter which Mr. Madison addressed to him on this subject from his residence in Orange county, on the 20th of August, 1784, though proceeding from a private and unofficial source, deserves, for the ability of its reasoning, and the variety and extent of its knowledge and research, to be ranked among the most remarkable diplomatic papers on record. We insert a single extract from it, as exhibiting not only his habitual largeness of views, but a minute and familiar acquaintance, rarely found among the public men of the present day, with the policy and relations, natural and conventional, of the various powers of the European world.

"Must not," he says, "the general interest of Europe, in all cases, influence the determination of any particular nation in Europe? and does not that interest, in the present case, clearly lie on our side? All the principal powers have, in a general view, more to gain than to lose by denying the right of those who hold the mouths of rivers to intercept a communication with those above. France, Great Britain, and Sweden have no opportunity of exerting such a right, and must wish a free passage for their merchandise in every country. Spain herself has no such opportunity, and has, besides, three of her principal rivers — one of them the seat of her metropolis — running through Portugal. Russia can have nothing to lose by denying this pretension, and is bound to do so in favor of her great rivers, the Dnieper, the Dniester, and the Don, which mouth in the Black Sea, and of the passage through the Dardanelles, which she extorted from the Turks. The emperor, in common with the inland States of Germany, and, moreover, by his possessions on the Maese and the Scheldt, has a similar interest. The possessions of the king of Prussia on the Rhine, the Elbe, and the Oder are pledges for his orthodoxy.

"The United Provinces hold, it is true, the mouths of the Maese, the Rhine, and the Scheldt; but a general freedom of trade is so much their policy, and they now carry on so much of it by the channel of rivers flowing through different dominions, that their weight can hardly be thrown into the wrong scale. The only powers that can have an interest in opposing the American doctrine are the Ottoman, which has already given up the point to Russia; Denmark, which is suffered to retain the entrance of the Baltic; Portugal, whose principal rivers head in Spain; Venice, which holds the mouth of the Po; and Dantzic, which commands that of the Vistula, if it is yet to be considered as a sovereign city. The prevailing disposition of Europe on this point once frustrated an attempt of Denmark to exact a toll at the mouth of the Elbe, by means of a fort on the Holstein side which commands it."

After two months of close application to his books in the seclusion of the country, Mr. Madison determined to devote the remainder of the legislative vacation to acquiring, by personal observation, a more extended knowledge of the different States of the confederacy. He had not yet been in the Eastern States, and he set out from home with the intention of making a tour of that portion of the Union. In Baltimore he met with the Marquis Lafayette, who, after an absence of two years from America, had returned to visit his friends and companions in arms and council, and to rejoice with them in the consummation of national independence, and in the opening prospects of the great empire he had assisted to found. The Marquis had already spent some time with his venerated chief at Mount Vernon, and was now on his way to visit his friends in the Middle and Eastern States, intending to rejoin General Washington in the capital of Virginia after the reassembling of the legislature.

Mr. Madison felt the highest satisfaction in meeting with this generous champion of American freedom, whom he had known and appreciated during the trying scenes of the war, and at once formed the plan of bearing him company in the tour which they equally had in view. Lafayette had been invited to attend a treaty to be held with the Indians at Fort Schuyler in the following month. The traditional influence of his nation, as well as his own personal popularity with these rude children of the forest, would, it was thought, enable him to serve the interests of the United States essentially in the approaching conference. Mr. Madison, on his arrival at New York, finding that he should not have time to accomplish his Eastern tour satisfactorily, decided to defer it to a future and more favorable period, and to proceed directly with Lafayette to Fort Schuyler.

His change of plan, and the attendant circumstances, he thus describes in a letter of the 15th of September, 1784, to Mr. Jefferson:—

"The information I have here received convinces me that I cannot accomplish the whole route I had planned within the time to which I am limited, nor go from this to Boston in the mode which I had reckoned upon. I shall therefore decline this part of my plan, at least for the present, and content myself with a trip to Fort Schuyler, in which I shall gratify my curiosity in several respects, and have the pleasure of the Marquis's company. We shall set off this afternoon in a barge up the North River. The Marquis has received in this city a continuation of those marks of cordial esteem and affection which were hinted in my last. The gazettes herewith enclosed will give you samples of them. Besides the personal homage he receives, his

49 *

presence has furnished occasion for fresh manifestations of those sentiments towards France which
have been so well merited by her, but which
her enemies pretended would soon give way to
returning affection for Great Britain."

The commissioners of the United States, appointed to hold the treaty with the Indians, were
Mr. Oliver Wolcott, Mr. Arthur Lee, and Mr. Richard Butler. The two travellers arrived in advance
of the commissioners at Fort Schuyler, and availed
themselves of the leisure thus gained to make a
visit to the nation of Oneidas, in their town
twenty miles beyond the fort. The appearance
of Lafayette produced the same outburst of enthusiasm among the red men of America —
to whom he was known under the familiar
name of Kayewla — that it had given rise to
among his brethren of European origin. At the
request of the commissioners, — though not without some demurring from the anti-Gallican jealousies of Dr. Lee, — he made a public address
to the different nations, when they were assembled in council.

The words of Kayewla were listened to with
profound sympathy and respect; and several of
the chiefs, in responding to him, as they did with
unbounded effusions of confidence and affection,
promised to follow his counsels, and live in peace
and brotherhood with the United States. Lafayette left this primeval congress with feelings gratified at the simple and untutored homage he had

received, as well as at the new opportunity which had been afforded him of evincing his zeal for the interests of America.[1] Mr. Madison parted with him at Albany, on their return, the Marquis proceeding to Boston to visit his friends in New England, while Mr. Madison pursued his way through New York and Philadelphia to attend the meeting of the legislature of Virginia, which was to take place in a few days at Richmond.

The free and unreserved intercourse with General Lafayette, on this excursion, presented an occasion for impressing upon his mind the vital importance of the navigation of the Mississippi to the interests of the United States, and the necessity of an earnest mediation of France with Spain on the subject, which one so thoughtful of the public welfare as Mr. Madison was not likely to leave unimproved. In writing to Mr. Jefferson, immediately after he fell in with Lafayette at Baltimore, he says : —

"The relation in which the Marquis stands to France and America has induced me to enter into a free conversation with him on the subject of the Mississippi. I have endeavoured emphatically to impress on him that the ideas of America and of Spain irreconcilably clash ; that, unless the mediation of France be effectually exerted,

---

[1] See an interesting account of the occurrences at this treaty in Mémoires de Lafayette, vol. II. pp. 98–104, and in a letter of Mr. Madison to Mr. Jefferson of the 17th of October, 1784.

an actual rupture is near at hand; that, in such an event, the connection between France and Spain will give the enemies of the former in America the fairest opportunity of involving her in our resentments against the latter, and of introducing Great Britain as a party with us against both; that America cannot possibly be diverted from her object, and therefore France is bound to set every engine at work to divert Spain from hers; and that France has, besides, a great interest in a trade with the Western country through the Mississippi."

These representations produced their natural and proper effect upon Lafayette. He recognized their justice and felt their force, and said he would write by the next packet to the Count de Vergennes on the subject. He was not unmindful of his word; and amid all the bustle and excitement of the enthusiastic reception he met with in New York, as in the other cities through which he passed, he found time to write a very pregnant, though brief letter to the French minister of foreign affairs on this critical and important question.[1]

The reader will be curious to know what impressions Mr. Madison formed, from a close and daily personal intercourse of a month's duration, with regard to the character of this remarkable man, who played so prominent a part in the affairs of Europe and America, and concerning

[1] See the letter in Mémoires de Lafayette, vol. II. pp. 107, 108.

whom so great a diversity of opinion has prevailed. In a confidential letter of the 17th of October, 1784, to Mr. Jefferson, he thus speaks of him : —

"The time I have lately passed with the Marquis has given me a pretty thorough insight into his character. With great natural frankness of temper he unites much address, and very considerable talents. In his politics, he says his three hobby-horses are the alliance between France and the United States, the union of the latter, and the manumission of the slaves. The two former are the dearer to him, as they are connected with his personal glory."

In another letter to Mr. Jefferson, written some months later, (the 20th of August, 1785,) we meet with this further sketch : —

"Subsequent to the date of mine in which I gave my idea of Lafayette, I had other opportunities of penetrating his character. Though his foibles did not disappear, all the favorable traits presented themselves in a stronger light, on closer inspection. He certainly possesses talents which might figure in any line. If he is ambitious, it is rather of the praise which virtue dedicates to merit than of the homage which fear renders to power. His disposition is naturally warm and affectionate, and his attachment to the United States unquestionable. Unless I am grossly deceived, you will find his zeal sincere and useful, whenever it can be employed on behalf of the

United States without opposition to the essential interests of France." [1]

[1] The foibles of Lafayette here referred to were, doubtless, those which sprang from what Mr. Jefferson denominated in him " a canine appetite for popularity and fame," (see Jefferson's Writings, vol. II. p. 89,) and what his distinguished countryman, Guizot, has more recently called " un besoin permanent et indistinct de faveur populaire," but which Mr. Madison more gently describes as an ambition of praise. The love of popularity was, unquestionably, a prominent trait in the character of Lafayette, and led him sometimes into weakness and error. He himself, on a memorable occasion, spoke of his popularity as dearer to him than life; but declared, at the same time, he would sacrifice both rather than fail in a duty and connive at a crime, and that he was persuaded no end could ever justify the employment of means which public or private morality disowned. The passage is so honorable to Lafayette, that it deserves to be cited in his own felicitous language. It was part of a general order issued by him as *commandant en chef* of the national guards in 1830, when the lives of the ex-ministers at the Luxembourg were threatened by an excited populace, and was in these words:—

" C'est ainsi que toujours ils le trouveront ce qu'il fut à dix-neuf ans, ce qu'il a été en 1789 et 1830,

ce qu'il sera pendant le peu d'années qui lui restent à vivre, — l'homme de la liberté et de l'ordre public, aimant sa popularité beaucoup plus que la vie, mais décidé à sacrifier l'une et l'autre plutôt que de manquer à un devoir et de souffrir un crime, et persuadé qu'aucun but ne justifie les moyens que la morale publique ou privée désavoue." Ordre du jour du 19 Décembre, 1830.

That love of the Union, in his system of American politics, which he spoke of in 1784 to Mr. Madison as one of the three cardinal principles of his cherished political creed, grew stronger and stronger in him as he advanced in years. It is so touchingly and eloquently expressed in a letter he addressed to the writer of these pages in the autumn of 1832, when the Union seemed to be threatened by the new theory of nullification, that we cannot forbear to give a brief extract from it to the reader:—

"For God's sake, my dear sir, tell our friends and fellow-citizens of every party, particularly those in public stations, that, in this critical situation of European politics, every speech or measure which threatens collision, separation, disorders, further than what is the appendage of republican debate in a free country, is eagerly made an argument against the diffusion of popular principles throughout this European part of the world; and

Mr. Madison did not arrive in Richmond until a fortnight after the period fixed for the meeting of the legislature, but in time for the commencement of business, as a quorum of the House was formed only the day before he took his seat. He was again put upon all the leading committees, and was now made chairman of the committee for courts of justice. As this is a position almost invariably assigned to a professional lawyer of reputation and experience, the appointment was a very marked compliment to the knowledge and attainments of Mr. Madison in a science he never professed, and to which he had but lately turned his attention as a necessary accomplishment of the legislator and statesman.

He took an active and leading part during the session in several questions which demanded an acquaintance with both positive and theoretical jurisprudence. In the general revision of the laws, for which he had taken the preliminary step at the last session of the legislature, he was not able to make any systematic advance, as the report of the revisors was not printed till near the close of the present session. Increased facilities, however, in the administration of justice being urgently required, in consequence of the immense accumulation of business and consequent delays in the general court, —

supposing a separation of the Union, which God forbid, was in futurity to take place, do wait at least until the last of those who have fought and bled in the revolutionary war has breathed his ultimate sigh." Manuscript letter of the 25th of September, 1832.

the great fountain of justice for the whole State,
—a resolution was adopted, declaring that, "for
the more convenient administration of justice
throughout the Commonwealth, circuit courts
ought to be established." A bill was ordered to be
brought in, pursuant to this resolution; and Mr.
Madison was placed at the head of a select committee, consisting of the ablest professional members of the House, to prepare and bring it in.[1]

The plan reported proposed to lay off the
State into a certain number of convenient districts or circuits, in each of which a court of
assize was to be held twice a year, at which all
issues and inquiries of damages, in suits depending before the general court, were to be tried
by juries duly empannelled in those courts. The
courts of assize were to be severally held by
two judges of the court of appeals, which tribunal consisted at that time of the judges of all
the higher courts united into one for the purpose of deciding appeals, and was thus composed
of the three judges of the high court of chancery, the three of the court of admiralty, and the
five of the general court. The judges were to
be assigned, by an order of the court of appeals
made from time to time, among the different circuits, for the purpose of holding the assize courts,
whose proceedings, with the verdicts found, were
to be certified into the general court, where final
judgment was to be entered.

[1] Journal of House of Delegates, October session, 1784, p. 43.

The plan was borrowed, with slight modifications, from that of the *Nisi Prius* courts in England, and promised to relieve the general court from the delays and inconveniences incident to the trial of all issues at its own bar, and thereby to render the administration of justice throughout the Commonwealth more expeditious and commodious, while insuring greater uniformity and the highest attainable grade of judicial wisdom in the decisions of the different courts. There was a numerous class of persons to whom no measure, contemplating the removal of delays in the administration of justice at that time, was likely to be acceptable. The bill reported by the committee was, therefore, not received with any special warmth of approbation, though it finally passed both Houses without any overt resistance. Mr. Madison, in a letter of the 9th of January, 1785, gives the following account of its reception and progress: —

"This act was carried through the House of Delegates against much secret repugnance, but without any direct and open opposition. It luckily happened that the latent opposition wanted both a mouth and a head. Mr. Henry had been previously elected governor, and was gone for his family. From his conversation since, I surmise that his presence might have been fatal. The act is formed precisely on the English pattern, and is nearly a transcript from the bill originally penned in 1776 by Mr. Pendleton, except that writs sent blank from the clerk of the general court are to issue in the district, but be returned to the general court. In the Senate, it became a consideration whether the assize courts ought not to be turned into so many courts of independent and complete jurisdiction, and admitting an appeal only to the court of appeals. If the fear of endangering the bill had not checked the experiment, such a proposition would probably have been sent down to the House of Delegates, where it would have been better relished by many than the assize plan."

There was another measure, of a somewhat novel, but highly important character, connected with the enforcement of justice in the exterior relations of the State, in which Mr. Madison took a very earnest and influential part. The pending discussions with Spain, respecting the navigation of the Mississippi, disposed many of the settlers in the western parts of Virginia, which then included Kentucky, to commit trespasses and acts of violence within the limits of the adjacent Spanish possessions. These proceedings were calculated not only to compromise the peace and tranquillity of the country, but to retard and render more doubtful the ultimate adjustment of the great national question at issue.

The legislature, immediately after its assembling, took a very wise and statesmanlike course to avert the threatened danger. On the third day of the session, the House of Delegates passed a resolution to the following effect: "That, for preserving the tranquillity of our western inhabitants, speedy and exemplary punishment ought to be inflicted on every person doing injury to the subjects of Spain or the Indians in that quarter, and that proper laws for that purpose ought to be enacted." This resolution they accompanied with another, declaring that "it is essential to the prosperity and happiness of the western inhabitants of this Commonwealth that they should enjoy the right of navigating the river Mississippi to the sea," and instructing the delegates. of the State in Congress "to move that honorable body to give directions (unless the same have been already given) to the American ministers in Europe to forward negotiations to obtain that end without loss of time." [1]

A committee was appointed, consisting of Mr. Matthews,—who had been chairman of the committee of the whole, in which these resolutions were agreed upon,—of Mr. Madison, Mr. Henry, Mr. Stuart, Mr. Corbin, Mr. Barbour, and Mr. Johnson, to prepare and bring in a bill in pursuance of the first-mentioned resolution. The bill, in the shape which it finally assumed, — after setting forth, in a well-conceived preamble, that "it is the desire of the good people of this Commonwealth, in all cases, to manifest their reverence for the law of nations, to cultivate peace and amity, as far as may depend on them, be-

[1] Journal of House of Delegates, October session, 1784, p. 9.

tween the United States and foreign powers, and
to support the dignity and energy of the federal constitution," — directs that if a citizen or
an inhabitant of Virginia shall commit, within
the jurisdiction of a foreign power at peace with
the United States, any crime for which, by the
law of nations or by treaty stipulations, he ought,
in the judgment of Congress, to be surrendered
to the offended power, such person, upon the
demand of the said power, duly sanctioned and
notified by Congress, shall be delivered to the
custody of such agent as Congress may approve,
in order to be tried and punished where the
alleged offence was committed.

The bill also contained provisions for punishing, in the courts of the State, offences committed by citizens of Virginia against the laws and
within the jurisdiction of a foreign power, "in like
manner as if they had been committed within
the body of some county of the Commonwealth";
and these provisions were extended to offences
committed in the territory of any Indian tribe,
equally with such as should be perpetrated
within the limits of a Christian or civilized nation.
The measure — suggested and proposed by Mr.
Madison — was vehemently opposed in every stage
of its progress. It was assailed, particularly, as
violating the eighth article of the Virginia Bill of
Rights, which guarantees to the accused, in criminal prosecutions, a trial by an impartial jury of
the vicinage, and declares that no man shall be

deprived of his liberty but by the law of the land or the judgment of his peers. At one time, amendments were made to it in committee of the whole which destroyed its principle; but, upon the renewal of the struggle in the House, those amendments were defeated, and the bill was finally carried by a majority of a single vote.[1]

Mr. Henry, while he remained in the House, warmly seconded Mr. Madison in the advocacy of this noble measure; but, having been elected governor, he left the House before the decisive battle was fought upon it. There is not to be found upon the statute-book of any civilized State a more honorable recognition of the principles of international justice and integrity, or a more emphatic denunciation and rebuke of those lawless enterprises which in modern times, under the name of *filibustering*,[2] have revived the license of a barbarous age, than this model act of the legislature of Virginia. We leave the further history and defence of it to the eloquent pen of Mr.

[1] See Journal of House of Delegates, pp. 41, 42, and Letter of Mr. Madison to Mr. Monroe of the 27th of November, 1784. For the act, see Hen. Stat. vol. XI. pp. 471, 472.

[2] This uncouth Americanism is, doubtless, derived through the Spanish from the French word *flibustier*, by which the French and English buccaneers of the seventeenth century were designated, and which was itself, probably, derived from the name of the species of light vessel, *fly-boat*, used by the buccaneers in their encounters with the larger Spanish vessels. For an interesting account of the French adventurers, with whom the life of buccaneering had its origin, and of the maritime equipments and mode of attack of the buccaneers, see Abbé Raynal's History of the Indies, Book x.

50 *

Madison, who, in his letter of the 9th of January, 1785, to Mr. Jefferson, thus speaks of it: —

"This measure was suggested by the danger of our being speedily embroiled with the nations contiguous to the United States, — particularly the Spaniards, — by the licentious and predatory spirit of some of our western people. In several instances, gross outrages are said to have been already committed. The measure was warmly patronized by Mr. Henry and most of the forensic members, and no less warmly opposed by the speaker, (Mr. Tyler,) and some others. The opponents contended that such surrenders were unknown to the law of nations, and were interdicted by our Bill of Rights. Vattel, however, is express as to the case of robbers, murderers, and incendiaries. Grotius quotes various instances in which great offenders have been given up by their proper sovereigns to be punished by the offended sovereigns. Puffendorf only refers to Grotius. I have had no opportunity of consulting other authorities.

"With regard to the Bill of Rights, it was alleged to be no more, or rather less, violated by considering crimes committed against other laws as not falling under the notice of our own, and sending our citizens to be tried where the cause of trial arose, than to try them under our own laws without a jury of the vicinage, and without being confronted with their accusers or witnesses; as must be the case, if they be tried at all for

such offences under our own laws. And to say
that such offenders should neither be given up
for punishment, nor be punished within their own
country, would amount to a license for every
aggression, and would sacrifice the peace of the
whole country to the impunity of the worst members of it. The necessity of a qualified interpretation of the Bill of Rights was also inferred
from the law of the confederacy which requires
the surrender of our citizens to the laws of other
States, in cases of treason, felony, and other high
misdemeanours. The act provides, however, for
a domestic trial, in cases where a surrender may
not be justified or insisted upon, and in cases of
aggressions on the Indians."

The triumph of this measure of peace and
justice furnished encouragement for another effort
to provide for the execution of the fourth article
of the treaty of peace with England by the removal of all existing impediments to the recovery of British debts. The resolutions passed at
the last session on the subject, by assuming to
the legislature of a State the right of determining in what contingencies a treaty solemnly entered into by the constitutional authority of the
Union should or should not be fulfilled, had
shocked the public sense of propriety, and created no small uneasiness in the minds of many
reflecting persons. Among the evidences of this
sober sentiment in portions of the constituent
body was a remarkable petition and remon-

strance presented to the House of Delegates from the county of Amherst, in which the petitioners say "they were deeply affected by certain resolutions passed at the last Assembly, which, they conceive, have an obvious tendency to introduce anarchy and confusion in our public councils, and to subvert the basis of the confederation, arrogating to this State the power of peace and war, which of right belongs to Congress, and pray that the said resolutions be rescinded."[1]

The opportunity for further reflection during the recess, and the exchange of ratifications of the treaty of peace in the interim, had also produced a sensible reaction in the representative body. All these favorable omens conspired to revive the hopes of those who stood in the minority at the last session, vainly urging the elevated policy of America's setting the example of a stainless public faith to her adversary. The proposition submitted at that time by Mr. Madison was now brought forward, with slight modifications of detail, by his friend Mr. Jones, and was acceded to, with but little opposition, in the House.

Resolutions were adopted, declaring that good faith required that the stipulations of the treaty of peace should be duly executed by the contracting parties, and that the impediments to the recovery of debts due to British subjects

[1] Journal of House of Delegates, October session, 1784, p. 15.

from citizens of the Commonwealth ought to be
removed; but that, as the calamities and devastations of the war had greatly impaired the ability
to make prompt payments, it would be conducive
to the interest of both creditors and debtors that
the balances due should be discharged in a
course of divided annual payments. The progressive extinguishment of the debts in seven annual
instalments, with the suspension of interest during
the interval between the commencement and termination of hostilities, was agreed upon as the
plan of adjustment most equitable and proper;
and a committee, of which both Mr. Jones and
Mr. Madison were members, was appointed to
prepare a bill in conformity to it.[1]

The bill passed readily through the House of
Delegates, but encountered difficulties and delays
in the Senate. An important amendment was
made to it in that body, which the House disagreed to. The two bodies adhering to their respective views, a conference finally took place
between them, which terminated in a compromise. What ensued, as well as some additional
particulars relating to the introduction and progress of the measure, we shall learn from Mr.
Madison's letter of the 9th of January, 1785,
written, immediately after the adjournment of
the legislature, to Mr. Jefferson.

"The subject of the British debts," he says,
"underwent a reconsideration, on the motion of

[1] Journal of House of Delegates, October session, 1784, p. 48.

Mr. Jones. Though no answer had been received from Congress to the resolutions passed at the last session, a material change had evidently taken place in the mind of the Assembly, proceeding in part from a more dispassionate view of the question, — in part from the intervening exchange of the ratifications of the treaty. Mr. Henry was out of the way. His previous conversation, I am told, favored a reconsideration. The speaker, (Mr. Tyler,) the other champion at the last session against the treaty, was, at least, half a proselyte."

After giving an account of the resolutions adopted and of the bill brought in, with the proceedings upon it in the Senate, and the subsequent conference between the two Houses, the letter proceeds: —

"The conference produced a proposition from the House of Delegates, to which the Senate assented; but, before the assent was notified, an incident happened which has left the bill in a very critical situation. The delays attending this measure had spun it out to the day preceding the one fixed for a final adjournment. Several of the members went over to Manchester [a village on the opposite side of the river] in the evening, with an intention, it is to be presumed, of returning the next morning. The severity of the night rendered their passage back the next morning impossible. The impatience of the members was such as might be supposed. Some were for stigmatizing the absentees, and adjourning. The rest were, some for one thing, some for another.

"At length, it was agreed to wait until the next day. The next day presented the same obstruction in the river. A canoe was sent over for inquiry by the Manchester party; but they did not choose to venture themselves. The impatience increased; warm resolutions were agitated. They ended, however, in an agreement to wait one day more. On the morning of the third day the prospect remained the same. Patience would hold out no longer; an adjournment to the last day of March" (equivalent to an adjournment *sine die*, as the official term of the legislature then expired) "ensued. The question to be decided is, whether a bill which had passed the House of Delegates and been assented to by the Senate, but not sent down to the House, nor enrolled, nor examined, nor signed by the two speakers, and consequently not of record, is or is not a law."

The *lex parliamentaria* was as inexorable as the unbridged torrent; and thus was unfortunately still left open a question which continued for years to be a source of bitter waters both in the foreign and domestic politics of America.

The question of a public provision for the support of religion, which was under the consideration of the legislature at its last session, was renewed at an early period of the present.

It was brought before the House upon a petition of a number of the inhabitants of Isle of Wight County, setting forth the concern they felt at seeing the countenance of the civil power wholly withdrawn from the support of religion, on the influence of which the happiness and prosperity of the country so essentially depend, —alleging that it is a principle as old as society itself, that whatever conduces to the advantage of all should be borne by all, and praying, therefore, that an act be passed to compel every one to contribute something, in proportion to his property, for the support of religion.[1]

This petition was referred to the committee of the whole House on the state of the Commonwealth. We learn from Mr. Madison's correspondence that Mr. Henry was the great champion of the proposition. In a few days the committee reported a resolution, drawn, doubtless, by Mr. Henry, declaring that "the people of the Commonwealth, according to their respective abilities, ought to pay a moderate tax or contribution for the support of the Christian religion, or of some Christian church, denomination, or communion of Christians, or of some form of Christian worship." The resolution was adopted in the House by a vote of 47 to 32, and a special committee, of which Mr. Henry was chairman, was appointed to bring in a bill in pursuance of it.[2]

[1] Journal of House of Delegates, October session, 1784, p. 11.
[2] Idem, p. 19.

Petitions continued to come in from other counties, urging the adoption of the measure by the same considerations which were set forth in the petition from Isle of Wight, and alleging, in addition, that "the rapid decline of religion within a few years past" proceeded, in the opinion of the petitioners, from the want of some general provision by the legislature for its support.[1] What is especially remarkable is, that in a memorial presented by the united clergy of the Presbyterian Church — a body which had hitherto distinguished itself by its zeal in favor of the principle of unlimited religious freedom — an opinion was now expressed, as cited in the Journal of the House of Delegates, that " a general assessment for the support of religion ought to be extended to those who profess the public worship of the Deity."[2] One exception only is shown by the Journal to the current of popular opinion which reached the legislature in the form of petitions; and that occurs in the petition of certain inhabitants of the county of Rockbridge, deprecating "the interference of the legislature in aid of religion, as unequal, impolitic, and beyond their power."[3]

It is, perhaps, not to be wondered at that, among a people accustomed from the earliest times to see religion lean for support on the

[1] Journal of House of Delegates, October session, 1784, p. 32.
[2] Idem, p. 21.
[3] Idem, p. 49.

arm of secular power, an apprehension should have been felt of its decline upon the withdrawal of that support; and that, under these circumstances, many enlightened minds did not, at first, perceive the departure from fundamental principles, as well as the dangerous precedent, in the measure now proposed. Besides Mr. Henry, who was the leading advocate and champion of the measure, it is known that General Washington and Richard Henry Lee [1] at first favored it; and in the House of Delegates, several of those rising and distinguished men who were the intimate friends of Mr. Madison, and almost invariably acted with him on public questions, — such as Henry Tazewell, John Marshall, and his late colleague in Congress, Mr. Jones, — now separated from him on the question of the general assessment.

It is an honorable proof of the firmness of his character, as well as of the depth of his views and of his acquaintance with the great lessons of history, that, amid the general favor and imposing sanction which this measure met with, he stood the unfaltering and, in debate, almost the solitary opponent of it. What adds to the weight of his testimony against the measure, and enhances the merit of his opposition to it, in a moral point of view, is, that to the cause

---

[1] Mr. Lee, having been elected one of the representatives of the State in Congress, at the last session of the legislature, did not take his seat in the House of Delegates at the present session.

of religion itself he was a sincere friend, as he was also an enlightened believer in the truth and divine authority of the Christian system. But in an enforced union between religion and the State he saw only omens of evil to both, and a fatal departure from principles which he held sacred.

We have no report of the speeches made by him in opposition to this measure; but among his papers is a relic of great interest, in the skeleton of what was probably his leading speech on the occasion, written on the torn back of a letter, in a very condensed hand and with many abbreviations. As a sample of the only kind of preparation he was in the habit of making even for his most elaborate parliamentary efforts, as well as on account of the intrinsic value of its contents, we subjoin this relic, for the instruction no less than the curiosity of the reader. It will be seen, small as is the space occupied by the written programme of the argument, that it contains the elements of a profound, comprehensive, and exhaustive discussion of the great subject in all its relations.

We learn from it that Mr. Madison contended, first, that the regulation of religion was not within the province of the civil power, and that every attempt of the kind tended necessarily to ultimate projects of compulsory uniformity; next, that religion stands in no need of artificial props, and that the history of the world proves that it

had been invariably corrupted by legal establishments, which propositions he illustrated and enforced by a review of primitive Christianity, of
the Reformation, and the general progress of religious liberty; that the interests of the State
would be seriously injured by the proposed measure, in discouraging the immigration into it of
those who set a proper value on religious freedom,
as well as by furnishing new motives for the emigration of many of its present inhabitants; that
the decay of public morals complained of was in
no degree attributable to the want of any legal
provision for the support of religion, but was the
result, in general, of a long-continued state of
war, of bad laws, and of a loose administration
of justice; and that the true and proper remedies would be found in the return and discipline
of peace, in laws cherishing virtue, in a more
regular administration of justice, and in the influence of good example and of voluntary religious associations. He then showed, that, as
the benefits of the proposed provision were to
be limited to *Christian* societies and churches, it
would devolve upon the courts of law to determine what constitutes Christianity, and thus,
amid the great diversity of creeds and sects, to
set up by their *fiat* a standard of orthodoxy on
the one hand and of heresy on the other, which
would be destructive of the rights of private
conscience. He argued, finally, that the proposition dishonored Christianity by resting it upon

a basis of mercenary support, and concluded with vindicating its holy character from such a reproach, contending that its true and best support was in the principle of universal and perfect liberty established by the Bill of Rights, and which was alone in consonance with its own pure and elevated precepts.[1]

A considerable period elapsed after the adoption of the resolution in favor of the principle of a general assessment, before any bill was reported to carry it into effect. This delay produced doubts whether the friends of the measure

[1] The following is the skeleton of Mr. Madison's speech, referred to in the text, as we find it among his papers: —

"I. Rel. not within purview of civil authority.

"Tendency of estabg Xnty — 1. to project of uniformity. 2. to penal laws for supports it.

"Progress of Gen. Assest proves this tendency.

"Difference between estabg and tolerating error.

"True question — not Is Rel. necessy, — but

"II. are Rel. Estabts necesy for Religion? No.

"1. propensity of man to Religion.

"2. Experience shews Rel. corrupted by Estabts.

"3. Downfall of States mentioned by Mr. Henry — happened, where there was estabt.

"4. Experience gives no model of Genl Asst.

"5. Case of Pa. explained — not solitary — N. J. See consts of it — R. I. — N. Y. — D.

"6. Case of primitive Xnty.
of Reformation.
of Dissenters formerly.

"7. Progress of Religious liberty.

"III. Policy —

"1. promote emigrations from State

"2. prevent immig. into it, as asylum.

"IV. Necessity of Estabt inferred from state of country.

"True causes of disease.

"1. war } common to other States,
"2. bad laws } and produce same complaints in N. E.

"3. pretext from taxes.

"4. state of administration of justice.

"5. transition from old to new plan.

"6. policy and hopes of friends to G. Asst.

"True remedies — not Estabt. — but, being out of war,

"1. Laws to cherish virtue.

"2. administration of justice.

"3. personal example — associations for Rel.

"4. By present vote, cut off hope of G. asst.

"5. Education of youth.

"V. Probable defects of Bill, when prepared.

"What is Xnty, courts of Law to decide.

"Is it Trinitarianism, Arianism, Socinianism? Is it salvation by faith or works also, &c. &c.

"Ends in what is orthodoxy, what heresy.

"VI. Dishonors christianity.

"panegyric on it, on our side.

"Decl. Rights."

51 *

would persist in it. Mr. Madison, writing to Mr. Monroe on the 14th of November, 1784, says: "The principal attention of the House has been and is still occupied with a scheme for a general assessment; — 47 have carried it against 32. In its present form, it excludes all but Christian sects. The Presbyterian clergy have remonstrated against any narrow principles, but indirectly favor a more comprehensive establishment. I think the bottom will be enlarged, and that a trial will be made of the practicability of the project."

Writing again to Mr. Monroe on the 27th of the same month, he says: "The bill for a religious assessment has not yet been brought in. Mr. Henry, the father of the scheme, is gone up to his seat for his family, and will no more sit in the House of Delegates, — a circumstance very inauspicious to his offspring." And in a letter, written on the same day, to another friend, he says: "You will have heard of the vote in favor of the general assessment. The bill is not yet brought in, and I question whether it will be; or if so, whether it will pass."

At length, however, on the 3d day of December, — three weeks after the adoption of the resolution, — the bill was introduced.[1] But, in the mean time, another subject involving the interests of religious societies, and which, in the sequel, appears to have exercised an important influence on the fate of the proposition for a

[1] See Journal of House of Delegates, October session, 1784, p. 52.

general assessment, was taken up. On the 17th
of November, 1784, a resolution had passed the
House of Delegates by a very large majority,
(62 to 23,) in favor of the "incorporation of all
societies of the Christian religion which may
apply for the ·same."[1] Mr. Madison here again
voted with the minority. On the same day, leave
was given to bring in a bill " to incorporate the·
clergy of the Protestant Episcopal Church "; and
a committee, of which Mr. Henry was the second-
named member, was appointed to prepare it.

This bill was not reported until Mr. Henry
had left the House and entered upon the duties
of the chief executive office, to which he had recently been again elected; but it was well known
that he favored the bill, having been, as we have
seen, the chief patron of a kindred measure
brought before the legislature at its last session.
The bill now reported was free from many of the
objections which were felt and urged against the
one presented on the former occasion. It was no
longer a bill to incorporate the " *clergy* of the Protestant Episcopal Church," as distinct from the laity,
— but to incorporate " the Protestant Episcopal
Church," embracing both clergy and laity. Other
amendments were made, or were supposed to have
been made, in its progress through the committee of the whole House, which still further lessened the objections to its passage; and it was
felt that there was one argument at least, of a

[1] See Journal of House of Delegates, October session, 1784, p. 27.

legitimate and practical nature, in its favor, arising from the necessity of some sort of incorporation to enable the church to hold and manage
its property.

But the consideration by which Mr. Madison
was induced finally to give a reluctant vote for
the passage of the measure was this. "A negative of the bill," he said, "would have doubled
the eagerness and pretexts for a much greater
evil, — a general assessment, — which, there is
good ground to believe, was parried by this partial gratification of its warmest votaries." [1] When
the impending danger of the greater evil was
ultimately averted, he took a decided and active
part in the movement which led, at an early
day, to the repeal of the incorporating act.

This measure being passed on the 22d of December, the House of Delegates, on the same
day, resolved itself into a committee of the whole
to consider the assessment bill, which had been
reported under the title of a bill "establishing a
provision for teachers of the Christian religion."
It was discussed for two days in committee of
the whole, and the opposition to it was renewed
with great spirit and vigor. Several amendments
were made; and on the second day, the bill,
with the amendments, was ordered to be en-
grossed and read the third time. On the succeeding day, (the 24th of December,) the opponents
of the measure, gallantly continuing the struggle

---

[1] Letter to Mr. Jefferson, of the 9th of January, 1785.

to the last, moved that the third reading of the bill be "postponed until the fourth Thursday in November next,"—a day beyond the term of the existing legislature. The motion was carried by a vote of 45 to 38.[1] This result, though not a final and decisive victory, was at least a drawn battle, which, considering the large numerical odds with which the contest opened against the opponents of the projected assessment, was matter of just felicitation to all who clung to the standard of an unqualified freedom in religion.

Mr. Madison, in writing to Mr. Jefferson immediately after the adjournment of the legislature, summed up the history of the long and arduous struggle in the following quiet manner, abstaining, with characteristic oblivion of self, from the slightest allusion to the leading and distinguished part he had borne in the transactions he records.

"A resolution for a legal provision for the 'teachers of the Christian religion' had, early in the session, been proposed by Mr. Henry, and, in spite of all the opposition that could be mustered, carried by 47 against 32 votes. Many petitions from below the Blue Ridge had prayed for such a law; and though several from the Presbyterian laity beyond it were in a contrary style, the clergy of that sect favored it. The other sects seemed to be passive. The resolution lay some weeks before a bill was brought

[1] See Journal of House of Delegates, October session, 1784, p. 82.

in, and the bill, some weeks before it was called
for. After the passage of the Incorporating Act,
it was taken up, and, on the third reading, ordered, by a small majority, to be printed for
consideration. The bill, in its present dress, pro-
poses a tax of —— *per cent.* on all taxable
property for support of teachers of the Christian
religion. Each person, when he pays his tax, is
to name the society to which he dedicates it;
and in case of refusal to do so, the tax is to be
applied to the maintenance of a school in the
county. As the bill stood for some time, the
application, in such cases, was to be made by the
legislature to pious uses."

Immediately after the vote which postponed
the further consideration of the subject to the
next session of the legislature, a motion was
made and carried that copies of the bill, together
with the ayes and noes on the question of postponement, be printed for distribution in the several counties of the Commonwealth, and that
" the people thereof be requested to signify their
opinion respecting the adoption of such a measure to the next session of the legislature." Thus
was an appeal formally taken, in this vital cause
of religious freedom, to the supreme and ultimate
tribunal in representative governments. With
what untiring zeal, and with what irresistible
force of eloquence and logic, Mr. Madison pleaded
the great cause before that tribunal, and what
was the final judgment pronounced by it, we
shall hereafter see.

CHAPTER XX.

Visit of Washington and Lafayette to the Legislature of Virginia —
Addresses to them, and their Replies — Washington takes a deep
Interest in the Improvement of the navigable Rivers of Virginia,
to command the Trade of the West — His able Letter to Governor
Harrison on the Subject laid before the Legislature — Leading
and active Part taken by Mr. Madison in Coöperation with him
— Washington appointed by the Legislature of Virginia a Commissioner to concert with the Legislature of Maryland the Provisions of a joint Act for improving and extending the Navigation
of the Potomac — Repairs to Annapolis — Remarkable Letter addressed by him to Mr. Madison in Explanation of the Proceedings
and Results of his Mission — Mr. Madison introduces Measures to
carry into full Effect the Arrangements agreed upon at Annapolis — Other Measures brought forward by Mr. Madison to complete the System of Interior Communications for the State —
Improvement of James River — Communication between Elizabeth
River and Albemarle Sound — Reflections of Mr. Madison upon
the vast Importance and future Consequences of these Public
Works — Homage rendered by him to Washington's Greatness of
Mind in so earnestly engaging in them — Brings in a Bill to
confer upon him, in the Name of the State, a number of Shares
in the Works authorized — Adjournment of the Legislature —
Agitation among the People on the Assessment Bill for Support
of Religious Teachers — Deep Interest felt by Mr. Madison in the
Progress of the Question — His Letters to Mr. Monroe on the Sub-

ject — Prepares "Memorial and Remonstrance" against the Assessment, to be circulated among the People — Memorial covered with Signatures in every Part of the State — It decides forever the Fate of the Proposition before the Legislature — Extraordinary Merits of the Paper — A Monument in itself of the Genius, Ability, and Love of Liberty of the Author.

THE proceedings of the legislature, during its present session, were agreeably diversified by a visit from General Washington and his friend and companion in arms, the gallant Lafayette. Washington arrived on the 14th of November, 1784, a few days before Lafayette. On the 15th, the House of Delegates adopted the following resolution, which bears evident traces of Mr. Madison's pen: —

"The House being informed of the arrival of General Washington in this city, —

"*Resolved, nemine contradicente,* That, as a mark of their reverence for his character and affection to his person, a committee of five be appointed to wait upon him, with the respectful regards of this House, to express to him the satisfaction they feel in the opportunity, afforded by his presence, of offering this tribute to his merits; and to assure him, that, as they not only retain the most lasting impressions of the transcendent services rendered in his late public character, but have, since his return to private life, experienced proofs that no change of situation can turn his thoughts from the welfare of his country, so his happiness can never cease to be an object of their most devout wishes and fervent supplications."

The committee appointed to perform this grateful duty consisted of Mr. Henry, Mr. Jones of King George, Mr. Madison, Mr. Carter Henry Harrison, and Colonel Edward Carrington. General Washington replied to the committee with blended dignity and modesty, and with that tact and gracefulness of expression, inspired by true feeling, which so remarkably distinguished his addresses on such occasions.

"My sensibility, gentlemen," he said, "is deeply affected by this distinguished mark of the affectionate regard of your House. I lament, upon this occasion, the want of those powers which would enable me to do justice to my feelings, and shall rely on your indulgent report to supply the defect. At the same time, I pray you to present for me the strongest assurances of unalterable affection and gratitude for this last pleasing and flattering attention of my country."

Lafayette arrived on the 18th of the month; and a committee, of which Mr. Madison was again named a member, was appointed to welcome him with the affectionate respects of the House of Delegates. The resolution adopted on the occasion contained an appropriate and well-merited tribute to the able military conduct of the youthful General during his command in Virginia, in the memorable campaign of 1781. The committee was instructed to assure him "that the General Assembly of Virginia could not review the scenes of blood and danger through which we have arrived at the blessings of peace, without being touched in the most lively manner with the recollection, not only of the invaluable services for which the United States at large are so much indebted to him, but of that conspicuous display of cool intrepidity and wise conduct during his command in the campaign of 1781, which, by having so essentially served this State in particular, have given him so just a title to its particular acknowledgments."

In his reply, the Marquis made the following handsome and feeling allusions to his service in Virginia, to the recollections which bound him affectionately to the State, and to his personal observation of her fidelity and exertions in the common cause.

"Through the continent, gentlemen," he said, "it is most pleasing to me to join with my friends in mutual congratulations; and I need not add what my sentiments must be in Virginia, where, step by step, have I so keenly felt for her distress, so eagerly enjoyed her recovery. Our armed force was obliged to retreat; but your patriotic hearts stood unshaken. And while, either at that period or in our better hours, my obligations to you are numberless, I am happy in this opportunity to observe that the excellent services of your militia were continued with unparalleled steadiness. Impressed with the necessity of federal union, I was the more pleased in the command of an army so peculiarly federal, as Virginia herself freely bled in defence of her sister States."

The visit of these illustrious guests at the capital of Virginia continued for a week, and was a rich feast of patriotism to all, while it lasted. On the part of Washington, besides the lively gratification of renewing his personal intercourse with friends from whom he had been long separated by the stern demands of public duty, the visit had a further motive in his desire to promote with the legislature some plan for connecting the Eastern and Western waters through Virginia, for the purpose of securing to her the share which nature designed for her in the vast future commerce of the West. This great interest, immediately after the close of the war, engaged at the same moment the meditations of Washington, Jefferson, and Madison, and had been the subject of correspondence and mutual consultation between them.[1]

A few days before the commencement of the present session of the legislature, General Wash-

[1] See manuscript letter of Mr. Jefferson to Mr. Madison of the 20th of February, 1784, — letters of Mr. Madison to Mr. Jefferson of the 16th of March and 25th of April, 1784, — letter of Mr. Jefferson to General Washington of the 15th of March, 1784, (extract in Marshall's Life of Washington, vol. II. p. 66,) — letter of General Washington to Mr. Jefferson of the 28th of March, 1784, (Sparks's Washington, vol. IX. p. 30,) — and correspondence between General Washington and Mr. Madison in November and December, 1784.

ington had addressed a very able letter to Colonel
Benjamin Harrison, then governor of the State,
exhibiting, in a striking and conclusive manner, the
immense importance of the proposed connection,
both in a commercial and political point of view;
and showing that the two great rivers of Virginia, which have their sources in the Apalachian
Mountains, if promptly and properly improved,
presented the shortest, easiest, and least expensive communications, between the tide-waters of
the Atlantic slope and the fertile regions of the
West and Northwest, of any which the continent
offered. In the close of his letter, he said, as if
prophetically, — "Upon the whole, the object, in
my estimation, is one of vast commercial and
political importance. In this light I think posterity will consider it, and regret, if our conduct
should give them cause, that the present favorable moment to secure so great a blessing to
them was neglected."

This communication, though not of an official
character, presented views of so much public interest and importance, and from a source commanding so much of the public consideration,
that the governor laid it before the General Assembly. Of the three distinguished men between
whom these views had been already freely interchanged in their private correspondence, with
that enlightened forecast and patriotic solicitude
for the future greatness and welfare of their
country which animated and directed them all,

Mr. Madison was the only one now in a position to render his assistance, through the action of the public authorities of the State, to carry them into effect.

In a letter of the 9th of January, 1785, to Mr. Jefferson, who was then one of the ministers of the United States in Europe, he gives the following interesting account of the passage of the "Act for opening and extending the navigation of the Potomac River." The act required the concurrence of the legislature of Maryland, — in obtaining which General Washington exhibited, in civil action, no small portion of the ardor, energy, and devotion that had been displayed by him in the battle-fields of Trenton, Princeton, and Monmouth.

"The subject of clearing the great rivers [Potomac and James] was brought forward early in the session under the auspices of General Washington, who had written an interesting private letter to Governor Harrison, which the latter communicated to the General Assembly. The conversation of the General, during a visit paid to Richmond in the course of the session, still further impressed the magnitude of the object on sundry members. Shortly after his departure, a joint memorial from a number of citizens of Virginia and Maryland, interested in the Potomac, was presented to the Assembly, stating the practicability and importance of the work, and praying for an act of incorporation and grant

of perpetual tolls to the undertakers of it. A
bill had been prepared at the same meeting
which produced the memorial, and was transmitted to Richmond at the same time. A like memorial and bill went to Annapolis, where the
legislature of Maryland was sitting.

"The Assembly here lent a ready ear to the
project; but a difficulty arose from the height
of the tolls proposed, the danger of destroying
the uniformity essential in the proceedings of
the two States by altering them, and the scar-
city of time for negotiating with Maryland a bill
satisfactory to both States. Short as the time
was, however, the attempt was decided on, and
the negotiation committed to Washington himself. General Gates, who happened to be in the
way, and Colonel Blackburn, were associated
with him. The latter did not act: the two
former pushed immediately to Annapolis, where
the sickness of General Gates threw the whole
agency on General Washington. By his exertions, in concert with committees of the two
branches of the legislature, an amendment of the
plan was digested in a few days, passed through
both Houses in one day with nine dissenting
voices only, and dispatched for Richmond just
in time for the session. A corresponding act was
immediately introduced, and passed without opposition."

The mission of General Washington to Annapolis on this errand of public beneficence, so soon

after the close of his great military career, forms
one of the most beautiful and instructive incidents in the drama of his life, and proves, by
the eloquence of a noble example, how true it
is that "peace hath her victories no less re-
nowned than war." The resolution which committed to him, with his two colleagues, the negotiation mentioned by Mr. Madison, was passed
by the legislature on the 14th of December, 1784.
Some days elapsed before it could be communicated to him at Mount Vernon. He lost no
time, after intelligence of his appointment, in setting off on his mission; and from his arrival at
Annapolis to the 28th of the month, he was incessantly and earnestly engaged in discussing and
arranging, with committees of the two Houses
of the Maryland legislature, the necessary but
complex details of the measure in hand, and
recommending its importance and advantages to
the favorable consideration of the members.

We have now before us an autograph letter
addressed by him to Mr. Madison on the last-
mentioned day—rendering an account of his
proceedings and the results of his mission—
which, in its hurried chirography, so unlike his
usual careful handwriting, and in the interlinea-
tions that mark its face, presents to the eye a
vivid picture of the fatigue and exhaustion which
the long-continued exertions and unremitted self-
devotion of the writer had at length brought in
their train. We cannot deny the reader the

gratification of perusing a few extracts from this rapid and unpretending production, which has hitherto rested unknown in a private repository, but which will be regarded by posterity, perhaps, as one of the most characteristic and interesting memorials of the unbounded energies and high civic talents of the great American, when called into action by a patriotic sense of duty.

"ANNAPOLIS, 28th December, 1784.

"DEAR SIR: I have been favored with your letter of 11th instant.

"The proceedings of the conference, and the act and resolutions of the legislature consequent thereupon, herewith transmitted to the Assembly, are so full, and explanatory of the motives which governed in this business, that it is scarcely necessary for me to say anything in addition to them, except that this State seems highly impressed with the importance of the objects which we have had under consideration, and is very desirous of seeing them accomplished. We have reduced most of the tolls from what they were in the first bill, and have added something to a few others. Upon the whole, we have made them as low as we conceived, from the best information before us, they can be fixed without hazarding the plan altogether. . . . . . .

"To secure success, and to give a vigor to the undertaking, it was judged advisable for each State to contribute (upon the terms of private subscribers) to the expense of it, especially as it might have a happy influence on the minds of the Western settlers; and it may be observed here that only part of this money can be called for immediately, provided the work goes on, and afterwards only in the proportion of its progression. Though there is no obligation on the State to adopt this, (if it is inconvenient, or repugnant to their wishes,) yet I should be highly pleased to hear that they had done so. Our advantages will, most assuredly, be equal to those of Maryland, and our public spirit ought not, in my opinion, to be less. . . . .

"Matters might, perhaps, have been better digested, if more time had been taken; but the fear of not getting the report to Richmond before the Assembly would have risen occasioned more hurry than accuracy, and even real despatch. But to alter the act now, further than to accommodate it to circumstances, where it is essential, or to remedy an obvious error, if any should be discovered, will not do. The bill passed this Assembly with only nine dissenting voices, and got through both Houses in a day, — so earnest were the members of getting it to you in time.

"It is now near twelve o'clock at night; and I am writing with an aching head, having been constantly employed in this business since the 22d instant, without assistance from my colleagues, — General Gates having been sick the whole time, and Colonel Blackburn not attending. But for this, I would be more explicit.

"I am, with great esteem and respect,

"Dear sir, your most ob't serv.,

"G. WASHINGTON.

"JAMES MADISON, ESQ.

"P. S. I am ashamed to send you such a letter, but cannot give you a fairer one.   G. W."

The head of Washington, so recently entwined with the laurel wreath of military triumph, aching over the details of a bill for the improvement of his native river, is a suggestive study for both patriotism and philosophy.

After providing for the improvement of the Potomac to the highest point to which it was susceptible of navigation, it was necessary, with a view to the great object of commanding the commerce of the West, that some communication should be opened between that point and the nearest navigable waters of the Ohio. Two routes of communication were in contemplation: one from the head of the Potomac to the Cheat or Monongahela River, and passing through the territory of Virginia or Maryland; the other from the mouth of Wills's Creek to the Yohioganey, and passing through the territory of Pennsylvania. It was agreed by Maryland and Virginia to open the first by appropriating a thousand pounds each to the undertaking, and appointing joint commissioners to superintend and direct the work.

For the second the requisite authority could be obtained only by an application to the legislature of Pennsylvania. Mr. Madison introduced resolutions providing for both objects, which were immediately passed.[1]

He also brought forward a proposition for representing to the State of Pennsylvania the great advantages that would result to her citizens from the proposed communication between the waters of the Potomac and the Ohio; and asking that, in consideration of those advantages and for the encouragement of the enterprise, she would grant a free transit for all produce or merchandise passing by the line of the improvement through her limits; and that articles imported into the State through that channel, for sale or consumption there, should be subjected to no other duties or imposts than they would be liable to, if imported by any other channel. This proposition was, in like manner, adopted.[2]

In conjunction with the measures for the improvement of the river Potomac and its connections, the attention of the legislature was naturally turned to that other great avenue for the commerce of the West with which the bounty of Providence had endowed Virginia. A bill for "opening and extending the navigation of James River" was brought in by Mr. Madison,[3] and

---

[1] See Journal of House of Delegates, October session, 1784, p. 101.
[2] Idem, p. 91.
[3] Idem, pp. 70 and 75.

finally passed with provisions analogous to those contained in the act for the improvement of the Potomac.

As a necessary complement of this measure, and still keeping in view the great object of a commercial intercourse with the West, Mr. Madison moved that commissioners be appointed to make an accurate examination and survey of the upper parts of James River, of the nearest navigable waters flowing into the Ohio, and of the best route of communication between the two, and to report the results of their examination to the next General Assembly, in order that proper steps be then taken to complete the connection. Looking, at the same time, to a commercial intercourse with the South through the channels which nature had provided for Virginia on that side of her territory, he moved also that an examination be made of the best course for a canal from the waters of Elizabeth River to those of Albemarle Sound, that the result be reported to the ensuing session of the legislature, and that the coöperation of North Carolina, if necessary, be invited in the execution of the work. All these propositions were adopted.[1]

Thus, by the direct agency of Mr. Madison in the legislature of Virginia, was the broad foundation laid of that whole system of internal improvements which has ever since been the cherished object of her policy, though, unfortu-

[1] See Journal of House of Delegates, October session, 1784, p. 102.

nately, not followed up by succeeding legislators with the energy and promptitude necessary to secure the prize that nature seemed to have designed for her. It is edifying to observe how quickly and earnestly the statesmen of the Revolution, uniting with the great chief whose operations they had sustained in the field, turned their attention to the fruitful and durable labors of peace, the moment the contest for national independence was ended. General Washington, by the weight of his opinions and his commanding influence in the country, and Mr. Madison, by his exertions in the legislature, inaugurated this noble career of civic wisdom and practical usefulness on the theatre of Virginia.

How truly Mr. Madison was penetrated with the dignity and importance of these labors, and with what sagacity he cast the horoscope of the fortunes of his native State as connected with them, if they had been carried forward with the requisite energy to a seasonable consummation, is shown by what he says, in a letter written at the time, of the agency of General Washington in them; much of which will ·be felt to be applicable to the writer himself, however sedulously he avoided the remotest allusion to the part, prominent as it was, he had performed in the common service.

"The earnestness," he says, "with which General Washington espouses the undertaking is hardly to be described, and shows that a mind like his, capable of great views, and which has long been occupied with them, cannot bear a vacancy. And surely he could not have chosen an occupation more worthy of succeeding to that of establishing the political rights of his country than the patronage of works for the extensive and lasting improvement of its natural advantages, — works which will double the value of half the • lands within the Commonwealth, will extend its commerce, link with its interests those of the Western States, and lessen the emigration of its citizens by enhancing the profitableness of situations which they now desert in search of better." [1]

The grateful sentiments of the legislature, evoked anew by the deep interest General Washington had shown in the permanent prosperity and improvement of his native State, sought some new and more substantial expression. By some persons a direct pension was proposed. But to Mr. Madison it seemed that the most delicate and appropriate form in which a reward could be presented to the sensitive mind of Washington, if he could be prevailed on to accept any, was to vest in him a certain interest in the stock of the companies that had just been established for the improvement of the two great rivers of the State, — public and noble enterprises on which he had already bestowed so much patriotic solicitude.

[1] See letter to Mr. Jefferson of the 9th of January, 1785.

On the motion of Mr. Madison, therefore, leave was given to bring in a bill for that purpose; and by the same order of the House he was appointed *sole* committee to prepare and bring it in.[1] The bill was immediately reported by him, and the day after, was unanimously passed by both branches of the legislature. It directed the treasurer of the State to make a special subscription of fifty shares in the Potomac Company, (of the value of $444 each share,) and of one hundred shares in the James River Company, (of the value of $200 each share,) in addition to the original subscription made on behalf of the State; and the additional shares, so to be subscribed for, were declared to be "vested in George Washington, Esq., his heirs and assigns forever, in as effectual a manner as if the said subscriptions had been made by himself or his attorney."

But the real value of this public recompense, to the mind of Washington, was in the preamble of the act by which it was offered. The pen of Mr. Madison was never more congenially or happily employed than in recording the praises of the great benefactor of his country. It thus nobly set forth in the preamble the motives of the grant: —

"Whereas it is the desire of the representatives of this Commonwealth to embrace every suitable occasion of testifying their sense of the

[1] Journal of House of Delegates, October session, 1784, p. 105.

unexampled merits of George Washington towards his country, and it is their wish in particular that those great works for its improvement, which, both as springing from the liberty which he has been instrumental in establishing, and as encouraged by his patronage, will be durable monuments of his glory, may be made monuments also of the gratitude of his country." Then follows the enactment.[1] With this graceful act of public sensibility and acknowledgment terminated, on the 5th of January, 1785, the session of the legislature.

It was not long after the adjournment of the legislature that the minds of the people began to be earnestly directed to the consideration of the bill proposing a general assessment for "the support of teachers of the Christian religion." This bill, we have seen, had passed through several stages of its parliamentary progress at the late session, and was then ordered to be "en-

[1] Hen. Stat. vol. xi. pp. 525, 526. This testimony of the appreciation of his native State was received by Washington with the same warmth of sensibility and acknowledgment that prompted it on the part of the legislature. But he declined to take any personal benefit from it, and consented to hold the stock vested in him by the act only as a trust fund, to be applied to some object of public and general utility. See his noble and graceful letter to the governor, Patrick Henry, dated the 29th of October, 1785, in Sparks's Washington, vol. ix. pp. 142, 143. The shares in the James River Company were applied by him to the better endowment of Liberty Hall Academy, at Lexington, in Rockbridge County, which afterwards assumed the name of Washington College; and the Potomac shares were set apart by his will, as well as by a previous assignment, in aid of the establishment of a university in the District of Columbia. See Idem, vol. xi. pp. 3, 4, 14–16, and 172, 173.

grossed"; but its third reading was finally postponed to the next meeting of the legislature,
which was to take place in the month of October
of the present year. Twenty-four copies of the
bill, with the ayes and noes on the question of
postponement, were ordered to be sent to each
county; and the people were requested to signify their sense, respecting its adoption, to the
ensuing Assembly.

Rarely has an issue of more vital importance
to the liberty and happiness of a free people —
and yet one which had already divided, and
might well continue to divide, the opinions of
good men — been submitted to the direct arbit-
rament of the popular will. Mr. Madison's convictions upon it were most profound. From
early manhood to this decisive moment, he had
been the earnest and steady champion of religious liberty in its widest latitude. He had stood
up nobly and manfully, during the late session
of the legislature, in opposition to the proposed
measure, against a most formidable array of talents, numbers, popularity, and influence. Allies,
too, on whom he had counted, as having taken
a most able and efficient part in the earlier
struggles for religious freedom, were now separated from their ancient standard, temporarily at
least, by the new and seductive form in which
the question was presented.

Under these circumstances, it may well be conceived with what deep interest and anxiety Mr.

Madison watched the progress of this great cause before the forum where it was to receive its final decision. We give the following extracts from his correspondence with Mr. Monroe, then a delegate in Congress from Virginia, as exhibiting the successive phases of the important trial. On the 12th of April, 1785, he writes to him: —

"The only proceeding of the late session of Assembly which makes a noise through the country, is that which relates to a general assessment. The Episcopal people are generally for it, though I think the zeal of some of them has cooled. The laity of the other sects are generally unanimous on the other side. So are all the clergy, except the Presbyterian, who seem as ready to set up an establishment which is to take them in as they were to pull down that which shut them out. I do not know a more shameful contrast than might be found between their memorials on the latter and former occasion."

On the 29th of May he writes: "The adversaries to the assessment begin to think the prospect here flattering to their wishes. The printed bill has excited great discussion, and is likely to prove the sense of the community to be in favor of the liberty now enjoyed. I have heard of several counties where the late representatives have been laid aside for voting for the bill, and not a single one where the reverse has happened. The Presbyterian clergy, too, who were in general friends to the scheme, are already in another tone, — either compelled by the laity of that sect, or alarmed at the probability of farther interference of the legislature if they begin to dictate in matters of religion."

On the 21st of June he again writes: "A very warm opposition will be made to this innovation [the general assessment] by the people of the middle and back counties, particularly the latter. They do not scruple to declare it an alarming usurpation on their fundamental rights; and that, though the General Assembly should give it the *form*, they will not give it the *validity* of a law. If there be any limitation to the power of the legislature, — particularly if this limitation is to be sought in our Declaration of Rights, or form of government, — I own the bill appears to me to warrant this language of the people."

It was soon felt that the opposition which had been manifested to this measure, with arguments of due weight to justify and strengthen the popular sentiment, should be embodied in a permanent and imposing form, and go before the legislature under the sign manual of the constituent body. The noble lead which Mr. Madison had taken in the question, and his superior and recognized ability, pointed him out at once for the task. At the instance of Colonel Mason, Mr. George Nicholas, and other distinguished friends of religious freedom, he prepared a "Memorial and Remonstrance" to the legislature against the proposed assessment, to be circulated among the people. In this masterly paper, he discussed the question of an establishment of religion by law from every possible point of view,—of natural right, the inherent limitations of the civil power, the interests of religion itself, the genius and precepts of Christianity, the warning lessons of history, the dictates of a wise and sober policy, —and treated them all with a consummate power of reasoning, and a force of appeal to the understandings and hearts of the people, that bore down every opposing prejudice, and precluded reply. It was diffused extensively through the State, and was rapidly covered with the signatures of the voters.

When the Assembly met in October, the table of the House of Delegates almost sunk under the weight of the accumulated copies of the memorial sent forward from the different counties, each with its long and dense column of subscribers. The fate of the assessment was sealed. The manifestation of the public judgment was too unequivocal and overwhelming to leave the faintest hope to the friends of the measure It was abandoned without a struggle.[1]

[1] Some very intelligent writers appear to have confounded the act "incorporating the Protestant Episcopal Church" with the General Assessment Bill. It has been stated, for example, that in 1785 the Rev. John Blair Smith was heard for three successive days, at the bar of the House of Delegates, in opposition to the assessment bill. (Evan. and Lit. Mag. vol. IX. pp. 43–47, cited by Mr. Howison in his interesting History of Virginia, vol. II. p. 298.) And yet another most respectable authority, belonging to the same religious denomination

Under cover of this signal victory won before the people by the irresistible voice of truth, the declaratory act for the "establishment of religious freedom," which had been drawn by Mr. Jefferson, as one of the committee of revisors, and presented to the legislature in 1779, with the rest of the revised bills, was taken up and passed into a law. The "Memorial and Remonstrance" had cleared away every obstruction, and so smoothed the ground before it that its passage became a matter of course.

When the early and conscientious zeal of Mr. Madison in the cause of religious freedom, so beautifully and strikingly displayed, even before the Revolution, in his correspondence with his friend Bradford; his sagacious and pregnant amendment to the Virginia Bill of Rights in 1776; his brave and manly struggle against the embattled hosts of the assessment in the legislature of 1784; and his glorious authorship of the "Memorial and Remonstrance" in 1785 — the crowning victory in the momentous contest — are considered; to him, of all the men of his age, posterity will award the meed of preëminence for long, earnest, persevering, and efficient exer-

with Dr. Smith, (Baird's Religion in America, p. 110,) relates that he had been won over by Patrick Henry in favor of the assessment. Dr. Smith was warmly opposed, as his correspondence with Mr. Madison shows, to the act incorporating the Protestant Episcopal Church; and the probability, therefore, is that the reported argument at the bar of the House was in opposition to that act more particularly, and in order to obtain its repeal, which took place a year afterwards.

tions in defence of one of the most precious rights of human nature — the basis of every other, and the indispensable guarantee of civil and political liberty.

As a triumphant plea in that great cause, never surpassed in power or eloquence by any which its stirring interests have called forth, and as a monument of the genius, ability, and love of liberty of the author, which, if he had left no other behind him, would suffice to transmit his name with honor to future ages, and ought to render it forever dear to his country, — we annex here this noble production of the mind and heart of Mr. Madison, that the reader may be enabled to form his own estimate of its merits, as well as to profit by its lessons of wisdom and justice.

Memorial and Remonstrance against the Bill " establishing a legal Provision for Teachers of the Christian Religion."

To the Honorable the General Assembly of the Commonwealth of Virginia : —

We the subscribers, citizens of the said Commonwealth, having taken into serious consideration a bill printed by order of the late session of the General Assembly, entitled " A Bill establishing a Provision for Teachers of the Christian Religion," and conceiving that the same, if finally armed with the sanctions of a law, will be a dangerous abuse of power, are bound, as faithful members of a free State, to remonstrate against it, and to declare the reasons by which we are determined. We remonstrate against the said bill ; —

Because we hold it for a fundamental and undeniable truth, " that religion, or the duty which we owe to our Creator, and the manner of discharging it, can be directed only by reason and conviction, not by force or violence." * The religion, then, of every man must be left to the conviction and conscience of every man; and it is the right of every man to exercise it as these may dictate. This right is, in its nature, an inalienable right. It is inalienable, because the opinions of men, depending only on the evidence contemplated by their own minds, cannot follow the dictates of other men; it is inalienable also, because what is here a right towards men is a duty towards the Creator. It is the duty of every man to render to the Creator such homage, and such only, as he believes to be acceptable to Him. This duty is precedent, both in order of time and in degree of obligation, to the claims of civil society. Before any man can be considered as a member of civil society, he must be considered as a subject of the Governor of the Universe; and if a member of civil society who enters into any subordinate association must always do it with a reservation of his duty to the general authority, much more must every man who becomes a member of any particular civil society, do it with a saving of his allegiance to the Universal Sovereign. We maintain, therefore, that, in matters of religion, no man's right is abridged by the institution of civil society, and that religion is wholly exempt from its cognizance. True it is that no other rule exists by which any question which may divide a society can be ultimately determined than the will of the majority; but it is also true that the majority may trespass on the rights of the minority.

Because, if religion be exempt from the authority of the society at large, still less can it be subject to that of the legislative body. The latter are but the creatures and vicegerents of the former. Their jurisdiction is both derivative and limited. It is limited with regard to the coördinate departments; more necessarily is it limited with regard to the constituent. The preservation of a free government requires, not merely that the metes and bounds which separate each department of power be invariably maintained, but more especially that neither of them be suffered to overleap the great barrier which defends the rights of the people. The rulers who are guilty of such an encroachment exceed the commission from which they derive their authority, and are tyrants. The people who submit to it are governed by laws made neither by themselves nor by an authority derived from them, and are slaves.

Because it is proper to take alarm at the first experiment on our liberties. We hold this prudent jealousy to be the first duty of citizens, and one of the noblest characteristics of the late Revolution. The

* Virginia Bill of Rights, art. 16.

freemen of America did not wait till usurped power had strengthened itself by exercise and entangled the question in precedents. They saw all the consequences in the principle; and they avoided the consequences by denying the principle. We revere this lesson too much soon to forget it. Who does not see that the same authority which can establish Christianity to the exclusion of all other religions may establish, with the same ease, any particular sect of Christians in exclusion of all other sects? that the same authority which can force a citizen to contribute threepence only of his property for the support of any one establishment may force him to conform to any other establishment, in all cases whatsoever?

Because the bill violates that equality which ought to be the basis of every law, and which is more indispensable in proportion as the validity or expediency of any law is more liable to be impeached. "If all men are by nature equally free and independent," [*] all men are to be considered as entering into society on equal conditions,—as relinquishing no more, and therefore retaining no less, one than another, of their natural rights. Above all, are they to be considered as retaining "an *equal* title to the free exercise of religion according to the dictates of conscience." [†] Whilst we assert for ourselves a freedom to embrace, to profess, and to observe the religion which we believe to be of divine origin, we cannot deny an equal freedom to those whose minds have not yet yielded to the evidence which has convinced us. If this freedom be abused, it is an offence against God, not against man. To God, therefore, not to man, must an account of it be rendered. As the bill violates equality by subjecting some to peculiar burdens, so it violates the same principle by granting to others peculiar exemptions. Are the Quakers and Menonists the only sects who think a compulsive support of their religions unnecessary and unwarrantable? Can their piety alone be intrusted with the care of public worship? Ought their religions to be endowed, above all others, with extraordinary privileges, by which proselytes may be enticed from all others? We think too favorably of the justice and good sense of these denominations to believe that they either covet preëminences over their fellow-citizens, or that they will be seduced by them from the common opposition to the measure.

Because the bill implies either that the civil magistrate is a competent judge of religious truth, or that he may employ religion as an engine of civil policy. The first is an arrogant pretension, falsified by the contradictory opinions of rulers in all ages and throughout the world; the second, an unhallowed perversion of the means of salvation.

* Virginia Bill of Rights, art. 1.   † Idem, art. 16.

Because the establishment proposed by the bill is not requisite for the support of the Christian religion. To say that it is, is a contradiction to the Christian religion itself; for every page of it disavows a dependence on the powers of this world. It is a contradiction to fact, for it is known that this religion both existed and flourished not only without the support of human laws, but in spite of every opposition from them, and not only during the period of miraculous aid, but long after it had been left to its own evidence and the ordinary care of Providence. Nay, it is a contradiction in terms; for a religion not invented by human policy must have preëxisted and been supported before it was established by human policy. Moreover, it is to weaken, in those who profess this religion, a pious confidence in its innate excellence and the patronage of its Author; and to foster, in those who still reject it, a suspicion that its friends are too conscious of its fallacies to trust it to its own merits.

Because experience witnesseth that ecclesiastical establishments, instead of maintaining the purity and efficacy of religion, have had a contrary operation. During almost fifteen centuries has the legal establishment of Christianity been on trial. What have been its fruits? More or less in all places, pride and indolence in the clergy, ignorance and servility in the laity; in both, superstition, bigotry, and persecution. Inquire of the teachers of Christianity for the ages in which it appeared in its greatest lustre: those of every sect point to the ages prior to its incorporation with civil policy. Propose a restoration of this primitive state, in which its teachers depended on the voluntary rewards of their flocks: many of them predict its downfall. On which side ought their testimony to have greatest weight? when for, or when against, their interest?

Because the establishment in question is not necessary for the support of civil government. If it be urged as necessary for the support of civil government only as it is a means of supporting religion, and it be not necessary for the latter purpose, it cannot be necessary for the former. If religion be not within the cognizance of civil government, how can its legal establishment be necessary to civil government? What influence, in fact, have ecclesiastical establishments had on civil society? In some instances they have been seen to erect a spiritual tyranny on the ruins of the civil authority; in many instances they have been seen upholding the thrones of political tyranny; in no instance have they been seen the guardians of the liberties of the people. Rulers who wished to subvert the public liberty may have found an established clergy convenient auxiliaries. A just government, insti-

tuted to secure and perpetuate it, needs them not. Such a government
will be best supported by protecting every citizen in the enjoyment of
his religion with the same equal hand which protects his person and
his property, — by neither invading the equal rights of any sect, nor
suffering any sect to invade those of another.

Because the proposed establishment is a departure from that generous policy which, offering an asylum to the persecuted and oppressed
of every nation and religion, promised a lustre to our country and an
accession to the number of its citizens. What a melancholy mark is
the bill of sudden degeneracy! Instead of holding forth an asylum
to the persecuted, it is itself a signal of persecution. It degrades from
the equal rank of citizens all those whose opinions in religion do not
bend to those of the legislative authority. Distant as it may be, in its
present form, from the Inquisition, it differs from it only in degree.
The one is the first step, the other the last, in the career of intolerance.
The magnanimous sufferer under this cruel scourge, in foreign regions,
must view the bill as a beacon on our coast, warning him to seek some
other haven, where liberty and philanthropy, in their due extent, may
offer a more certain repose from his troubles.

Because it will have a like tendency to banish our citizens. The
allurements presented by other situations are every day thinning their
number. To superadd a fresh motive to emigration, by revoking the
liberty which they now enjoy, would be the same species of folly which
has dishonored and depopulated flourishing kingdoms.

Because it will destroy that moderation and harmony which the forbearance of our laws to intermeddle with religion has produced among
its several sects. Torrents of blood have been spilled in the Old World,
in consequence of vain attempts of the secular arm to extinguish religious discord by proscribing all differences in religious opinion. Time
has at length revealed the true remedy. Every relaxation of narrow
and rigorous policy, wherever it has been tried, has been found to as-
suage the disease. The American theatre has exhibited proofs that
equal and complete liberty, if it does not wholly eradicate it, sufficiently destroys its malignant influence on the health and prosperity
of the State. If, with the salutary effects of this system under our
own eyes, we begin to contract the bounds of religious freedom, we
know no name which will too severely reproach our folly. At least,
let warning be taken at the first fruits of the threatened innovation.
The very appearance of the bill has transformed "that Christian forbearance, love, and charity" * which of late mutually prevailed into

* Virginia Bill of Rights, art. 16.

animosities and jealousies which may not soon be appeased. What mischiefs may not be dreaded, should this enemy to the public quiet be armed with the force of a law?

Because the policy of the bill is adverse to the diffusion of the light of Christianity. The first wish of those who enjoy this precious gift ought to be that it may be imparted to the whole race of mankind. Compare the number of those who have as yet received it with the number still remaining under the dominion of false religions, and how small is the former! Does the policy of the bill tend to lessen the disproportion? No; it at once discourages those who are strangers to the light of revelation from coming into the region of it, and countenances by example the nations who continue in darkness in shutting out those who might convey it to them. Instead of levelling, as far as possible, every obstacle to the victorious progress of truth, the bill, with an ignoble and unchristian timidity, would circumscribe it with a wall of defence against the encroachments of error.

Because attempts to enforce, by legal sanctions, acts obnoxious to so great a proportion of citizens, tend to enervate the laws in general, and to slacken the bonds of society. If it be difficult to execute any law which is not generally deemed necessary or salutary, what must be the case where it is deemed invalid and dangerous? And what may be the effect of so striking an example of impotency in the government on its general authority?

Because a measure of such singular magnitude and delicacy ought not to be imposed without the clearest evidence that it is called for by a majority of citizens; and no satisfactory method is yet proposed by which the voice of the majority, in this case, may be determined, or its influence secured. "The people of the respective counties," indeed, "are requested to signify their opinion respecting the adoption of the bill to the next session of the Assembly." But the representation must be made equal before the voice either of the representatives or of the counties will be that of the people. Our hope is that neither of the former will, after due consideration, espouse the dangerous principle of the bill. Should the event disappoint us, it will still leave us in full confidence that a fair appeal to the latter will reverse the sentence against our liberties.

Because, finally, "the equal right of every citizen to the free exercise of his religion according to the dictates of conscience" is held by the same tenure with all our other rights. If we recur to its origin, it is equally the gift of Nature; if we weigh its importance, it cannot be less dear to us; if we consult the declaration of those rights "which pertain to the good people of Virginia as the basis and foundation of government," * it is enumerated with equal solemnity, or rather with studied emphasis. Either, then, we must say that the will of the legislature is the only measure of their authority, and that, in the plenitude of that authority, they may sweep away all our fundamental rights; or that they are bound to leave this particular right untouched and sacred. Either we must say that they may control the freedom of the press, may abolish the trial by jury, may swallow up the executive and judiciary powers of the State, — nay, that they may despoil us of our very right of suffrage, and erect themselves into an independent and hereditary assembly, — or we must say that they have no authority to enact into a law the bill under consideration.

We, the subscribers, say that the General Assembly of this Commonwealth have no such authority; and in order that no effort may be omitted on our part against so dangerous a usurpation, we oppose to it this remonstrance, earnestly praying, as we are in duty bound, that the Supreme Lawgiver of the Universe, by illuminating those to whom it is addressed, may, on the one hand, turn their councils from every act which would affront His holy prerogative or violate the trust committed to them, and, on the other, guide them into every measure which may be worthy of His blessing, redound to their own praise, and establish more firmly the liberties, the prosperity, and the happiness of the Commonwealth.

* Bill of Rights, preamble.

APPENDIX.

A. See page 35.

MR. MADISON'S THEOLOGICAL CATALOGUE FOR THE LIBRARY OF
THE UNIVERSITY.

IT was in 1824, when the University of Virginia was soon to be
opened, that Mr. Jefferson, the Rector, applied to Mr. Madison for his
aid in making out a catalogue of books on theology for the library.
In a letter of the 8th of August, 1824, he says to Mr. Madison: "The
chapter in which I am most at a loss is that of divinity; and knowing
that in your early days you bestowed attention on this subject, I wish
you could suggest to me any works really worthy of a place in the catalogue. The good moral writers, Christian as well as pagan, I have
set down; but there are writers of celebrity in religious metaphysics,
such as Duns Scotus *et alii tales*, whom you can suggest. Pray think
of it, and help me." Mr. Madison answered on the 16th of the same
month: "I will endeavour to make out a list of theological works, but
am less qualified for the task than you seem to think, and fear also that
my catalogues are less copious than might be wished. There is a difficulty in marking the proper limit to so inexhaustible a chapter, whether
with a view to the library in its infant or more mature state."

On the 3d of September, Mr. Jefferson wrote again to Mr. Madison: "I am near closing my catalogue, and it is important I should
receive the kindness of your theological supplement by the first or
second mail, or its insertion will be impracticable. Be so good as to
expedite it as much as possible." On the 10th of the month, Mr. Madison wrote the following answer, and accompanied it with the desired
catalogue : —

"MONTPELIER, September 10th, 1824.

"DEAR SIR: On the receipt of yours of August 8th, I turned my
thoughts to its request on the subject of a theological catalogue for the

54 *

library of the University; and not being aware that so early an answer was wished as I now find was the case, I had proceeded very leisurely in noting such authors as seemed proper for the catalogue. Supposing also that, although theology was not to be taught in the University, its library ought to contain pretty full information for such as might voluntarily seek it in that branch of learning, I had contemplated as much of a comprehensive and systematic selection as my scanty materials admitted, and had gone through the five first centuries of Christianity when yours of the 3d instant came to hand, which was the evening before the last. This conveyed to me more distinctly the limited object your letter had in view, and relieved me from a task which I found extremely tedious, especially considering the intermixture of the doctrinal and controversial part of divinity with the metaphysical and moral part, and the immense extent of the whole.

"I send you the list I had made out, with an addition, on the same paper, of such books as a hasty glance at a few catalogues and my recollection suggested. Perhaps some of them may not have occurred to you, and may suit the blank you have not filled. I am sorry I could not make a fair copy without failing to comply with the time pointed out.

"I find by a letter from Lafayette, in answer to a few lines I wrote him on his arrival at New York, that he means to see us before the 19th of October, as you have probably learned from himself. His visit to the United States will make an *annus mirabilis* in the history of liberty. Affectionately yours,

"JAMES MADISON.

"MR. JEFFERSON."

The following is the catalogue enclosed: —

CENTURY I. — Polyglott. Clement's Epistles to the Corinthians, published at Cambridge, 1788.

Ignatius, Epistles. Amsterdam, 1607.

Cotelier, Recueil de Monumens des Pères dans les Temps apostoliques. Edit. par Le Clerc. Amsterdam, 1724.

Flavius Josephus (in English, by Whiston). Amsterdam, 1726. 2 v. fol.

Philo Judæus (Greek and Latin). English Edition, 1742. 2 v. fol.

Lucian's Works. Amsterdam, 1743. 8 v. 4to.

Fabricius, Bibl. Græc. Delectus, etc. See Mosheim, v. I. p. 106.

CENT. II. — Justin Martyr's Apology, etc. Ed. by Prudent Maran, Benedictine.

Hermias. Oxford, 1700. 8vo.

Athenagoras. Oxford, 1706. 8vo.

Clemens Alexandrinus. Ed. by Potter. Oxford, 1715. 2 v. fol.

Tertullian. Venice, 1746. 1 v. fol.

Theophilus of Antioch (first adopted the term Trinity). 1742. 1 v. fol.

Irenæus. Ed. by Grabe. 1702. 1 v. fol.

Tatian, against the Gentiles. Oxford, 1700. 8vo.

Ammonius Saccas's Harmony of the Evangelists.

Celsus translated par Bonhereau. Amsterdam, 1700. 4to.

CENT. III. — Minutius Felix (translated by Reeves). Leyden, 1672. 8vo.

Origen. Gr. and Lat. 4 v. fol.

Cyprian (translated into French by Lambert). 1 v. fol.

Gregory Thaumaturgus. Gr. and Lat. 1626. 1 v. fol.

Arnobius Africanus. Amsterdam, 1651. 1 v. 4to.

Anatolius. Antwerp, 1634. 1 v. fol.

Methodius Eubulius. Rome, 1656. 8vo.

Philostratus — Life of Apollonius Tyanæus. Gr. and Lat., with notes by Godefroy Olearius. Leipsic.

CENT. IV. — Lactantius. Edit. by Linglet. Paris, 1748. 2 v. 4to.

Eusebius of Cæsarea.

Athanasius, par Montfauçon. 1698. 3 v. fol.

Antonius, (founder of the monastic order,) Seven Letters, etc. Latin.

St. Cyril (of Jerusalem). Gr. and Lat. Paris, 1720. 1 v. fol.

St. Hilary. Ed. by Maffei. Verona, 1730.

Lucifer, Bishop of Cagliari. Paris, 1568. 1 v. 8vo.

Epiphanius. Gr. and Lat. Edit. Père Petau. 1622. 2 v. fol.

Optatus. Ed. by Dupin. 1700. fol.

Pacianus. Paris, 1538. 4to.

Basil (Bishop of Cæsarea). Gr. and Lat. 1721. 3 v. fol.

Gregory (of Nazianzen). Gr. and Lat. Paris, 1609. 2 v. fol.

——— (of Nyssa). 1615. 2 v. fol.

Ambrosius. Paris, 1690. 2 v. fol.

Jerome. Paris, 1693–1706. 5 v. fol.

Rufinus. Paris, 1580. 1 v. fol.

Augustin. 1679–1700. 8 v. fol.

Chrysostom, John. Gr. and Lat. 10 v. fol.

Ammianus Marcellinus.

Julian's Works.

CENT. V. — Sulpitius Severus. Verona, 1754. 2 v. 4to.

Isidorus (of Pelusium). Paris, 1638. Gr. and Lat. 1 v. fol.

Cyril (of Alexandria). Gr. and Lat. 6 v. fol.

Orosius. Leyden, 1738. 4to.

Theodoret. Edit. by Père Simond. Gr. and Lat. 6 v. fol.

Philostorgius, by Godefroi. Gr. and Lat. 1642. 1 v. 4to.

Vincentius Lirinensis. Rome. 4to.

Socrates's Eccles. History.

Sozomen's do. do.

Leo (the Great), by Quesnel. Lyons, 1700. fol.

Æneas (of Gaza). Greek, with Latin version by Barthiris. 1655. 4to.

MISCELLANEOUS. Thomas Aquinas, (Doct. Angelicus,) Head of the Thomists, 12 v. fol. Duns Scotus, (Doctor Subtilis,) Head of the Scotists, 12 v. fol. The Koran. Cave's Lives of the Fathers. Daille's Use and Abuse of them. Erasmus. Luther. Calvin. Socinus. Bellarmin. Chillingworth. Council of Trent, by F. Paul; by Pallavicini; by Basnage. Grotius on Truth of Christian Religion. Sherlock's Sermons. Tillotson's Sermons. Tillemont. Baronius. Lardner. Hooker's Ecclesiastical Polity. Pearson on the Creed. Burnet on Thirty-Nine Articles. Pascal's Lettres Provinciales ; Pensées. Fénelon. Bossuet. Bourdaloué. Saurin. Fléchier. Massillon. Warburton's Divine Legation. Hannah Adams's View of all Religions. Stackhouse's History of the Bible. Sir Isaac Newton's Works on Religious Subjects. Locke's ditto. Stillingfleet's Controversy with him on the Possibility of endowing Matter with Thought. Clarke on the Being and Attributes of God ; his Sermons. Butler's Analogy. Eight Sermons at Boyle's Lecture, by Bentley. Whitby on the Five Points. Whiston's Theological Works. Taylor's (Jeremy) Sermons. John Taylor (of Norwich) against Original Sin. Edwards, in answer; on Free Will; on Virtue. Soame Jenyns's Inquiry into the Nature and Origin of Evil. Liturgy for King's Chapel, Boston. Mather's Essays to do Good. Price on Morals. Wollaston's Religion of Nature delineated. Barclay's Apology for Quakers. William Penn's Works. King's (William) Essay on Origin of Evil; notes by Law. Wesley on Original Sin. King's Inquiry into the Constitution, Discipline, etc., of the Church within the Three First Centuries. Priestley's and Horsley's Controversies. Historical View of Controversy on Intermediate State of the Soul, by Dean Blackburne. The Confessional, by the same. Jones's Method of settling the Canonical Scriptures of New Testament. Leibnitz on Goodness of God, Liberty of Man, and Origin of Evil. Paley's Works. Warburton's Principles of Natural and Revealed Religion. Blair's Sermons. Buckminster's (of Boston) Sermons. Necker's Importance of Religion. Latrobe's (Benjamin) Doctrine of the Moravians. Ray's Wisdom of God in the Creation. Durham's Astro-theology. Bibliotheca Fratrum Polonorum, 9 v. fol.

B. See pp. 137-146.

SUCCESSIVE DRAUGHTS OF VIRGINIA DECLARATION OF RIGHTS.

Original Draught of George Mason.	*Draught reported by Committee.[*]*
A Declaration of Rights made by the Representatives of the good people of Virginia, assembled in full and free convention, which rights do per-	A Declaration of Rights made by the Representatives of the good people of Virginia, assembled in full and free convention, which rights do

[*] We have marked in *Italics*, in order to indicate them the more readily to the reader, the verbal variations of this draught from that of Colonel Mason.

tain to them and their posterity, as the basis and foundation of government.

1. That all men are created equally free and independent, and have certain inherent natural rights, of which they cannot, by any compact, deprive or divest their posterity; among which are the enjoyment of life and liberty, with the means of acquiring and possessing property, and pursuing and obtaining happiness and safety.

2. That all power is by God and Nature vested in, and consequently derived from, the people; that magistrates are their trustees and servants, and at all times amenable to them.

3. That government is, or ought to be, instituted for the common benefit, protection, and security of the people, nation, or community. Of all the various modes and forms of government, that is best which is capable of producing the greatest degree of happiness and safety, and is most effectually secured against the danger of maladministration; and that whenever any government shall be found inadequate or contrary to these purposes, a majority of the community hath an indubitable, unalienable, and indefeasible right to reform, alter, or abolish it, in such manner as shall be judged most conducive to the public weal.

4. That no man, or set of men, are entitled to exclusive or separate emoluments or privileges from the community, but in consideration of public services; which not being descendible, neither ought the offices of magistrate, legislator, or judge to be hereditary.

5. That the legislative and executive powers of the State should be separate and distinct from the judicial; and that the members of the two first may be restrained from oppression by feeling and participating the burthens of the people, they should, at fixed peri-

pertain to *us* and *our* posterity, as the basis and foundation of government.

1. That all men are *born* equally free and independent, and have certain inherent natural rights, of which they cannot, by any compact, deprive their posterity; among which are the enjoyment of life and liberty, with the means of acquiring and possessing property, and pursuing and obtaining happiness and safety.

2. [The same as the original draught of George Mason, except that the clause " by God and Nature " is stricken out.]

3. [The same in all respects.]

4. That no man, or set of men, are entitled to exclusive or separate emoluments or privileges from the community, but in consideration of public services; which not being descendible *or hereditary, the idea of a man born a magistrate, a legislator, or a judge is unnatural and absurd.*

5. [The same, except that the word *judicative* is substituted for " judicial," and the conjunction " and," after the words " private station," is stricken out.]

eds, be reduced to a private station, and return into that body from which they were originally taken. and the vacancies be supplied by frequent, certain, and regular elections.

6. That elections of members to serve as representatives of the people in the legislature ought to be free, and that all men, having sufficient evidence of permanent common interest with and attachment to the community, have the right of suffrage, and cannot be taxed, or deprived of their property for public uses, without their own consent, or that of their representatives so elected, nor bound by any law to which they have not, in like manner, assented for the common good.

7. That all power of suspending laws, or the execution of laws, by any authority, without consent of the representatives of the people, is injurious to their rights, and ought not to be exercised.

8. That in all capital or criminal prosecutions, a man hath a right to demand the cause and nature of his accusation, to be confronted with the accusers and witnesses, to call for evidence in his favor, and to a speedy trial by an impartial jury of his vicinage, without whose unanimous consent he cannot be found guilty, nor can he be compelled to give evidence against himself; and that no man be deprived of his liberty, except by the law of the land or the judgment of his peers.

9. That excessive bail ought not to be required, nor excessive fines imposed, nor cruel and unusual punishments inflicted.

6. That elections of members to serve as representatives of the people in *Assembly* ought to be free, and that all men, having sufficient evidence of permanent common interest with and attachment to the community, have the right of suffrage.

7. *That no part of a man's property can be taken from him or applied to* public uses without *his* own consent or that of *his legal* representatives; nor *are the people* bound by any *laws but such as* they have, in like manner, assented to for *their* common good.

8. [The same.]

9. That laws having retrospect to crimes, and punishing offences committed before the existence of such laws, are generally oppressive, and ought to be avoided.

10. [The same, with the single exception of the disjunctive *or* being substituted for "and" between the words "accusers" and "witnesses."]

11. [The same.]

12. That warrants, unsupported by evidence, whereby any officer or messenger may be commanded or required to search suspected places, or to seize any person or persons, his or their

10. That in controversies respecting property, and in suits between man and man, the ancient trial by jury is preferable to any other, and ought to be held sacred.

11. That the freedom of the Press is one of the great bulwarks of liberty, and can never be restrained but by despotic governments.

12. That a well regulated militia, composed of the body of the people, trained to arms, is the proper, natural, and safe defence of a free State; that standing armies in time of peace should be avoided, as dangerous to liberty; and that, in all cases, the military should be under strict subordination to, and governed by, the civil power.

13. That no free government, or the blessing of liberty, can be preserved to any people but by a firm adherence to justice, moderation, temperance, frugality, and virtue, and by frequent recurrence to fundamental principles.

14. That religion, or the duty which we owe to our Creator, and the manner of discharging it, can be directed only by reason and conviction, not by force or violence; and, therefore, that all men should enjoy the fullest toleration in the exercise of religion, according to the dictates of conscience, unpunished and unrestrained by the magistrate, unless, under color of religion, any man disturb the peace, the happiness, or the safety of society. And that it is the mutual duty of all to practise Christian forbearance, love, and charity towards each other.

property, not particularly described, are grievous and oppressive, and ought not to be granted.

13. [The same.]

14. [The same.]

15. [The same.]

16. That the people have a right to uniform government; and, therefore, that no government separate from, or independent of, the government of *Virginia*, ought, of right, to be erected or established within the limits thereof.

17. [The same.]

18. [The same.]

It will be seen, upon a comparison of the preceding draughts, that the committee added three entirely new articles (Nos. 9, 12, and 16) to the original draught of Colonel Mason, and subdivided one of his articles (No. 6) into two, thereby making eighteen articles of their draught for the fourteen of his. In the Declaration, as finally adopted, the convention incorporated two of the additional articles reported by the committee, and restored the unity of the 6th article of Colonel Mason's draught; so that the Declaration, in its ultimate form, consisted of sixteen articles. It is not deemed necessary to insert it here as it was finally adopted, and as it now stands at the head of the present constitution, and has unchangeably stood at the head of all the successive constitutions of Virginia. With the exception of the two added articles mentioned above, a brief additional clause at the end of the 5th article, and the amendment of the last article made on the motion of Mr. Madison, it is, in every essential particular, identical with the draught of Colonel Mason.

C. See pp. 149–152, and 158–165.

PARALLEL BETWEEN THE FIRST DRAUGHT OF THE VIRGINIA CONSTITUTION OF 1776 AND THE FORM IN WHICH IT WAS FINALLY ADOPTED.

First Draught of Constitution, or Plan of Government, laid before Select Committee.	*Constitution as agreed to and adopted by the Convention.*
1. Let the legislative, executive, and judicative departments be separate and distinct, so that neither exercise the powers properly belonging to the other.	1. The legislative, executive, and judiciary departments shall be separate and distinct, so that neither exercise the powers properly belonging to the other; nor shall any person exercise the powers of more than one of them at the same time, except that the justices of the county courts shall be eligible to either House of the Assembly.
2. Let the legislative be formed of two distinct branches, who together shall be a complete legislature. They shall meet once, or oftener, every year, and shall be called the General Assembly of Virginia.	2. The legislature shall be formed of two distinct branches, who together shall be a complete legislature. They shall meet once, or oftener, every year, and shall be called the General Assembly of Virginia.
3. Let one of these be called the Lower House of Assembly, and consist of two delegates or representatives, chosen for each county annually, by such men as have resided in the same for a year last past, are freeholders of	3. One of these shall be called the House of Delegates, and consist of two representatives to be chosen for each county, and for the district of West Augusta, annually, of such men as actually reside in and are freeholders of

the county, possess an estate of inheritance of land in Virginia of at least one thousand pounds value, and are upwards of twenty-four years of age.

4. Let the other be called the Upper House of Assembly, and consist of twenty-four members; for whose election, let the different counties be divided into twenty-four districts, and each county of the respective district, at the time of the election of its delegates for the Lower House, choose twelve deputies or sub-electors, being freeholders residing therein, and having an estate of inheritance of lands within the district of at least five hundred pounds value. In case of dispute, the qualifications to be determined by the majority of the said deputies. Let these deputies choose, by ballot, one member of the Upper House of Assembly, who is a freeholder of the district, hath been a resident therein for one year last past, possesses an estate of inheritance in lands in Virginia of at least two thousand pounds value, and is upwards of twenty-eight years of age. To keep up this assembly by rotation, let the districts be equally divided into four classes, and numbered. At the end of one year after the general election, let the six members elected by the first division be displaced, rendered ineligible for four years, and the vacancies be supplied in the manner aforesaid. Let this rotation be applied to each division ac-

the same, or duly qualified according to law, and also one delegate or representative to be chosen annually for the city of Williamsburg, and one for the borough of Norfolk, and a representative for each of such other cities and boroughs as may hereafter be allowed particular representation by the legislature; but when any city or borough shall so decrease as that the number of persons having right of suffrage therein shall have been, for the space of seven years successively, less than half the number of voters in some one county in Virginia, such city or borough thenceforward shall cease to send a delegate or representative to the Assembly.

4. The other shall be called the Senate, and consist of twenty-four members, of whom thirteen shall constitute a House to proceed on business; for whose election the different counties shall be divided into twenty-four districts, and each county of the respective districts, at the time of the election of its delegates, shall vote for one senator, who is actually a resident and freeholder within the district, or duly qualified according to law, and is upwards of twenty-five years of age; and the sheriffs of each county, within five days at farthest after the last county election in the district, shall meet at some convenient place, and, from the poll so taken in their respective counties, return as a senator the man who shall have the greatest number of votes in the whole district. To keep up this assembly by rotation, the districts shall be equally divided into four classes, and numbered by lot. At the end of one year after the general election, the six members elected by the first division shall be displaced, and the vacancies thereby occasioned supplied from such class or division by new election in the manner aforesaid. This rotation shall be applied to each division according to its number, and continued in due order annually.

cording to its number, and continued in due order annually.

5. Let each House settle its own rules of proceeding, direct writs of election for supplying intermediate vacancies; and let the right of suffrage, both in the election of members of the Lower House and of deputies for the districts, be extended to those having leases for land in which there is an unexpired term of seven years, and to every housekeeper who hath resided for one year last past in the county, and hath been the father of three children in this country.

6. Let all laws originate in the Lower House; to be approved or rejected by the Upper House, or to be amended with the consent of the Lower House, except money bills, which in no instance shall be altered by the Upper House, but wholly approved or rejected.

7. Let a governor or chief magistrate be chosen annually by joint ballot of both Houses, who shall not continue in that office longer than three years successively, and then be ineligible for the next three years. Let an adequate, but moderate salary be settled on him, during his continuance in office; and let him, with the advice of a council of state, exercise the executive powers of government, and the power of proroguing or adjourning the General Assembly, or of calling it upon emergencies, and of granting reprieves or pardons, except in cases where the prosecution shall have been carried on by the Lower House of Assembly.

5. The right of suffrage in the election of members for both Houses shall remain as exercised at present; and each House shall choose its own speaker, appoint its own officers, settle its own rules of proceeding, and direct writs of election for supplying intermediate vacancies.

6. All laws shall originate in the House of Delegates, to be approved or rejected by the Senate, or to be amended with the consent of the House of Delegates; except money bills, which, in no instance, shall be altered by the Senate, but wholly approved or rejected.

7. A governor or chief magistrate shall be chosen annually by joint ballot of both Houses, to be taken in each House respectively, deposited in the conference-room, the boxes examined jointly by a committee of each House, and the numbers severally reported to them that the appointments may be entered, (which shall be the mode of taking the joint ballot of both Houses in all cases,) who shall not continue in that office longer than three years successively, nor be eligible until the expiration of four years after he shall have been out of that office. An adequate, but moderate salary shall be settled on him during his continuance in office; and he shall, with the advice of a council of state, exercise the executive powers of government, according to the laws of this Commonwealth; and shall not, under any pretence, exercise any power or prerogative by virtue of any law, statute, or custom of England; but he shall, with the advice of the council of state, have the power of granting reprieves or pardons, except where the prosecution shall

have been carried on by the House of Delegates, or the law shall otherwise particularly direct; in which cases, no reprieve or pardon shall be granted but by resolve of the House of Delegates.

Either House of the General Assembly may adjourn themselves respectively. The governor shall not prorogue or adjourn the Assembly during their sitting, nor dissolve them at any time; but he shall, if necessary, either by advice of the council of state, or on application of a majority of the House of Delegates, call them before the time to which they stand prorogued or adjourned.

8. Let a privy council, or council of state, consisting of eight members, be chosen by joint ballot of both Houses of Assembly, promiscuously from their own members or the people at large, to assist in the administration of government. Let the governor be president of this council; but let them annually choose one of their own members as vice-president, who, in case of the death or absence of the governor, shall act as lieutenant-governor. Let three members be sufficient to act, and their advice be entered of record in their proceedings. Let them appoint their own clerk, who shall have a salary settled by law, and take an oath of secrecy in such matters as he shall be directed by the board to conceal, unless called upon by the Lower House of Assembly for information. Let a sum of money, appropriated to that purpose, be divided annually among the members, in proportion to their attendance; and let them be incapable, during their continuance in office, of sitting in either House of Assembly. Let two members be removed, by ballot of their own board, at the end of every three years, and be ineligible for the three next years. Let this be regularly continued, by rotation, so as that no member be removed before he hath been three years in the council; and let these vacancies, as well as those occasioned by

8. A privy council, or council of state, consisting of eight members, shall be chosen by joint ballot of both Houses of Assembly, either from their own members or the people at large, to assist in the administration of government. They shall annually choose out of their own members a president, who, in case of the death, inability, or necessary absence of the governor from the government, shall act as lieutenant-governor. Four members shall be sufficient to act, and their advice and proceedings shall be entered of record, and signed by the members present, (to any part whereof any member may enter his dissent,) to be laid before the General Assembly, when called for by them. This council may appoint their own clerk, who shall have a salary settled by law, and take an oath of secrecy in such matters as he shall be directed by the board to conceal. A sum of money, appropriated to that purpose, shall be divided annually among the members, in proportion to their attendance; and they shall be incapable, during their continuance in office, of sitting in either House of Assembly. Two members shall be removed by joint ballot of both Houses of Assembly at the end of every three years, and be ineligible for the three next years. These vacancies, as well as those occasioned by death or inca-

death or incapacity, be supplied by new elections, in the same manner as the first.

9. Let the governor, with the advice of the privy council, have the appointment of the militia officers, and the government of the militia, under the laws of the country.

10. Let the two Houses of Assembly, by joint ballot, appoint judges of the supreme court, judges in chancery, judges of admiralty, and the attorney-general, — to be commissioned by the governor, and continue in office during good behaviour. In case of death or incapacity, let the governor, with the advice of the privy council, appoint persons to succeed in office *pro tempore*, to be approved or displaced by both Houses. Let these officers have fixed and adequate salaries, and be incapable of having a seat in either House of Assembly, or in the privy council, except the attorney-general and the treasurer, who may be permitted to a seat in the Lower House of Assembly.

11. Let the governor and privy council appoint justices of the peace for the counties. Let the clerks of all the courts, the sheriffs, and coroners be nominated by the respective courts, approved by the governor and privy council, and commissioned by the governor. Let the clerks be continued

pacity, shall be supplied by new elections in the same manner.

The delegates, for Virginia to the Continental Congress shall be chosen annually, or superseded in the mean time, by joint ballot of both Houses of Assembly.

9. The present militia officers shall be continued, and vacancies supplied by appointment of the governor, with the advice of the privy council, on recommendation from the respective county courts; but the governor and council shall have a power of suspending any officer, and ordering a court martial on complaint of misbehaviour or inability, or to supply vacancies of officers happening when in actual service. The governor may embody the militia, with the advice of the privy council, and, when embodied, shall alone have the direction of the militia under the laws of the country.

10. The two Houses of Assembly shall, by joint ballot, appoint judges of the supreme court of appeals and general court, judges in chancery, judges of admiralty, secretary, and the attorney-general, — to be commissioned by the governor, and continue in office during good behaviour. In case of death, incapacity, or resignation, the governor, with the advice of the privy council, shall appoint persons to succeed in office, to be approved or displaced by both Houses. These officers shall have fixed and adequate salaries, and, together with all others holding lucrative offices, and all ministers of the gospel of every denomination, be incapable of being elected members of either House of Assembly, or the privy council.

11. The governor, with the advice of the privy council, shall appoint justices of the peace for the counties; and in case of vacancies, or a necessity of increasing the number hereafter, such appointments to be made upon the recommendation of the respective county courts. The present

during good behaviour, and all fees be regulated by law. Let the justices appoint constables.

acting secretary in Virginia, and clerks of all the county courts, shall continue in office. In case of vacancies, either by death, incapacity, or resignation, a secretary shall be appointed as before directed, and the clerks by the respective courts. The present and future clerks shall hold their offices during good behaviour, to be judged of and determined in the general court. The sheriffs and coroners shall be nominated by the respective courts, approved by the governor with the advice of the privy council, and commissioned by the governor. The justices shall appoint constables, and all fees of the aforesaid officers be regulated by law.

12. Let the governor, any of the privy councillors, judges of the supreme court, and all other officers of government, for mal-administration, or corruption, be prosecuted by the Lower House of Assembly, (to be carried on by the attorney-general, or such other person as the House may appoint,) in the supreme court of common law. If found guilty, let him or them be either removed from office, or forever disabled to hold any office under the government, or subjected to such pains or penalties as the laws shall direct.

12. The governor, when he is out of office, and others offending against the State, either by mal-administration, corruption, or other means by which the safety of the State may be endangered, shall be impeachable by the House of Delegates. Such impeachment to be prosecuted by the attorney-general, or such other person or persons as the House may appoint, in the general court, according to the laws of the land. If found guilty, he or they shall either be forever disabled to hold any office under government, or removed from such office *pro tempore*, or subjected to such pains or penalties as the law may direct. — If all or any of the judges of the general court shall, on good grounds, (to be judged of by the House of Delegates,) be accused of any of the crimes or offences before mentioned, such House of Delegates may, in like manner, impeach the judge or judges so accused, to be prosecuted in the court of appeals; and he or they, if found guilty, shall be punished in the same manner as is prescribed in the preceding clause.

13. Let all commissions run in the name of the *Commonwealth of Virginia*, and be tested by the governor, with the seal of the Commonwealth annexed. Let writs run in the same manner, and be tested by the clerks of

13. Commissions and grants shall run, *In the name of the Commonwealth of Virginia*, and bear test by the governor, with the seal of the Commonwealth annexed. Writs shall run in the same manner, and bear test by the

55 *

the several courts. Let indictments conclude, *Against the peace and dignity of the Commonwealth.*

14. Let a treasurer be appointed annually, by joint ballot of both Houses.

clerks of the several courts. Indictments shall conclude, *Against the peace and dignity of the Commonwealth.*

14. A treasurer shall be appointed annually, by joint ballot of both Houses.

All escheats, penalties, and forfeitures, heretofore going to the King, shall go to the Commonwealth, save only such as the legislature may abolish, or otherwise provide for.

The territories contained within the charters erecting the Colonies of Maryland, Pennsylvania, North and South Carolina, are hereby ceded, released, and forever confirmed to the people of those Colonies respectively, with all the rights of property, jurisdiction, and government, and all other rights whatsoever, which might at any time heretofore have been claimed by Virginia, except the free navigation and use of the rivers Potomac and Pohomoke, with the property of the Virginia shores or strands bordering on either of the said rivers, and all improvements which have been or shall be made thereon. The western and northern extent of Virginia shall, in all other respects, stand as fixed by the charter of King James the First, in the year one thousand six hundred and nine, and by the public treaty of peace between the courts of Great Britain and France in the year one thousand seven hundred and sixty-three; unless, by act of legislature, one or more territories shall hereafter be laid off, and governments established westward of the Alleghany Mountains. And no purchase of lands shall be made of the Indian natives but on behalf of the public, by authority of the General Assembly.

15. In order to introduce this government, let the representatives of the people, now met in convention, choose twenty-four members to be an Upper House; and let both Houses, by joint ballot, choose a governor and privy council; the Upper House to continue until the last day of March next, and

15. In order to introduce this government, the representatives of the people, met in convention, shall choose a governor and privy council; also such other officers directed to be chosen by both Houses as may be judged necessary to be immediately appointed. The Senate to be first chosen by the

the other officers until the end of the succeeding session of Assembly. In cases of vacancies, the president to issue writs for new elections.

people, to continue until the last day of March next, and the other officers until the end of the succeeding session of Assembly. In case of vacancies, the speaker of either House shall issue writs for new elections.

D. See p. 360.

MONSIEUR RAYNEVAL'S LETTER TO MR. MONROE, VINDICATING THE CONDUCT OF FRANCE IN THE NEGOTIATIONS FOR PEACE IN 1782.

PARIS, le 14 Novembre, 1795.

MONSIEUR: J'ai reçu la lettre que vous m'avez fait l'honneur de m'écrire le 30 du mois dernier. Je suis, on ne peut pas plus, flatté de la marque de confiance que vous voulez bien me donner; et je crois ne pouvoir y mieux répondre qu'en vous transmettant, avec la plus scrupuleuse exactitude, les explications que vous me demandez. Je suis d'autant plus en mesure de vous satisfaire, que les faits, dont il est question, me sont en quelque sorte personnels; et je le dois, puisque le ministère, avec qui je les ai partagés, n'existe plus. D'ailleurs, c'est une dette que je m'empresse d'acquitter envers ma patrie, qu'on a cherché à calomnier, avec une intention qu'il n'est pas difficile de pénétrer.

Votre lettre, Monsieur, renferme le passage suivant: "Vous savez que les ministres Américains ont signé avec ceux de l'Angleterre un traité provisoire, à l'insçu du cabinet Français, et contre les instructions qu'ils avaient du Congrès, lequel traité ne devait pas avoir son effet, jusqu'à ce qu'il fût conclu un traité entre la France et l'Angleterre. Comme on cherchait à s'informer des motifs de cette démarche, il était dit, d'après ce que j'ai souvent entendu, que la France, témoignant de l'indifference sur plusieurs points de nos réclamations, vis-à-vis l'Angleterre, débattus pour lors par nos ministres, avait même pris le parti de cette puissance contre nous, en cherchant à écarter nos reclamations relatives à la pêche, aux limites, et au Mississippi; et qu'elle vous avait envoyé en Angleterre expressément pour décider le Marquis de Lansdowne dans son opposition à nos demandes sur ces points, de laquelle mission vous vous êtes acquitté dans les conférences personnelles que vous avez eu avec ce ministre; et qu'enfin, si nos négociateurs ont réussi sur les points que je viens de nommer, ils devaient leur succès à la politique libérale de l'Angleterre, — qui, en rejettant les conseils de la France, a préféré nous accorder nos demandes, tandis-qu'instruite qu'elle était des vœux de la France, à cet égard, elle aurait pu s'y refuser, — et à leur propre adresse à découvrir et à déjouer les intrigues du gouvernement Français, en terminant le traité de la manière et aux conditions déjà citées."

Voilà, Monsieur, les faits sur lesquels vous me demandez des éclaircissements, et voici ma réponse : —

Vous vous rappelez sûrement, Monsieur, qu'au combat naval qui eut lieu en Avril, 1782, dans les Antilles à la hauteur de la Dominique, M. De Grasse, fait prisonnier, fut conduit en Angleterre. Cet amiral eut des entretiens avec Milord Shelburne, et à son retour en France en Septembre, 1782, il fit entendre que ce ministre lui avait fait des overtures de paix : il remit même une note des conditions qu'il disait lui avoir été proposées. Cette annonce causa beaucoup d'étonnement ; et l'on n'était pas sans défiance sur l'exactitude du rapport. Toutefois, on jugea devoir éclaircir les faits ; et on se détermina à m'envoyer pour cet effet secrètement en Angleterre. Mes instructions étaient aussi simples que laconiques : elles portaient que je devais demander l'aveu ou le désaveu de la note remise par M. De Grasse.

Le premier article de cette note concernait l'indépendance de l'Amérique. Je joins ici un extrait du rapport que je fis lors de mon retour. Il renferme textuellement ce que s'est dit à l'égard des affaires Américaines : il est de la fin du mois de Septembre, 1782. Vous y trouverez : 1° que l'article fondamental de mes instructions était l'indépendance des États-Unis, et qu'il ne m'a rien été prescrit relativement aux autres conditions à convenir avec les commissaires Américains ; 2° que je n'ai provoqué aucune conversation, aucune discussion sur cet objet, et que lorsque le ministre Anglais en a parlé de lui-même, je me suis renfermé dans mon ignorance et dans mon défaut d'autorisation ; 3° que dans les opinions que j'ai énoncés, j'ai plutôt appuyé qu'affaibli les demandes des commissaires Américains. Je crois devoir observer que le langage que j'ai tenu à l'égard des affaires Américaines, je l'ai tenu également à l'égard de celles de l'Espagne, parceque j'étais de même sans autorisation de la part de cette puissance.

Après mon retour en France, les négociations reprirent toute leur activité pour ce qui concernait la France. Je joins ici l'extrait des pièces concernant la pêche de la Terre Neuve. Vous ne verrez, Monsieur, pas un mot qui ait le moindre rapport aux intérêts des États-Unis. Pour la parfaite intelligence de ces pièces, je crois devoir vous donner l'explication suivante.